THE GUIDE TO BELONGING IN LAW SCHOOL

■ ■ ■

Russell A. McClain (He/Him)
Law School Professor
Associate Dean for Diversity and Inclusion
Director, Academic Achievement Program
University of Maryland Francis King Carey School of Law

WEST
ACADEMIC
PUBLISHING

© 2020 LEG, Inc. d/b/a West Academic
    444 Cedar Street, Suite 700
    St. Paul, MN 55101
    1-877-888-1330

West, West Academic Publishing, and West Academic are trademarks of West Publishing Corporation, used under license.

Printed in the United States of America

ISBN: 978-1-68328-379-9

To Kishka, thank you for your love and support.

*To Melina and Alana, have a Growth Mindset
and know you can do anything.*

*To my colleagues at Maryland Carey Law, thank you for
giving me mentorship, room to grow, and the
freedom to pursue my passion.*

*To my many academic support colleagues and friends,
thank you for believing in and encouraging me.*

RAM

SYLLABUS

———

Below, you can find a suggested schedule for proceeding through this book. I suggest that you follow the suggested pace. Moving through the material too quickly actually will cheat you of the opportunity to experience some authenticity in absorbing the material as you would over a few weeks in a law school course.

In addition to the assignments below, there are various assignments embedded within each chapter. Take your time to do all of the assignments and exercises in this book.

———

Day	Assignment

1	Read:
	   • Introduction
	   • Chapter 1: The Legacy of Minorities in the Law
	   • Chapter 2: The Law School Experience

2	Read:
	   • Chapter 3: Invisible Influences
	   • Chapter 4: Legal Sources and Structures

3	Read:
	   • Chapter 5: Introduction to Contracts
	   • Chapter 6: Preparing for Class
	   • Class 1 Reading (Appendix)

4	Pre-Class Review for Class 1
5	Read: • Chapter 7: Class One Watch: Class 1 (Website)

6	Read:
	   • Chapter 8: Introduction to Legal Analysis
	   • Class 2 Reading (Appendix)

7	Read: • Chapter 9: Class Two Watch Class 2 (Website) Post-Class Review for Class 2

		Read:
		    • Chapter 10: Preparing for Exams
		    • Class 3 Reading (Appendix)

8		*[BREAK]*
9		Pre-Class Review for Class 3

10		Read:
		    • Chapter 11: Class Three
		    • Chapter 12: How to Take a Law School Exam (Stop before Midterm Exam.)
		Watch Class 3 (Website)

11		Prepare for Midterm Exam
12		Read: • Remainder of Chapter 12 (Midterm Exam and Following) Take Midterm
13		*[BREAK]*
14		Read: • Class 4 Materials
15		Pre-Class Review for Class 4

16		Read:
		    • Chapter 13: Class Four
		Watch Class 4 (Website)
		Read:
		    • Chapter 14: Class Five (Beginning Only)
		    • Class 5 Reading (Appendix)

17		Pre-Class Review for Class 5
18		Watch Class 5 Read: • Chapter 14: Class Five (Remainder) Exam Preparation—Day 1
19		Exam Preparation—Day 2
20		Exam Preparation—Day 3

21		Read:
		    • Chapter 15: The Final Exam
		    • Final Words

SUMMARY OF CONTENTS

TABLE OF CONTENTS

THE GUIDE TO BELONGING IN LAW SCHOOL

INTRODUCTION

■ ■ ■

There are many good books written about law school. They offer guidance on how to learn effectively in law school, including how to read and study effectively, how to prepare for class and take notes, and how to study for and take law school exams. Other books give you a basic overview of or introduction to substantive topics.

But very few books address the special dynamics people from marginalized groups will face in law school. That is why I chose to write this book. I will do some of the things addressed above, but I also have included special content to help readers navigate a distinct set of experiences you will encounter in law school.

A.   Why a Special Book?

This book is addressed to those who are statistical minorities in the legal profession. This includes people of color, ethnic minorities, women, religious minorities, people who are non-binary, LGBTQIA students, first generation law students, and others. I have struggled greatly with the title of this book, because nearly every term we might use to refer to people who are not white males can carry with it a sense of othering or minimization. Words like minorities, marginalized, outsiders, underrepresented, underserved, and outsiders all suggest powerlessness and exclusion, a sense that these groups do not truly belong. You may find that I use these words from time to time, but my ultimate goal is to leave you with one conclusion by the time you finish this book:

> ## *YOU BELONG IN LAW SCHOOL, AND YOU CAN AND WILL SUCCEED IN BECOMING PART OF THE LEGAL PROFESSION.*

Historically, people from non-white racial and ethnic groups (African-Americans, Latinos and Hispanics, American Indians, and others), women, and people from less affluent socioeconomic backgrounds have been excluded from law schools and, hence, the legal profession. Women were not admitted in significant numbers to law schools until the mid-1900s. It

1

was not until the mid-to-late 1960s that African Americans began to break through the barriers to law school admission. Other historically marginalized racial, ethnic, and gender minority groups followed thereafter. At the time the legal profession started paying serious attention to this issue—in the mid-to-late twentieth century—the legal profession was dominated by white males. It still is.

These histories of exclusion and oppression can make the law school experience different for members these groups. As I will discuss in Chapter 2, being a statistical minority can dramatically affect learning experiences. When you are in the minority, you experience greater pressure to speak for your group, to succeed, to prove that you belong. These pressures do not begin in law school; they can be felt in the formative childhood years.[1] And they continue throughout one's life. In education, these dynamics can interfere with learning, increasing in intensity as one reaches higher levels of education. If ignored, they can prevent minorities from realizing their full academic and professional potential.

This book is designed to explain and address these unique challenges, to demystify the law school experience, and to equip readers with fundamental skills that can help you manage the academic challenges that law school presents. I will walk you through various aspects of the law school experience, so you know what to expect at each turn and how to handle each challenge you encounter.

B.   Every Reader Is Different

Even though there are commonalities to experiences of law students from underrepresented groups, not all minorities are the same. We are multidimensional beings, existing across a range of backgrounds. I, for example, am an African American who uses he/him pronouns, but that is not all I am. I am male, middle-class, suburban, educated, and I possess a range of characteristics and experiences that help explain and define who I am. In some ways, I am extremely privileged. In other ways, I am oppressed.

You, likewise, are complex. You exist among intersections of your age, race, ethnicity, sexuality, gender identity, socioeconomic status, religion, and a host of other identity characteristics. In many ways, your make-up is a byproduct of when you were born, where you have lived, your familial, social, and other life experiences, and myriad other tangible and invisible influences. No one thing defines or explains who you are—nor should it.

Nor will all of your law school experiences be identical. You may go to an elite school, or your school may be in the top, middle, or bottom tier. Your school may be predominately white, or you might attend an institution devoted to the education of people of color, like a Historically Black College or University. Your faculty may be comprised of mostly conservative or mostly liberal faculty members. Teaching at your chosen law school might be focused on legal theory, or your law school may be devoted to teaching you strict rules (as we call them, "black letter law") in order to help you master the rules and pass the bar exam. You might attend as a full or part-time student. You might get scholarships, or you may have to pay your own way. Each of these variables will color your law school experience.

Throughout the book, I will try to explore the variety of experiences readers may face, but I recognize the challenges in attempting to create a one-size-fits-all book. My hope is that every reader will find something valuable in these pages that can increase your ability to deal with the challenges of law school successfully.

C.   Methodology

My approach for this book is to try to approximate the law school experience for you. To do that, I will ask you to learn about two weeks' worth of what you would cover in a single class. As we move through that material, I hope to teach you how to:

(1)   Read law school material;

(2)   Prepare for class;

(3)   Listen effectively in class;

(4)   Take proper notes;

(5)   Review effectively after class;

(6)   Study for exams;

(7)   Read a law school exam question;

(8)   Write an exam answer; and

(9)   Evaluate your own work.

Along the way, I hope to introduce you to the reality of law school and help you learn to navigate its intellectual and psychological complexities.

As you read through this book, please look for three things:

- Accompanying Website. Throughout the book, you will find references to www.belonginginlawschool.com. On this website you will find supplemental materials, class instruction, and other information created to work with this text. To get the most value out of this book, please use the materials on the website.

- "First Things First." Throughout the book, I have provided exercises designed to address some of the psychological dynamics that can interfere with learning. I encourage you to take full advantage of these exercises.

- <u>"We Belong."</u> In addition, you will find a few narratives about lawyers from a range of backgrounds. You will read their stories and receive some of their advice.

I hope you will find this book rewarding and informative. Most of all, I hope that by the time you finish working through this book, you will have the utmost confidence that you can succeed in law school and beyond.

A Word About COVID-19

As this book is being published, the entire planet is suffering from the COVID-19 pandemic. At this moment, there is no telling how law school education might be changed by this global event. You may find that, at least for the short-term future, more classes are taught remotely. However you end up learning in law school, the tools provided in this book should be helpful to support you during your studies.

FIRST THINGS FIRST

Before we start, I would like you to think (and write) about a couple of things. I am going to ask you two questions below. Do not start writing right away. Take a few minutes to think about each of these questions and then answer in the space provided.

Question 1: What are your core values? What makes you who you are?

_____

_____

_____

_____

_____

_____

_____

_____

_____

_____

_____

_____

_____

_____

_____

_____

_____

_____

_____

_____

_____

_____

_____

_____

_____

_____

Question 2: How did your core values lead you to choose law school?

_____

_____

_____

_____

_____

_____

_____

_____

_____

_____

_____

_____

_____

_____

_____

_____

_____

_____

_____

_____

_____

_____

_____

_____

_____

_____

_____

_____

_____

You are going to law school for a reason. Maybe you have decided on law school because you want to help the oppressed. Maybe you want to make a difference. Maybe you want to apply yourself to something really challenging. Perhaps you want to be a prosecutor, or a public defender, or a tax lawyer, or a judge, or an immigration lawyer, or a mergers and acquisitions attorney. Maybe you want to make money at a large firm, or you may wish to work representing the poor. All of these are valid and viable paths for you.

Whatever your motivation, remember to hold onto these reasons. I encourage you to revisit these pages and remind yourself regularly why you have chosen law school. This will help sustain you as you navigate the challenges of law school that confront every law student by reminding you that you are doing this for a reason, that you are capable and talented, and that you can achieve anything you put your mind to.

---

[1] The classic study, relied on by the Supreme Court of the United States in *Brown v. Board of Education*, 347 U.S. 483 (1954), is the infamous "doll experiment," where children as young as three years old demonstrated a "well-developed knowledge of the concept of racial difference . . . ." Kenneth, B., & Clark, M. P., *Racial Identification and Preference in Negro Children*, READINGS IN SOCIAL PSYCHOLOGY, 602 (1947).

CHAPTER 1

THE LEGACY OF MINORITIES IN THE LAW

■ ■ ■

The history of underrepresentation of women and racial and ethnic minorities in the legal profession is staggering. Prior to the 20th century, the legal profession was almost exclusively white men.

By the 1970s, law schools affirmatively sought to diversify themselves, admitting women and minorities—at the time, the latter primarily were African Americans—in greater numbers. Over the last five decades, these efforts have ebbed and flowed, but African Americans, Latinx Americans, American Indians, Asian Americans, LGBTQIA people, and women still remain woefully underrepresented in the legal profession.

In the late 1960s, census data showed that Blacks, who then constituted roughly 11 percent of the U.S. population, were less than one percent of the legal profession. Of course, a few hundred years of slavery, followed by Jim Crow exclusion and oppression contributed to this statistic. Even as late as the 1950s, most law schools in the south were totally white and not open to Blacks at all.[1]

Women, who really did not have full citizenship status until the 1920s, have been systematically excluded from the practice of law.[2] Even though there have been many high achieving women in law schools, women have been kept from advancing in the profession. Famously, women like Justice Ruth Bader Ginsburg, Justice Sandra Day O'Connor, and many other high-achieving women graduated from elite schools but nevertheless were denied entry in to the profession. Even though there are many high-achieving women in law practice today, women still are underrepresented among law firm partnerships and in other high-profile law positions. The underrepresentation is even more significant among women of color.

Data on Lesbian, Gay, Bisexual, Transgender, Queer/Questioning, Intersexed, and/or Asexual people is less than perfect in the United States. Our nation's history of discrimination and violence against this collection of identities has made it difficult to get precise measures of people in these categories, but current estimates are that roughly 4.5% of our adult population fit within this collection of identities. According to the National Association for Law Placement, less than 3% of lawyers identify as LGBT.[3]

By focusing on these groups, I do not mean to ignore the many others that matter greatly.

Authors have addressed the issue of underrepresentation in books, articles, blog posts, and elsewhere. In this book, I will not try to restate the points others have made. Instead, I hope to shine a light on a handful of examples of the thousands of people who, like you, thought of law school as an option. These amazing attorneys have come from all walks of life, have gone to all kinds of law schools, and they have taken a wide variety of paths to success in their legal careers.

Look for stories like these throughout this book:

We Belong

MARILYN, the only child of a preacher, grew up in the poorest part of St. Louis in the mid-20th century. She spent her summers in the cotton fields of the deep south. Growing up in the Jim Crow era, Marilyn went to segregated schools as a child. She was the first of her family to go to college, and then she moved on to law school in New Jersey.

Marilyn was among the first Black lawyers to work on Wall Street. In a world where women were second class—and African-American women held even lower status—Marilyn had her first child on a Friday and returned to work on the following Monday. Ultimately, Marilyn became a tenured law professor.

Marilyn's Advice: ***Congratulations on your acceptance to law school. You were chosen because your application stood out among thousands of others who applied. You already are smart and capable, and you don't have to prove that to anybody. You already have everything it takes to succeed in law school.***

---

[1]   *See* Henry W. McGee, Jr., *Minority Students in Law School: Black Lawyers and the Struggle for Racial Justice in the American Social Order*, 20 BUFF. L. REV. 423 (1971). McGee describes how, "Northern law schools, 'nominally open to Negro applicants,' were until recently virtually lily-white, and 'except for the occasional "Jim Crow" institution, Southern law schools were completely closed to the Negro until the 1950's.'" *Id.* at 424 (quoting Ernest Gellhorn, *The Law Schools and the Negro*, 1968 DUKE L. J. 1069, 1069 (1968)).

[2]   See Bowman, Cynthia Grant, "Women in the Legal Profession from the 1920s to the 1970s: What Can We Learn From Their Experience About Law and Social Change?" (2009). Cornell Law Faculty Publications. Paper 12. http://scholarship.law.cornell.edu/facpub/12.

[3]   LGBT Representation Among Lawyers in 2017, NALP Bulletin, January 2018, available from https://www.nalp.org/0118research.

CHAPTER 2

THE LAW SCHOOL EXPERIENCE

■ ■ ■

I. WHAT TO DO BEFORE YOU GET TO LAW SCHOOL

I often get the following question from prospective law students: What should I do prior to starting law school to prepare? There are many kinds of advice lawyers and law professors will give you in response to this question, some of which will focus on your preparation in college and/or in the years leading up to law school. I will focus on the summer before law school, and what you can do to get ready.

As we will explore in more detail in the following pages, law school can be extremely rigorous. So much of my advice will be based on getting yourself ready to understand and handle that challenge. In general, my advice is to spend your summer mentally and physically preparing to handle the work ahead. Here are a few specific suggestions that I hope will help you accomplish that general goal:

(1) **Rest.** You will work *really hard* in law school. Many law students view themselves as working harder in law school than they have ever worked before. For that reason, it is important not to wear yourself out before you start. So I would not recommend that you do a full summer's worth of intensive work that will just have you tired before you begin law school. On the other hand, there are some amazing "bridge" programs, like summer courses offered by the Council on Legal Education Opportunity, law school bridge programs or boot camps, and other law school prep offerings. Whether or not you choose to do some kind of bridge program, it is important that you start law school refreshed, energetic, and ready to work. Take time, therefore, to get enough rest and to make sure that you are not worn out before you begin.

(2) **Have Fun.** Make sure that you enjoy yourself before law school starts. Law school can be a lot of fun—you will meet many interesting people, make friends, and you can engage in a wide range of law school activities (trial team, moot court, etc.) that can be thoroughly engaging and rewarding. That said, you should make sure that you spend some time enjoying yourself during the

summer leading up to law school. Take a vacation, go see movies, and spend time with friends and family. You may feel that the time you have to do some of those things will be limited once law school starts, so take advantage of the time that summer provides and make sure you create opportunities to relax and have a good time.

(3) **Work Out**. It is important to take care of yourself physically. Some people go to the gym, or walk, or run, or take yoga. Working out can benefit you by reducing stress and giving you additional energy. Unfortunately, because law school can keep students so busy, students may end up sacrificing some of the most important things that keep them mentally and physically healthy. Developing healthy routines that you can take with you to law school will help you get through the experience more effectively, helping you thrive rather than simply survive.

(4) **Read This Book**. I would not have written this book if I did not believe it would help you prepare for law school. If you follow this book at the pace I have suggested, I expect that you will find it will give you a realistic and effective approximation of the law school learning experience. (I have not attempted to approximate the law school workload, because there will be enough time in the next few months for you to become super busy.)

(5) **Make a Plan for Success**. Success in law school does not happen accidentally. If you are to succeed in law school, you must approach it intentionally. Once you have finished this book, and before you have started law school, you should visualize and then write down a plan for success.

II. WHAT LAW SCHOOL IS REALLY LIKE (THE BAD NEWS)

In this section, I hope to give you an unvarnished look at what your law school experience can be like. I do not want to sugar-coat my description of the experience, so I will deliberately try to point out some of the toughest parts of law school. I do not do this to scare you, but to let you know, as realistically as possible, how intense this experience can be. It can be overwhelming if you do not go into the experience with open eyes and a prepared mind. That said, if you are prepared, law school can be a fantastic, rewarding, and enjoyable experience. Make sure to stay tuned to the end of this section for the good news!

Workload. As I said above, you may feel like you work harder in law school than you ever have before. Typically, in your first year, you will take four or five courses each semester. One course is usually a course in legal writing. The other courses are what we call "doctrinal" courses—classes like Contracts, Criminal Law, Torts, Civil Procedure, Property, and Constitutional Law. I will discuss the writing course separately below, so for now I will focus on the workload in doctrinal courses.

Each book for your doctrinal courses can be a thousand pages or more, and you will be asked to read most of those pages. In the early weeks of law school, you can expect that you will be given something like 30–50 pages to read per week, per class, which translates into a total of 150–200 or so pages across three to four classes. And this reading is not like reading a novel or other pleasure reading. Some of the cases you read were written a hundred years ago or more, and even those that were written more recently may be difficult to follow. You likely will find that you'll have to read these pages more than once. If we assume that your normal reading speed will be cut in half—which may be an underestimation—then we're talking about the time equivalent of reading 300–400 pages a week. Later in the semester, your reading assignments will increase in volume—it is not uncommon for professors to assign 50–100 pages per week. This can feel overwhelming. It will take you many hours to finish all of this reading and actually understand it.

On top of your reading, you will have assignments to work on in your writing courses. In addition, roughly halfway through the semester, you will begin a process called "outlining" (a big deal in law school that I will discuss later), which involves exam preparation and will continue for the rest of the semester. These will add even more hours to your already packed schedule.

Altogether, you should expect to spend an average of 50–60 hours per week outside of class.[1] This is a lot of work, and it will feel like it.

Classroom. Your classroom experiences may be different than those from your past. Your prior teachers may have spent a great deal of class time explaining assignments and going over what you were expected to learn since the previous class meeting. In law school, your professors often expect you to teach yourself from the reading, and then they spend time building on the reading rather than reiterating the lessons to be learned from the reading.

One way in which your law professors will evaluate your understanding of class readings is to ask you questions designed to have you apply what you have learned to new situations. (We will explore this in more detail later in the book.) Many professors do "cold-calling," or unannounced calling on students that puts them on the spot for a few minutes or longer. These cold-calling moments can feel extremely stressful, because you are trying to listen to the professor's question, remember what you've read, try to appear calm, and avoid embarrassing yourself in front of your classmates. Your adrenaline starts pumping, your mouth dries out, and your mind suddenly goes blank. Many students hate this experience.

Depending on the size of your classes, this experience may happen only a few times per class each semester.

Feedback and Exams. One of the hardest things about law school is that you get very little feedback. Depending on your school, you may find that most classes do not have quizzes, midterms, or any other kind of homework assignments to help you know how you are doing. In fact many if not most classes will have one exam at the end of the semester, and that exam will be your entire grade.

The prototypical law school exam probably not what you are used to. You'll never be asked the question, "Is there a contract?" or "Did the defendant commit first degree murder?" or "Who has the property rights to Greenacre?" Instead, you will read hypothetical fact patterns—short stories with several characters who interact with each other in various ways—and you will be expected to identify the questions (or "spot the issues") as well as the answers to those questions. We will discuss the way to issue spot and write exam answers in Chapter 11.

Although there are some take-home exams, many exams are limited to several hours. The time given to the exams is often just barely enough to allow you to get through if you know the material really well.

Exams are usually graded comparatively, so that the best **written** exams get the highest grades. What this means is that even though most students work really hard and go into the exam knowing the material, not all students will get As. This can be demoralizing for some students, who often are used to getting higher grades. Exams end up, then, not really being a measure of how hard you work or how well you know the material. Instead, exams measure how well you meet the expectations of your professor under extremely tight timed conditions.

Legal Writing. For the first year, at least, you will be enrolled in a writing course. In the first semester, typically, you will be asked to write two or three memoranda—papers in which you provide objective analysis of a legal problem. These memoranda usually are based on a small case file that you will be given. The case file will contain some basic facts about a legal situation that has arisen between two parties, and it will provide you with cases to use to try to figure out what the correct outcome should be. One little twist, and this will be a common theme in law school as you will discover, the answer may not always be clear, and you may be required to account for more than one possible outcome.

The second semester writing program, like the first semester, will have you doing more written legal analysis. This time, however, you probably will be writing one or two briefs—legal papers where you argue and provide persuasive analysis for a particular party in a case. Like the memoranda, you will be given factual background and some cases. In some circumstances, you will be required to do some legal research and find your own legal authorities.

You will find that these writing assignments take up a lot of your time, especially in the days before assignments are due. It will be important for you to spread out the writing so that you do not get overwhelmed leading up to the due date.

Self-Regulation. Another uniquely challenging aspect to law school is that you have to monitor your own progress.[2] Especially given the fact that you usually don't have quizzes, midterms, homework to turn in (except in legal writing), or other ways to determine how you are doing, you must find ways to effectively measure your own progress. There are varying ways to do this that we will explore over the course of this book. But keep in mind that no one else is keeping a close eye on you to see how you are doing. You must be prepared not only to do the readings and attend the classes, but also to evaluate yourself over the course of the semester so that you reach the end fully prepared for your exams.

Dealing with Challenges and Setbacks/Mindset. Everybody faces challenges in law school. What is important is how you deal with those challenges. There is no way to know ahead of time what your challenges will be. Maybe you didn't get the grade you were expecting on a paper. Perhaps a cold call didn't go well. Maybe you're having trouble understanding a particularly difficult case. Whatever it is, you will encounter something difficult during your time in law school. These setbacks are not the end of the world, but you have to know how to deal with them.

To preview material from a later chapter, it is important to have a growth mindset when you encounter difficulty. A growth mindset views setbacks as opportunities to learn and grow. In other words, don't let problems in law school get you down too much. They happen to everyone. You just need to roll with the punches.

Social Life/Relationships. Relationships are a key to healthy living. It is important to have the support of one's family and friends at normal times, and it is even more true to maintain and nourish relationships while one is a law student. Relationships in and out of law school are necessary to help you stay grounded and sane. Unfortunately, law school also can place a lot of stress on your relationships. The primary reason for this is that the amount of time you must spend on your schoolwork demands sacrifices of your time elsewhere. It is easy, then, to call your family fewer times each week, or to spend less time with your significant other.

While you cannot avoid all of the strain that law school will place on your time and relationships, you should be intentional about spending time with the people who are important in your life.

Financial Planning. Law school can be very expensive. At the lowest end, the cost of law school is about $13,000 per year, and at the high end, it can cost about $70,000 per year.[3] That means that three years of tuition and fees will range from nearly $40,000 to $210,000 by the time you graduate law school. To those numbers you must add the cost of living—housing, food, and other miscellaneous costs. Conservatively, that can add another $30,000 to the total cost. In addition, you have to plan to live through the summer after you graduate so that you can study for and pass the bar exam. That is a few months more of living expenses, costs of a bar review program (anywhere from $1500 to $4000). As you can see, the costs add up. Law school will cost you at least tens of thousands of dollars and possibly hundreds of thousands of dollars. This will be a significant financial investment.

To pay these costs, some students get scholarships. Others take out loans to pay for law school. Some try to find part-time jobs to defray the cost. Whatever choices you make, it's good to go into this with your eyes wide open. It's important for you to be thoughtful about the costs you are incurring and to think about ways to minimize your debt when you graduate.

Extra Challenges for Part-Time Students. Part-time students should factor in a few additional issues into their consideration. Many part-time students have families, full-time jobs, and attend law school in the evenings. Schedules that are already full become jam-packed. I have taught many students who get up at 6:00 a.m., get to work by 8:00, work 8–9 hours, commute to law school by 6:00, stay in class for three hours a night, and try to get home by 10:00 p.m. Somewhere in there, these students find time to eat, hope to kiss their kids goodnight, and look for time to study during lunch breaks and on weekends. These part-time students are among the most admirable law students, in my opinion. They carry a much heavier load than the rest of us.

III. THE GOOD NEWS

As I said above, I did not write the previous section in order to scare you away from law school. But I do want you to know what you are getting into. And, I want you to know that, should you choose to go to law school, you can handle it. In this book, I will do my best to give you advice to help you navigate many of the challenges I have raised.

---

[1]   Michael Hunter Schwartz and Paula J. Manning, EXPERT LEARNING FOR LAW STUDENTS at 241 (Carolina Academic Press)(3d. Ed. 2019).

[2]   Professors Schwartz and Manning call this Self-Regulation. Id. at 7.

[3]   *See* Ilana Kowarski, *See the Price, Payoff of Law School Before Enrolling*, U.S. News and World Report, March 12, 2019, available from https://www.usnews.com/education/best-graduate-schools/top-law-schools/articles/law-school-cost-starting-salary.

CHAPTER 3

INVISIBLE INFLUENCES

■ ■ ■

Imagine you are sitting in a classroom with 75 other people. In this large group, you are one of only a few people of your (racial, ethnic, gender, religious) group. You are called on by a professor to answer a question. Even though you worked really hard to understand the reading and felt really prepared coming into the classroom, you have trouble answering the question.

The professor, obviously disappointed in your response, calls on one of your colleagues, a non-minority student. This student also has trouble answering the question, but the professor, instead of moving on to someone else, follows up and keeps trying with that student. Eventually, after a long interaction, the professor leads the other student around to the right answer.

How do you feel about this interaction? Unsteady? Embarrassed? Hurt? Angry? Motivated? Stressed? Are you experiencing some degree of self-doubt?

Imagine what you or someone else in a similar position might be thinking about this interaction:

- Why didn't the professor ask *me* any follow-up questions?
- Does she think I'm not smart enough?
- I prepared as hard as I could have, but I still didn't get it. What else could I have done?
- What must this professor think of me?
- What must all of these other students think about me?
- What must they all think about my (racial, ethnic, gender, religious) group?
- I'm going to prove them all wrong!
- Maybe I'm not cut out for this?
- Maybe I don't belong here.

You might not think of all of these things, but some of them might hover at the edge of your conscious thinking. And this can be true even if—perhaps especially if—you are the most confident, self-driven person ever.

I. THE INSIDIOUS EFFECTS OF IMPLICIT BIAS AND STEREOTYPE THREAT

There are two psychological dynamics that can have a negative effect on the academic success of minorities in law school. They are implicit bias and stereotype threat. As I will discuss below, these dynamics can work together to make law school a rough experience, especially if they are ignored.

A. IMPLICIT BIAS

Implicit (sometimes referred to as unconscious or subconscious) bias refers, generally, to subconscious "snap judgments" that we all make concerning our environment.[1] The study of implicit bias is rooted in Information Processing Theory,[2] which views our brains like computers.

Like a computer, your brain takes in information and processes that information. Some of that information is lost, but large portions of what you encounter are retained and stored in long-term memory.

Given the sheer volume of information our brains take in at any given moment, it is impossible for all of that processing to happen consciously. At this moment, try to identify the range of things your senses are taking in:

(1) You're reading the words on this page, obviously, but pay attention to the various visual inputs that surround you. Even though you are not paying conscious attention to them all the time, your mind is aware of them.

(2) Close your eyes for a second and listen to the ambient noises you probably weren't even noticing. (For example, as I type this, I can hear traffic outside, a clock ticking, the air conditioner blowing, someone rustling in the another room, a television in the distance, and children laughing.)

(3) Think about the temperature in the room. What smells do you notice? Take in the feel of your chair, the fit of your clothes, and whether or not you feel hungry, tired, or uncomfortable.

Think about how long it took us to work through this consciously. Then realize that our brains are processing, evaluating, reevaluating, organizing, and reorganizing constantly. Imagine how many additional inputs you encounter when you are out in the world and not reading a book.

There is no way we can handle all of that information consciously. So our brains deal with a lot of this information behind the scenes, subconsciously. In order to manage that information, the brain looks for patterns. Things that are alike are grouped together and assigned common characteristics.

Professor Jerry Kang introduced a classic way for you to think of how this works: to consider chairs.[3] If you are sitting down right now, you probably did not bother to consider whether the thing you are sitting on is a chair. You just sat down. This is likely true every time you sit down in a chair. Why? Because you have encountered many chairs in your life. Even though many of them are different, they have certain things in common. Over your life, you have seen enough variations of chairs that you can, subconsciously, group them all together in a category called "Chairs."

Not only does your brain put chairs in a category, but it also assigns common characteristics to that category.[4] Chairs are stable; they support your weight; they generally have a flat surface roughly 18–20 inches high; they have a base, often touching the floor in four places; there often is a vertical component, adjacent to the flat surface, that is roughly 12–20 inches high and 15–18 inches wide. Now, as you read this, you will recognize immediately that not all chairs conform to this description: Formal chairs are different than benches, rocking chairs are different than office chairs, bar stools are different from toddler chairs. But your brain groups these things together and assigns these characteristics to them, whether or not they all apply.

I once was mowing a lawn, and I encountered a bed of baby snakes in my lawn. I actually like snakes, and, consciously, they do not particularly scare me. When I saw them, I could have thought about all of the things I know about snakes: I prefer constrictors to biters, of course, but I think snakes are pretty cool. They are slippery, squirmy, scaly, and often colorful. There are very few poisonous snakes in the geographical area where I live, so the likelihood of encountering a problem was low. But, in the moment, I thought of none of these things. Because embedded deep within in my subconscious brain I have a category: "Small Things Moving Quickly on the Ground." And my brain assigns at least one clear characteristic to this category: "Dangerous." So, when I encountered the snakes, and before I had time to think, my heart started racing, I shouted, and I jumped away. This was a normal and useful subconscious reaction. But this normal and necessary operation of the brain also can operate in insidious ways.

In addition to all of the other things we process, our brains categorize people also, based on the collective input we receive over the course of our lives.[5] And the input we receive is problematic, to say the least:

(1) In movies, television, and in advertising—

   • People of color are disproportionately portrayed in movies and television as criminal, dangerous, and low-achieving;[6]

   • People of color are stereotyped;[7]

- Women are often shown in weaker roles and dependent on men;[8]

- Gays, lesbians, women, and minorities get only token roles;

- Religious minorities are often portrayed as dangerous (often terroristic) characters.[9]

(2) In video games—

- People of color are portrayed as dangerous more often than white characters;[10]

- Women tend to be cast as objects of sexual desire.[11]

(3) In our society, women and minorities are the exception among leadership roles—

- There are relatively few women and people of color who are CEOs of large businesses;[12]

- University faculties and leadership are overwhelmingly white;[13]

- Educational institutions are disproportionately white;[14]

- Our government leadership is populated largely by white men—including all but one President of the United States.

In sum, we are bombarded with positive, high-achieving, white male images and overt or subtle images of women and people of color as subordinate.

The consequences of this input are that we, as a society, tend subconsciously to group white males, people of color, women, people who are gay and lesbian, transgender people, and religious and ethnic minorities into separate categories.[15] And we subconsciously assign characteristics to each of these categories, so that people in our society tend to:

(1) Associate images of Whites with positive ideas than they can associate images of Blacks with those ideas;

(2) More easily connect African-Americans with negative ideas—including weapons—than Whites;

(3) View religious minorities, particularly Muslims, as dangerous;

(4) Form negative associations with people who are perceived as homosexual or transgender;

(5) See women in liberal arts professions and not in math and science careers.

These tendencies have been measured on large-scale testing,[16] but much other research connects these subconscious associations with over-policing (suspicion, stop, search, and arrest, prosecution, and imprisonment) of people of color,[17] excessive discipline of students of color in public schools,[18] disparate diagnoses and treatment of women and minorities in medicine,[19] disparities in hiring,[20] differences in consumer behavior,[21] and an increased likelihood among juries in remembering bad facts about minority defendants.

In light of this, it is easy to see how a professor may be influenced by implicit bias. Even an inclusively-minded professor can have subconscious biases, and in the story above, the professor could have been biased against the first student. If so, then the bias could have caused the professor to have lower expectations of the first student, so that the professor moved away from that student in order to prevent the student from embarrassing themselves. The professor's bias may have been more positive toward the second student, which would explain why the professor endured with that student notwithstanding the similarities in the second student's initial responses to questioning.

So there is no doubt that implicit bias presents great potential for harm on its own. But in addition, while biased conduct affects us from the outside, there also are additional, internal consequences for women and minorities who are subjected to biases and stereotypes.

B. STEREOTYPE THREAT

Stereotype thereat, simply put, is the fear of confirming negative stereotypes.[22] When you are a part of a group about which there is a negative stereotype, it can affect how you think and act. Particularly in academic settings, studies show that the fear of confirming negative stereotypes can affect cognition, limiting subjects' ability to perform up to their full potential. Although stereotype threat has been studied relative to many stereotypes, two primary negative stereotypes have been the subject of research.

One of the two most studied negative stereotypes involves women and math. There is a pervasive negative stereotype that women are not as good at math as men. A study evaluated at women who were very good at math—i.e., planning to go to graduate school in mathematics.[23] The women were required to complete a challenging portion of the math section of the Graduate Record Examinations (GRE). Prior to taking the exam, one group of women was instructed that the test tended to show differences between men and women. You can imagine that this would trigger, in the minds of these women, a concern about the negative math-gender stereotype. As it turns out, the women who were given this triggering instruction performed worse on the test than equally capable women who were not given the instruction.[24]

The other most studied negative stereotype is also intelligence-based. There is a pervasive negative stereotype that African Americans are not as intelligent as Whites. In stereotype threat studies, college-age African Americans were given a challenging portion of the verbal part of the GRE.[25] One group was primed with a trigger instruction that the test was "diagnostic of intellectual ability." This of course, made the negative, intelligence-based stereotype relevant. Predictably, the African Americans who were given this instruction performed worse on the test than those who were not given the instruction.[26]

Stereotype threat has a significant effect on cognition. The fear of confirming a negative stereotype creates anxiety—what research call an "excessive cognitive load"—that interferes with the brain's ability to process.[27] If you imagine your brain as a computer with limited operating space, then it is not at all surprising that if some of that operating space is occupied by worry about confirming a negative stereotype, that one's ability to think clearly would be affected. Indeed, studies show that stereotype threat interferes with working memory,[28] motivation,[29] and confidence.[30]

In simple terms, stereotype threat undermines the capacity of the brain to process information. And the threat has been shown to affect not just women and African-Americans. The threat affects academic performance across a range of racial, ethnic, and socio-economic groups.

Claude Steele, one of the original and primary researchers of stereotype threat, summarized just how significant stereotype threat is:

> When a stereotype indicts the intellectual abilities of your group, the implication is that, as a member of that group . . . you lack a critical fixed ability. It's a narrative that makes any frustration a plausible sign that you can't do the work, that you don't belong there. And it discourages your taking on academic challenges, for fear you'd confirm the fixed limitation alleged in the stereotype.[31]

If left unchecked, stereotype threat can significantly hinder academic performance. And if you experience stereotype threat, you might perceive it in one or more different ways:

(1) "It's too much!"

> Stereotype threat can create anxiety that leaves you feeling overwhelmed. The anxiety can cause you to feel like there is more than you can handle. This can lead to an emotional shutdown and cause students to disengage from their studies.

(2) "Cloudy"

Stereotype threat can lead to something called cognitive overload, which can affect a person's ability to access short-term memory or stay focused. Obviously, this can make it tough to perform in high-pressure situations, like when a student gets called on in class or is taking a high-stakes exam.

(3) "Why try at all?"

The anxiety caused by stereotype threat can cause some people to give up. Sometimes, this can be just because the stress feels like too much. Other times, it can operate as a self-protection or coping mechanism. In other words, a person might feel like saying, "If I don't try my best, I can blame any lack of success on my lack of trying instead of lack of ability." Unfortunately, this lack of effort can lead to the very result (low performance) the student feared.

(4) "Try even harder"

Others might react in exactly the opposite way. Sometimes, the reaction might be to say, "I'm going to prove everybody wrong." In this situation, students tense up, determined to show the world that they can handle anything that comes their way. But this tensing up can actually backfire and restrict the student's ability to operate at peak potential.

The student in our story above could have been significantly affected by stereotype threat. Being a statistical minority could cause that student to experience not only the normal stress of class questioning, but also the additional anxiety imposed by the risk of confirming the negative stereotype that people in the minority subgroup are not as capable as white students could, as described above, interfere with the student's ability to think clearly and respond to the professor's questions.

II. HOW YOU CAN DEAL WITH IMPLICIT BIAS AND STEREOTYPE THREAT IN LAW SCHOOL

Implicit bias are everywhere, and law school is no exception. And, because it is important to be—or, at least, to appear to be—smart in law school, intelligence-based stereotype threats can thrive. The more you care about doing well, the more likely you are to be threatened by the fear of not being up to the task.[32] I do not say this to terrify you; instead, I hope you will be able to recognize these dynamics at play so you can stop them from interfering with your academic progress.

A. HOW YOU MIGHT EXPERIENCE IMPLICIT BIAS AND STEREOTYPE THREAT IN LAW SCHOOL

Implicit bias might show up in a few ways in law school. Implicit bias can lead a professor to have lower expectations of you and not be as tough on you when asking questions of you in class. Or other students may overlook you when forming study groups, for example.

These kinds of occurrences can cause you to experience stereotype threat. "Are they not inviting me to the study group because they think I'm not smart enough?" "Did the professor just take it easy on me because she thinks I can't handle tough questions?"

The work in law school is tough enough that nearly all students feel themselves questioning their own intelligence. The reading is challenging both in substance and volume. Sometimes, you will find yourself reading judicial opinions that were written in pre-colonial England, in language that is challenging to follow. Other cases, even though they were written in the U.S., still are more than a hundred years old and can be difficult to understand. Regardless, you will be expected read hundreds of pages each week, and it's not easy reading. Especially at first, you'll read pages and occasionally feel like you have no idea what judges are talking about. (This will change over time, as you learn the language of the law.)

With that difficulty can come doubt. "Do I really belong here?" "Maybe they made a mistake admitting me." "No one else seems to be struggling like I am." These are things you may never say out loud. You might not even admit them to yourself. And you might respond to all of this by saying, "I will prove them all wrong and work harder." This is a reasonable response to your awareness of negative stereotypes. But this doubling down, the tension created by the "prove them all wrong" attitude, is a part of the cognitive noise that can actually be the problem. As all of this bounces around in your head, it causes cognitive interference, preventing your brain from operating at its fullest potential.

The good news is: ***It is within your control to limit the effects these dynamics can have on your performance***.

B. HOW YOU CAN MINIMIZE THE EFFECTS OF STEREOTYPE THREAT

Given that the primary effect of stereotype threat is to create cognitive noise, many of the best interventions are designed to quiet that noise.

Reflective Writing. One way to reduce stress and improve performance is to engage in activities like the values writing exercise you did in the introduction to this book. Writing about your own values can reduce the effects of stereotype threat and improve academic performance for those subject to stereotype threat.[33] Taking a few minutes to write about the nature of intelligence—in other words, whether intelligence and ability are fixed or capable of growth—also works. (Pay close attention to the discussion of growth mindset, discussed below.) Or, you might try writing a letter to a future law student like you, providing words of encouragement about how to succeed.

Mindfulness. Engaging in mindfulness meditation has been shown to help reduce stress and enhance focus.[34] There are websites and smartphone apps dedicated to mindfulness meditation. (Insight Timer, Calm, and Headspace are apps that provide mindfulness exercises. There are many other mindfulness resources, including apps websites, and YouTube videos.) This is not meditation in a religious sense. It really is just a way to get your mind focused and to rid yourself of other things that can interfere with clear thinking. Studies have shown that mindfulness has, generally, an impact on growth

Working on a Growth Mindset. Whatever you do to work on minimizing the effects of stereotype threat, work on this one. For the last two decades or more, researchers have looked at differences in performance and how that is connected to having what is called a "Growth Mindset."[35] "Growth Mindset" and its opposite, "Fixed Mindset," are terms used to refer to two distinct ways of thinking about intelligence.

A fixed mindset views intelligence and ability as fixed. Under this mindset, a person is either capable of doing something or not. You are smart or you aren't. You are good at something, or you're not. Fixed mindsets consider aptitude to be limited, so if you're not cut out for something, you'll never be good at cut out for it.

A growth mindset, on the other hand, views intelligence and ability as capable of growth or improvement. When a person has a growth mindset, they believe that people can acquire ability and increase intellectual capability, with the right kind of effort and guidance. A growth mindset views failures as setbacks, not as proof of inability. A growth mindset says, "I can learn from my mistakes and improve," "I can learn how to do this," and "I may not be great at this task *yet*, but I can be."

Why is this important? Well, in law school, you will experience self-doubt and encounter difficulty. You will be inundated with readings and challenged intellectually. Sometimes, you will feel like you are in over your head. And, because everybody who is admitted to law school is capable, *including you*, not everyone will receive all A+ grades. So there is the chance that you might have setbacks. The question is how you deal with these setbacks.

So, when you encounter feelings of disappointment, discouragement, or doubt, here are a few things you should remember:

NEGATIVE THOUGHT	GROWTH MINDSET RESPONSE
• I'm the only one who doesn't get it.	• Everyone in law school feels this way at some point. What I am experiencing is normal.
• This reading is too hard	• I can persevere, using the right techniques, and figure this out.
• This grade I got on a writing assignment is evidence that I'm a bad writer.	• I can learn from my mistakes and the feedback I got from my writing professor.
• This material is too hard for me.	• Nothing is too hard for me. I can figure out how to get through this material and understand it.
• I don't know if I'm cut out for this.	• I am as capable as any of the other students in this law school.
• I'm bad at (multiple choice/ writing/exams)	• I can learn to do anything if I put my mind to it and approach it in the right way.
• Maybe I'm just not smart enough.	• Intelligence is not a fixed characteristic. I can study, work hard, and seek help when I need it in order to master the skills and knowledge necessary to succeed.

Finally, do not be afraid to ask for help. Most likely, your school has an academic support professional who is there to help you find ways to reach your full potential academically. The academic support person is eager to help you discover your particular path to success.

Here is the bottom line: Even though the information you encounter may seem like rocket science at times, it's not. You're just learning a new language—new grammar, new syntax, new rules of construction. And that can take time. You are bound to make a few mistakes, have a few misunderstandings, and trip over a few things. Even though it can be a little frustrating, you can learn the language and become fluent, an expert.

> ### *We Belong*
>
> AYO is an African American who grew up in the upper middle class suburbs of a major east coast city. His father was a doctor and their mother was a lawyer. Ayo went to college in Pittsburgh, and law school back in his home state. After graduating from law school, Ayo became a solo practitioner and has maintained a solo law practice for nearly 25 years.
>
> *Ayo's Advice:* **Visit your local courthouse. If you do, you will see that people like us exist at all levels of the profession. Sit in on cases. Take the opportunity to speak with court personnel, law clerks, lawyers and judges about what they do. It is valuable to see how what you will learn in school applies practically. And you will see that you have the ability to succeed, just like those who came before you.**

---

[1]   *See* Jerry Kang, *Trojan Horses of Race*, 118 HARV. L. REV. 1489 (2005).

[2]   Atkinson, R.C. and Shiffrin, R.M., *Human Memory: A Proposed System and Its Control Processes.* 2 PSYCHOLOGY OF LEARNING AND MOTIVATION 89 (1968); Newell, A. and Simon, H.A., *Simulation of Human Thinking and Problem Solving*, MONOGRAPHS OF THE SOCIETY FOR RESEARCH IN CHILD DEVELOPMENT (1962).

[3]   Kang, *Trojan Horses of Race* at 1498–1499.

[4]   Id.

[5]   Id.

[6]   Eschholz, S., Bufkin, J., & Long, J. (2002). Symbolic Reality Bites: Women And Racial/Ethnic Minorities In Modern Film. *Sociological Spectrum, 22*(3), 299–334.

[7]   Bristor, J. M., Lee, R. G., & Hunt, M. R. (1995). Race and ideology: African-American images in television advertising. *Journal of Public Policy & Marketing*, 48–59.

[8]   Eschholz, S., Bufkin, J., & Long, J. (2002).

[9]   Alsultany, E. (2012). *Arabs and Muslims in the Media: Race and Representation after 9/11.* NYU Press; Ahmed, A. (2002). Hello, Hollywood: Your Images Affect Muslims Everywhere. *New Perspectives Quarterly, 19*(2), 73–75.

[10]   Burgess, M. C., Dill, K. E., Stermer, S. P., Burgess, S. R., & Brown, B. P. (2011). Playing With Prejudice: The Prevalence and Consequences of Racial Stereotypes in Video Games. *Media Psychology, 14*(3), 289–311.

[11]   Dickerman, C., Christensen, J., & Kerl-McClain, S. B. (2008). Big Breasts and Bad Guys: Depictions of Gender and Race in Video Games. *Journal of Creativity in Mental Health, 3*(1), 20–29.

[12]   Giscombe, K., & Mattis, M. C. (2002). Leveling the Playing Field for Women of Color in Corporate Management: Is the Business Case Enough?. *Journal Of Business Ethics, 37*(1), 103–119; Fairfax, L. M. (2005). Lisa M. Fairfax, Some Reflections on the Diversity of Corporate Boards: Women, People of Color, and the Unique Issues Associated With Women of Color, 79 St. John's L. Rev. 1105 (2006); Cook, A., & Glass, C., *Above the Glass Ceiling: When Are Women and Racial/Ethnic Minorities Promoted to CEO?. 35*(7) STRATEGIC MANAGEMENT J., 1080 (2014).

[13]   Fang, D., Moy, E., Colburn, L., & Hurley, J. (2000). Racial and Ethnic Disparities in Faculty Promotion in Academic Medicine. *Jama, 284*(9), 1085–1092; Peterson, N. B., Friedman, R. H., Ash, A. S., Franco, S., & Carr, P. L. (2004). Faculty Self-Reported Experience With Racial and Ethnic Discrimination in Academic Medicine. *Journal Of General Internal Medicine, 19*(3), 259–265; Xu, Y. J. (2008). Gender Disparity in STEM Disciplines: A Study of Faculty Attrition and

Turnover Intentions. *Research In Higher Education, 49*(7), 607–624; Allen, W. R., Epps, E. G., Guillory, E. A., Suh, S. A., & Bonous-Hammarth, M. (2000). The Black Academic: Faculty Status Among African Americans in US Higher Education. *Journal Of Negro Education*, 112–127.

14 Reardon, S. F., Baker, R., & Klasik, D. (2012). Race, Income, and Enrollment Patterns in Highly Selective Colleges, 1982–2004. *Center for Education Policy Analysis, Stanford University. Retrieved from http://cepa.stanford.edu/content/race-income-and-enrollment-patterns-highly-selective-colleges-1982-2004.*

15 It is important to note that not all people fall neatly into only one of these categories. So the categories or characteristics subconsciously applied may depend on the salient context or external perception.

16 Banaji, M.R. and Greenwald, A.G. (1995). Implicit Social cognition: Attitudes, Self-Esteem, and Stereotypes. Psychological Review, 102(1), 4–27.

17 Michael Selmi, *Statistical Inequality and Intentional (Not Implicit) Discrimination*, 79 Law & Contemp. Probs. 199 (2016); L. Song Richardson, *Implicit Racial Bias and Racial Anxiety: Implications for Stops and Frisks*, 15 Ohio St. J. Crim. L. 73 (2017); Michael Selmi, *Statistical Inequality and Intentional (Not Implicit) Discrimination*, 79 Law & Contemp. Probs. 199 (2016).

18 Josh Gupta-Kagan, *The School-to-Prison Pipeline's Legal Architecture: Lessons From the Spring Valley Incident and its Aftermath*, 45 Fordham Urb. L.J. 83 (2017).

19 Chapman, et al., Physicians and Implicit Bias: How Doctors May Unwittingly Perpetuate Health Care Disparities, 28 J. Gen. Intern. Med. 1504 (2013).

20 Bertrand, M., & Mullainathan, S. (2004). Are Emily and Greg More Employable Than Lakisha and Jamal? A Field Experiment on Labor Market Discrimination. *American economic review, 94*(4), 991–1013.

21 Jennifer L. Doleac and Luke C.D. Stein, *The Visible Hand: Race and Online Market Outcomes*, 123 Econ. 469 (2013).

22 Claude M. Steele, *A Threat in the Air: How Stereotypes Shape Intellectual Identity and Performance*, 52 AM. PSYCHOLOGIST 613 (1997); Claude M. Steele, WHISTLING VIVALDI: AND OTHER CLUES TO HOW STEREOTYPES AFFECT US (W.W. Norton & Co. 2010).

23 Steven J. Spencer et al., *Stereotype Threat and Women's Math Performance*, 35 J. EXPERIMENTAL SOC. PSYCHOL. 4 (1999); Ryan P. Brown & Robert A. Josephs, *A Burden of Proof: Stereotype Relevance and Gender Differences in Math Performance*, 76 J. PERSONALITY & SOC. PSYCHOL. 246 (1999); Michael Johns et al., *Knowing Is Half the Battle: Teaching Stereotype Threat as a Means of Improving Women's Math Performance*, 16 PSYCHOL. SCI. 175 (2005).

24 Spencer, footnote 23 supra.

25 A Threat in the Air, at 613–29; Claude M. Steele, Thin Ice: "Stereotype Threat" and Black College Students, ATLANTIC MONTHLY, Aug. 1999; Claude M. Steele & Joshua Aronson, Stereotype Threat and the Intellectual Test Performance of African Americans, 69 J. PERSONALITY & SOC. PSYCHOL. 797 (1995).

26 Steele, A Threat in the Air.

27 Jean-Claude Croizet, et al., *Stereotype Threat Undermines Intellectual Performance by Triggering a Disruptive Mental Load*, 30 PERSONALITY & SOC. PSYCHOL. BULL. 721 (2004).

28 Toni Schmader & Michael Johns, *Converging Evidence that Stereotype Threat Reduces Working Memory Capacity*, 85 J. PERSONALITY & SOC. PSYCHOL. 440 (2003); Sian L. Beilock, *Stereotype Threat and Working Memory: Mechanisms, Alleviation, and Spillover*, 136 J. EXPERIMENTAL PSYCHOL. 256 (2007).

29 *See, e.g.*, Jeremy P. Jamieson & Stephen G. Harkins, *Mere Effort and Stereotype Threat Performance Effects*, 93 J. PERSONALITY & SOC. PSYCHOL. 544 (2007).

30 Joshua Aronson & Michael Inzlicht, *The Ups and Downs of Attributional Ambiguity: Stereotype Vulnerability and the Academic Self-Knowledge of African American College Students*, 15 PSYCHOL. SCI. 829 (2004).

31 Claude M. Steele, WHISTLING VIVALDI: AND OTHER CLUES TO HOW STEREOTYPES AFFECT US (W.W. Norton & Co. 2010).

32 Johannes Keller, *Stereotype Threat in Classroom Settings: The Interactive Effect of Domain Identification, Task Difficulty and Stereotype Threat on Female Students' Maths Performance*, 77 BRIT. J. EDUC. PSYCHOL. 323 (2010).

33 Steele, WHISTLING VIVALDI; Joshua Aronson et al., *Reducing the Effects of Stereotype Threat on African American College Students by Shaping Theories of Intelligence*, 38 J. EXPERIMENTAL SOC. PSYCHOL. 113 (2002); Lisa S. Blackwell et al., *Implicit Theories of Intelligence*

Predict Achievement Across an Adolescent Transition: A Longitudinal Study and an Intervention, 78 CHILD DEV. 246 (2007).

[34] Ulrich W. Weger et al., *Mindful Maths: Reducing the Impact of Stereotype Threat Through a Mindfulness Exercise*, 21 CONSCIOUSNESS & COGNITION 471 (2012)

[35] Carol S. Dweck, MINDSET: THE NEW PSYCHOLOGY OF SUCCESS (Random House 2016).

CHAPTER 4

LEGAL SOURCES AND STRUCTURES

■ ■ ■

In this chapter, I wish to provide you with a context for much of the academic subject matter you will encounter in law school. Of course, this is law school, so much of what you will read involves law. But where does law come from? Who creates, interprets, and enforces the rules that we call "law?" What I will provide below is a simplified, but I think helpful, explanation of the basics you need to know in order to get started with your law study. (There is much more nuance that you will learn during your time in law school, but I will not explore all of that nuance here.)

I. STRUCTURE OF GOVERNMENT

Most readers know that the basic structure of government in the United States involves the interaction of three branches of government: Executive, Legislative, and Judicial. (Although some consider "Agencies" a virtual fourth branch, that is outside of the scope of this introduction.) These structures have parallels on the state and local levels. We usually think of the legislative branch as making the laws, the executive branch as enforcing laws, and the judicial branch as evaluating and applying laws in order to resolve disputes. In reality, these relationships are much more complex.

II. SOURCES OF AMERICAN LAW

"Laws," as we think of them—rules that structure relationships and govern behavior—come from a range of sources. These sources interact with each other to set boundaries on behaviors, to establish rights and responsibilities, and to create a relatively stable set of structures and ground rules within which our society operates.[1]

A. CONSTITUTIONS

Constitutions exist at varying levels of government. Indeed, they establish governments and the paramount principles that dominate all other rules. I expect you are familiar with the Constitution of the United States, which established our federal governmental structure, and from which, through the bill of rights, we derive freedoms of speech and religion, the right to be free from unreasonable searches and seizures, the right to vote, the right to privacy, and numerous additional rights and freedoms that guarantee us the liberty the Constitution promises.

States also have constitutions that are similar in form to the U.S. Constitution. These state constitutions establish their executive, legislative, and court structures. State constitutions also may provide additional rights to their citizens, beyond those guaranteed by the U.S. Constitution.

Even local governments may have constitutional types of documents. Many cities and counties have charters that establish their own governmental structures (mayors, city councils, county executives, etc.) and authorize them to make laws (e.g., city ordinances) that regulate conduct within their borders.

B. STATUTES

On both the federal and state levels, legislatures enact statutes that establish rules. On the federal level, a bicameral (i.e., the House of Representatives and the Senate) legislative process is used to pass bills that then must be signed by the President in order to become laws. (Of course, the President may veto any bill, and the legislature may override the veto with a two-thirds majority in each house of Congress.) Many states have similar legislative processes.

Statutes are subject to constitutional processes. At the federal level, the Constitution provides the U.S. Congress with regulatory authority over specific areas. For example, Congress has the constitutional authority to pass laws that regulate interstate commerce, but it does not have the power to exercise general police powers. State legislatures, on the other hand, can regulate based on general police powers unless doing so violates the state constitution or federal law (including the U.S. Constitution).

When the validity of statutes is challenged, the challengers often allege that a statute is unconstitutional, meaning, usually, that they either exceeded a legislature's authority to regulate or that they violate some constitutionally-imposed constraint.

C. REGULATIONS

Sometimes, although legislatures have the authority to regulate in certain areas, they pass that authority on (or "delegate" it) to an agency— located either within the executive branch or independent of any branch— to regulate the area. This happens because, among other reasons, these agencies generally have specialized expertise that legislators do not have. Agencies then issue detailed regulations that govern within their particular areas of expertise. At the federal level, examples include the Internal Revenue Service, an executive branch agency that issues a range of regulations relating to taxes, and the Environmental Protection Agency, an executive branch that issues regulations relating to environmental standards. The Federal Trade Commission, an independent agency, issues regulations and ruling related to how businesses conduct themselves in the market.

Regulations that are properly authorized and enacted have the same force as laws passed by the legislature. They also are subject to the same constitutional limits.

D. COURT DECISIONS

Much of the law you study in law school comes from court decisions (judicial opinions). It will be important for you to understand how courts are structured and how they interpret and create law.

1. Structure of Courts

Court systems usually are structured into a three-level hierarchy. On the lowest level are trial courts. Above that are intermediate courts of appeal. At the top level are super-appellate (i.e., supreme) courts.

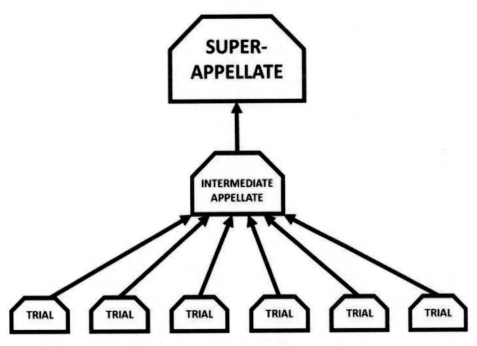

Federal courts are organized, for example, into District Courts (trial), Circuit Courts (intermediate-appellate), and the Supreme Court of the United States (super-appellate). State courts have similar structures, but the names might be different. (For example, a trial court in the state of New York is called the Supreme Court, and the highest court is the New

York Court of Appeals.) So, it is important to pay attention to which level court authored an opinion you are reading.

Trial courts often are the first to hear disputes between parties. Parties present evidence in the form of documents and witnesses, and, after the parties make their arguments, trial courts render initial decisions. Trial courts—often relying on the fact-finding conducted by juries—are in the best position to evaluate credibility of witnesses and to make choices about disputed facts in a dispute. Trial judges also issue legal rulings, including evidentiary rulings in the course of trials, and these rulings often provide a basis for the party that loses to appeal.

Intermediate appellate courts generally are the first available opportunity for appellate review of trial court decisions. After a trial is over, an party dissatisfied with the outcome may appeal in order to change the outcome—assuming that they have a legitimate legal argument for appealing the decision. (An important exception is the state, which cannot appeal an acquittal in a criminal proceeding—due to constitutional double jeopardy concerns.) Rather than evaluating evidence, appellate courts typically evaluate a trial court's determination of the governing legal rules and their application to the facts of a case. In other words, the trial court is generally regarded as being in the best position to evaluate the facts, and the appellate court is considered better able to evaluate the law.

In many cases, parties are entitled or may be permitted to appeal from an unfavorable outcome issued by an intermediate-appellate court. These appeals are decided by supreme (super-appellate) courts. These courts have ultimate authority to resolve disputes of law within their jurisdictions. For example, on the federal level, the Supreme Court of the United States has ultimate authority to resolve questions of federal law.

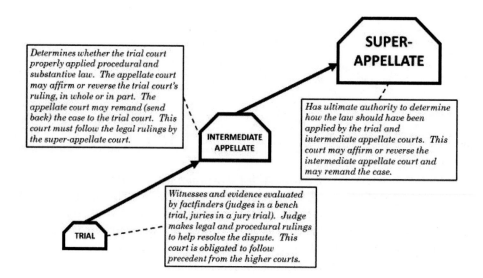

2.   Function of Courts

Courts are often called upon to interpret laws. Using rules of constitutional or statutory interpretation, judges and justices determine the meaning of words in statutes, constitutions, and regulations. Judges use these interpretations to resolve the disputes before them.

Sometimes, disputes arise in contexts where there is no relevant, governing law, or where open legal questions remain that must be resolved. In these cases, courts create law, often with the resolved legal question forming the basis for precedent. These cases serve two simultaneous functions: (1) resolving disputes between the parties before the court, and (2) establishing legal rules to be used as precedent in later cases.

Much of what you will study in the first year of law school will be based on this court-created law. If you imagine a world where statutes and regulations do not regulate particular areas of conduct—or where they cover the general area yet fail to resolve particular issues, you can better understand how disputes arise. But if there is insufficient law available to address a specific dispute, courts must create (or derive) that law in order reach a resolution. The resulting judicially created law is called "common law."

Common law grows to regulate areas over time, often decades or even hundreds of years. In your first year, you can expect to read judicial opinions from pre-Colonial England up to and including the present, in the subject areas of Contracts, Torts, Criminal Law, and Property.

A kind of common law also arises in the context of constitutional interpretation. Constitutional law is the body of case law, centering on the United States Supreme Court, arising from the resolution of various provisions set out in the U.S. Constitution.

3.   Relationships Among Court Systems

Above, we discussed the relationships within court systems (trial, intermediate appellate, and super appellate courts). It is also important to understand the relationships between and among different court systems. During your studies, you will learn about federal, state, and international courts, and you may even study the judicial systems of other nations. The most important set of relationships you will encounter is between the federal courts and the state courts. Among the biggest questions in this very complex relationship is which system has primary authority to resolve particular kinds of disputes and issue controlling rulings in those areas.

A superficial answer to this question might suggest that federal courts have primary authority to resolve disputes relating to federal law, and state courts have primary authority to resolve disputes relating to state law. But the fact is that each set of courts has some ability to hear and resolve disputes arising under the law of the other. Some cases may be resolved only by a particular court system—we call this exclusive jurisdiction. In other cases, multiple court systems may have jurisdiction to resolve certain kinds of disputes—this is called concurrent jurisdiction.

Federal courts have primary jurisdiction over disputes arising under the Constitution and laws of the United States. With respect to certain areas of federal law, federal courts have exclusive jurisdiction. Federal courts also have concurrent jurisdiction to hear a range of other kinds of disputes, including significant disputes between citizens of different states. (You will learn about this in a course called "Civil Procedure.")

State courts generally have primary jurisdiction over cases arising under their laws and constitutions. If the state-law-based cases do not fall within the "disputes between citizens of different states" area of federal court jurisdiction, or if the dispute does not challenge the constitutionality of a state law, then this jurisdiction is likely to be exclusive to state courts. State courts also have concurrent jurisdiction to hear certain kinds of cases arising under federal law.

E. OTHER SOURCES OF LAW

In addition to reading judicial opinions, statutes, and regulations, you also will encounter other resources that help us understand the operation of the law in various circumstances. Unlike the other sources of law we discussed above, which are binding, these sources are not binding (unless an appropriate lawmaking body elects to adopt the rules as its own), but they may inform us about the way laws should be applied to certain kinds of problems.

Restatements. Sometimes, experts in a particular area of law get together to explain that area of law to the rest of the world. One way in which experts do this is to write volumes of rules called "restatements of the law," which are produced by the American Law Institute. These restatements contain what the experts agree should be the rules to govern disputes within a doctrinal area. These suggestions are not law at all, but they often influence courts and policymakers. When the rules regarding a particular kind of legal problem are unsettled, courts might consult restatements to get expert guidance on the law. Restatements exist in a range of doctrinal areas. During your first year, you are most likely to encounter restatements in you courses on Contracts, Torts, and Property.

Uniform Codes. There are certain areas of law where it makes sense for the law to be the same or similar across jurisdictions. For that reason, uniform codes emerged as a method to make it easy for jurisdictions to adopt rules that help in the process of coordinating legal rules across states. Like restatements, uniform codes are developed by doctrinal experts who agree on what rules should govern a particular area of law. Uniform codes are usually comprehensive, covering an entire area of law. Even so, once these codes are adopted in jurisdictions, they may be supplemented by the common law in that jurisdiction.

In order for these rules to become law, however, they must be adopted by each relevant jurisdiction. Uniform codes usually are adopted by legislatures, but some uniform codes (like codes of lawyers' ethics) are adopted by courts. Sometimes, when jurisdictions adopt rules, they adopt them wholesale. At other times, jurisdictions may modify some of the rules to conform to their own views of the law.

Examples of uniform codes include (i) the Uniform Commercial Code (UCC), a set of rules governing various kinds of commercial transactions; (ii) the Model Penal Code, rules defining a full range of crimes; and (iii) the Model Rules of Professional Conduct, a code of ethics for lawyers.

Scholarly Writings. The law also can be influenced by experts in a different way. Law professors in every law school in the nation produce articles addressing cutting edge developments in the law. Sometimes, judges rely on these articles for guidance as they strive to determine what law should be applied in the cases before them. You likely will read excerpts from some of these articles in your casebooks, and you may find that these articles help a great deal as you learn about the law and the theory behind it.

You will encounter many of these types of law in your few years of study in law school.

---

[1]   This is not to say that these structures are all fair and equitable, but, at the very least, we have a set of structures and rules that we understand. We can vote for government representatives, we can lobby legislatures to change laws, and we can go to courts to seek redress for wrongs. Even though we may not always be happy with the outcomes, these structures are generally stable.

CHAPTER 5

INTRODUCTION TO CONTRACTS

■ ■ ■

Before we begin learning about Promissory Estoppel—the substantive topic we will cover in this book—it is important to provide some context for the topic we are learning. In this section, I will introduce you to some of the basics of contract law that will help you understand where the doctrine of promissory estoppel fits and why it matters.

Contract law is built on the basic notion that parties can agree to an exchange of promises and/or obligations. In general, the formation of the contractual relationship is built on two pillars: (1) Mutual Assent, and (2) Consideration. We will discuss these concepts in the pages that follow.

I.   Mutual Assent

Of course, it makes sense that if we are going to talk about contracts, or agreements, it is essential that the parties actually **agree to something**. I use this phrase deliberately, because when resolving whether parties have formed a contract we look both for the *agreement* (the parties' commitment) and the *something* (substance of the agreement).

A.   Making a Commitment

1.   Manifestation of Assent—Technical Aspects

To form a contract, parties must express their unequivocal commitment to the terms of the agreement. Often (but not always), this occurs in the form of an offer and an acceptance.

An offer is made by one party, called the offeror, to another, called the offeree. The offeror must express a commitment and terms so definitely that the offeree may simply say "yes" in order to form a contract. Once an offer is made, the offeree acquires the power of acceptance. This power continues until the offer is withdrawn, expires, or is rejected by the offeree. The offeror generally has the power to withdraw (or revoke) an offer at any time after it is made. The offer expires (or lapses) when a sufficient amount of time has passed or when the offeror has given the offeree a deadline for making a response. Once the power of acceptance has been terminated, it cannot be revived except through the expression of a new offer.

For many contracts, the offeree's response must be an unequivocal yes in order to be an acceptance. If the response varies the terms of the offer at all, then the response is considered to be a counteroffer. (There is an exception for contracts involving the sale of goods, but we will not address that here.) A counteroffer has two effects: (i) it operates as a rejection of the initial offer, and (ii) it creates a new offer, so that the person who was the offeree becomes the offeror.

Once the parties agree to the same thing at the same time—we sometimes call this a "meeting of the minds"—the mutual assent requirement has been met.

The following examples will demonstrate how these technical rules of contract formation work.

EXAMPLE A

In the following diagram, we see the simplest form of contract formation. A offers terms to B, who accepts those terms. At that moment, a contract has been formed.

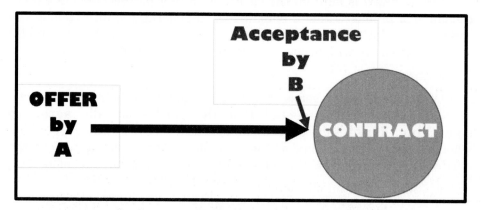

EXAMPLE B

This illustration is nearly identical to the previous example. I have added information to show you that, once B accepts A's offer, A has lost the power to revoke that offer.

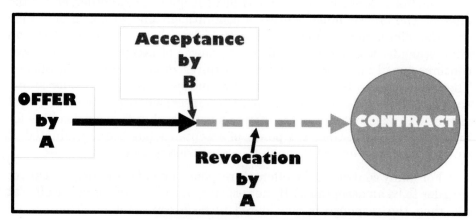

EXAMPLE C

If A's offer lapses because too much time has passed—either because a reasonable time has passed or because a deadline set by A has passed—B has lost the power of acceptance, and no contract is formed.

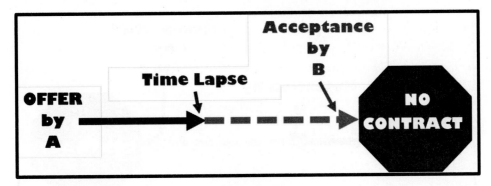

EXAMPLE D

Like the previous example, once A has revoked the offer, B has lost the power of acceptance, and there is no contract.

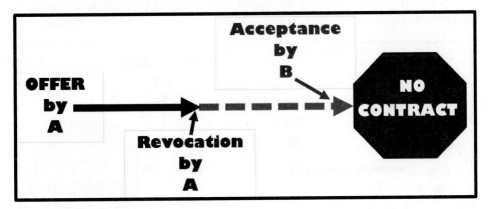

EXAMPLE E

If B rejects A's offer, the offer is no longer valid, and B has lost the power of acceptance. If B changes their mind later, they may not accept, and no contract is formed.

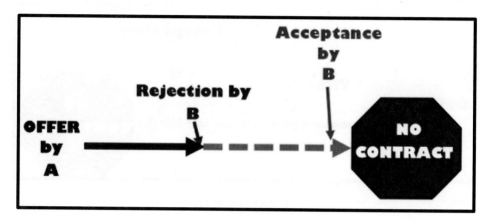

EXAMPLE F

A counteroffer operates the same as a rejection, so far as A's offer is concerned. Once B counters, B may no longer accept A's original offer.

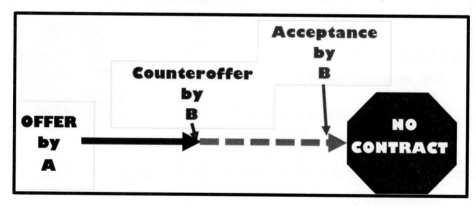

EXERCISES

1.   Bill wants to buy a car. He goes onto Craigslist and sees an ad saying, "FOR SALE. Vintage 1976 Volkswagen Beetle. Mint Condition. Classic Yellow. 25,000 original miles." Bill e-mails the seller, saying, "I want to buy this car." The seller replies, saying, "Glad to hear it. We have a deal." *Have the parties manifested assent to an agreement? Why or why not?*

2. Dev offers to Irit: "I offer to paint your house for $5000 plus the cost of materials." Irit responds: "How about $4000?" Dev: "No deal." Irit: "Okay, then I accept the $5000." *Have the parties manifested assent to an agreement? Why or why not?*

3. Andre offers to Drew: "I offer to paint your house for $5000 plus the cost of materials." Drew does not respond for six months, at which time she says, "I accept your offer." *Have the parties manifested assent to an agreement? Why or why not?*

4. Pat offers to Shira: "I offer to paint your house for $5000 plus the cost of materials." Three hours later, Pat says to Shira, "Never mind, I'm not going to be able to do it for that price." Shira immediately responds, "I accept your offer." *Have the parties manifested assent to an agreement? Why or why not?*

5. Buyer makes a written offer to buy property from Seller. Seller modifies and then signs the offer sheet, returning it to Buyer. Buyer does not respond immediately. Seller agrees to terms with a second buyer, notifying the first Buyer that Seller's version of the offer sheet is revoked. Buyer signs Seller's offer sheet as modified. *Have the parties manifested assent to an agreement? Why or why not?*

(Answers are on the following page.)

ANSWERS TO EXERCISES

1. No, the parties have not manifested assent to the agreement. Bill's e-mail saying, "I want to buy this car" was not unequivocal. "I want" is similar to saying "I'm interested" but different from saying "I offer to" or "I promise to." Even though Seller says, unequivocally, "We have a deal," there was no offer to be accepted. No contract is formed.

2. No, the parties have not manifested assent to the agreement. Dev's initial statement was an unequivocal statement of an intention to be bound, and thus it constituted an offer. When Irit tried to change the terms from $5000 to $4000, Irit made a counteroffer. The counteroffer both rejects Dev's offer and creates a new offer by Irit. The implicit rejection of Dev's offer terminated Irit's power of acceptance, so Irit could not "accept the $5000." Note: Dev's rejection of Irit's counteroffer also terminated that offer.

3. No, it is not likely that the parties have manifested assent. Although both Andre's offer and Drew's response were unequivocal, it is likely that Andre's offer lapsed during the six months Drew waited to respond. This terminated Drew's power of acceptance, and there is no contract.

4. No, the parties have not manifested assent to the agreement. Even though Pat's offer was unequivocal, Pat revoked the offer three hours later. Once Pat revoked the offer, Shira's power of acceptance was terminated, so her response has no effect. No contract was formed.

5. No. Buyer's initial offer was rejected when Seller modified it. Seller's response was a counteroffer. Seller revoked its counteroffer before it was accepted. Buyer did not have the power to accept the offer. (See *Normile v. Miller*, 326 S.E.2d 11 (NC 1985).)

2. Objective Approach to Evaluating Assent

To determine whether parties have assented to an agreement, we interpret their words and actions objectively. In simple terms, this means that we care what they say and/or do, not what they think. The question we ask is, "What would a reasonable person think the words and/or actions of the parties mean?" Aside from the way that parties act (so long as those actions are voluntary), we do not generally concern ourselves with their actual intention to be bound. In other words, it is the manifestation we care about rather than the intent.

The following examples should clarify how to understand this.

EXAMPLES

A. Business, through an online portal, engages with a search engine company to appear at the top of relevant searches. Business scrolled through terms and conditions, but did not read them. At the end of the terms and conditions, Business clicked on an "I AGREE" button. If business had read the terms, it would have realized that the cost could have been more expensive than it predicted. *If Business did not read the terms, can it be bound by those terms?*

ANSWER: Yes, Business can be bound. We interpret the conduct of Business objectively. By clicking "I AGREE," Business objectively manifested its assent to the terms of the agreement, whether it read the terms or not. (See *Feldman v. Google, Inc.*, 513 F.Supp.2d 229 (E.D.Pa 2007).)

B. Home Builder signs agreement to build home for Customer. The written agreement attached specifications, which Builder signed. Builder did not read the specifications, mistakenly believing they were an earlier version of the specifications. Builder's honest, but unexpressed, intention, was to commit to the earlier version of the specifications. *Is Builder bound by the terms of the agreement, including the attached (revised) specifications?*

ANSWER: Yes, Builder is bound. Absent some misconduct by the other contracting party, we interpret Builder's conduct objectively. It does not matter what Builder thought it was agreeing to. What matters is how a reasonable person would interpret Builder's actions. (See *Ray v. William G. Eurice & Bros., Inc.*, 93 A.2d 272 (Md. 1952).)

C. Property Seller takes out ad in newspaper seeking inquiries from those interested in selling property. Buyer responds to Seller asking for details about the property and purchase process. Seller responds with additional information and says, "You need to act quickly, because I have a lot of interested buyers." Buyer writes to Owner saying, "I agree to your terms." *Have the parties manifested assent to the agreement?*

ANSWER: No. Although Buyer manifested an intention to be bound, Seller never unequivocally manifested such an intention. Saying, "You need to act quickly" is not the same as saying, "I offer these terms to you." (See *Lonergan v. Scolnick*, 276 P.2d 8 (Cal. App. 1954).)

EXERCISES

1. Darrell promises to store Carlos's belongings for one month for the price of $500. Carlos agrees to these terms, but, unbeknownst to Darrell, Carlos has his finger crossed behind his back. (This means that Carlos secretly does not mean what he is saying.) *Have Darrell and Carlos manifested assent to an agreement?*

2.   Felix signs up for a social media membership with MyFace. Felix clicked "I Agree" when signing up for the membership, but was not given the opportunity to read the terms and conditions, which were not visible on the page when Felix signed up. *Have Felix and MyFace manifested assent to an agreement?*

(Answers are on the following page.)

ANSWERS TO EXERCISES

1. Yes, the parties have manifested assent to the agreement. Even though Carlos has his fingers crossed and did not actually mean what he said, we evaluated Carlos's behavior objectively, not subjectively. A reasonable person in Darrell's position would believe that Carlos was manifesting assent to the agreement, given that Carlos hid his true intentions. Therefore, a contract was formed.

2. This is a close call, but the parties likely did not manifest assent to the hidden terms. Unlike the *Feldman v. Google, Inc.* case, Felix did not have the opportunity to review the terms before clicking "I Agree." Therefore, viewed objectively, there is no manifestation that Felix assented to those terms. (The lines in these cases vary across jurisdictions, so the answer may vary in different courts.)

B. Essential Terms

The parties get to decide what contract terms matter to them, and if either party deems a term important enough, a contract cannot be formed until the parties agree to that term. But there are some terms that must be agreed to before a contract has been formed: (1) Parties, (2) subject matter, (3) price, and (4) time.

Parties. The contracting parties must agree to who holds the benefits and obligations under the contract.

Subject Matter. They must agree to the obligations required under the contract.

Price. They must agree to the cost to be paid under the contract. Cost may be paid in money, but it also may be paid in a corresponding obligation.

Time. Historically, the parties also had to agree to the time period within which the obligations under a contract must be performed. Where the parties do not agree to a time, modern courts will impose a "reasonable time" obligation.

EXERCISES

1. Krisha and Selma agree that Krisha will paint the exterior of Selma's home next weekend. *Have Krisha and Selma manifested assent to an agreement? Why or why not?*

2. Max and Sam agree that Max will work for Sam from 6 a.m. until 10 p.m. next Saturday for the price of $2000. *Have Max and Sam manifested assent to an agreement? Why or why not?*

3. Bria and Felicia agree that Felicia will mow Bria's lawn for $50? *Have Bria and Felicia manifested assent to an agreement? Why or why not?*

ANSWERS TO EXERCISES

1.   No, they have not manifested assent to an agreement. The parties have not yet agreed to a price. Price is an essential term.

2.   No, they have not manifested assent to an agreement. The subject matter is not clear—there is no indication what work Max will be doing in exchange for the $2000. Subject matter is an essential term.

3.   No and Yes are appropriate answers to this question. Under Common Law, the absence of a time for performance would mean that the parties have not yet agreed to an essential term. Modern courts likely would impose a "reasonable time" term on the agreement and would enforce it.

II. Consideration

Even though the parties may agree to terms, their contract is not complete unless their agreement contains consideration. There are two ways of looking at consideration. One view is that consideration exists when there is a bargained for exchange between the parties. The other view is that a promise is supported by consideration when the agreement provides a benefit to the promisor or a detriment to the promisee.

Bargained for Exchange: The most common of these types of exchanges involves each party giving something of value to the other. As experts have put it: "A performance or return promise is bargained for if it is sought by the promisor in exchange for his promise and is given by the promisee in exchange for that promise." (Restatement (2nd) Contracts § 71.) For example, A and B might agree that A will wash B's car for $200. In this case, both A and B have bargained for an exchange of promises. A has promised to wash B's car, and B has promised to pay $200 to A.

Benefit or Detriment. Another way of looking at consideration is to look to see whether a promise that is made is connected to some benefit or detriment. In the same example above, A's promise to wash B's car is connected to the benefit of receiving $200. Or, we might look at this and say that B's entitlement to enforce A's promise is supported by the detriment to B of having to pay $200 to A.

EXAMPLES

Consider the following situations:

A. Uncle promises 21 year-old Nephew that Uncle will pay Nephew $1000 if Nephew will refrain from drinking until the age of 25. Nephew agrees to this arrangement. ***Is there consideration?***

ANSWER: Yes. Consideration exists using a benefit/detriment analysis. Nephew agreed to relinquish a legal right—the right to drink once a person is 21 years old. This is treated as a legal detriment. (See *Hamer v. Sidway*, 27 N.E. 256 (N.Y. 1891).) Under the detriment approach in *Hamer v. Sidway*, a legal detriment-and, therefore, consideration—exists where a party relinquishes (or agrees to relinquish) a legal right.

B. Oil refinery agrees to give oil sludge, for free, to a recycling company, which will recycle the sludge into usable products. Oil refinery saves itself the cost of disposing of the sludge, which is hazardous waste. ***Is there consideration?***

ANSWER: Yes. Although the recycling company did not suffer a detriment (the sludge was free), the refinery received a benefit through saving the expense of having to dispose of the waste. This benefit to the refinery is sufficient consideration to support its promise. (See *Pennsy Supply, Inc. v. American Ash Recycling Corp of Pennsylvania*, 895 A.2d 1184 (Pa. Super. 2007).)

C. Aunt loves nephew so much that she promises to provide for him in her will. Nephew agrees to this arrangement. ***Is there valid consideration?***

ANSWER: No. There is no consideration to support the aunt's gratuitous promise. She has received no benefit from the nephew, nor has he suffered a detriment. Looking at this another way, there is no bargained for exchange of promises here. (See *Dougherty v. Salt*, 125 N.E. 94 (N.Y. 1919).)

D. A Coin collector is missing a 2015 penny from their collection. The collector enters into a bargain with a neighbor whereby the collector agrees to give a priceless 1700's coin to the neighbor in exchange for a 2015 penny the neighbor pulled from under a sofa cushion. ***Is there valid consideration?***

ANSWER: Yes. Even though the 2015 penny has little actual value, it is valuable to the collector, who bargained for it in this exchange. So long as the exchange is bargained for, there is no requirement that there be any equivalence in the exchange. (See Restatement (2nd) Contracts § 79; *Batsakis v. Demotsis*, 226 S.W.2d 673 (Tex.App. 1949).)

E.   Auto Dealership and Mobile Car Wash Service agree that Service will wash as many cars as Dealership chooses to have washed during a month for a price of $200 per car. *Is there valid consideration?*

ANSWER: No. At first glance, there appears to be a bargained for exchange here, but Dealership has the option of choosing zero cars to be washed, meaning that it has not committed to anything. The absence of any obligation on Dealership's part makes its promise illusory. (Restatement (2nd) Contracts § 77.)

EXERCISES

1.   Professor walks into the law school lobby and sees a hungry law student. Professor says, "If you walk over to the food truck across the street, I'll buy you lunch." *Is there valid consideration? Why or why not?*

2.   After moving into a home, a new homeowner offers to give moving boxes to a neighbor who is moving out. The neighbor agrees to take the boxes. The new homeowner could have left the boxes at the curb, where the city trash and recycling agency would have removed it for free. *Is there valid consideration? Why or why not?*

3.   Company X and Company Y agree that company X will purchase from Company Y "as many widgets as Company X shall choose to order, up to a maximum of 5000 widgets" *Is there valid consideration? Why or why not?*

4.   A and B are negotiating over the sale of a home. A offers to sell the home for $1.2 million. B, undecided, offers to place $10,000 into escrow as a "good faith deposit" towards the purchase of a home if A will keep the offer open (and exclusive to B) for 10 days. The parties agree to these terms. Under the agreement, the deposit is fully refundable if for any reason, A and B do not go through with the transaction. *Is there valid consideration? Why or why not?*

(Answers are on the following page.)

ANSWERS TO EXERCISES

1.   No, there is no consideration. The professor is making a gratuitous promise to student. The fact that the student must cross the street is simply the cost of accessing the gift. Student is not incurring any obligation or bargaining for any exchange.

2.   No, there is no consideration. There was no exchange bargained for here. Looked at another way, there is no benefit given to the new homeowner by the neighbor's removal of the boxes. The boxes would have been removed for free by the city anyway.

3.   No, there is no consideration. By reserving the right to order as many as it would choose to order, X did not commit to anything. (i.e., X could choose to order zero widgets.) This was an illusory promise, creating no actual obligation.

4.   Yes, there is consideration. B's deposit was fully refundable, which makes it look as though there is no cost to B. However, B lost the ability to use those funds for 10 days. B has suffered a detriment by giving up the legal right to use those funds.

III. Why This Matters

Given that this book will not focus on the traditional methods of contract formation discussed in this chapter, you might wonder why I have bothered devoting a whole chapter to it. Promissory estoppel, the topic we *will* discuss in this book, is an alternative theory of contract formation (or enforcement of promises). As an alternative claim, promissory estoppel usually is employed when traditional contract formation theories will not work. This is often the case when there is a failure in one of the pillars of contract formation.

As you read the cases we will discuss in the chapters ahead, it will be important for you to understand why the courts choose to focus on promissory estoppel rather than traditional theories. In some cases, you will see that courts are prevented from using the traditional contract approach. This can lead to outcomes that seem unfair in light of the circumstances. Using a promissory estoppel approach can lead to more just outcomes in certain cases.

CHAPTER 6

PREPARING FOR CLASS

■ ■ ■

In this chapter, you will learn how to read a judicial opinion effectively. This is the skill you will spend most of your time on, especially during the first year of law school. And, although writing and other skills are very important, virtually everything you do in law school is dependent upon your ability to read—and to understand—the materials (primarily judicial opinions) that are assigned as a part of your reading.

I. READING JUDICIAL OPINIONS

Before we get into reading and understanding, however, it will be useful for you just to learn the structure and contents of a judicial opinion. To learn this, we will focus on the *Aceves v. U.S. Bank, N.A.* opinion, which you can find in the appendix of this book. (You may want to locate that opinion and place a bookmark there, as you will bounce back and forth from the opinion to these instructions as you work through this chapter.) The *Aceves* opinion is not the first case we will study in our upcoming classes, but it is good for learning how to read.

A Little Background

Before we take a closer look at the Aceves *case, we need a little context.*

You would read this case about a month and a half or so into a Contracts course, depending on how the course is taught. You might spend the first bit of time in the course learning about what makes a contract. Among the things that you will learn is that for an enforceable contract to exist, parties must agree to a concrete set of obligations, and those obligations (generally) must be mutual— meaning that each party has made promises or obligations in a negotiated exchange for the other's. (Caveat: I have just dramatically and unfairly oversimplified contract formation.)

So, when you encounter this case, you will have entered a different section in the course that focuses on when promises can be enforced even when no contract has been formed under the previously stated rules. Your casebook probably will have a section or chapter devoted to this topic, which is called Promissory Estoppel.

Even though not all opinions are the same, there are some basic components to most opinions you must familiarize yourself with:

THE CAPTION

The caption will tell you several important things about a case, including the names of some or all of the parties, the name and level (trial or appellate) of the court deciding the opinion, and the year the opinion was written. Take a look at the caption of the *Aceves* case.

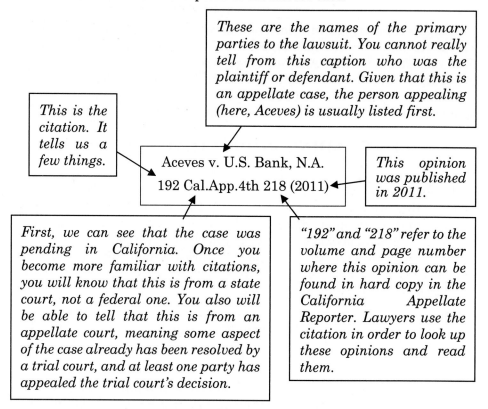

These are the names of the primary parties to the lawsuit. You cannot really tell from this caption who was the plaintiff or defendant. Given that this is an appellate case, the person appealing (here, Aceves) is usually listed first.

This is the citation. It tells us a few things.

Aceves v. U.S. Bank, N.A.

192 Cal.App.4th 218 (2011)

This opinion was published in 2011.

First, we can see that the case was pending in California. Once you become more familiar with citations, you will know that this is from a state court, not a federal one. You also will be able to tell that this is from an appellate court, meaning some aspect of the case already has been resolved by a trial court, and at least one party has appealed the trial court's decision.

"192" and "218" refer to the volume and page number where this opinion can be found in hard copy in the California Appellate Reporter. Lawyers use the citation in order to look up these opinions and read them.

It's probably also useful to note that the way the opinion begins tells us the name of the judge who wrote the opinion:

MALLANO, P. J.

PROCEDURAL HISTORY

Courts generally also will explain the process the parties went through in order to get the case to the court that is rendering this decision.

A.   Complaint

This action was filed on April 1, 2009. Two months later, a first amended complaint was filed. On August 17, 2009, after the sustaining of a demurrer, a second amended complaint (complaint) was filed. * * *

* * *

B. Demurrer

U.S. Bank filed a demurrer separately attacking each cause of action and the requested remedies. Aceves filed opposition.

At the hearing on the demurrer, Aceves's attorney argued that Aceves and her husband "could have saved their house through bankruptcy," but "due to the promises of the bank, they didn't go those routes to save their house. [¶] . . . [¶] . . . [T]hat's the whole essence of promissory estoppel. [¶] . . . [¶] Prior to [American Home's November 12, 2008] letter, there's numerous phone contacts and conversations with [American Home], which was the agent for U.S. Bank, regarding, 'Yes, once we get leave, we will work with you, . . . and they did not work with her at all.'" The trial court replied: "The foreclosure took place. There's no promissory fraud or anything that deluded [Aceves] under the circumstances."

On October 29, 2009, the trial court entered an order sustaining the demurrer without leave to amend and a judgment in favor of U.S. Bank. Aceves filed this appeal.

This describes how the lawsuit began. Here, we see when the initial pleading (a complaint) was filed. There is other information here about the original procedural history, including a first amended complaint, a demurrer, and a second amended complaint. When you first start reading cases, you will have to look up definitions for words like "demurrer." It often will be important for you to note the order in which things happened.

This describes what else happened while the case was pending before the trial court. We see that U.S. Bank filed another demurrer, which the trial judge sustained, entering judgment for U.S. Bank. This means Aceves lost. So, Aceves appealed that decision.

FACTS

Most judicial opinions will tell you the story of what happened between the parties to lead to the dispute that is being litigated in the courts. Sometimes, the facts will be long and complicated. Other times, courts will be more succinct and tell only the truly relevant parts of the story. When you read these stories, you may have to sift through the facts in order to get to the relevant parts of the story.

In the Aceves case, here is where the court explains the facts:

---

* * *

Plaintiff Claudia Aceves, a married woman, obtained a loan from Option One Mortgage Corporation (Option One) on April 20, 2006. The loan was evidenced by a note secured by a deed of trust on Aceves's residence. Aceves borrowed $845,000 at an initial rate of 6.35 percent. After two years, the rate became adjustable. The term of the loan was 30 years. Aceves's initial monthly payments were $4,857.09.

On March 25, 2008, Option One, the mortgagee, transferred its entire interest under the deed of trust to defendant U.S. Bank, National Association, as the "Trustee for the Certificateholders of Asset Backed Securities Corporation Home Equity Loan Trust, Series OOMC 2006-HE5" (U.S. Bank). * * *

In January 2008, Aceves could no longer afford the monthly payments on the loan. On March 26, 2008, Quality Loan Service recorded a "Notice of Default and Election to Sell Under Deed of Trust." (See Civ.Code, § 2924.) Shortly thereafter, Aceves filed for bankruptcy protection under chapter 7 of the Bankruptcy Code (11 U.S.C. §§ 701–784), imposing an automatic stay on the foreclosure proceedings (see 11 U.S.C. § 362(a)). Aceves contacted U.S. Bank and was told that, once her loan was out of bankruptcy, the bank "would work with her on a mortgage reinstatement and loan modification." She was asked to submit documents to U.S. Bank for its consideration.

Aceves intended to convert her chapter 7 bankruptcy case to a chapter 13 case (see 11 U.S.C. §§ 1301–1330) and to rely on the financial resources of her husband "to save her home" under chapter 13. In general, chapter 7, entitled "Liquidation," permits a debtor to discharge unpaid debts, but a debtor who discharges an unpaid home loan cannot keep the home; chapter 13, entitled "Adjustment of Debts of an Individual with Regular Income," allows a homeowner in default to reinstate the original loan payments, pay the arrearages over time, avoid foreclosure, and retain the home. (See 1 Collier on Bankruptcy (16th ed. 2010) ¶¶ 1.07[1][a] to 1.07[1][g], 1.07[5][a] to 1.07 [5][e], pp. 1-25 to 1–30, 1–43 to 1–45.)

U.S. Bank filed a motion in the bankruptcy court to lift the stay so it could proceed with a nonjudicial foreclosure.

On or about November 12, 2008, Aceves's bankruptcy attorney received a letter from counsel for the company servicing the loan, American Home Mortgage Servicing, Inc. (American Home). The letter requested that Aceves's attorney agree in writing to allow American Home to contact Aceves directly to "explore Loss Mitigation possibilities." Thereafter, Aceves contacted American Home's counsel and was told they could not speak to her before the motion to lift the bankruptcy stay had been granted.

In reliance on U.S. Bank's promise to work with her to reinstate and modify the loan, Aceves did not oppose the motion to lift the bankruptcy stay and decided not to seek bankruptcy relief under chapter 13. On December 4, 2008, the bankruptcy court lifted the stay. On December 9, 2008, although neither U.S. Bank nor American Home had contacted Aceves to discuss the reinstatement and modification of the loan, U.S. Bank scheduled Aceves's home for public auction on January 9, 2009.

On December 10, 2008, Aceves sent documents to American Home related to reinstating and modifying the loan. On December 23, 2008, American Home informed Aceves that a "negotiator" would contact her on or before January 13, 2009—four days after the auction of her residence. On December 29, 2008, Aceves received a telephone call from "Samantha," a negotiator from American Home. Samantha said to forget about any assistance in avoiding foreclosure because the "file" had been "discharged" in bankruptcy. On January 2, 2009, Samantha contacted Aceves again, saying that American Home had mistakenly decided not to offer her any assistance: American Home incorrectly thought Aceves's loan had been discharged in bankruptcy; instead, Aceves had merely filed for bankruptcy. Samantha said that, as a result of American Home's mistake, it would reconsider a loss mitigation proposal. On January 8, 2009, the day before the auction, Samantha called Aceves's bankruptcy attorney and stated that the new balance on the loan was $965,926.22; the new monthly payment would be more than $7,200; and a $6,500 deposit was due immediately via Western Union. Samantha refused to put any of those terms in writing. Aceves did not accept the offer.

On January 9, 2009, Aceves's home was sold at a trustee's sale to U.S. Bank. On February 11, 2009, U.S. Bank served Aceves with a three-day notice to vacate the premises and, a month later, filed an unlawful detainer action against her and her husband (U.S. Bank, N.A. v. Aceves (Super.Ct.L.A.County, 2009, No. 09H00857)). Apparently, Aceves and her husband vacated the premises during the eviction proceedings.

> U.S. Bank never intended to work with Aceves to reinstate and modify the loan. The bank so promised only to convince Aceves to forgo further bankruptcy proceedings, thereby permitting the bank to lift the automatic stay and foreclose on the property.
>
> * * *

There are a lot of facts here. When you read them at first, it might be difficult to determine which are the most important. We'll try to figure that out together soon, but for now, you might just notice that Claudia Aceves took out an adjustable rate mortgage loan, defaulted two years later, filed for bankruptcy, and tried to work it out with the bank but couldn't. There probably are more facts that are relevant, but it will be hard to figure them out until you read the rest of the opinion and see which facts the court relies upon to make its decision. But understanding the story will help you follow the court's rationale.

A. ISSUE(S)

For a court to resolve a case, it has to answer a legal question, which we call an issue. Sometimes, a court will be explicit about what the issue is, saying, "The question we must answer is . . ." or "The issue in this case is . . ." or "Appellant asks us to determine whether . . ." or a dozen variations of these phrases. At other times, you may have to read between the lines to figure out what the legal issue is.

In this case, we get a bit of a clue when the court says, "Aceves focuses primarily on her claim for promissory estoppel, arguing it is adequately pleaded." It might be a little hard to interpret this at first, but we might understand here that the issue, generally stated, is *whether the facts alleged by Aceves are sufficient to support a claim under the legal theory of promissory estoppel.*

RULES

Every opinion in your casebooks will have at least one rule in it. Some will have several, or even the single rule might have several parts to it. Rules are principles or standards that govern how a case should be resolved.

When you are looking for rules, look for clues. Sometimes, the court might lead up to a rule by saying something like, "When determining whether . . . we consider the following . . . ." Or, you might see a list of factors or considerations—or things we in law call "elements"—that make up the parts of a claim.

In *Aceves*, there are a lot of rule statements, so let's look at them closely so you can recognize them in other cases. The discussion starts with a really obvious rule statement:

" 'The elements of a promissory estoppel claim are "(1) a promise clear and unambiguous in its terms; (2) reliance by the party to whom the promise is made; (3) [the] reliance must be both reasonable and foreseeable; and (4) the party asserting the estoppel must be injured by his reliance." ' "

There are a few important things you want to pay attention to here. First, you can see that there is a list of four elements. You should also notice the word "and" before the last element. This means you need all four elements in order to establish a claim for promissory estoppel. Not all rules are structured this way, so you want to make sure that you pay attention to grammar, syntax, and punctuation, all of which can affect the meaning of a sentence or paragraph.

Next, notice that the opinion is quoting language from another opinion, the *Advanced Choices, Inc.* case, which was decided a year before *Aceves*. We call this earlier case "precedent." So that people can behave in predictable ways and be able to tell how cases should play out, courts follow precedent—in other words, courts tend to stick to the principles established in earlier cases, unless there is something about the new case that is different enough to justify a departure.

Finally, it's also useful to observe that even though you recognize all of the words—like "promise," "reliance," "reasonable," "foreseeable," and "injured"—they may have specific meanings. You may need to look up the meanings of these words in a legal dictionary, but, more likely, you will need to read the opinions carefully to see how the courts interpret the words used.

There are more rules throughout the *Aceves* opinion that actually explain how you can understand each element. It is critical for you to understand, in detail, each subtle aspects of the way these rules and sub-rules work together. Without trying to repeat all of these rules here, you should read and understand them carefully, because understanding the rules is just the beginning, as we will explore later.

DECISION

Of course, it is really important when reading a judicial opinion to figure out what happens with the case. This is usually at or near the very end of the opinion, although many judges also will let you know the outcome at the beginning.

As you read through the *Aceves* opinion, you will see a number of clues that will suggest that Aceves will be the winner:

"This is a clear and unambiguous promise."

". . . U.S. Bank broke its promise to negotiate with her toward a mutually agreeable modification."

"Aceves relied on U.S. Bank's promise by declining to convert her chapter 7 bankruptcy proceeding . . . ."

"We conclude Aceves reasonably relied on U.S. Bank's promise; U.S. Bank reasonably expected her to so rely; and it was foreseeable she would do so."

"We accept the truth of Aceves's allegations over U.S. Bank's speculation."

At the very end of the opinion, you will see this language: "The order and the judgment are reversed to the extent they dismissed the claims for promissory estoppel and fraud." To understand this sentence, you have to remember the procedural history—that the trial court sustained a demurrer, ending Aceves's case. So a reversal on the promissory estoppel and fraud claims allowed her case to continue.

THE HIDDEN STORY

When you read this case in the casebook, it is easy to get focused on the doctrine of promissory estoppel. And you have to do that, of course. But there are narratives behind many of the cases that we read that often go unnoticed.

Take the Aceves case. If you look closely, you may see that Aceves bought her home in 2006, during the peak of the housing bubble. This was during a time when banks were freely making loans, especially variable rate loans. Many of these loans were predatory, meaning banks were targeting people of color and people from lower socioeconomic strata, often making loans without requiring supporting documentation (i.e., proof of ability to pay). Banks were willing to take these risks because, just as in this case, these loans were bundled together and sold off as securities, effectively shifting the risk to the markets. The result? A financial crisis not seen since The Great Depression. Many of the same poor people and people of color went into default and ended up losing their homes to foreclosure.

So, if you look closely, the story in this case is also one that involves social justice issues.

You may find that some casebook authors fail to acknowledge these kinds of issues in cases. Your professors might overlook them sometimes also. This is not always—and indeed it may not often be the case—the result of malice on the part of the authors or professors. Sometimes, your well-meaning professors may feel inadequately prepared to deal with topics that are more challenging or controversial, and they may choose to avoid them in order to avoid making mistakes or letting classroom discussion get out of control. I say this by way of explanation, not by way of excuse—it is your professors' responsibility to deal with these issues or, at least, to be prepared to manage a classroom conversation around these topics.

If these topics are not raised by your professors, it is up to you what to do next. You should not feel like you have to bear the weight of bringing up these topics issues every time they are overlooked (or avoided). On the other hand, you have every right to shine a light on these issues. This is your choice.

B. PREPARING FOR CLASS

Now that you know how the basic structure of a judicial opinion, you are ready to move on to class preparation. While every stage in law school learning is important, class preparation is critical. Preparing for class lays the foundation for the rest of learning.

In law school classes, professors generally expect that students will come to class already having learned the material. This is not to say that professors expect that students will know everything or appreciate every nuance laced throughout reading assignments, but students should enter the classroom prepared to converse with the professor as experts on the law. This conversation, commonly known as Socratic dialogue and which is a part of many law school courses, is discussed in more detail in a later chapter. For now, you should understand that you will be expected to know the subject matter well enough to be able to expertly participate in class discussion. Law school Socratic dialogue is different from what some students experience in undergraduate study, where class time is devoted to restating the information that was in the reading. Instead, law professors expect you already to have learned the information. Class time is spent reinforcing and building on what you already have learned. Reading for class is the first step in developing the level of expertise expected of law students.

In this section, we will explore further the fundamentals of reading and understanding cases and other legal materials.

- **STAGE 1 (Reading the Law)**

The first step in preparing for class is reading. In preparing for class, first-year law students generally are required to read through many pages of material, which may be comprised of statutes or other rules, legal opinions (especially judicial opinions), or other sources of law.

In Stage 1 (Reading the Law), you should break up your reading into two steps. First, skim the entire body of material that you are about to read. Then, follow up that skim with a careful reading of the material.

- ### Step 1—Skim the Reading

Note: if you plan to move through the rest of this lesson, you should set aside two to three hours. You also may spend about half an hour just on the skimming portion of this lesson. Then, find another time where you have two to three hours, so you can "re-skim" the reading quickly and then read it carefully.

<u>THE PLAN</u>: You are trying to get through this reading quickly. You will read it again, and there is no need to take notes at this time. For now, do the following:

1. Read the beginning of the opinion to try to find out who the parties are and what the case is about.

2. Jump to the end of the opinion and try to find out how the case is resolved (i.e., who won);

3. Jump back to the middle and look for the location of the rules, perhaps reading those quickly.

   a. Look for lists

   b. Look for citations

4. Read the headings;

5. Quickly read the introductory paragraphs after each heading; and

6. Scan other paragraphs, looking for other points of emphasis (e.g., words that are **bold**, *italicized*, or <u>underlined</u> for emphasis).

<u>THE GOAL</u>: **Context.** When skimming, you are not trying to fully understand the material. So, you should allow yourself the freedom to skip over challenging passages or even move quickly through readings without appreciating every detail. You may see words or parts of discussions that you do not understand immediately, and that is acceptable. At most, you are trying to determine what the reading is about. If you can state, in a few words or a sentence, the general subject matter of the reading, you have accomplished your purpose for this session.

<u>Exercise 1</u>: Let's start by skimming the *Aceves* case. Because we already have looked at a lot of it, you can probably do this easily, but try to pretend as though you have not read the case before. Please spend no more than ten minutes skimming the Aceves opinion. When you are finished, please continue reading and answer the following questions. Complete the answers to the questions and then move on to the next page.

1. **What is the main topic of discussion?**

2. **What is promissory estoppel?**

3. **How many elements are there to a promissory estoppel claim?**

4. **Can you physically locate where the rules in this opinion are located?**

5. **Who prevails in this case?**

After you have answered these questions for yourself, please proceed to the following page.

You may have answered these questions kind of like this:

1. What is the main topic of discussion? *Promissory estoppel.*

2. What is promissory estoppel? *A claim to allow recovery where a person is injured because they relied on someone else's promise.*

3. How many elements are there to a promissory estoppel claim? *Four.*

4. Can you physically locate where the rules in this opinion are located? (Please place a check mark or asterisk in the margin next to the rules.) *Yes/Done.*

5. Who prevails in this case? *Aceves.*

You might feel like this was too easy (because we covered *Aceves* already), but now I would like you to do this same exercise with the Week 1 Reading at the back of this book. Remember, you aren't supposed to take notes yet. All you really need to get from the reading is *context*. Hopefully, by the end, you understood at least the basic context of the reading: The reading is about promissory estoppel. If you get nothing else than this, you are doing just fine.

The comforting thing about skimming is that it requires very little of you. As stated above, you can rest assured that you are going to follow up the skimming immediately with careful reading of the passage.

- **Step 2—Careful Reading**

THE PLAN: There are two primary foci you should have as you read through the assignment carefully. First, you are trying to understand what you are reading. Given that you are new to law school reading, this may take more time than you expect, even though the reading is (in law school standards) relatively short. You should set aside at least two hours for this reading. Depending on your pace of reading, you may need as many as three hours. Though it may be ideal for you to read this all at once, as you might in law school, you may break up the reading into two parts if that suits your schedule better.

Second, you must memorialize what it is that you understand from the reading. Ideally, you will not have to come back and re-read this passage again. So, note-taking and other techniques to help you remember what you read and understood are critical. Accordingly, as you read the assignment, you should do the following:

1. **Pay attention to your environment**. If you find that reading while in a prone position across your bed causes you to fall asleep, then you should try sitting at a desk. If reading in a room with a television or iPod playing, you should consider turning those devices off or going to another location without those distractions. If you are distracted by e-mails or web pages on your computer, consider turning your computer off or disabling web applications while you are studying.

2. **Read everything**, and do not skip any portion of the assignment. This does not mean, however, that you must read the assignment "like it is a novel."[1] In fact, it might make sense for you to read any judicial opinions first, then any rules or statutes, followed by other materials (e.g., law review articles). Before you are read judicial opinions, you might employ some of the skimming skills you learned in the previous section;

3. **Highlight** the passages that you think are important. Ultimately, you want to avoid over-highlighting, but do not worry about that right now;

4. As you highlight important passages, **write notes** in the margin of the book to summarize (i) what each passage says, and (ii) why you thought it was important enough to highlight.

5. When you read judicial opinions, you must note several things:

    a. the parties to the litigation;

    b. the court where the litigation is occurring;

    c. the procedural history of the case—what happened (to the case, not to the people) to get the case to the court issuing the opinion;

    d. the facts—identify which *important* facts affect the outcome of the case;

    e. the issue—identify what the main legal problem is in the opinion;

f. the rule(s)—find the principle(s) the court relies upon to reach its decision; and

g. how the court uses the rule to reach a conclusion.

THE GOAL: **Comprehension.** When you are reading carefully, you are attempting to understand what you are reading. You may not appreciate *everything* you read, but you are trying your best to make sure that you get all of the main points from the reading. In the next section, you will learn how to take what you learned from the first reading and reinforce that understanding as you prepare for class. Unlike the skimming step, you should expect, after you have finished this stage, to be able to summarize the theme(s) of the reading in a few sentences. You also should be able to, when consulting your notes, explain to someone else the details of the reading.

Exercise 2: **Read the entirety of the *Aceves* opinion. Do not be surprised if you need to read it more than once to understand it fully. It would be completely normal for you to take an hour or more to make sure you completely understand the opinion, especially if this is the first time you are ever reading a full judicial opinion. When you have finished reading this assignment, proceed to the next step.**

- **Step 3: Recording Your Understanding of the Law**

In order to retain the information you have read, you must record what you learned from the reading. Typically, students organize their understanding by doing two primary tasks. First, students prepare case briefs to record the important aspects of cases. Second, they prepare pre-class notes to summarize their understanding of the reading.

1. Case Briefs

Case briefs, as we call them in law school, are simple documents that students create in order to easily identify key aspects of the judicial opinions that they read. Case briefs serve two purposes. Primarily, students use case briefs to be used during class, in case professors call on them and ask them questions about the opinions. Case briefs also become a useful studying tool later on in the semester, because students can use the briefs to remind themselves quickly about the key points of cases, rather than having to re-read the cases.

In general, these are the kinds of things you should look for when reading judicial opinions:

(i) What it the **name** of the case?

(ii) Who are the **parties**? (Plaintiff, Defendant, Appellant, Appellee, etc.)

(iii)   What is the **<u>procedural history</u>**? (I.e., how did the case get to this court? Who filed the claim? Was there a trial? Was it appealed?)

(iv)   What does the court view as being the important **<u>facts</u>**? (I.e., what are the facts that are important to the resolution of the legal issue?)

(v)   What does the court see as the important legal **<u>issue</u>**?

(vi)   What rule does the court deem to be the controlling **<u>rule</u>**?

-    Or, if the court does not use an existing rule (or even if it does), does the court establish a new one (or modify an old one)?

(vii)   What **<u>reasoning</u>** affects the court's use of the FACTS and the RULE to resolve the legal dispute?

(viii)   What is the **<u>holding</u>** of the case?

-    I.e., what is the court's conclusion about this specific case in a way that it can be understood and applied in future cases?

-    Think of stating it in this way: "When (X) happens, (Y) should be the result." You fill in the (X) and (Y).

(ix)   What is **<u>your opinion</u>** about the case? What do you think about the way the court resolved the dispute?

-    Do you think the court resolved the dispute correctly? Why or why not?

-    How might this rule be applied in other factual circumstances?

Here is an example of a case brief for the <u>Aceves</u> case:

Name	*Aceves v. U.S. Bank, N.A.*
Parties	Claudia Aceves: Plaintiff/Appellant (P) U.S. Bank, N.A.: Defendant/Appellee (D)
Procedural History	• P filed complaint, then a first amended complaint • D filed demurrer, sustained by court • P filed second amended complaint • D filed demurrer • Court sustained demurrer without leave to amend and entered judgment for D • P appealed

Facts	• P took out adjustable rate loan from bank (Option One) • OO sold loan to D • P defaulted less than 2 years later, got foreclosure notice • P filed for Chapter 7 (can't keep the home) bankruptcy, intended to convert to Chapter 13 (can keep the home) • D says it will negotiate if she does not convert to Ch. 13 • D says it cannot negotiate if "stay" is in place • P does not convert and does not oppose motion to lift stay • D forecloses
Issue	Whether these facts are sufficient to state claim for promissory estoppel.
Rule(s)	The elements of a promissory estoppel claim are "(1) a promise clear and unambiguous in its terms; (2) reliance by the party to whom the promise is made; (3)[the] reliance must be both reasonable and foreseeable; and (4) the party asserting the estoppel must be injured by his reliance." ' "
Reasoning	Basic idea is that the court reasons that the facts support the conclusion that D made promises on purposes to lead P into not opposing what D wanted, which allowed D a free path to foreclosure.
Holding	Where a borrower alleges that a bank promised to negotiate the terms of a loan for which a borrower is in default, and the borrower forgoes bankruptcy protection in reliance on that promise, thereby enabling the bank to foreclose on the home, the borrower has stated a claim for promissory estoppel.
My own opinions	Where do we draw the line between personal responsibility and reliance? I feel sorry for Aceves, but is it the bank's fault that she defaulted? (On the other hand, I guess, why did the bank make a loan to someone who might not be able to pay?) If the bank did not promise to renegotiate the loan but to negotiate about renegotiating, was it reasonable for her to rely on their "promise"?

Using a template like the one above is not the only way to brief cases. Some law students do something called "book briefing" which involves highlighting and making notes within the casebook. To see examples of book briefs, please go to www.belonginginlawschool.com, click on "Study Materials," and then on "Contracts (Promissory Estoppel)."

Although most students start out making case briefs in law school, some students gravitate towards other methods of recording their understanding of the reading materials. Some create pre-class notes that contain the important information you got from the readings (i.e., not just the judicial opinions). Some students rely simply on highlighting and on the notes that they made in the margins of the reading—book briefing, as shown above. (Visual learners may find it helpful to use this approach.) Other students will record notes on their computers. There is no one right way to take reading notes. What is important is that you find a way to record everything you think is important from the reading. Whether you use a case brief, make margin notes ("book brief"), or record notes in another way, it is critical to memorialize what you got out of the reading.

ASSIGNMENT: **Please skim, read, and prepare a case brief for each of the three opinions assigned for Class 1. These cases are (i)** *Kirksey v. Kirksey*, **(ii)** *Harvey v. Dow*, **and (iii)** *Greiner v. Greiner*. **(You will find these cases at the back of the book.) blank templates for the briefs are available at the end of this chapter. You also can find electronic versions of these documents on www.belongingin lawschool.com.**

TIMELINE—**You should spread this step over three days:**

Day 1 (Today)—Reading. Give yourself a few hours to read this carefully and to write your briefs and notes. Then, it is important for you to take a break. Your brain actually needs time to process the information you have just learned. You will learn better if you take a break now. *(Time Estimate: 3 hours.)*

Day 2 (Tomorrow)—Pre-Class Review. Review your briefs and notes. You do not need to reread the entire assignment, because hopefully you read it carefully enough to understand it the first time and then made briefs and notes that captured your understanding. But it may be useful for you to reread important passages in addition to reading your notes in order to refresh your recollection of what you read the day before. *(Time Estimate: 30–45 minutes.)*

Day 3 (Day After Tomorrow)—Class. Go to Chapter 7.

Try to follow this schedule if you can. It is important to space this out because your brain actually learns information better—meaning that you will both understand it better and develop long-term recollection of that information—if you if you interact with information in different ways and at different times. As Professor Louis Schulze explains, this "spaced repetition" involves "revisiting information at specified intervals [and] solidifies memory and ultimately drastically increases knowledge and understanding.[2] If you are really trying to master a topic, you are way better off spreading out your study rather than spending a longer time in a single setting "cramming" on that same information.

This is not always intuitive. Many of us have crammed for exams, spending hours, maybe even staying up all night, reading and rereading whatever it is we are studying. We may even have had success using this approach in the past. But there are three significant problems with using this approach.

First, when you cram the night before an exam, you are only putting that information in your short term memory. You will be able to recall the information that you studied during the exam that next morning, which is all you are trying to do. In undergraduate settings, you probably can do reasonably well on an exam. But if you tried to take that exam just a day later, you would not do as well. A week later, you would perform even worse. A month later, you surely would not remember most of what you need in order to give even a minimally sufficient job on the exam. To do well in law school, you need to develop long-term cognitive connections. You cannot expect to read something in week 3 of the semester and then remember anything meaningful when you take your exam in week 15. And, even if you review that information in week 13 as you prepare for your exam, you won't remember enough and you will have to start over, relearning the material. This will be too time consuming.

Second, there is simply too much information in every law school class for you to try to cram it all into your short-term memory immediately prior to a law school exam. You may have three or four exams in any given semester, and for each of those exams, you will have read as many as a thousand pages or more during the semester. It is impossible for you to try to cram the night before—or even the week or two before—the exam. You must spend weeks preparing.

Third, although cramming can give a person success in situations where simple recall is called for, law school classes (and, ultimately, law school exams) do not depend on your ability to recall information. Instead, they require you to apply the information you have learned during the semester, not just to recall it. If you cram immediately before a law school class, you may remember the facts of a case, or even the outcome, but you should have no expectation that you have developed the expertise necessary to apply the law effectively. And if you fail to do that as you prepare for classes, you can expect limited expertise on your exams also.

The best chance you have of excelling in your law school classes and on your law school exams is to build long-term mastery over time. To do this, you must space your learning up front and keep coming back to review information over the course of the semester (we will discuss this in a later chapter). If you do this, you will be a much more efficient and effective learner.

Case Name	*Kirksey v. Kirksey*
Parties	
Procedural History	
Facts	
Issue	
Rule(s)	
Reasoning	
Holding	
My own opinions	

Case Name	*Harvey v. Dow*
Parties	
Procedural History	
Facts	
Issue	
Rule(s)	
Reasoning	
Holding	
My own opinions	

Case Name	*Greiner v. Greiner*
Parties	
Procedural History	
Facts	
Issue	
Rule(s)	
Reasoning	
Holding	
My own opinions	

[1]   I use this analogy often with students. Reading like the assignment is a novel means reading from front to back, taking nothing out of order. If you were to imagine reading a mystery novel, you would never want to read the ending, for example, because it would ruin the book. All of the hidden clues would stand out to you, and there would be no surprise at the end, because you already would know "who done it." But, that is exactly what you want from reading a casebook. You want to know all of the clues that lead to the conclusions. So feel free to experiment with how you approach the reading. See, generally, Ruth Ann McKinney, Reading Like a Lawyer (Carolina Academic Press 2005).

[2]   Louis N. Schulze, Jr., *Using Science to Build Better Learners: One School's Successful Efforts to Raise Its Bar Passage Rates in an Era of Decline*, 68 J. LEGAL EDUC. 230, 243 (2019).

CHAPTER 7

CLASS ONE

∎ ∎ ∎

Now that you have prepared for your first class, it is time to go to class. This is a book, and there is no good way to approximate in print what a class really will be like. So, you will be able to go online to participate in simulated classes on www.belonginginlawschool.com. There are five classes connected to this book.

The Socratic Method

As discussed briefly in Chapter 3, law school classes can be a lot different than other classroom experiences. Instead of explaining information to students, law professors traditionally expect students to come to class already having understood the reading. They spend their time, then, drawing students' knowledge out through a process of iterative questioning called Socratic dialogue.

With Socratic questioning, rather than asking you specific questions about your recent reading assignments, professors are more likely to ask questions designed to require you to apply what you have learned to new, hypothetical situations. You usually have no advance notice of what these questions will be, and you often do not even have notice that you will be called upon to answer these questions. This is "cold-calling," as we discussed earlier, where professors call on students unexpectedly. This process can be more than a little unnerving, of course.

Fortunately, you can anticipate some of the questions. At least at the outset, the questions may draw upon your reading. You may be asked to answer questions about the cases you read—for example, what are the important facts, what was the procedural history, what is the rule, and what was the holding. If you read carefully and created traditional case briefs, book briefs, or good pre-class notes, you should be able to answer many of these questions. So, in anticipation of receiving these questions, think now about where you would look and how you might answer them.

The next series of questions can be more difficult. After you go through the basics of how a particular case was decided, the dialogue will shift to exploring how well you understand the rule and its application. The way your professors will test this is to ask you "what if" (or hypothetical) questions that contain facts that differ in some big or small way from the case you read. These "what if" questions are fundamental to your learning in law school, so pay close attention.

Professors will ask hypothetical questions to test your understanding of the boundaries of the rules you have studied. It is not enough to know the "law," or rules, from a given case. You have to think about the underlying principles supporting that rule, the court's rationale for using that rule. Understanding those supporting ideas will help you figure out how to apply the law to other situations.

For example, let's take a closer look at *Harvey v. Dow*. In that case, you learned about a daughter who claimed she was entitled to land on her parent's property. There are several rules from that case, but let's focus on this one quote from the opinion:

> "The promise relied on by the promisee need not be express but may be implied from a party's conduct."

It is not enough for you to simply know this quote, even though this is where we start. We call this kind of explicit rule "Black Letter Law." From this quote, we know that a person can make a promise by either words or conduct. But what kind of conduct is sufficient to constitute a promise? To answer that question, we must think about how that rule worked in the context of this particular case. Let's start by looking at what facts were important to this court and why:

> In sum, on the facts found by the Superior Court, Teresa's reliance on the Dows' general promise to give her land at some time, when coupled with their affirmative actions in allowing her to build a substantial house on a particular piece of their land, would seem to be eminently foreseeable and reasonable. From those actions, a promise by the Dows to convey that specific site could be fairly implied.

From this particular quote, we can see that the court valued a few facts:

- The Dows let Teresa build a house;
- The house Teresa built was substantial; and
- The house was built on a specific site on the Dow's land.

If we read the opinion closely, including the way the court tells the story at the beginning of the opinion, we can also see a host of other facts that probably influenced the court's opinion:

- Teresa was the Dow's daughter;
- The Dow's owned a 125-acre homestead;
- The Dow children had always expressed a desire to build on the homestead;

- There appeared to be a long understanding that the Dow children would be allowed to have a home on the Dow's property;

- The Dow's agreed to help Teresa finance the property;

- Teresa initially attempted to get zoning approval to build the house; and

- Mr. Dow eventually applied for and received zoning to build the house.

(Were all of these facts in your case brief? Seeing all of these facts should reinforce for you the importance of reading the opinion closely.)

Now that we understand what facts seem to matter to the court, we can start to think about how we might change the real facts into some "what if" facts. Let's put the original facts into a chart and see how we might vary the story in order to test the operation of the rule. I have filled in half of the "what if" facts. See if you can fill in the remainder with "what if" facts of your own:

Original Fact	**"What If" Fact**
The Dows let Teresa build a house.	The Dows let Teresa park her Winnebago trailer on the land.
The house Teresa built was substantial.	The house was a tree house.
The house was built on a specific site on the Dows land.	The house was moveable, and they kept moving it around to different places on the Dows' property.
Teresa was the Dow's daughter.	
The Dows owned a 125-acre homestead.	
The Dow children had always expressed a desire to build on the homestead.	
There appeared to be a long understanding that the Dow children would be allowed to have a home on the Dows' property.	No such long-term understanding existed.

The Dows agreed to help Teresa finance the property.	Teresa financed the building on her own, without the help of her parents.
Teresa initially attempted to get zoning approval to build the house.	Teresa never attempted to get zoning.
Mr. Dow eventually applied for and received zoning to build the house.	

You might have filled in the blanks with something like you see below:

Original Fact	"What If" Fact
The Dows let Teresa build a house.	The Dows let Teresa park her Winnebago trailer on the land.
The house Teresa built was substantial.	The house was a tree house.
The house was built on a specific site on the Dows land.	The house was moveable, and they kept moving it around to different places on the Dows' property.
Teresa was the Dow's daughter.	*Teresa was the Dows' friend.*
The Dows owned a 125-acre homestead.	*The Dows had a .25 acre lot.*
The Dow children had always expressed a desire to build on the homestead.	*This had never been discussed.*
There appeared to be a long understanding that the Dow children would be allowed to have a home on the Dows' property.	No such long-term understanding existed.
The Dows agreed to help Teresa finance the property.	Teresa financed the building on her own, without the help of her parents.
Teresa initially attempted to get zoning approval to build the house.	Teresa never attempted to get zoning.
Mr. Dow eventually applied for and received zoning to build the house.	*Mr. Dow never applied for zoning approval, and there was no such approval.*

Project how the outcome might be different if you changed one of the original facts into one of the "what if" facts. Does each factual alteration affect the projected outcome in the same way? How about if you changed two or three of the original facts into "what if" facts? Does the combination of facts matter? What if you changed all of the original facts into the "what if" facts? And what if we considered other "what if" facts not listed above? This is the exploration you will do in many of your classes, especially in the first year.

Rather than trying to explain this further, let's just jump into the classroom. But before we do that . . . .

FIRST THINGS FIRST

Before you go to class, it is important to get your mind right. To do this, I would like you to spend a few minutes reflecting on and then writing about the following:

Please re-read the section earlier in this book about Growth Mindset. After reading it, please respond to this below: What, in your view, does it take to be a successful law student? Natural Intelligence? Hard Work? Perseverance? Something else?

_____

_____

_____

_____

_____

_____

_____

_____

_____

_____

_____

_____

_____

_____

_____

_____

_____

_____

_____

_____

CLASS 1

There is no better way to understand what class is like except to sit in class. So I'm going to try to let you in on the classroom experience. To do this next step, you'll need to use your phone, computer, or tablet. I recommend using the largest screen you can so that you can feel as much as possible as though you are really in the classroom.

On your computer, please go to www.belonginginlawschool.com, click on "Classes," then on "Contracts (Promissory Estoppel)," and then on "Class 1." You will return to this web page for our future classes, so you may want to bookmark the page.

The one thing we cannot really approximate is cold-calling, which we discussed a bit earlier. You will hear the professor in this video cold-call several students, so you will get a good feel for what it is like. But you should also try to participate as much as you can. So listen for those moments when the professor calls on someone else. (At times, there will be cues to pause the video so you can attempt to answer questions.) When that happens, pause the recording for a moment and see if you can answer the question for yourself.

We will talk soon about how to take notes, but for now, please just do your best.

When you are ready to begin, please click the play button and take your first class.

When you are finished, please proceed to the next page.

Class 1 Debrief

After participating in Class 1, I'd like to ask you a few questions about your experience. I've given you a little space to write answers below, if you like.

(1) How was that experience for you? Was it what you expected?

(2) Did you notice all of the hypotheticals the professor used when interacting with the class?

(3) Did you notice how much detail the professor drew from the readings?

(4) Did the professor dig into the material deeper than you expected or not as much?

(5) How prepared did you feel for class?

(6) What do you think would have helped you better prepare for class?

We Belong

KATHRYN: Kathryn is an openly gay woman who went to Georgetown University Law Center as a public interest law scholar. Knowing there were out LGBTQ faculty at the school was very encouraging. While she had wonderful faculty mentors during her higher education, she found her social scene outside of law school. Once she graduated, she did a judicial clerkship and then practiced health law in San Francisco. She later went back to school to get an LLM in health care law and then returned to practice in Washington DC. Finally, she moved in-house, working as counsel to two community hospitals in the largest health care system in her region.

Notwithstanding that she has never been closeted, she still finds that colleagues presume she has a husband. She enjoys correcting them to tell them that her spouse is her wife.

Kathryn's Advice: **The law can be a powerful tool, and we need all voices at the table. Professional networks matter, so be bold in expanding yours. Find mentors and join professional organizations while you are in law school. Be patient as you go; law is tedious but impactful. Never give up!**

TAKING NOTES

Taking notes, like everything else we will discuss in the book, is a learned skill. There is no one right method for doing this, so it is important for you to know and use the approach the works best for you. That said, there are some guidelines you might consider when thinking about how to take notes.

Goals: When taking notes, it helps to have a goal in mind. If you do not approach note-taking with a purpose, you will be unsure what to pay attention to in class. The lack of a goal drives some students to take too many notes—they try to write down everything a professor says. This reflects that these students do not have a great idea about what is or isn't important. On the other hand, if you have a goal, you will pay attention to certain parts of class and relegate other parts to the margins. So let's think about what goals are important:

(1) *Themes.* The cases you read and the discussions in class should relate to an overall theme or set of themes. If you pay attention, you will notice those themes. Try to see more than what is said about a particular case. How are the cases similar or different? What ideas connect them?

(2) *Conceptual Relationships.* As you listen to the ideas shared in class, pay attention to how the concepts relate to each other. It is important to know the elements of a rule; it is just as important to see how those elements relate to each other. Likewise, it is important for you to see the relationships between and among cases, what differences in facts lead courts to similar or different outcomes?

(3) *Rules.* Of course, you want to make sure that you write (or type) the rules—what we earlier called "Black Letter Law"— discussed in class. If you did a good job preparing for class, this information already should be in your pre-class notes or briefs. In that case, you can simply highlight or mark those notes rather than taking new notes.

(4) *Process.* Like the rules (and sometimes, but not always, following the rules exactly), it is important for you to pay attention to the process used to answer legal questions. How does the professor show you how to address legal issues? Are there steps? What is the structure for thinking through a particular legal problem? What kind of logic is applied?

(5) *Hypotheticals.* These are the "what if" scenarios that professors spin during the class. Sometimes, professors will make up new stories to test your ability to apply a legal standard. It is important to take close note of these stories,

because they give you insight into how a professor might ask questions on an exam. (We will discuss exams later, but typical law school exams generally are hypothetical stories that you must analyze with the rules you have learned over the course of a semester.)

(6) *Complement.* The ultimate goal of class is to complement (add to) your understanding of the law. You came to class having prepared effectively, so now is your opportunity to check what you got right, what you misunderstood, and also to add to that new information that the professor shares with the class. There are bound to be things that you did not anticipate or glean from the reading. Expect that, and use your note-taking to make sure you record that new information.

Listening: Perhaps the most important part of note-taking is listening. If you have prepared effectively for class, you should feel more comfortable listening for the things that are important enough to write down or type. Thus, the biggest skill you can learn to help with note-taking is how to prepare for class effectively. For this, please see the preceding chapters on reading and class preparation. If you go into class feeling like you already understand the material, you will see where you are right and where you are wrong. Write *that* stuff down.

Medium: Law students and, even more, law professors fret over what is the best way to take notes. Should you type or handwrite? Should you record your classes and watch or listen to them again and again? I don't think most of this matters. What matters is that you really think through the approaches discussed above. If you can listen effectively and write down the things that are important, noting themes, structures, process, relationships, and hypotheticals, then you will take good notes no matter what approach you use.

ASSIGNMENT: Please re-watch Class 1, taking notes (again) following the guidelines outlined above. Listen first, paying attention to what you think is important. Make choices about what you want to write down or type.

CHAPTER 8

INTRODUCTION TO LEGAL ANALYSIS

■ ■ ■

In this chapter, we will focus less on learning the law and more on how to use the law to resolve legal issues (even though you may find that focusing on using the law actually can help you learn it better.) In this chapter, we will focus on simple legal analysis. In a later chapter, in preparation for our midterm exam, we will introduce more complex legal analysis, like that you do on law school exams.

Quality legal analysis depends on your employing solid logic, which will lead you to have good structure. In addition, your content must be thorough. We will explore both of these in the section below.

I. USING BASIC LOGIC

The Basic Logical Form

Throughout your law school and professional career, you will be required to think logically—to understand the guidelines that govern legal issues and apply that logic to resolve legal issues. Although entire courses are taught on logic in some undergraduate and graduate majors, law schools, for the most part, are short on actually teaching logic. Instead, your law professors simply assume that you think logically. (Logic is an essential skill applied on the LSAT, so that assumption is not entirely unreasonable.) And your law professors all think logically—or at least they *think* they think logically—and they expect you to do the same. So it is necessary for you to be able to meet that expectation.

Let's start with diagramming a logical proof, which we call a syllogism. A basic syllogism is made up of three parts: a major premise, a minor premise, and a conclusion. Here is a simple example:

> Major Premise: If A, then B.
>
> Minor Premise: A.
>
> Conclusion: Therefore, B.

How should we understand this logical proof? The major premise establishes a general principle telling us the outcome if a particular factual condition exists—in this case telling us that in the event that condition A exists, then the outcome will be B. The minor premise establishes for us the factual condition—here, that the condition A does exist. Finally, the conclusion shows the outcome, in light of the general principle and the factual condition.

Let's look at this same syllogism in prose:

Major Premise: If condition A exists, then the result will be B.

Minor Premise: Condition A exists.

Conclusion: The result is B.

Using words like "condition" and "outcome" can make this seem a little more formal than necessary, but it is important for us to understand this structure. Now let's see what this structure looks like using plain language.

Major Premise: If a person jumps in a lake, they will get wet.

Minor Premise: Mary just jumped in a lake.

Conclusion: Therefore, Mary just got wet.

Or, try this:

Major Premise: All cats have four paws.

Minor Premise: Tom is a cat.

Conclusion: Therefore, Tom has four paws.

What you should notice from all of these patterns is that if the major premise is true and the minor premise is true, then the conclusion must be true. It is unavoidable. That is the nature of logic: that certain conclusions or outcomes are inescapable in light of certain inputs.

Before we move on, let's double check to make sure that you understand how this works. Please fill in the blanks in the examples below:

Example 1

Major Premise: If a person travels more than 10 miles over the speed limit, they deserve a speeding ticket.

Minor Premise: Jim traveled more than 10 miles over the posted speed limit.

Conclusion: Therefore, _____.

Example 2

Major Premise: If you eat expired potato salad, you will get sick.

Minor Premise: Tanya ate expired potato salad.

Conclusion: Therefore, _____.

Example 3

Major Premise: If you show up to work late, you will lose your job.

Minor Premise: Kendrick showed up to work late.

Conclusion: Therefore, _____.

NOTE: For this proof structure to work, both the major premise and the minor premise must be true.

Variations on the Basic Logical Form[1]

Not every logical proof takes the "If A, then B" form. There are many variations on the forms syllogisms can take. Let's look at a few:

Negative Condition. Rather than looking for the presence of a condition, this proof depends on looking for the absence of a condition. For example:

Major Premise: If no A, then B.

Minor Premise: No A.

Conclusion: Therefore, B.

This proof depends on our focusing on the absence of condition A. So long as we do not see condition A present, then conclusion B is unavoidable. Here it is, in plain language:

Major Premise: If Donald does not work out in the morning, he will get tired later in the afternoon.

Minor Premise: Donald did not work out this morning.

Conclusion: Therefore, Donald will get tired later this afternoon.

Given that we were looking for the absence of Donald's workout and saw it was not there, we reach the necessary conclusion that Donald will get tired.

Exclusive Condition. In this approach, as in our basic syllogism, we are looking for the existence of a condition. In this case, the existence or absence of that condition will make a difference in the outcome. Here, we see what happens if the condition is present:

Major Premise: If A, and only if A, then B.

Minor Premise: A.

Conclusion: Therefore, B.

Another way of thinking about this syllogism might be to phrase it as follows: If A, then B, but if not A, then not B. (Put this way, it is like a combination of the basic form and the negative condition form.) Here is an example of this syllogism, in plain language:

Major Premise: If you clean your room, and only if you clean your room, you are entitled to your allowance. *(Or, as my mother might have put it, "You're not getting that that allowance unless you clean your room!")*

Minor Premise: You cleaned your room.

Conclusion: Therefore, you are entitled to your allowance.

Note that if we use the same major premise but change the minor premise, then we will find a different conclusion:

Major Premise: If A, and only if A, then B.

Minor Premise: Not A.

Conclusion: Therefore, not B.

Or, in common terms:

Major Premise: If you clean your room, and only if you clean your room, you are entitled to your allowance.

Minor Premise: You did not clean your room.

Conclusion: Therefore, you are not entitled to your allowance.

Exclusive Rule with Exceptions. In this case, we have a necessary single condition. Without the existence of that condition, we cannot satisfy the premise, unless other conditions (exceptions) exist. This can be stated positively, negatively, and/or exclusively.

Major Premise: If and only if A, then X, unless B.

Minor Premise: No A, but B.

Conclusion: Therefore, X.

A plain language example:

Major Premise: You may play video games only if you already have done your homework, unless the next day is a school holiday.

Minor Premise: You did not do your homework, but tomorrow is a school holiday.

Conclusion: Therefore, you may play video games.

Conjunctive Conditions. In this syllogism, our outcome depends upon the existence of multiple conditions in order for the major premise to be satisfied.

Major Premise:	If A, B, and C, then X.
Minor Premise:	A, B, and C.
Conclusion:	Therefore, X.

Or, in common terms:

Major Premise:	If you go to all classes, study hard, and take practice exams, you can perform at your peak capacity.
Minor Premise:	You went to all of your classes, studied hard, and you took practice exams.
Conclusion:	Therefore, you will perform at peak capacity.

Disjunctive Conditions. Here, we are looking for the existence of <u>at least</u> one of several possible conditions.

Major Premise:	If A, B, or C, then X.
Minor Premise:	B, but not A or C.
Conclusion:	Therefore, X.

A plain language example:

Major Premise:	If you clean your room, if you do the dishes, or if you take out the trash, you are entitled to your allowance.
Minor Premise:	You did the dishes, but you did not clean your room or take out the trash.
Conclusion:	Therefore, you are entitled to your allowance.

Compound Conditions. There are many other variations on the proofs we discussed above. Many of the variants involve combinations of the above proofs.

<u>Logical Ambiguity</u>

There are many legal fallacies that can interfere with logical reasoning. I will not try to explore all of those here, but you should guard against reaching conclusions that are not expressly required by the premises. One of the biggest potential problems, however, is accepting or using premises that are not correct.

If you pay close attention to the syllogisms discussed above, you can see that they do not work at all if either of the premises are inaccurate. It is, thus, important to have precise major and minor premises in order to reach logical conclusions.

As we will discuss in more detail below, ambiguity in one or both premises is not devastating to legal analysis. Instead, it really makes the analysis more complex, because alternative premises can lead to alternative conclusions. Much of legal analysis, especially in law school, requires you to deal with that ambiguity. The better you are at noticing ambiguities and dealing with alternative arguments, the better you will do with your legal analysis overall.

II. LEGAL PROOFS AS LOGICAL PROOFS

A. LEGAL RULES AS MAJOR PREMISES

Analysis of the law can resemble the logical proofs we discussed above. You simply must learn to recognize the patterns. As we saw above, the type of proof depends greatly on the form of the major premise. And legal rules work just like the major premises we saw above—they set a structure for the way we look at the logical proof.

Let's take a look at a few rules[2] and see if we can recognize their structure:

The Basic Form

Legal Rule:	If a claim arises under the U.S. Constitution, federal courts have jurisdiction over the claim.
Major Premise:	If A, then B.
Explanation:	This is a simple major premise. In this case, we are looking for just one condition—whether the claim arises under the U.S. Constitution. In the event that the condition exists, we would conclude that the federal courts have jurisdiction.

Negative Condition

Legal Rule:	If a search is not executed pursuant to a warrant, any evidence discovered is inadmissible.
Major Premise:	If not A, then B.
Explanation:	Here, we are looking for the absence of a condition—a warrant. The absence of the

warrant leads to a conclusion that evidence discovered is inadmissible.

Exclusive Condition

Legal Rule: A person may practice law in the state if and only if they are admitted to practice in that jurisdiction.

Major Premise: If and only if A, then B.

Explanation: The condition—here admission to practice—must exist in order for a person to practice law.

Exclusive Condition with Exceptions

Legal Rule: A lawyer may reveal confidential information if and only if the client gives the lawyer permission, unless revealing the information is necessary to protect a person from substantial bodily harm.

Major Premise: If and only if A, then X, unless B.

Explanation: Here, we are looking for the existence of the necessary condition. In the absence of that condition, the rule cannot be satisfied, unless the exception is satisfied.

Conjunctive Conditions

Legal Rule: Burglary is the breaking and entering into the dwelling of another in the nighttime with the intent to commit a felony therein.

Major Premise: If A, B, C, D, and E, then X.

Explanation: All of the conditions—(i) breaking, (ii) entering, (iii) dwelling, (iv) another, (v) night time, (vi) intent to commit a felony therein—must be satisfied in order to establish the conclusion that burglary has been committed. (Note: this really is an exclusive and conjunctive rule.)

Disjunctive Conditions

Legal Rule: A lawyer has a conflict of interest if there is a significant risk that the lawyer's ability to represent a client effectively will be substantially limited by the lawyer's duties to another client, a former client, a third

	party, or the lawyer's own personal interests.
Major Premise:	If A, B, C, or D, then X.
Explanation:	The presence of any one of the conditions— limitation by duties to (i) another client, (ii) a former client, (iii) a third party, or (iv) the lawyer's own personal interests.

B. SIMPLE LEGAL PROOFS

Now that you understand basic logical structure and can see how legal rules follow the same forms as major premises, we can start to focus on basic legal analysis.

Simple legal analysis follows the same logical structure as the proofs we saw above. So, we can begin to construct legal analysis by using that structure. Let's revisit the basic logical structure:

Major Premise:	If A, then B.
Minor Premise:	A.
Conclusion:	Therefore, B.

Now, let's show an example of that structure in a legal context:

Major Premise:	If a matter involves interstate commerce, then Congress may regulate it.
Minor Premise:	The sale of tires involves interstate commerce.
Conclusion:	Therefore, Congress may regulate it.

This is simple legal analysis, and it follows exactly the same structure as the syllogisms we discussed above. In law school, we have shortened the names of the two premises each part of the proof, so that they look like this:

RULE:	If a matter involves interstate commerce, then Congress may regulate it.
APPLICATION:	The sale of tires involves interstate commerce.
CONCLUSION:	Therefore, Congress may regulate it.

We also add, up front, the question we are trying to answer, calling it an "Issue":

ISSUE:	May Congress regulate the sale of tires?
RULE:	If a matter involves interstate commerce, then Congress may regulate it.

APPLICATION: The sale of tires involves interstate commerce.

CONCLUSION: Therefore, Congress may regulate it.

We shorten this basic structure to "**IRAC**"—you will hear this acronym a lot in law school. A version of IRAC will be taught to you in your legal writing classes, and you will be expected to apply this approach on your law school exams. This latter purpose is why we are focused on it here.

EXERCISE: In each syllogism below, I have left blanks in the analysis. Please fill in the blanks with the sentence that logically fits. Answers will follow.

(A)   Issue: Does Lonnie Lawyer have a conflict of interest?

        Rule: A lawyer has a conflict of interest if a new client wishes to sue the lawyer's existing client.

        Application: Lonnie's new client, Andie, wishes to sue Carson, Lonnie's current client.

        Conclusion: _____

                            _____

                            _____

(B)   Issue: Is Allie entitled to an interest in the family home as a part of a divorce resolution?

        Rule: A spouse is entitled to an interest in a family home if the home was acquired during the marriage.

        Application: _____

                            _____

                            _____

        Conclusion: Therefore, Allie is entitled to an interest in the family home.

(C)   Issue: Did Mary have capacity to enter into the contract?

        Rule: _____

                            _____

                            _____

        Application: Mary was under 18 at the time she entered into the contract.

Conclusion: Therefore, Mary did not have capacity to enter into a contract.

(D) Issue: _____

_____

_____

Rule: Material is abnormally dangerous if (i) the danger it presents is lethal, and (ii) even with the use of reasonable care, the danger cannot be eliminated.

Application: The danger dynamite presents is lethal, and that danger cannot be eliminated with the use of reasonable care.

Conclusion: Therefore, dynamite is abnormally dangerous.

ANSWERS

(A) Therefore, Lonnie has a conflict of interest.

(B) Allie and their spouse acquired the family home during the marriage.

(C) If a person was under the age of 18 when they entered into a contract, they do not have the capacity to enter into the contract.

(D) Is dynamite abnormally dangerous?

Before we move on, let's make sure you can recognize language as either Issue, Rule, Application, or Conclusion. Here are the characteristics we are looking for:

Issue: The question we are trying to answer. Sometimes presented as an actual question.

Rule: The generic principle that helps us answer the question. No reference to specific facts.

Application: The reference to the particular situation we are dealing with. Sometimes characterized by the use of "here" or "in this case."

Conclusion: A short statement that presents us with the result. Often begins with "Therefore."

EXERCISE: Write "I," "R," "A," or "C" next to each sentence below, to indicate whether you think it is an Issue, a Rule, an Application, or a Conclusion. Answers will follow.

1. _____ Here, there is no evidence to support one of the critical elements of Plaintiff's trespass claim, namely that Defendant was not authorized, explicitly or tacitly, to enter the property.

2. _____ Therefore, A adversely possessed Blackacre.

3. _____ To form a joint venture, all that is required is that the parties agree to engage in a specific business enterprise. No written agreement is required.

4. _____ The fumes not only escaped into the air, but they also drifted across the lake and onto the Smith's property, killing their livestock.

5. _____ We must resolve whether ABC, Inc. is a "person" within the meaning of the statute.

6. _____ Hearsay is an out of court statement offered to prove the truth of the matter asserted.

7. _____ Even though Damon gave nothing to Max in support of the promise, he detrimentally relied on Max's promise when he quit his job and sold his car.

8. _____ No governmental actor may unconstitutionally infringe upon a citizen's free exercise of religion.

9. _____ First, we have to determine whether the assessment is a criminal penalty or a civil fine.

10. _____ When Judy pointed the gun at Jill and pulled the trigger, saying, "I'm going to kill you now," that showed that her actions were intentional.

11. _____ Thus, X owed no duty to Y.

12. _____ To have standing to bring a qui tam action, a party must have personal knowledge of the wrongful conduct. No showing of personal harm is required.

13. _____ It is well-settled that even minimal consideration is sufficient to support a contract.

14. _____ In this case, the copyright violation is shown insofar as the text from Chapter 2 of Barnes's book is identical to that of Chapter 8 of Noble's.

15. _____ When the contract is between merchants, the proposed additions can automatically become part of the contract.

ANSWERS

1. A
2. C
3. R
4. A
5. I
6. R
7. A
8. R
9. I
10. A
11. C
12. R
13. R
14. A
15. R

C. ANALYZING SIMPLE LEGAL ISSUES

Now we can begin to apply this logic to the issues we have been discussing. In order to do that, let's start with a short hypothetical scenario:

Karla and Michael Jenkins had one child, Damon. Karla and Michael knew that Damon wanted their car when he turned 18. They never said clearly that they would give it to him, but when Damon turned 17, they handed him a set of keys to the car. The keys were on a keychain that had been personalized with Damon's initials. Over the next year, Karla and Michael had Damon pay the insurance on the car, and they allowed him to drive it to and from school each day. Damon paid to have the car painted, and he also paid for some substantial improvements to the sound system, engine, and wheels. In all, Damon spent about $8,000 on insurance and improvements. A year later, Damon asked his parents to give him the title to the car. Karla and Michael refused.

When you read this story, you may see similarities to one or more of the cases we read for Class 1. If so, well done. If not, that's okay. For now, we just want to answer one legal question: Did Karla and Michael Jenkins make a promise to Damon?

Answer this question in the space below, based only on the law we have learned so far:

Issue:	Did Karla and Michael Jenkins make a promise to Damon?
Rule:	
Application:	
Conclusion:	

Your first attempt might look like this:

Issue:	Did Karla and Michael Jenkins make a promise to Damon?
Rule:	A promise does not have to "be express but may be implied from a party's conduct."
Application:	Here, Karla and Michael's conduct amounted to a promise.
Conclusion:	Therefore, they made a promise.

This is a good first attempt. In law school, we will ask a little more of you, however. This is true in the case of the "Rule" section of the analysis and even more so for the "Application" section.

1. Improving the Rule

The rule statement from our first attempt is completely true. But it is not truly complete. Let's look at the rule we used again:

A promise does not have to "be express but may be implied from a party's conduct."

This is good, but it doesn't get us all the way there. Any lawyer would ask at least one follow up question if given this rule: What kind of conduct is sufficient to demonstrate a promise? So we have to answer that question as a part of our rule statement. How do we answer it? Well, we have guidance from the Harvey v. Dow case.

As you remember, the Dows and their children, including daughter Teresa Harvey, had talked about each of the children building a home on the Dow's property. But the Dows never explicitly promised this to the kids. The Dows did, however, allow Teresa and her husband move onto the property and live on it in a mobile home. They also helped Teresa select a lot on the property and pursue plans to build a home. They agreed to help finance the new home by taking out a second mortgage. These, and other things, led the court to conclude that the Dows had promised, through their conduct, to provide Teresa with a parcel of land on which she could build a home.

Let's try to summarize this into a concise explanation of the kind of situation that would lead a court to conclude that a promise had been made by conduct. What are the characteristics? First, we see a general understanding among the parties that the Dows would give land to their children. Then we see several actions taken by the Dows that are consistent with that understanding. How might we summarize this? Here is an attempt:

> Where there is a general, albeit not explicit, understanding between parties, and the alleged promisor takes multiple actions consistent with that understanding, the promisor's conduct can be viewed as a promise.

This does a good job of summarizing the analysis in Harvey v. Dow. We can use this when we put the rest of our analysis together.

2.   Improving the Application

The application in our first attempt is what we would call conclusory. We call it conclusory because the statement that "Karla and Michael's conduct amounted to a promise" is not supported by an argument. It is a statement (really a conclusion) given without any justification.

To strengthen the application, it is important to think of three important terms. The first term is FACTS. The second term is FACTS. The third term is FACTS. This joke is usually funnier when I deliver it in person, but I use it to emphasize three things you need to do with legal analysis:

(1)   Identify what FACTS are relevant to the analysis;

(2)   Explain why those <u>FACTS</u> are relevant; and

(3)   Show how the <u>FACTS</u> lead to your conclusion.

Let's explore how to do this effectively. This time I will let you go first. Please follow the instructions below to start to build your application:

(1)   Please list ***all*** of the FACTS that are relevant to the legal question we are trying to answer? (You should be looking for any facts that make it look like Karla and Michael made a promise to Damon ***and*** any facts that make it look like they did not make a promise to him.)

(2)   Why do you think those FACTS are relevant? (What made you list the facts in response to the previous question? How do they relate to the issue you are trying to resolve?)

(3)   How do those FACTS lead to your conclusion? (Taken together, do the facts lead you to a definite outcome? Can you explain how they caused you to reach that outcome?)

You might have answered these questions this way:

(1) *Please list all of the FACTS that are relevant to the legal question we are trying to answer? (You should be looking for any facts that make it look like Karla and Michael made a promise to Damon **and** any facts that make it look like they did not make a promise to him.)*

- They knew Damon wanted their car.

- They never said clearly that they would give it to him.

- They handed him keys when he turned 18.

- The keys were on a personalized keychain.

- Damon paid the insurance for a year.

- Damon drove the car to and from school everyday.

- Damon paid to have the car painted.

- Damon paid for improvements.

- Damon spent $8000 on the car during the year.

(2) *Why do you think those FACTS are relevant? (What made you list the facts in response to the previous question? How do they relate to the issue you are trying to resolve? Do the facts support your conclusion or not? Is there more than one way to look at the facts?)*

FACT	RELEVANCE
- They knew Damon wanted their car.	*Provides a context for their subsequent actions.*
- They never said clearly that they would give it to him.	*Tends to show they did <u>not</u> make a promise.*
- They handed him keys when he turned 18.	*Tends to support a promise, but alone really doesn't show anything except that they allowed him to drive it.*
- The keys were on a personalized keychain.	*Tends to support a promise, but really is just evidence that they were giving him his own set of keys, not the entire car.*
- Damon paid the insurance for a year.	*This seems like a sign of ownership. It is not conclusive, but he is spending his own money on this.*

-	Damon drove the car to and from school everyday.	*Possession/use shows possible ownership, but parents let older children drive cars without giving them title all the time.*
-	Damon paid to have the car painted.	*Paying to improve the condition of the car suggests ownership. Presumably he did this with his parent's knowledge. They had to see the new paint job and the new wheels at least.*
-	Damon paid for improvements.	*Same.*
-	Damon spent $8000 on the car during the year.	*Same. The amount spent seems large for someone who did not own the car.*

Let's put these ideas into text:

Several facts support the idea that Karla and Michael, by their conduct, promised to give Damon their car. First, they knew he wanted the car. With that as background, they (i) gave him keys on a personalized keychain, (ii) let him pay the insurance, (iii) allowed him to drive the car daily, (iv) observed (presumably) as he paid for paint and other improvements to the car at a cost of $8000. Taken together, it seems like Karla and Michael, knowing Damon wanted the car, gave him every indication that they were, indeed, giving it to him.

The above paragraph is sufficient to support our conclusion, but our analysis will be even stronger if we acknowledge the opposite viewpoint. We call the other view a *counterargument*, and it would look something like this:

On the other hand, Karla and Michael might argue that the actions they took were more consistent with what parents would do for a child coming of age and were not a promise to give him a car. Parents give children car keys all the time without giving them title to a car, and having Damon do things like pay for insurance are ways to teach responsibility, or at least these actions can be viewed as such.

This seems to capture all of the facts that are relevant to the analysis. So now we can move on to the third step.

(3) *How do those FACTS lead to your conclusion? (Taken together, do the facts lead you to a definite outcome? Can you explain how they caused you to reach that outcome? If there is more than one way to look at the facts—i.e., if there is a*

counterargument—which perspective do you think is stronger?)

One way we might look at these arguments is this:

If you look at the facts together, in context, it looks like Damon's parents gave him every indication that the car was his. Although some of the facts can be interpreted in more than one way, together (especially within the context that they knew Damon always wanted them to give him the car) it looks like they communicated to him that the car was his. If not by words, they did it by their conduct. The argument that the parents were merely teaching him responsibility does not hold water, especially given the great expense Damon undertook.

It also might be reasonable to reach the alternate conclusion that Karla and Michael did not make a promise by their conduct. The outcome you reach actually is less important than the application of the law to the facts.

3. Revising the Analysis

Finally, we can revise the analysis with our improved rule and application:

> Did Karla and Michael Jenkins make a promise to Damon?
>
> A promise does not have to "be express but may be implied from a party's conduct." Where there is a general, albeit not explicit, understanding between parties, and the alleged promisor takes multiple actions consistent with that understanding, the promisor's conduct can be viewed as a promise.
>
> Several facts support the idea that Karla and Michael, by their conduct, promised to give Damon their car. First, they knew he wanted the car. With that as background, they (i) gave him keys on a personalized keychain, (ii) let him pay the insurance, (iii) allowed him to drive the car daily, (iv) observed (presumably) as he paid for paint and other improvements to the car at a cost of $8000. Taken together, it seems like Karla and Michael, knowing Damon wanted the car, gave him every indication that they were, indeed, giving it to him.
>
> On the other hand, Karla and Michael might argue that the actions they took were more consistent with what parents would do for a child coming of age and were not a promise to give him a car. Parents give children car keys all the time without giving them title to a car, and having Damon do

things like pay for insurance are ways to teach responsibility, or at least these actions can be viewed as such.

If you look at the facts together, in context, it looks like Damon's parents gave him every indication that the car was his. Although some of the facts can be interpreted in more than one way, together (especially within the context that they knew Damon always wanted them to give him the car) it looks like they communicated to him that the car was his. If not by words, they did it by their conduct. The argument that the parents were merely teaching him responsibility does not hold water, especially given the great expense Damon undertook.

Therefore, they made a promise.

Compare the above to our first attempt, reproduced here:

Did Karla and Michael Jenkins make a promise to Damon?

A promise does not have to "be express but may be implied from a party's conduct."

Here, Karla and Michael's conduct amounted to a promise.

Therefore, they made a promise.

Which do you think is better? Why? Which is more complete and thorough?

In law school (and in law practice), analysis is better if it (i) states the rule clearly and completely, (ii) identifies the relevant facts and explains their relevance, (iii) articulates and examines any counterarguments, and (iv) briefly states a conclusion. It is ***imperative*** that you learn to write the more comprehensive legal analysis, like the one we have developed above. Doing so will improve your chances of succeeding in law school greatly.

We will work a lot more on building your understanding of analysis in upcoming chapters.

ASSIGNMENT: You need to prepare for Class Two, which is coming next. Please skim, read, and prepare a case brief for each of the opinions assigned for Class 2.

<u>**TIMELINE**</u>**—You should spread this step over three days:**

Day 1 (Today)—<u>Preparation and Reading</u>. Give yourself a few hours to read this carefully and to write your briefs and notes. Then, it is important for you to take a break. Your brain actually needs time to process the information you have just learned. You will learn better if you take a break now. *(Time Estimate: 3 hours.)*

Day 2 (Tomorrow)—<u>Pre-Class Review</u>. Review your briefs and notes. You do not need to reread the entire assignment, because hopefully you read it carefully enough to understand it the first time and then made briefs and notes that captured your understanding. But it may be useful for you to reread important passages in addition to reading your notes in order to refresh your recollection of what you read the day before. *(Time Estimate: 30–45 minutes.)*

Day 3 (Day After Tomorrow)—<u>Class</u>. Move on to the next chapter.

<u>*We Belong*</u>

CAROLINE, who immigrated to the U.S. as a child, was the first person in her large extended family to go to college. According to her family, the only way she could live the American dream was to become a doctor or a lawyer. She ended up going to the University of California, Berkeley for law school. According to Caroline, "Law literally opened my eyes to the possibilities—which are endless!" After practicing law for a few years, Caroline went to business school and since has worked in private equity as an executive for several corporations.

Caroline's Advice: ***Believe in the possibilities. Law school and the path it put me on was probably the best decision I have ever made. It shaped my future—the tangible one, as viewed through my career progression, but more importantly the intangible one, allowing me to take calculated risks and explore the many paths that have opened up as a result of my education.***

---

[1]   For a discussion of rule structures, see Linda H. Edwards, LEGAL WRITING: PROCESS: ANALYSIS, AND ORGANIZATION, 3d. Ed. (Aspen 2002).

[2]   Some of the rules in this section are incomplete. I am using them to demonstrate rule structure.

CHAPTER 9

CLASS TWO

■ ■ ■

FIRST THINGS FIRST

Before you go to your next class, let's explore a way to calm your mind before going to class. Studies show that spending just a few minutes calming your mind through mindfulness meditation can improve academic performance. Mindfulness meditation involves focusing your mind on the present. When you do that, it can liberate your brain, allowing you to focus on the task in front of you.

Here's what I'd like you to do:

Go to one of the following websites or apps (Calm, Headspace, or Insight Timer) and find a 5–10 minute, free(!) mindfulness exercise to do. After doing the exercise, please answer the following questions:

1. Was that your first time trying mindfulness?

2. How was that experience for you?

3. Do you notice a difference in how you feel after doing the exercise as compared to how you felt before? If so, how so?

CLASS 2

You have read and prepared for class, you have calmed your mind, and now you are ready to take on your second class. Please go to www.belonging inlawschool.com, click on "Classes," then on "Contracts (Promissory Estoppel)," and then on "Class 2."

Please remember your goals for note-taking. Look for (i) themes, (ii) conceptual relationships, (iii) rules, (iv) process, (v) hypotheticals, and (vi) information that will complement your notes.

POST-CLASS REVIEW

Congratulations on finishing your second class. Before we move forward to the next topic, let's add one more technique to complete our learning cycle. So far, we have learned about (1) reading for class, (2) pre-class review, and (3) class. Finally, we want to focus on post-class review.

Let's start by remembering our goals for the first three stages of the class learning cycle:

STAGE	TASK	GOAL
1	Skim	**Context**—You are just trying to identify the topic you are writing about. If you can, read quickly the beginning and end of cases to see what the dispute is about and which party prevailed. You are **_not_** trying to read or understand anything fully.
	Read	**Comprehension**—Immediately after skimming, you read carefully. You are reading to understand the material. This means that you have to spend enough time with the material to understand it. It is important to record your understanding in notes and/or briefs.
2	Pre-Class Review	**Confidence**—Here, you review the notes and briefs you created in Stage 1. No need to re-read the reading, though you may want to revisit important passages. From here, you should go to class feeling

		as though you have taught yourself everything you can learn on your own.
3	Class	**Complement**—Class should add to your understanding, clarify any misunderstanding, confirm information you learned. Take notes, focusing on listening first.

After class, you want to make sure to wrap up the cycle with a quick review. By the end of this review, you want to feel assured that you learned and understand everything you were expected to learn during the class cycle. You don't want any questions left unanswered. To accomplish this, you want to do several things:

(1) **Fill in any gaps in your notes**. If you missed anything during class, figure out what you missed. Fill in the gaps so you are not leaving yourself to fill them in later, when things are not fresh in your memory.

(2) **Ask questions**. If, despite reading, attending class, and taking good notes, you find that there still is something you do not fully understand, then never be afraid to ask questions. In law school, this means going to your professors during office hours and talking to them specifically about issues raised during class.

(3) **Write out answers to the in-class hypotheticals asked by your professors**. This is an excellent way to test (i) your knowledge of the subject matter, and (ii) your ability to apply the law you have learned. If you remember, part of our note-taking plan is to write or type all hypotheticals, verbatim if possible. After class, you can use some of your time to write answers to those hypotheticals, using the IRAC structure we have learned above. (We will continue to work on that structure in the next chapter.)

GOAL: Completion. After you do this, you should feel as though you completely understand the material. You are not saving anything to figure out later. You understand it, and you have memorialized it in your notes.

ASSIGNMENT: Conduct a post-class review of the material from Classes 1 and 2. Try to write out brief IRAC analysis for at least 2 of the hypotheticals the professor raised in class.

TIMELINE—You should spend about 30–45 minutes on this task. You should do it the same day you completed Class 2.

CHAPTER 10

PREPARING FOR EXAMS

■ ■ ■

I. THE KEYS TO EXAM SUCCESS

In the pages that follow, I will walk you through how to prepare for law school exams. There is a lot of truly important information in this chapter, and you probably will want to come back to this chapter during your time at law school.

If you get nothing else from this chapter, pay attention to this:

> *Taking exams involves skills that you must develop. In the same way that you study the law that you learn, you must study how to apply that law effectively. You will maximize your potential in law school when you combine expertise in the knowledge of the law with expertise in the practical application of that law.*

DEGREES OF KNOWLEDGE

To help you appreciate what I mean by this, I would like you to think for a moment about a story of three students in medical school. All three of these medical students are taking a surgery class, and, at the end of the semester, their surgical skill will be assessed with a final evaluation. Over the course of the semester, they will learn how to perform 15–20 separate surgical procedures. For this final evaluation, they must perform a particular surgery on a cadaver, but they do not know which of the 15–20 they will be required to perform. As a result, they must be prepared to do any one of these procedures without any notice. The exam is open book, and their entire grade depends not only on whether they competently perform the surgery, but on how well they perform the procedure compared when compared to each other.

All three students are hard-working, diligent students—they are <u>not</u> slackers who are unwilling to put forward the effort necessary to succeed. So, let's take a look at how they prepare, focusing first on Student 1 and Student 2:

Student 1: Student 1 really wants to excel in medical school. He goes to all of his classes, does all of the readings, takes notes, and he studies really hard. In preparation for his final evaluation, he reviews all of his notes and makes a comprehensive list of every step he needs to take in order to perform each procedure perfectly. *During his final, he plans to keep the list in front of him and consult it as necessary to ensure that he does every step perfectly.*

Student 2: Student 2 really wants to excel in medical school. She goes to all of her classes, does all of the readings, takes notes, and she studies really hard. In preparation for her final evaluation, she reviews all of her notes and makes a comprehensive list of every step she needs to take in order to perform each procedure perfectly. *In order to ensure that she does well on the final, she memorizes the list of steps for each procedure so that she will automatically know what to do when her final evaluation happens.*

First, I'd like you to see that these students are both industrious and committed to doing well. And, if given <u>unlimited</u> time, you also should see that these students could do equally well on the final evaluation. Why? Because they each could take their time and access their own lists of steps (one physical, one mental), and they would do roughly the same quality work.

If, however, they are graded not only on how well they perform the procedure, but also on how <u>quickly</u> they can do it, can you see that Student 2 will do better than Student 1? The reason that Student 2 will do better, in simple terms, is that she will not have to stop after every step to consult her notes. She knows every step by memory and can simply consult her brain. All other things being equal, she will be able to perform the same quality work more quickly than Student 1.

Now, let's compare Students 1 and 2 to a third student:

Student 3: Student 3 really wants to excel in medical school. They go to all of their classes, do all of the readings, take notes, and they study really hard. In preparation for the final evaluation, they review all of their notes and make a comprehensive list of every step they need to take in order to perform each procedure perfectly. They also memorize the list of steps for each procedure so that they will automatically know what to do when the final evaluation happens. *In addition to this, Student 3 also practices each procedure several times over the course of the semester, so that they can see what it feels like to do each procedure. By the time the final evaluation occurs, Student 3 has developed a muscle memory for each procedure.*

When we add Student 3 to the mix, we could expect the quality of Student 3's work to outshine that of Students 1 and 2, even in an unlimited time setting. Whatever the procedure, Student 3 has not only studied it, but they have actually practiced it, giving them the opportunity to experience their knowledge put into action.

But there is no question that, if the students were evaluated both on quality and on speed, Student 3's performance would **overwhelm** that of Students 1 and 2. Given that Student 3 has not only the knowledge, but the practical experience, they can do higher quality work, and they can do it much more quickly than the other two.

Although you are not planning on medical school, I think this analogy describes almost exactly the way law school works. Over the course of a semester, you are taught "the law," the rules (or procedures) that you must use to resolve legal problems. Much of what you are taught helps you learn to apply those rules in different contexts, i.e., how to use your knowledge to perform "surgery" on these legal problems.

Like our analogy, in law school, you are evaluated on your ability to apply your knowledge to new and unexpected legal problems. There usually are no quizzes or midterms, and your grade usually depends on a single exam at the end of the semester. Those exams are usually timed, and the volume number of problems you must address is usually quite large. In other words, like the med students above, you will be evaluated on your ability to analyze these legal problems well, and you are expected to do that analysis quickly and efficiently.

Another important thing to remember is that your grades in law school typically depend not only on how well you analyze these problems, but on how well your analysis compares to that of your colleagues. In other words, not everyone can or will get A pluses (assuming your law school uses grades). Even when you do good work, you grade depends on how many other people do good work, how many people do really good work, how many people do really, really good work, and how many people do excellent work.

It is important, therefore, that you maximize your potential by trying to be like Student 3 above. Of course, you should do all of your class readings, go to class, take notes, study, and create study tools to help you prepare for exams, like Student 1. You will learn even better if you memorize the information in those study tools, like Student 2. And you will become an expert if you also practice applying that knowledge by taking practice exams and doing other work that will help you not only learn information but master the skills needed to use that information effectively.

II. OUTLINING—WHAT IT IS AND WHY EVERYONE GOES CRAZY ABOUT IT

From the first day that you enter law school, you will hear a buzz about something called "outlining":

"Have you started outlining?"

"I've started outlining all of my classes already."

"My outline is soooooooo long!"

All of this buzz stresses students out, not only because they feel like they should be doing something that they are not doing, but because they don't even know what outlining is. In this section, I will explain what outlining is and will show you a few ways to approach it.

Outlining is not something magical. It is a version of something you have been doing most of your life: studying. For some reason, we use a special word for it in law school, and the mystery behind it freaks everyone out. Outlines are simply exam preparation, study tools that help students organize information they need to know in order to do well on their exams.

Outlining well depends on your understanding a few key guiding principles:

- Outlines help you create a comprehensive list of possible exam issues;

- Outlines give you structure and process for analyzing particular issues; and

- Outlines help you identify facts that trigger issues.

Let's consider each of these.

A. ISSUE LIST

During a full semester in a law school course, you will study dozens of topics, so outlining becomes an important tool for helping you master the universe of topics studied over the term. Part of this mastery is simply identifying all of the topics—an outline should contain a comprehensive list of all of the topics and subtopics you have studied. The reason that this is important is that it will assist us in forming a mental checklist of issues to look for on the exam.

In half a semester of contracts, your topic list might look something like this:

> - Formation
> - Promissory Estoppel
> - Statute of Frauds

Once you start adding subtopics, your list might show more detail looking like this:

- Formation
  - Objective Theory of Contracts
  - Offer
  - Acceptance
  - Essential Terms
  - Sufficient Definiteness
  - Consideration
- Promissory Estoppel
  - Contract Theory (Restatement)
  - Detrimental Reliance
  - Areas of Application
    - Family
    - Business
    - Charity
- Statute of Frauds
  - Areas of Application
    - Contracts for Interest in Land
    - Contracts Not to Be Performed in One Year
    - Marriage as Consideration
    - Surety
    - Goods Contracts for $500 or More
  - Requirements
    - Writing
    - Signed by Party Against Whom Enforcement Is Sought
  - Exceptions
    - Partial Performance
    - Merchants (Goods Contracts)

In this book, we really are learning about only one topic, <u>Promissory Estoppel</u>. There are, of course, a number of areas where we have seen this doctrine applied, including reading several cases within the family context and others within a business context. So our issue list should look something like this for now:

> - Promissory Estoppel
>   - Contract Theory (Restatement)
>   - Detrimental Reliance
>   - Areas of Application
>   - Family
>   - Charity

This list will help us keep an eye out for various issues on exams. We are more likely to recognize them if we are looking for them.

B. STRUCTURE AND PROCESS

Once we have listed the possible issues that might arise on an exam, we have to know how to analyze them. This is where the rules we learned from our readings and classes will come in handy. We can use our outline to help establish the structure we must use for each issue that arises on the exam and the process for analyzing each of them. This structure will be a guide for us as we prepare for the exam.

As we begin to look at the issues that might come up on the exam, we can look at the rules that we have pulled from our casebook and classes. So let's start to do that. The main rule we have learned is from the Restatement (2nd) of Contracts, Section 90:

> A promise which the promisor should reasonably expect to induce action or forbearance on the part of the promisee or a third person and which does induce such action or forbearance is binding if injustice can be avoided only by enforcement of the promise. The remedy granted for breach may be limited as justice requires.

Knowing this paragraph is great, but we have to break it up into its parts, known as "elements," in order to use it effectively. Let's try to see each part of the paragraph:

> **A promise** which the **promisor should reasonably expect to induce action or forbearance** on the part of the promisee or a third person and which **does induce such action or forbearance** is binding if **injustice can be avoided only by enforcement** of the promise. The **remedy granted for breach may be limited as justice requires**.

You'll notice that I did not highlight all of the language above. That does not necessarily mean that the language is not important, but it may not be necessary for us to highlight every word in the paragraph. For example, the language "on the part of the promise or a third person" is not highlighted, but it is important for us to understand whose "action or forebearance" matters. But if we look closely, the phrase "promise or a third person" is very broad, rather than limiting. The important language is the language highlighted in orange, which lets us know that what matters is if the reliance (by anyone) should have been foreseen. So we will keep our eye on the language that has not been highlighted, but we'll keep it from being an element for now.

Using the language highlighted above, we can see four or five elements to a claim for promissory estoppel:

(1) There must be a promise;

(2) The person making the promise should have expected that someone would rely on the promise;

(3) Someone must actually have relied on that promise;

(4) Injustice can be avoided only by enforcement of the promise; and

(5) The promise should be enforced only so much as is necessary to meet justice.

You probably notice that I have put this in my own words. Using one's own words is an important aspect of understanding rules. Everyone can quote a rule, but if you can paraphrase the elements *without changing its meaning*, that is an indication that you understand what you are reading or quoting.

So now we have the structure for analyzing a claim of promissory estoppel, so we can add that to our outline:

```
■  Promissory Estoppel

   •  Elements
      1)  Promise
      2)  Foreseeable Reliance
      3)  Actual Reliance
      4)  Justice Requires Enforcement
      5)  Justice Can Limit Enforcement

   •  Contract Theory (Restatement)
   •  ~~Detrimental Reliance~~
   •  Areas of Application
      o  Family
      o  Charity
```

You can see that I crossed out "Detrimental Reliance." That is because I noticed that reliance is an element of the claim. So I figure that part of the rule captures that subject. (I might be wrong, but I can put it back if my view on this changes as I continue to work on my outline.) Although this might seem like a minor point, it is important so you can see that your outline is not rigid. You should expect it to change as you work on it—you are constantly revising and improving it.

Notice how we started with a certain level of detail and then added more detail. As we continue to work on the outline, we will continue to add more and more detail to the outline. For example, element 1) requires a promise. But what is a promise? Restatement section 2 defines a promise as follows:

> A promise is a manifestation of intention to act or refrain from acting in a specified way, so made as to justify a promisee in understanding that a commitment has been made.

As we did with Section 90, we can break this down into parts:

> A promise is a **manifestation of intention to act or refrain from acting** in a specified way, so made as to **justify a promisee in understanding that a commitment has been made**.

Here, we see two elements, so we can add this information to our overall outline to make it more detailed:

- Promissory Estoppel

  - Elements
    1) Promise
       a. Manifestation of intention to act or refrain from acting; that
       b. Justifies promisee in determining that a commitment has been made.
    2) Foreseeable Reliance
    3) Actual Reliance
    4) Justice Requires Enforcement
    5) Justice Can Limit Enforcement

  - Contract Theory (Restatement)
  - Areas of Application
    o Family
    o Charity

C. THE IMPORTANCE OF CASES

You also should note that we have not yet included any cases in our outline. The structure of our outline is driven by topics and rules, not cases. But the cases will be helpful as we build more detail into our outline. With each case, we can add information that we think will help our understanding of the rules and process for analyzing legal issues.

Consider the *Harvey v. Dow* case. What can that add to our outline? Well, one thing you can do is consult your brief to see what rules you got from the case. You probably will find the following statements are relevant to your outline:

- "General promises alone are not sufficient to support a claim of promissory estoppel."

- "General promises plus encouragement of reliance will support the claim."

- "The promise relied on by the promisee need not be express but may be implied from a party's conduct."

All three of these rules help us understand the nature of a promise. So we can add them to our outline:

- Promissory Estoppel

  - Elements
    1) Promise
       a. Manifestation of intention to act or refrain from acting; that
       b. Justifies promisee in determining that a commitment has been made.
          o General promises insufficient
            ▪ Added encouragement may suffice;
          o Promise may be express or implied from conduct.
    2) Foreseeable Reliance
    3) Actual Reliance
    4) Justice Requires Enforcement
    5) Justice Can Limit Enforcement

  - Contract Theory (Restatement)
  - Areas of Application
    o Family
    o Charity

You can see our outline gaining more detail and really taking shape.

Now it is your turn. Take the next case we read, Greiner v. Greiner, along with your pre-class and class notes, and add in any information you think is relevant to help you understand the structure and process for analyzing the issues we have studied so far. When you are ready, proceed below.

———————

We've done the above outline in a particular way in this chapter, but there is more than one way to outline. You could use flash cards, flow charts, mindmaps, or a range of other kinds of study tools. All of these should be used to help you achieve the same goals. To see other examples of outlines, please go to www.belonginginlawschool.com, click on "Study Materials," and then on "Contracts (Promissory Estoppel)."

———————

D. TRIGGER FACTS

In addition to the above, it can be a very useful exam preparation tool to think ahead of time about what kinds of facts should cause you to do certain kinds of analysis. If, for example, we are looking at the issue of promissory estoppel, you could think of <u>types</u> of facts that might be used to cause you to analyze that topic:

-   A story where somebody promises something to someone else.

-   The other person makes a decision based on that promise.

You can also think of <u>examples</u> of those kinds of facts.

-   A story where somebody promises something to someone else.

    o   "I'll give you a million dollars."

    o   "I'll pay for your college."

-   The other person makes a decision based on that promise.

    o   Other person buys a house.

    o   Person uses college money for something else.

So you could go ahead and add notes about this into your outline.

- Promissory Estoppel
    - Elements
        1) Promise
            a. Manifestation of intention to act or refrain from acting; that
            b. Justifies promisee in determining that a commitment has been made.
        2) Foreseeable Reliance
        3) Actual Reliance
        4) Justice Requires Enforcement
        5) Justice Can Limit Enforcement
    - Contract Theory (Restatement)
    - Areas of Application
        o Family
        o Charity

Look for somebody promising something to someone else *(I'll give you a million dollars/I'll buy you a car)*

Look for somebody doing something because the promise was made *(X buys a house/Y goes to car dealer and signs a contract)*

OUTLINING MISTAKES

There are several common mistakes that students make when outlining. You should look out for these mistakes, especially when you are outlining in your first semester of law school. Here are some of the most common errors:

(1) Organizing outlines by case, rather than by topic;

(2) Planning on using the outline during the exam rather than memorizing the material;

(3) Insufficient detail; and

(4) Too much detail.

ASSIGNMENT: Finish your outline for the material we have covered so far.

Then, you need to prepare for Class 3.

TIMELINE—**You should spread this step over three days:**

Day 1 (Today)—**Outlining.** Using the guidelines above, prepare a study tool (outline) for the material we have covered so far. *(Time estimate: 2 hours)*

Preparation and Reading. Prepare for Class 3 *(Time Estimate: 3 hours.)*

Day 2 (Tomorrow)—**Pre-Class Review.** Review your briefs and notes for the Class 3 materials. *(Time Estimate: 30–45 minutes.)*

Day 3 (Day After Tomorrow)—**Class.** Proceed to the next chapter.

CHAPTER 11

CLASS THREE

■ ■ ■

Before you move on to Class 3, let's spend a few minutes getting grounded.

FIRST THINGS FIRST

Before you go to class, it is important to get your mind right. To do this, I would like you to spend a few minutes reflecting on and then writing about the following:

Imagine yourself as a successful (however you define that) lawyer in five or ten years. Describe the path that took you to success. What barriers did you overcome? How did you persevere?

CLASS 3

You have read and prepared for class, you have grounded yourself, and now you are ready for your third class. Please go to www.belonginginlaw school.com, click on "Classes," then on "Contracts (Promissory Estoppel)," and then on "Class 3."

Please remember your goals for note-taking. Look for (i) themes, (ii) conceptual relationships, (iii) rules, (iv) process, (v) hypotheticals, and (vi) information that will complement your notes.

POST-CLASS REVIEW

Congratulations on finishing your third class. There is a lot to do before we move on to the next chapter.

ASSIGNMENT:

(1) **Conduct a post-class review of the material from Class 3.**

(2) **Update your study tool/outline with new insights and information you got from preparing for and attending Class 3.**

TIMELINE:

(1) **Post-Class Review (30 Minutes).**

(2) **Updating Outline (1 Hour).**

We Belong

SAM is nonbinary and queer. When entering law school, Sam wasn't sure whether they would come out as nonbinary to anyone. Law school was a big culture shock, and it took Sam some time to get their feet under them. Sam also wanted to let people get to know them a bit before introducing others to a potentially unfamiliar gender identity. There was one other trans student at the school, and that gave Sam a lot of courage in starting to talk to people about their identity.

Sam was pleasantly surprised by how supportive the law students and professors were. Certainly not everyone understood, but they had an amazing network of people who helped them educate others and advocate for more trans-inclusive policies at the school. They even got the school to build a multi-stall, all-genders restroom, and some professors began introducing themselves with pronouns and addressing ways the law affects people of different genders. Sam made lifelong friends whom they trust and love dearly. The positive reception in law school cemented Sam's confidence in being out in the legal profession and working to be seen and recognized for who they are. After graduating, Sam's path includes a federal district court and federal appellate court clerkships as well as a prestigious fellowship working to address LGBTQ youth homelessness.

Sam's Advice: Our profession still has a long way to go to become inclusive, but there are a lot of people willing to learn how to get there. Being involved in community was critical to my mental health while in law school. I deliberately connected with other LGBTQ students and lawyers, saw an LGBTQ therapist, and I also kept in touch with friends outside law school. Being surrounded by people who get your experiences can make a huge difference when you're harmed, misunderstood, or feeling isolated. Finding a way to set down the work and inevitable drama of law school is also crucial to being able to recharge. After law school, I've found more ways to cultivate joy in my life. It's hard to do when law school is so overwhelming, so I'd recommend finding time before school starts to focus on finding what brings you joy.

CHAPTER 12

HOW TO TAKE A LAW SCHOOL EXAM

■ ■ ■

Exams are among the top stressors in law school. In many courses, there is only one law school exam at the end of the semester. And, your entire grade is based on that single exam. So taking an exam is among the top skills you must master in law school.

In this chapter, you will learn how to take a law school exam in two major parts: (1) Reading an exam question, and (2) Writing an exam answer.

I. READING AN EXAM QUESTION

THE PLAN: Unlike other kinds of exams, most law school exams generally do not tell you what issues you are expected to address. Instead, you are presented with hypothetical stories—longer versions of the hypotheticals we looked at in earlier chapters. When you read an exam question, it is important to read it carefully, so that you can identify all of the issues you are expected to write about in your answer. This is called "Issue Spotting." You are expected to read the facts in these hypos and create a list of issues to analyze. We will discuss analyzing these issues in the next section. For now, you should do the following:

(1) Read through the question carefully. Make sure to read every word. As you read, ask yourself the following questions:

   a. Why did the professor put this fact into the question?

   b. What issue(s) are suggested by this fact?

   Example: In an exam question, you read that "Person A tells Person X that A will pay X's college tuition." That should cause you to start thinking about a promise, perhaps in the context of promissory estoppel.

(2) Every time you see an issue suggested by the facts in the hypo, circle or underline the fact and write a note in the margin identifying the issue.

   Example: You would underline the sentence referenced above and write "Promise for Promissory Estoppel." To save time, you might develop a shorthand and write, "P/E—Prom." or something like that.

(3) Do the above for the entire question, circling, underlining and making margin notes along the way. You may find that you do not spot issues for every sentence. Some sentences are background to move the story along, but you should consider every sentence and clause to determine whether they bear some relationship to the issues you are required to discuss.

(4) When you are finished with the question, make sure you read the call of the question. This is the sentence or paragraph usually found at the end of the hypo that tells you what to do.

> *Example: At the end of a hypo, you might see a sentence that says, "Please analyze the issues raised by this question," or, "What possible claims does A have against B?" or, "You have been asked by your senior partner to evaluate the contractual issues presented by this problem and write a memorandum explaining your analysis." Each of these calls of the question is instructing you to do the same thing—spot all of the relevant issues and analyze them.*

(5) Once you have read through the entire question and the call of the question, repeat steps (1) and (2) above. Though you should re-read every sentence of the question again, make sure to pay special attention to any sentences or phrases you did not underline or circle and confirm whether any issues are raised by those facts. Note any new issues in the margins.

As you read, make sure that you look for all of the topics you have studied. If you don't see a topic that you covered in class, double check to make sure you haven't overlooked it. Finally, once you have spotted big issues, make sure to look for facts that relate to each of their elements.

THE GOAL: Precision. This is your only opportunity to identify and list all of the issues raised by the exam question. Make sure that you do this step carefully.

Exercise 11-1: Please read and mark up the Practice Exam Question on the following page.

Practice Exam Question

Serenity Sibling had many brothers and sisters and loved them all dearly. Recently, Serenity won the lottery and wanted to help out their family. Serenity told Bobbi, one of Serenity's siblings, that Serenity wanted to help Bobbi have a car to drive. Bobbi, who lived in an apartment far from their workplace, had a beat down pickup truck that had significant engine damage and was about to die permanently. The failing car had broken down so many times on Bobbi's way to work that Bobbi had nearly lost a job as a result of being chronically late. Serenity offered to give Bobbi $100,000 in order to get reliable transportation. Afterward, Serenity took Bobbi to several car dealerships to look at high-end, brand new pickup trucks. Witnesses can confirm that Serenity told Bobby when looking at these vehicles, "You can have your pick of these, you've got $100,000 to spend." Serenity then helped Bobbi take the old pickup truck to the salvage yard (it was not worth anything in its condition).

The day after these events, Bobbi decided to enter into a binding contract to purchase a condominium that was within walking distance to Bobbi's workplace. The price for the condominium was $300,000, which Bobby could afford if $100,000 were used as a down payment. When told about the condominium purchase, Serenity refused to give Bobbi the $100,000.

When you have finished marking up this exam question, please go online to www.belonginginlawschool.com, click on "Exams" and then on "Contracts (Promissory Estoppel)."

When reading the exam question, you should have observed all of the things that have been noted in the margins of the marked up version of this exam. For a color version of this mark-up, please go to www.belongingin lawschool.com, click on "Exams" and then on "Contracts (Promissory Estoppel)."

II. WRITING AN EXAM ESSAY ANSWER

One of the biggest mistakes law students make is a failure to take practice exams. Most students show up for their exams having studied and "knowing" the material,[1] but they do not appreciate how to write the answers or, perhaps, manage their time on exams. They end up with incomplete or poorly written answers, even if they knew the substantive law very well. In other words, even smart, hard-working, well-meaning students can get low grades on exams if they do not know how to write the answers properly.

The only way to develop the skill of writing answers to law school exams is to practice writing them. In this section, you will focus on writing answers to the question you read in the previous section.

THE PLAN: You should have a deliberate approach for reading and writing answers to traditional law school exams (i.e., those that present hypothetical situations and ask for comprehensive analysis). Once you have spotted the issues as you did in the previous section, then you should turn your attention to writing the analysis for each issue. You should do this in several steps:

1. Create a heading for each issue and each sub-issue. It is not particularly critical, but you may wish to use traditional outline headings (I, A, 1, a).

2. For each heading that you have, make sure your analysis is complete using I-R-A-C as a model. For review, here is a reminder of what I-R-A-C should accomplish:

    a. The **ISSUE** should be stated in the heading, and it also may be stated in the first sentence of the analysis. Some students will state the issue as a conclusion: "John did not owe a duty to warn Mary of potential harm."

    b. Follow the issue with a complete statement of the **RULES** or principles that govern, this part of the analysis. Make sure that the rule is fully addressed and that you do not save parts of the rule for later in your discussion. All of the rules for each issue (or sub-issue) should be stated at the beginning of each section/sub-section.

    c. Follow the rule statement with **ANALYSIS** that applies the law to the facts. Here, you should explain what facts are important, why they matter to the analysis, and how they lead to a conclusion. It is imperative that you acknowledge and articulate any counterarguments that may exist, even if you do not agree with them.[2] State the arguments and then explain which argument you believe will prevail and why you think so.

    d. State a brief **CONCLUSION**. Sometimes, there is more than one possible conclusion. You should acknowledge that in your discussion. In connection with your analysis, discussed in the preceding paragraph, make sure to explain why you think one outcome is more likely than another.

THE GOAL: Practice. This may be the first time that you have written this kind of exam answer. If so, you may find it to be challenging. A key to preparedness on exams is becoming very familiar with the process of exam writing. Hopefully, after practicing writing a few answers, you will develop comfort with the process and feel as though you can perform effectively on your final exam. In law school, you must develop this comfort through practice for every class that you take.

Exercise 11-2: Write an exam answer analyzing every issue you identified in Practice Midterm Exam Question 1, using the skills discussed above. When you are finished, you may proceed to the following page.

Your answer should look similar to what you see below. In the margins below, see comments on what makes this a good exam answer:

Headings that clearly communicate the **ISSUE** being discussed, including any subtopics.

A statement of the **ISSUE** to be discussed

A statement of the **RULE**. Given that this rule has five subparts, we should expect to see (and do see) five sections of the analysis devoted to this topic.

MODEL ANSWER TO MIDTERM EXAM

Model Answer to Practice Exam Question 1

Bobbi's Claim Against Serenity—Promissory Estoppel

To establish a right to recovery under a theory of promissory estoppel, a plaintiff must show that (i) the defendant made a promise to the plaintiff, (ii) the defendant should have known that the plaintiff would rely on that promise, (iii) the defendant actually relied on the promise, (iv) the defendant's reliance was reasonable, and (v) justice requires enforcement of the promise. Rest. s90.

A.   Serenity Made a Promise

A promise is a manifestation of intention to act or not to act, that justifies in the promise that the promisor has made a commitment. Rest. s2. The promise can be words, but it does not have to be. Actions—alone or in combination with words—can be sufficient to create a promise.

Here, Bobbi will argue that Serenity made statements and actions that would justify Bobbi in believing that Serenity made a commitment to give Bobbi $100,000. First, they "offered to give Bobbi $100,000 in order to get reliable transportation." Second, they took Bobbi to dealers to look at cars. When looking at the cars, Serenity said, in front of several people, "[Y]ou've got $100,000 to spend." Finally, Serenity helped Bobbi get rid of Bobbi's pickup truck. This combination

A complete statement of the **RULES/** principles that apply to this issue.

of words and promises was a definite source of commitment.

Serenity will argue, on the other hand, that there was no promise to give Bobbi $100,000 to spend as Bobbi wished. Instead, the promise, if there was one, was to help Bobbi acquire a car, not to give Bobbi $100,000 in cash. This is supported by the facts that Serenity's offer was to give money "in order [for Bobbi] to get reliable transportation" and that Serenity's second reference to the money was in the context of a car purchase—"You can have your pick of these . . . ." This suggests that, at most, there was a promise to buy a car, not to give cash to Bobbi.

Analysis that identifies all of the relevant facts and explains why those facts matter.

A concise **CONCLUSION.**

Bobbi's argument is stronger that a promise was made. (Serenity may have a decent argument about the nature of the promise, but that likely is more relevant to the reasonableness of Bobbi's reliance, as discussed in section D below.) Therefore, a promise was made.

B. Serenity Should Have Known Bobbi Would Rely on That Promise

Whether Serenity should have known that Bobbi would rely on Serenity's promise is a factual inquiry.

Here, everything about Serenity's actions was designed to get Bobbi to rely on the promise. From the words (described above), to the actions of taking Bobbi to the dealership to look at cars, to the final act of helping Bobbi dispose of the old pickup, Serenity certainly should have known that Bobbi would need to do something in order to keep the job.

Note how the answer quickly deals with issues that are less important and devotes more energy to important issues.

Therefore, this was the kind of promise on which Serenity should have known Bobbi would rely.

C. Bobbi Relied on Serenity's Promise

Whether Bobbi relied on Serenity's promise is a question of fact.

Here, the facts demonstrate that Bobbi actually relied on Serenity's promise. Bobbi took the old pickup truck to the junkyard. The proximity of this act, right after Serenity took Bobbi to the dealership to look at new cars, suggests that the two occurrences are connected. Again, "the day after these events," Bobbi bought a condo that Bobbi could not have afforded without the $100,000.

All of this supports a conclusion that Bobbi relied on Serenity's promise.

D. Bobbi's Reliance Was Reasonable

Even if the promisee actually relies on the promise, that reliance must be reasonable. There is a significant question about whether Bobbi's reliance was reasonable.

As discussed above, there was a relatively clear promise by Serenity to help Bobbi buy a car. Serenity will argue that there was never a promise to give Bobbi $100,000 outside of the context of buying a car. The cash and the car were the same, not separate. Thus, Bobbi's purchase of a home (rather than a car) was unreasonable.

> Note that the analysis here discusses both sides of the issue. You must be able to discuss arguments and counter-arguments effectively.

For Bobbi's part, Bobbi will argue that, even if the promise was to give $100,000 for a car only, Bobbi still could reasonably rely on that to purchase a home instead. The purpose of the $100,000 gift was for the underlying purpose of ensuring that Bobbi could get to work reliably. Purchasing the home satisfied that underlying purpose. And, for that matter, Bobbi could have purchased a car and immediately sold it, using the proceeds of the sale as Bobbi hoped to use a direct cash gift. Consequently, cutting out the middle step is not particularly meaningful.

Bobbi's argument is stronger, in my opinion. Therefore, Bobbi's reliance was reasonable.

E. Justice Requires Enforcement

The final consideration is whether justice requires enforcement of Serenity's promise. Essentially, the question here is whether Bobbi suffered a legal detriment. A detriment is the undertaking of an act or obligation one is not already legally

> obligated to undertake (i.e., doing or agreeing to do something one is not already required to do) or the relinquishment of a legal right (i.e., agreeing not to do something one is entitled to do).
>
> Here, there are two possible detriments. First, Bobbi changed position by getting rid of the old pickup. Bobbi certainly was not obligated to get rid of the truck, and that act was undertaken (as discussed above, in response to the Serenity's promise. That, however, was not a significant loss, as the truck had no value. Second, Bobbi entered into a contract to purchase the condo. This binding obligation is a detriment, as Bobbi has significantly changed position incurring this new legal obligation.
>
> Justice requires enforcement of Serenity's promise, insofar as Bobbi incurred a $300,000 obligation in reliance on that promise.
>
> For all of the aforementioned reasons, Bobbi has a valid claim for recovery under the doctrine of promissory estoppel.

III. MORE STUDYING AND PRACTICE

After you have completed a practice exam, you may realize that you did not understand the law as well as you thought, or you may realize that your ability to recall the law is not as good as you had hoped. In order to do well on exams, you want to study and practice until you have achieved a level of mastery that allows you to operate with automaticity.[3] In other words, you are ready when you can respond to questions automatically—reacting to issues rather than thinking about them.

THE PLAN: Keep studying and practicing until you believe that you can execute effectively on the final exam. Do the following:

1. Note any areas where you did not correctly apply the law on a previous practice question;

2. Study the portions of your outline where you have not yet achieved complete mastery;

3. Take more practice questions.

4. Revisit your checklist and edit if necessary.

5. Repeat this process as necessary.

THE GOAL: Mastery. By the time that you have finished studying, you should feel as though you can analyze any relevant issue with expertise.

Exercise 11-3:

Study and take another exam. Read and write answers to Practice Midterm Question 2, using the skills discussed above. Compare your answers to the sample provided after the exam question. Only when you believe that you have achieved a sufficient level of mastery, proceed to the next page.

FIRST THINGS FIRST

Please go to a website or app (e.g., Calm, Headspace, Insight Timer) and do another mindfulness exercise for 5–10 minutes.

Now that you are relaxed and ready, please proceed to the following page to take the midterm exam.

Mid-Term Exam (90 Minutes)

Tired of all of the poverty in his city, Phil Anthropist, an eccentric billionaire, decided to do something about it. In order to make a difference, Phil decided to do three things.

First, Phil sought the advice of Lara Learned, a social work professor who worked at a prominent university within the city. Lara was a 40 year-old, tenured faculty member, meaning that she had an incredible amount of job security and essentially could keep her position for at least the next three decades. Lara earned $150,000 per year as a professor. When Phil and Laura met, they discussed several ways that Phil could have a direct impact on reducing poverty in the city. Given that this was Laura's area of expertise, Phil was delighted with the advice she gave. After their meeting, and grateful for the time and ideas that Lara shared with him, Phil told Lara, "I'd like to give you $5 million to start your own foundation." He pointed out of the window to another building in the city, and said, "I own that abandoned building. You can have it. You will do amazing things." Immediately after their meeting, Lara went back to her school and promptly resigned her position as a faculty member.

Second, Phil held a press conference, telling the entire city that he was going to buy school uniforms for every child in the city's public school system and that he was going to ensure that there was a computer in school for every child. He said, "Think of the freedom that will give families, who will not have to worry about a clothes or technology budget for their children!" Using a directory provided him by the public school system, Phil mailed out personal, handwritten letters to every family in the school district, telling them the same things that he had said publicly.

Third, Phil decided to attack the city's congestion and flailing green spaces. Phil bought a square mile of abandoned properties in the middle of the city and announced that he was going to create a massive, central park, and that he would create a biking and pedestrian system throughout the city. The biking and pedestrian system would allow people within the city to use publicly available bikes and scooters, free of charge, to get anywhere within the city without a car. At the same press conference referenced earlier—to which he invited city officials, all of whom attended, he held a ground breaking ceremony for the park and promised to provide whatever funds were necessary to widen roads and create bike lanes. Of course, he would need government approval for a massive undertaking like this, but he also had the ability to donate millions to the reelection campaigns of several prominent elected public officials.

Based on the statements Phil made at the press conference, many families in the city redirected their school clothing and technology budgets to pay for other necessary items. In addition, some families who previously lived outside of the city decided to move into the city, so they could take advantage of the park, pedestrian and bike paths, and the upgraded school system. In many cases, this meant that families made down payments of tens of thousands of dollars to buy homes in the city.

Unfortunately, Phil changed his mind and decided to buy his own personal island and move away from the city altogether. He refused to give Lara the $5 million or to do any of the things he said he would do for the city and school system.

Please analyze.

IV. SELF-EVALUATION

An important aspect of exam writing is developing the ability to evaluate your own work. This can be challenging at the beginning, because you do not necessarily know what to look for. Nor do you always know what your professors are expecting.

That said, there are some basic aspects of exam writing that you should be able to evaluate on your own. To learn the process of self-evaluation, we will take three steps. First, I am going to ask you to evaluate your answer. Second, I am going to have you read the model answer. Finally, I will ask you to re-evaluate your answer in light of the model.

A. EVALUATING YOUR OWN ANSWER

There are two steps to evaluating your exam answers in a practice context. A first step is to do an activity I call a "Cross-Out" task. For this, you will need to have a copy of your exam answer and a copy of the question above.

ASSIGNMENT: Place a copy of your exam answer and the exam question in front of you. Read through your answer. Every time your answer mentions a fact that is in the question, cross out that fact on the exam question. Then, see what facts remain that are not crossed out. Ask yourself whether the facts that are not crossed out are relevant to any of the analysis in your answer. If so, ask whether you should have included those facts in your answer.

Doing the exercise above will help you see whether you have been as inclusive in your discussion of the facts as you should have. *(Remember my earlier admonition about FACTS, FACTS, and FACTS being critical to your analysis.)*

Next, you should assess your own work. We will keep this simple. Use the chart below to evaluate aspects of your work.

ASSIGNMENT: Please evaluate yourself in the following categories on a scale of 1 to 5 by identifying how true the following statements are. (5 = Totally True, 4 = Relatively True, 3 = Somewhat True, 2 = Partially True, 1 = Not Very True)

Self-Evaluation (Midterm)					
	1	2	3	4	5
I spotted all of the relevant issues.					
I discussed each claim separately.					
I used IRAC format.					
I clearly articulated all of the relevant rules.					
I used all of the facts that were relevant to each part of the analysis.					
I included counter-arguments, where appropriate.					
I stated a conclusion for each issue and sub-issue.					

How you answer these questions will give you the first insight into how you think you did on the exam. This is important, because you do want or need to wait for someone else's evaluation of your work, though that will come in law school. It is most important that you are paying attention to what you are doing and that you are deliberate and methodical about implementing your exam-taking plan.

B. READING THE MODEL ANSWER

Our second step in the process is to read the model answer. As you read, please note the topics discussed (i.e., issues that were spotted), organization, and inclusion of facts. It is not that important that you arrived at the same conclusion as the author of the model answer. It is, however, very important to have discussed both sides of the issues raised in your answer, where applicable, and for you to have been thorough in your analysis.

You should not expect however, that your answer—as someone who is just learning how to do this—will be as comprehensive as the model answer, which was written by an expert. The model answer is something you should aspire to. You will grow in your ability to do this as you practice, practice, and practice some more.

Assignment: Please read through the model answer below. Compare it to your answer as you read and note any meaningful differences.

Model Answer to Midterm Exam

There are four parties (or groups of parties) who may have claims against Phil Anthropist. I will discuss each claim below.

I. Promissory Estoppel (Lara v. Phil)

To prove a claim of promissory estoppel, a plaintiff must show (i) that the defendant made a promise, (ii) the defendant knew or should have known that the plaintiff would rely upon that promise, (iii) the defendant actually relied on the promise, (iv) the defendant's reliance was reasonable, and (v) justice requires enforcement of the promise.

A. Promise

"A promise is a manifestation of intention to act or refrain from acting in a specified way, so made as to justify a promisee in understanding that a commitment has been made." Rest. § 2. Although promises can be made expressly (i.e. in words), conduct can also effect a promise if that conduct (i) exists in a context where a promise can be understood, or (ii) the gravity of the conduct taken in its totality reflects that a promise was made. (See Harvey v. Dow, where parents took a number of actions consistent with a promise.)

Here, Lara would argue that Phil made Lara a promise. He did this expressly. The context of meeting about reducing poverty in the city, Phil told Lara, "I'd like to give you $5 million" for a foundation. In addition, he pointed out a building and told her she could have it, and he told her that she "will do amazing things." These statements reflect a promise being made by Phil to Lara, she would argue.

On the other hand, Phil would argue that none of his statements or conduct, taken separately or together, do not rise to the level of expressing a true commitment in what appears to be their first conversation about addressing poverty. First, Phil said, "I would like," which is different than "I will" or "I promise." Second, Phil merely said "you can have it" about the building. He really did not say anything else to her. These two statements cannot possibly rise to the level of a promise. Moreover, he took no actions in further support of these ideas. At best, it seems Phil was suggesting a proposed course of action or opening a discourse.

Phil has the stronger argument. Without more definitive words or conduct in support of those words, it does not appear that a promise has been made.

B.   Foreseeable Reliance

For the promise to be enforceable under a promissory estoppel theory, the plaintiff's reliance must be foreseeable.

Phil would argue that it is not foreseeable that anyone would rely on the two sentences he uttered at the meeting between him and Lara. Anyone expecting funds to start a foundation would not rely on that promise (if one were made). Certainly, it would not be foreseeable that a person hearing those two sentences would quit their job immediately

Therefore, there was no reasonable reliance.

C.   Actual Reliance

To satisfy this element, the plaintiff must have relied on the promise to their detriment. In other words, because of the promise, the promisee must have taken some action or refrained from acting in a particular way.

Here, assuming there was a promise, Lara relied on that promise by quitting her job.

This element is satisfied.

D.   Reasonable Reliance

The plaintiff's reliance also must be reasonable. The question we should ask here is whether a reasonable person would have relied on the defendant's promise in the way that the plaintiff did.

Here, Lara will argue that, assuming a promise of $5 million was made, her actions were eminently reasonable. Assuming that the money would be given, it is reasonable to begin preparations for starting the foundation.

Phil would argue that, even if he promised 5 million, no reasonable person would quit summarily a tenured position paying $150 thousand a year. A reasonable person would keep that job and wait for the logistics to be worked out. Phil never said when he would fund the foundation or how the funding would work (cash, annual payments, an endowment, or some other kind of funding mechanism). There was too much left to be worked out to justify this kind of reliance.

Phil has the better argument here. For that reason, the reliance was unreasonable.

E.   Justice Requires Enforcement

In light of the above discussion, there is no justification for enforcing the promise.

F.   Ultimate Conclusion on P/E

Lara will not prevail on a claim of promissory estoppel.

II.   Charitable Contribution—Lara v. Phil

Under Restatement Section 90, a charitable pledge is binding without proof that it induced action or forbearance. Not every jurisdiction adheres to this rule, so some jurisdictions require a charity to prove an entitlement to recovery under a promissory estoppel theory. (See above rules on promissory estoppel.)

Here, Lara might try to argue that she is entitled to recovery because Phil's "promise" was a charitable pledge. But at the time Phil made the statements to Lara, she was not a charity. There was no charity. The discussion was about starting a charitable enterprise, but none was yet in existence. So this was not a pledge to a charity.

(See above for discussion on promissory estoppel.)

For these reasons, Lara cannot recover under a charitable pledge theory.

III.   Promissory Estoppel (School District Families v. Phil))

The families in the city's public school district may have a claim against Phil. (See above rules on promissory estoppel.)

A.   Promise

(See above rules on promise.)

Here, the families in the school system would claim that Phil made a promise to them that he would give school uniforms and provide computers for every child in the school system. They will argue that his public statements constituted a promise. He said that he "was going to buy" and "was going to ensure" that these things would not be an issue. Indeed, he articulated that the families "will not have to worry about a clothes or technology budget."

Phil might argue that public statements cannot be considered promises to any particular person. The families would observe that Phil not only made public statements, but he made identical promises in "personal, handwritten letters" to every family in the school district. In other words, Phil went beyond saying these things publicly—he made a direct promise to each of these families.

Phil's actions in making public statements and following up with direct letters to families would justify these families in believing that Phil was making a commitment.

For these reasons, there was a promise.

B. Foreseeable Reliance

(See above rules.)

It certainly was foreseeable that people would rely on Phil's promise to provide clothing and computers. Phil's statement that they "will not have to worry" about their clothing and technology budgets makes it foreseeable that these people would forego purchasing clothing and computers. And, given that Phil understood the poverty within the city, it also is foreseeable that these funds would be redirected to address other needs.

Reliance was foreseeable here.

C. Actual Reliance

(See above rules.)

The families in the city actually relied on Phil's promise by redirecting "their school clothing and technology budgets to pay for other necessary items." This is a change in position in response to the promise. According to the facts, "many families" did this, so this analysis would apply only to the families that made this change.

For these reasons, there was actual reliance.

D. Reasonable Reliance

For the same reasons addressed above, the reliance by these families was reasonable. They did not quit their jobs or go buy fancy cars or homes. The extent of their reliance was to redirect their budgets to buy other necessary items. In other words, the harm to them was limited only to the amount they had budgeted for the items promised by Phil.

E. Justice Requires Enforcement

Based on the above analysis, justice requires enforcement of the promise Phil made. For the families that redirected their school budgets to other items, the promise should be enforced.

F. Ultimate Conclusion on P/E

For all of the reasons stated above, the people in the county can prevail on a claim of promissory estoppel.

IV. Promissory Estoppel (Outside of the City Families v. Phil)

The families who lived outside of the city have comparable claims to those of the families within the city, but the outcome is likely to be different. (See above analysis and rules.) I will discuss this briefly below.

A. Promise

In addition to the rules already stated above, it is important to note that a promisee is the person to whom a manifestation of a commitment is made. In other words, a promise must be made to someone who then may be justified in attempting to enforce that promise.

The families will argue that Phil promised to build a park and that he was going to create a biking and pedestrian system throughout the city. He took action in furtherance of this promise by buying the property, holding a press conference, and having a ground breaking ceremony. He also promised to do whatever it took to make this happen. These families will argue that they were justified in believing that Phil had made a commitment.

Phil will argue that these were not promises and that, even if they were, they were not promises to the people who lived outside of the city. It was clear that Phil's plan would need government approval in order to happen, so there was no guarantee that his plan would happen, even though he was able to "donate millions" to reelection campaigns.

And, even if there was a promise, it was not made to the people outside of the city. This was merely a public declaration. Unlike the situation with the people within the city school district, there were no personal letters sent. There was nothing directed at the people outside of the city.

There was no promise.

B. Foreseeable Reliance

It is not foreseeable that people who lived outside of the city would rely on the statements made at the press conference, especially when he had no direct contact with them.

C. Actual Reliance

Assuming there was a promise, the people outside of the city actually relied on the promise by moving into the city and making down payments in the tens of thousands of dollars on homes in the city.

D. Reasonable Reliance

The reliance by the people outside of the city was not reasonable. At best, their purchases of homes was speculation. They were hoping to gain an overflow benefit from promises made to others.

E. Justice Requires Enforcement

There is no justification for enforcing the promise Phil made regarding parks, etc. for the people who lived outside of the city.

F. Ultimate Conclusion on P/E

The people in the city cannot prevail on the claim of Promissory Estoppel.

V.   Charitable Pledge (City v. Phil)

There is an argument that Phil made a charitable pledge to the city.

(See above rules.)

Phil invited all city officials to his press conference, and they all attended. If the city qualifies as a charity, it is possible that his statements and conduct (invitations, press conference, and ground breaking ceremony) could qualify as a promise (pledge) made to the city. If our jurisdiction follows the rule in Restatement Section 90, the city might recover.

If the jurisdiction does not follow the rule in Section 90, then it is not at all likely that the city could recover under the promissory estoppel theory. Even though a promise arguably was made, there is nothing in the facts to suggest that the city detrimentally relied on that promise. Without more to go on, the city would not succeed under this theory.

C. RE-EVALUATION

Now that you have had the opportunity to read through the model answer and compare it to your answer, you probably have learned a little about where you have areas to grow. Perhaps you did not spot all of the issues—i.e., all of the various claims by all of the various parties against Phil. Or, you may not have stated the law as comprehensively. You might not have organized your answer as well as you hoped. Or, maybe you did not include as many facts in your analysis as you should.

As I stated before you starting reading the model answer, do not worry if your answer is not of the same quality as this model. The point of this book is for you to experiment and learn. Mistakes are actually good; you will learn from them. But let's take an opportunity for you to re-evaluate your work, now that you have more information.

Assignment: Please evaluate yourself in the following categories on a scale of 1 to 5 by identifying how true the following statements are. (5 = Totally True, 4 = Relatively True, 3 = Somewhat True, 2 = Partially True, 1 = Not Very True)

Self-Evaluation (Midterm)					
	1	2	3	4	5
I spotted all of the relevant issues.					
I discussed each claim separately.					
I used IRAC format.					
I clearly articulated all of the relevant rules.					
I used all of the facts that were relevant to each part of the analysis.					
I included counter-arguments, where appropriate.					
I stated a conclusion for each issue and sub-issue.					

How did your answers to these questions change once you had the opportunity to compare your answer to the model?

Assignment: In the space that follows, please reflect on what you have learned about exam writing, what you still want to work on, and how you can begin to grow in this skill.

> *We Belong*
>
> MONICA *grew up right near the border of Kansas and Missouri, in a conservative Midwestern family. Her mother grew up on a pecan and dairy farm in Oklahoma with 13 brothers and sisters and her father was the grandson of a sharecropper. When the time came for college, Monica wanted to spread her wings, so she chose a liberal arts school thousands of miles from home in California. There, she excelled as a creative writer, and after spending her junior year in France she almost left college to pursue an acting career in Europe. However, she was driven to go to law school because she saw it as a way to build her independence. Monica went to a top tier law school on the East Coast, and then she went to work for one of the largest law firms in the world, practicing in the area of corporate mergers and acquisitions (M&A). She left that law firm to go to another large law firm, where she became a partner in the corporate group. Monica currently is one of the top corporate attorneys in California.*
>
> *Monica's Advice:* **Don't be afraid. Ask questions, be curious, try and connect with the material that you are learning.**

This has been an incredibly busy chapter for you. Congratulations on completing your first midterm. Please take a break. Rest a full day and come back to this book the day after tomorrow.

TAKE A BREAK!

---

[1] See discussion in Chapter 5 concerning levels of mastery.

[2] See Richard Michael Fischl and Jeremy Paul, GETTING TO MAYBE: HOW TO EXCEL ON LAW SCHOOL EXAMS 234–238 (Carolina Academic Press 2009).

[3] See Schwartz and Manning, Expert Learning for Law Students. Professors Schwartz and Manning describe automaticity like this: It is like driving a path you have driven dozens of times before. There are times when fifteen or twenty minutes have passed, and you barely remember having done the driving. In those situations, your brain has engaged in the activity so many times that it can operate at a high level even when your mind is focused on other things.

CHAPTER 13

CLASS FOUR

■ ■ ■

In this chapter, we will prepare for and attend a new class, and we will add some additional post-class instruction. Given that we took a break after the midterm, you will have to prepare for class, so let's start that process immediately.

ASSIGNMENT: Prepare for Class 4.

TIMELINE—You should spread this step over three days:

Day 1 (Today)—Preparation and Reading. Read for Class 3 *(Time Estimate: 3 hours.)*

Day 2 (Tomorrow)—Pre-Class Review. Review your briefs and notes for the Class 3 materials. *(Time Estimate: 30–45 minutes.)*

Day 3 (Day After Tomorrow)—Class. Proceed below.

CLASS 4

You have read and prepared for class, and now you are ready for your fourth class. Please go to www.belonginginlawschool.com, click on "Classes," then on "Contracts (Promissory Estoppel)," and then on "Class 4."

Please remember your goals for note-taking. Look for (i) themes, (ii) conceptual relationships, (iii) rules, (iv) process, (v) hypotheticals, and (vi) information that will complement your notes.

POST-CLASS REVIEW

Congratulations on finishing your fourth class. Before we move on to the next class, you should do your post-class review. In addition to the things we have learned already in post-class review, there is another task to explore.

Creating Your Own Short Hypotheticals

As you have seen in your classes and on the midterm, a primary way that professors test your knowledge of material is to present you with hypotheticals. Hypotheticals test your understanding of the material, rather than rote memorization. In other words, if you understand it, you will be able to apply it to new situations. Hypotheticals will help show where students do or do not fully understand the law they are learning.

Of course, answering questions presented by your professors helps, as does using practice questions. Another tool that will help you, however, is to create your own hypotheticals. Now, you do not have to write full-length exam questions, but you can benefit a lot from creating short hypotheticals.

Why does this process work? Because in order to create a hypothetical testing an area of law, you have to understand the law. You will see this as we engage in the task set forth below.

> **Background**: To create exams or in-class questions, professors use the same process we are about to learn. We ask ourselves, "On what rules do I want to test my students' knowledge?" Then we proceed to draft hypotheticals that contain the right story elements to cause you to have to apply the law we are testing.

In order to create hypotheticals, we will follow three steps:

(1) We will decide what we want to test;

(2) We will look at the rule and decide what kind of facts trigger analysis that will require the use of that rule.

(3) We will craft a short story that uses the kind of facts we need.

Here is an example of how this will work, taken from another area of contracts:

(1) <u>Rule</u>: An offer may be revoked up until the moment it is accepted.

(2) <u>Facts Needed</u>: You need an offer, a response that may or may not be an acceptance, and then you need a revocation of the offer.

(3) <u>Hypo</u>: *On Monday, Quincy offered to sell his house to Bria for $450,000. Monday afternoon, Bria responded by saying, "I am very interested in accepting your offer. I have one question. Does your offer include the appliances in the home?" Quincy responded, "No. And I now withdraw my offer." Bria immediately responded, "I accept your offer."*

Right now, the answer to this hypo is not as important as the fact that we have written a short paragraph that tests the rule. It is clear, however, that Bria is not actually accepting the offer. She is asking a preliminary question and may plan to accept. And, in light of the rule, we see that Quincy revoked the offer before Bria finally accepted the offer.

Note that we can play with this hypothetical to change the outcome. Look at the following altered hypo:

> *On Monday, Quincy offered to sell his house to Bria for $450,000. Monday afternoon, Bria responded by saying, "This sounds great. I accept your offer." Quincy responded, "You know what? Never mind. No deal."*

In this version, we have changed Bria's response so that Quincy's attempted revocation comes too late.

Here is another short hypo example, taken from the area of professional responsibility (lawyers' ethics):

(1) <u>Rule</u>: A fee agreement is not proper if the fee is contingent upon the lawyer's securing a divorce or upon the amount of alimony or support. (Note: A contingent fee would be okay if the representation involved collecting on past due support, because the fee is not contingent upon the "amount of alimony or support.")

(2) <u>Facts Needed</u>: You need a contingent fee agreement. The matter has to be a domestic relations matter. The fee has to be contingent on either the prohibited things (securing a divorce/alimony or support) or not.

(3) <u>Hypo</u>: *Steve was granted a divorce three years ago and was awarded a fixed amount of permanent alimony and child support. Steve's ex-wife was delinquent on the alimony and child support payments. The delinquency was not a big deal until recently, when Steve lost his job. Steve hired Lana Lawyer to represent Steve in a matter involving his ex-wife. Steve wanted Lana to sue the ex-wife for (i) payment of past-due alimony and child support, and (ii) adjustment of the amount of alimony and support. Lana agreed to take the case on a contingent fee.*

Now it's your turn.

ASSIGNMENT: On the following page, please follow the steps to create your own short hypothetical fact pattern. Use any rule (or part of a rule) that we studied in Class 4.

Create Your Own Hypo

Step 1:   Pick a topic area: _____

Step 2:   Look at the rule. What fact(s) are needed for this rule to be involved?

_____

_____

_____

_____

_____

Step 3:   Write a very short (3–5 sentence) story that involves these facts.

_____

_____

_____

_____

_____

_____

_____

_____

_____

_____

_____

_____

_____

_____

_____

_____

Drafting a hypothetical can be challenging the first time you do it. But I hope you noticed how you really had to understand the rule in order to create a good question. And that is where a significant benefit exists from doing this exercise—it gives you yet another way to interact with the rule and make sure you understand it. But it also helps you prepare for exams and begin to recognize the kinds of facts that will be triggers for analysis on exams.

On your own, I would like you to try a few more of these as part of your post-class review. (Remember to do everything else that is a part of that post-class review also.)

ASSIGNMENTS: (1) Continue your post-class review, including drafting three additional short hypotheticals. (2) Update your outline to include information learned in Class 4. (3) Prepare for Class 5.

TIMELINE—**You should spread this step over three days:**

Day 1 (Today)—Complete Post-Class Review of Class 4. *(Time Estimate: 1 hour.)*

      Preparation and Reading. Read for Class 5. *(Time Estimate: 3 hours.)*

Day 2 (Tomorrow)—Pre-Class Review. Review your briefs and notes for the Class 5 materials. *(Time Estimate: 30–45 minutes.)*

Day 3 (Day After Tomorrow)—Class. Proceed to the next chapter.

CHAPTER 14

CLASS FIVE

■ ■ ■

In this chapter, we will complete our final class and begin our preparations for the final exam. The number of pages we devote to this chapter are small, but you will need to devote substantial time to the tasks presented, particularly and the end of this chapter.

First, let's go to class.

CLASS 5

You have read and prepared for class, and now you are ready for your fourth class. Please go to www.belonginginlawschool.com, click on "Classes," then on "Contracts (Promissory Estoppel)," and then on "Class 5."

Please remember your goals for note-taking. Look for (i) themes, (ii) conceptual relationships, (iii) rules, (iv) process, (v) hypotheticals, and (vi) information that will complement your notes.

POST-CLASS REVIEW

Congratulations on finishing your fifth class. Before we move on to the final exam, you should do your post-class review for this class, remembering to do more short hypotheticals.

ASSIGNMENT: Do post-class review for Class 5, including drafting three additional short hypotheticals.

FINAL EXAM PREPARATION

Given that you already have prepared for the midterm, you have some idea about what it will take to prepare for the final exam. But here, we want to take our preparation to a new level.

There are several things you need to do in order to get ready for the midterm, most of which you already have learned to do. Where there is a need for additional guidance, I have included additional instructions below:

(1) <u>Complete Your Outline</u>. Incorporate all of the remaining information your outline from Chapter 5 into your outline.

(2) <u>Study Your Outline</u>. Read the outline through, critically asking yourself what you understand and what you do not. If there is anything you do not understand, take the time to go back to your brief, class notes, or the lecture to try to figure out what you are missing. Do this several times (in other words read and re-read and re-re-read your outline.) Each time, use highlighters and make notes in the margin until you are very confident that you understand the material.

(3) <u>Memorize Your Outline</u>. Many law school exams are closed book exams, meaning you will not have the benefit of relying on your notes or outlines during the exam. You should prepare for your final here with that same idea in mind. You want to be able to take the final exam without needing notes. This requires you to go beyond simply understanding the material. You must commit it to memory so that you have instant recall. This requires reading the outline again and again. Perhaps it means creating other memory tools, like flashcards. This memorization is hard work in law school, especially at the end of a long semester when you have read and discussed thousands of pages of information. Here, we have focused on a relatively narrow topic, so memorization should be more manageable.

(4) <u>Take Practice Exams</u>. Once you have committed the information you have learned to memory, the best way to test how ready you are for the exam is to take practice exams. Get used to the pace of an exam. For practice exams connected to this course, please go to www.belonginginlawschool.com, click on "Exams," and then on "Contracts (Promissory Estoppel)." There, you will see a list of several practice exams you can take in preparation for the final. As you take each practice exam, remember to evaluate yourself. Ask yourself what you have missed and whether there are things you still do not understand clearly. For those topics, go back and review your outline to ensure that you fully understand the material. One quick thing you can do is to write short answers to the short hypotheticals you created in the last couple of chapters. As you take practice exams, you should evaluate your work on substance (did I understand the material?) and style (did I write effectively?)

(5) <u>Create a Topic Checklist and Memorize It</u>. One important exam preparation tool is creating a list of topics that may be

on the test. This will help you remember what you are looking for on the exam. Commit this list to memory, and you will have a mental list against which you can compare your issue spotting. (Imagine saying to yourself, "I haven't seen a charitable pledge. Maybe I should go back and look for that, just in case.) It is not likely that you will be tested on every issue you have studied, but having this list operates as a safety net for you during the exam.

ASSIGNMENTS—Do your final exam preparation: **(1) Update your outline to include information learned in Class 5. (2) Study your outline. (3) Memorize Your Outline. (4) Take Practice Exams. (5) Create and Memorize a Topic Checklist.**

<u>TIMELINE</u>—**You should spread these tasks over 3 days:**

Day 1 <u>Complete Your Outline</u>. *(Time Estimate: 2 hours.)*

<u>Read Through Your Outline</u>. Take notes, highlight, paying attention to things you do not fully understand. *(Time Estimate: 2 hours.)*

<u>Write Answers to Your Short Hypos</u>. *(Time Estimate: 1 hour.)*

Day 2 <u>Re-Read Your Outline</u>. *(Time Estimate: 1 hour.)*

<u>Take a Practice Exam</u>. Do this untimed and using your notes to help you with things you do not remember. Evaluate your mastery of the subject matter **<u>and</u>** your writing. *(Time Estimate: 2–3 hours.)*

<u>Re-Read and Memorize Your Outline</u>. Focusing especially on things you did not get exactly right on the practice exam, review your outline again to refresh your understanding of the material. Work on memorization, perhaps creating flashcards. *(Time Estimate: 2 hours.)*

<u>Take Another Practice Exam</u>. Do another untimed exam. Keep your notes nearby, but consult them only if you have difficulty remembering something specific. Evaluate your mastery of the subject matter **<u>and</u>** your writing. *(Time Estimate: 2–3 hours.)*

<u>Create a Topic Checklist</u>. *(Time Estimate: 1 hour.)*

Day 3	<u>**Re-Read Your Outline or Other Study Tool**</u>. *(Time Estimate: 30 minutes hour.)*

Take a Practice Exam. Do an exam under timed conditions and without notes. Evaluate your mastery of the subject matter <u>***and***</u> your writing. *(Time Estimate: 2–3 hours.)*

Revisit Your Outline. Focusing especially on things you did not get exactly right on the practice exam, review your outline again to refresh your understanding of the material. *(Time Estimate: 1 hour.)*

Take Another Practice Exam. Do another timed exam. Evaluate your mastery of the subject matter <u>***and***</u> your writing. *(Time Estimate: 2–3 hours.)*

Revisit Your Outline. Take one last look at the outline or study tool to look at anything you may still be working through. *(Time Estimate: 1 hour.)*

We Belong

JOE was placed in an orphanage at birth and then spent time shuttling between foster parents and the orphanage. During the fourth grade, Joe attended three different primary schools. When he was 13, he was adopted by foster parents who had six children of their own, all but one of whom ended up serving prison time for committing felonies.

As a senior in high school, Joe moved out of his home and lived with a series of friends until he graduated. As a high school senior, he was content just to graduate and get a full time job—at the time he was a swimming pool salesman. But during a senior Civics class, Joe had a teacher who convinced him that he had much more to offer the world and to consider college and possibly law school. This mentor encouraged Joe along a much better educational and professional path.

After law school, Joe worked for the United States Securities and Exchange Commission in Washington, D.C., ultimately becoming a Special Counsel to The Division of Corporation Finance. He subsequently joined a large, New York based law firm. After practicing law for ten years, Joe joined a client as an Investment Banker and ultimately rose to be the Head of Investment Banking at a large bulge bracket investment bank.

Joe's Advice: **You are only limited by your own fears. I recall when I was going to Washington to interview with the SEC that no one from my law school had ever worked at the SEC. Most of my friends, while supportive, believed I had very little chance of succeeding. There was, however, one professor who believed that I had the right drive and skill set to succeed and aggressively pushed me to try for a position with the SEC. I applied, was ultimately offered a position, and that set me on a path to a very long and successful career on Wall Street. For me, finding people that believed in me, and learning from and leaning on them was critical. Going back to my senior year in high school, I had someone who believed in me and pushed me. If I hadn't listened to their advice along the way, I am sure I would have been a successful swimming pool salesman in Akron, Ohio.**

REST AND GET READY TO TAKE THE FINAL EXAM *TOMORROW*!

CHAPTER 15

THE FINAL EXAM

■ ■ ■

Okay. You now have learned everything in the book, and it is time to put it to use. Before you take the final exam, let's do one more practice test. Below, you will find a practice final exam to take. As you prepare to practice, remember the steps to taking the exam:

(1) <u>Issue Spotting</u>

    (a) React to the facts. (Why did the professor put this fact in the question?)

    (b) Remember your checklist. (Be on the lookout for issues you have studied.)

    (c) Elements. (Once you spot legal issues, look for facts relating to each element.)

(2) <u>Organization</u>

    (a) Analyze one issue/sub-issue at a time.

    (b) Use I-R-A-C to present a logical proof for each issue/sub-issue.

        (i)   Issue—concisely identify the issue/sub-issue you are discussing.

        (ii) Rule—Use all of the relevant legal rules that apply to the issue you are addressing.

        (iii) Application—Remember "FACTS, FACTS, FACTS."

            •   What are all of the relevant facts for this issue?

            •   Why are those facts relevant?

            •   How do those facts lead to a conclusion?

            •   *[DO NOT FORGET TO INCLUDE COUNTERARGUMENTS!]*

        (iv) Conclusion—State a brief conclusion.

FIRST THINGS FIRST

Before you take your final exam, I would like you to perform one final reflection exercise. In light of what you have learned from reading this book, I would like you to write a letter to a future law student—someone who will start law school several years from now. This should be a letter of encouragement and wisdom. Let them know what law school will be like, the challenges they will face, the ways to overcome those challenges, and any other thoughts they can carry with them to sustain them while they study.

_____

_____

_____

_____

_____

_____

_____

_____

_____

_____

_____

_____

_____

_____

_____

_____

_____

_____

_____

_____

_____

_____

_____

_____

_____

_____

_____

_____

_____

_____

_____

_____

_____

_____

_____

_____

_____

_____

_____

_____

_____

_____

_____

_____

_____

_____

_____

_____

_____

_____

_____

_____

_____

_____

_____

———————

Now you are ready for the final exam.

Assignment: When you are ready, turn the page and take the final exam.

Time Estimate: Two Hours.

EXAM QUESTION—TWO HOURS (120 MINUTES)

Pauline Prepper was convinced that the world would end as the result of a zombie apocalypse. And she was not alone—there was a whole culture of doomsday preppers who were getting ready for the fall of civilization.

The head of the End of Days Movement was Lon Leader. On the EDM website, Lon posted the following message:

> *If you are a prepper like me, you need protection. I am building a compound, and you can have a spot. All you need to do is show up, and a home within our compound is yours. We have brand new, state of the art, 2-bedroom homes, sitting on one acre of land each. There are no strings attached.*

Seeing this message on the EDM website, Pauline immediately abandoned her current home, packed up all of her necessary belongings in her car, and drove to the EDM compound.

When Pauline arrived at the EDM compound, she discovered that, while there was space available for her, the "homes" were actually small, one-room shacks that appeared to have been built hastily and poorly. The shacks were just feet apart from each other—not on one-acre lots—and they had dirt floors and there was no electricity, heat, air conditioning, or indoor plumbing. When she asked Lon about the conditions of the homes, Lon told her, "This is all real preppers need. Learn to live with it."

After Pauline moved to the EDM compound, news began to spread about a growing, worldwide pandemic. Due to global warming and the resulting changes in the migratory patterns of wild animals, conditions were perfect to foster the growth of a new and terrible disease. The disease turned ordinary humans into rabid monsters that would attack other humans and try to bite and eat them (particularly their brains). Naturally, Pauline was extremely worried about the danger presented by the disease and those who contracted it. She approached Lon, saying that she was considering leaving the compound to find an unpopulated area in the mountains. Lon reassured Pauline that she did not have to worry. He walked with her around the entire compound, spray-painting a line on the ground as they walked, and told her that he was going to build a great wall along that line that would be impenetrable by outsiders. He described the wall in detail, explaining that it would be made of concrete and steel, that it would be extremely tall, and that no one would be able to get through, over, under, or around it. Based on this description, Pauline decided to stay in the compound.

Lon actually ended up having the members of the compound gather as many sticks and branches as they could find, and they erected what can be described only as a rudimentary fence. Soon thereafter, the fence was overrun easily by a horde of flesh-eating monsters. Pauline escaped, but only with her life. She lost all of her belongings in the rampage. Lon also escaped, but only because he had a personal, secure underground bunker in which he could ride out the zombie storm.

Having nowhere to go, Pauline borrowed a phone and reached out to her family for help. Immediately, her parents responded that she could come and live in their home. "Honey, we love you more than anything. We want you to be safe and happy for the rest of your life. You can move back in with us and have your old room as long as you need it," her parents told her. Pauline immediately headed back to her home town, walking hundreds of miles with the clothes on her back as her only possessions. But when she arrived at her home, her parents took one look at her and told her that they had changed their minds because they were concerned about her mental state. They handed her a piece of cake and then closed the door in her face, saying, "Good luck, honey. We love you. Enjoy the cake."

Devastated, Pauline ate the cake and then decided to take matters into her own hands. She went to a bank and took out a small business loan. With the money, she decided to open up a doomsday prepper store called "Prepper's Preparations." To open the store, she needed inventory. She contacted a wholesaler of prepper goods (durable clothes, non-perishable foods, and weapons of all kinds) and explained her business plan. They negotiated on and off for several weeks. Though they never reached an agreement on exactly what she would buy, the wholesaler repeatedly reassured Pauline that it could provide her with whatever supplies she needed. When Pauline explained that she needed to use her loan to buy a store location, the wholesaler responded, "That's okay, we can work out very comfortable repayment terms. You can buy on credit and pay us back in installments once you get on your feet." The wholesaler followed up with a "sample contract," saying, "This is not a binding agreement, but you can look at this to see the credit terms that we are willing to agree to. Once you have your location, let us know, and we can move forward with a formal agreement." Based on this, Pauline used all of her remaining funds to make a down payment on buying a small building on the main road in her town.

Once she had the building, Pauline sent an order to the wholesaler for the goods, but the wholesaler said that they had changed their minds and decided not to sell her any goods. Pauline tried to get goods elsewhere, but no one would sell her goods on credit. Without inventory, Pauline could not open her store. Without the store, she could not pay the mortgage on the building. Ultimately, the bank foreclosed on the building, and Pauline was left with nothing.

Please analyze.

LAST WORDS

■ ■ ■

Law school can be challenging. It is hard work, there are many stressors, and invisible barriers can try to get in your way. But you are strong and prepared. You have the capacity, the mindset, and the tools to succeed.

I hope that this book has provided you with a taste of what law school will be like. My deep desire is that you will know that there is a place for you in the legal profession. If this is the path you have chosen, know that you can accomplish your goal of succeeding in law school, passing the bar, and becoming a practicing lawyer.

The skills you have spent so much energy learning in this book will serve as a foundation for you when you begin law school. You will build on them each day of your schooling. Commit yourself to doing the hard work of learning the law. Spend the hours, do the readings, go to your classes, and do all you must to learn effectively.

Because this book is devoted to the law school learning process, I have not emphasized as much as I would like that you should remember to enjoy yourself. Law school can be a great three or four years. You will make friends that you will have for life, you will have countless memories of the time you spent there. So take the time to have a good time, participate in extra-curricular activities, network, work out, eat out, and make sure to have a full life experience.

Always keep in mind that you belong in law school, and you can and will succeed.

APPENDIX

READINGS

■ ■ ■

READING ASSIGNMENT 1

KIRKSEY V. KIRKSEY
Supreme Court of Alabama
8 Ala. 131 (1845)

ASSUMPSIT by the defendant, against the plaintiff in error. The question is presented in this Court, upon a case agreed, which shows the following facts:

The plaintiff was the wife of defendant's brother, but had for some time been a widow, and had several children. In 1840, the plaintiff resided on public land, under a contract of lease, she had held over, and was comfortably settled, and would have attempted to secure the land she lived on. The defendant resided in Talladega county, some sixty, or seventy miles off. On the 10th October, 1840, he wrote to her the following letter:

> "Dear sister Antillico—Much to my mortification, I heard, that brother Henry was dead, and one of his children. I know that your situation is one of grief, and difficulty. You had a bad chance before, but a great deal worse now. I should like to come and see you, but cannot with convenience at present. * * * I do not know whether you have a preference on the place you live on, or not. If you had, I would advise you to obtain your preference, and sell the land and quit the country, as I understand it is very unhealthy, and I know society is very bad. If you will come down and see me, I will let you have a place to raise your family, and I have more open land than I can tend; and on the account of your situation, and that of your family, I feel like I want you and the children to do well."

Within a month or two after the receipt of this letter, the plaintiff abandoned her possession, without disposing of it, and removed with her family, to the residence of the defendant, who put her in comfortable houses, and gave her land to cultivate for two years, at the end of which time he notified her to remove, and put her in a house, not comfortable, in the woods, which he afterwards required her to leave.

A verdict being found for the plaintiff, for two hundred dollars, the above facts were agreed, and if they will sustain the action, the judgment is to be affirmed, otherwise it is to be reversed.

ORMOND, J.

The inclination of my mind, is, that the loss and inconvenience, which the plaintiff sustained in breaking up, and moving to the defendant's, a distance of sixty miles, is a sufficient consideration to support the promise, to furnish her with a house, and land to cultivate, until she could raise her family. My brothers, however think, that the promise on the part of the defendant, was a mere gratuity, and that an action will not lie for its breach. The judgment of the Court below must therefore be reversed, pursuant to the agreement of the parties.

HARVEY V. DOW

Supreme Judicial Court of Maine
962 A.2d 322 (2008)

MEAD, J.

Teresa L. Harvey appeals from a judgment entered by the Superior Court (Penobscot County, *Hjelm, J.*) in favor of Jeffrey B. Dow Sr. and Kathryn L. Dow on Harvey's complaint seeking to compel the Dows to convey to her the land on which she built a house, or for damages based on the value of the house. Harvey contends that she is entitled to a judgment on theories of promissory estoppel or the existence of a confidential relationship. We note that the findings of the Superior Court do not address the actions of the Dows beyond their generalized statements of intent and the possible application of section 90 of the Restatement of Contracts thereto. We vacate the judgment and remand for further proceedings.

I.   FACTS AND PROCEDURE

Jeffrey Dow Sr. and Kathryn Dow are the parents of Teresa Harvey. The Dows own 125 acres of land in Corinth in two adjoining parcels, one fifty acres and the other seventy-five acres. They, their daughter Teresa, and their son Jeffrey Dow Jr. each have homes on the property. From the time they were young, Teresa and her brother talked about the houses they would eventually like to build on the homestead; Teresa said she wanted her home to be located near a spring, close to where it now sits. For their part, the Dows saw the land as their children's heritage that would be left to them or given to them when they were older. Jeffrey Sr. testified that when the children were teenagers, he believed that his wife had promised them some land in the future, and the subject of the children living on the homestead was commonly discussed within the family.

The Superior Court found that the Dows had a general, non-specific plan to transfer land to the children at some undetermined time. In the court's words, the "evidence at most reveals that Jeffrey Sr. expressed an intention to enter into an agreement to convey property sometime in the future," and "Kathryn had made it clear that eventually, both Teresa and Jeffrey Jr. would end up with all or part of the two parcels."

In 1999, Teresa and her future husband, Jarrod Harvey, installed a mobile home on her parents' land with their permission at the location where her brother's mobile home is now located. She did not pay rent and did not ask her parents for a deed. Later, she and Jarrod built a garage near the mobile home, again with the Dows' permission.

Around January 2003, Teresa and Jarrod, by then married, decided to build a house on the lot where their mobile home then stood. At the Harveys' request, the Dows agreed to use their home equity line of credit to initially finance the house. At trial, Teresa testified that part of the plan for repaying her parents included having them convey the building site to her by deed once the house was completed. Jeffrey Sr. denied any discussion of a deed at that time. In March 2003, Jarrod Harvey died in a motorcycle accident. Following his death, Teresa decided to finance the house with life insurance proceeds rather than use her parents' home equity line.

When it came time to do site preparation work for the new house, Teresa, her father, and her grandfather determined that it would cost no more to build further back on the property where Teresa had always wanted her house to be. Jeffrey Sr. agreed that she could build the house at its current site. Before construction began, Teresa and Jeffrey Sr. went to obtain a building permit from the town. There was no discussion of Teresa obtaining a deed at that point; she testified at trial that she did not ask her father for one directly because she did not need it then. The town initially denied Teresa a permit because she would not have the requisite amount of road frontage. A permit was eventually issued to Jeffrey Sr. for him to build another house on his property. Teresa testified that her father told her he would execute a deed to her for the property after the house was built; Jeffrey Sr. said there was no discussion about a deed.

Construction of the new house began in the summer of 2003 and was completed in May 2004 at a cost to Teresa of about $200,000. Jeffrey Sr. did a substantial amount of the construction himself, including much of the foundation work, and the carpentry, and helped to get underground electrical lines installed. In January 2004, while construction of the house was underway, Teresa lent $25,000 to her brother, Jeffrey Dow Jr. The record indicates that by the spring of 2004, around the time the house was completed, the relationship between Teresa and her parents and brother began to deteriorate over when and how the loan from Teresa to Jeffrey was to be repaid, and over the Dows' dissatisfaction with Teresa's partner, who lived with her. Eventually Teresa sued Jeffrey Jr. for the money, and the Dows filed a grandparents' rights action to see Teresa's children.

At some point after moving into her new house, Teresa began to ask Jeffrey Sr. for a deed so that she could obtain a mortgage to finance other projects. After a period of discussion, it became clear that the Dows were not going to execute a deed. At the time of trial, Teresa was paying the taxes on the house itself, but she was not paying the property taxes or any rent. Both Kathryn Dow and Jeffrey Jr. testified that they had no knowledge of Jeffrey Sr. ever offering or agreeing to deed any land to Teresa.

In March 2006, Teresa filed a seven-count complaint in the Superior Court, primarily seeking a judgment compelling the Dows to convey unspecified real property to her, or for damages on her claims of breach of contract, breach of fiduciary duty, and fraud. The Dows counterclaimed, seeking a judgment declaring that Teresa had no rights in their property. Following a two-day bench trial, the court found for the Dows on the real property claims and on their request for a declaratory judgment. Based on her assertion that the court failed to address whether she was entitled to a judgment on a theory of promissory estoppel, Teresa filed motions for further findings, to amend the judgment, and for a new trial. In a written decision, the court recognized that Teresa's argument was properly raised and then rejected it, finding that "[the Dows'] statements were not promises that could be enforced even if they were the subject of detrimental reliance," and concluding that "the plaintiffs have not established that Harvey received an offer or promise that can be enforced in this action." This appeal followed.

II. DISCUSSION

A. Existence of an Enforceable Promise

Teresa contends that the Dows, having made general promises to convey land to her at some point and then assenting to her building a $200,000 house on their property in reliance on those promises, are now estopped from asserting that she has no rights to the land the house is located on. The Superior Court agreed that the Dows made general promises to convey land to Teresa, but concluded that they were too indefinite to enforce because there was no agreement on basic elements such as the boundaries or size of the property involved. We review the court's factual findings for clear error, and its legal conclusion that those facts do not make out a claim of promissory estoppel de novo. *Daigle Commercial Group, Inc. v. St. Laurent,* 1999 ME 107, ¶ 13, 734 A.2d 667, 672.

The doctrine of promissory estoppel "applies to promises that are otherwise unenforceable," and is "invoked to enforce [such] promises . . . so as to avoid injustice." *Id.* ¶ 14, 734 A.2d at 672 (quotation marks omitted); *Cottle Enters., Inc. v. Town of Farmington,* 1997 ME 78, ¶ 17 n. 6, 693 A.2d 330,

335. It is an accepted doctrine in Maine. *June Roberts Agency, Inc. v. Venture Props., Inc.*, 676 A.2d 46, 49 (Me.1996). We have adopted the definition of promissory estoppel set out in the Restatement (Second) of Contracts, which states:

> A promise which the promisor should reasonably expect to induce action or forbearance on the part of the promisee or a third person and which does induce such action or forbearance is binding if injustice can be avoided only by enforcement of the promise. The remedy granted for breach may be limited as justice requires.

Restatement (Second) of Contracts § 90(1) (1981); *Bracale v. Gibbs,* 2007 ME 7, ¶ 14, 914 A.2d 1112, 1115.

Here, the record supports the trial court's finding that although they made general promises to Teresa that she would at some time receive some of their land as a gift or inheritance, the Dows did not make an express promise to convey a parcel of land of any specified size, or with any defined boundaries, at any time certain. The court was correct in finding that the existence of a promise to convey property was an essential element of Teresa's claim, and in holding that if there was no promise on which Teresa could rely, then her claim of promissory estoppel failed. *See Tarbuck v. Jaeckel,* 2000 ME 105, ¶¶ 17, 18, 752 A.2d 176, 181 (stating that "[t]he court's finding that there was no promise on which [the party] could rely thereby foreclosed her argument of promissory estoppel"); *Gagne v. Stevens,* 1997 ME 88, ¶ 13, 696 A.2d 411, 416 (holding that claim of promissory estoppel failed when plaintiff "made no promise specific enough to enforce").

If the evidence consisted only of the Dows' general promises to convey land as a gift or inheritance, we would agree that Teresa's claim of promissory estoppel should be denied. However, the evidence included an important second component: the Dows' acquiescence, support, and encouragement of Teresa's construction of a house upon the property and the application of section 90 of the Restatement of Contracts to those facts. Neither the initial decision and judgment nor the order on Teresa's motion for findings of fact addressed these critical points.

Against the backdrop of the parties' general understanding that Teresa would one day receive property as a gift or inheritance from her parents, she decided to build a new house on their land. Jeffrey Dow Sr. agreed to the location, obtained a building permit to allow construction at that site, and not only acquiesced in the house being built, but built a large portion of it himself. In a promissory estoppel analysis, "[t]he promise relied on by the promisee need not be express but may be implied from a party's conduct." *June Roberts Agency, Inc.,* 676 A.2d at 50; *see Nappi v. Nappi Distribs.,* 1997 ME 54, ¶ 9, 691 A.2d 1198, 1200 (stating that promise may be implied from a party's conduct).

At least as to the land on which Teresa's house now sits, a promise by Jeffrey Dow Sr. to convey that specific parcel could be implied from his conduct, and if that implication is made, given that Teresa now has an immobile $200,000 asset on that parcel, "[t]he circumstances [are] such that the refusal to enforce the promise to make a gift would work a fraud upon the donee." *Tozier v. Tozier,* 437 A.2d 645, 648–49 (Me.1981); *see Nappi,* 1997 ME 54, ¶ 9, 691 A.2d at 1200 (stating that when applying the doctrine of promissory estoppel "[i]n the context of the transfer of land, when the donee has made substantial improvements to the land in reliance upon the promise to convey the land, courts will enforce the promise to convey." (quotation marks omitted)). Under these circumstances, a promise is enforceable notwithstanding a lack of consideration. *See Nappi,* 1997 ME 54, ¶ 9, 691 A.2d at 1200.

In *Tozier,* a father told his son that he could have a parcel of land to live on. 437 A.2d at 646. The son moved from where he had been living and built a house on the parcel with his father's help. *Id.* Years after the father's death, the son's brother made a claim to the property and eventually filed an action for possession. *Id.* at 646–47.

Analyzing the father's original parol promise to give his son a parcel of land, we said:

> [T]he enforceability of a promise *to make a gift* of land depends not upon contract principles, but upon principles of fraud. A mere showing that a donee incurred *some* detriment at the instance of the donor is insufficient to enforce a parol gift. When the donee, however, has made substantial improvements to the land, and the donee has made the improvements in reliance upon the promise to convey the land, courts will enforce the promise to convey.

Id. at 648 (emphasis in original). We then held that building a house constituted a "valuable and permanent improvement[ ]" such that "[t]o deny the [son] his rights in the property . . . would be both unjust and inequitable." *Id.* at 649. The same equities are applicable in this case.

The Restatement (Second) of Contracts also lends support to the inference that the Dows might have made an enforceable promise to convey the site of Teresa's house to her. It defines a "promise" as "a manifestation of intention to act or refrain from acting in a specified way, so made as to justify a promisee in understanding that a commitment has been made." Restatement (Second) of Contracts § 2(1) (1981); *see* § 90, reporters' note cmt. a (stating that "[o]n the meaning of 'promise,' see § 2"). Jeffrey Dow Sr.'s actions in approving the site of Teresa's house, obtaining a building permit for it, and then building a substantial part of it himself at that location would seem to be "manifestation[s] of [his] intention to act . . . in a specified way"—namely a manifestation of his intent to confirm his general promise to convey land to Teresa and to direct it to that specific parcel.

In addition to giving a general definition of the term "promise," section 90 specifically discusses promises to make a gift. It explains that "[s]uch a promise is ordinarily enforced by virtue of the promisee's reliance only if his conduct is foreseeable and reasonable and involves a definite and substantial change of position which would not have occurred if the promise had not been made." Restatement (Second) of Contracts § 90 cmt. f. An illustration to that discussion describes a scenario analogous to the one presented here:

> A orally promises to give her son B a tract of land to live on. As A intended, B gives up a homestead elsewhere, takes possession of the land, lives there for a year and makes substantial improvements. A's promise is binding.

Restatement (Second) of Contracts § 90 cmt. f, illus. 16.

In sum, on the facts found by the Superior Court, Teresa's reliance on the Dows' general promise to give her land at some time, when coupled with their affirmative actions in allowing her to build a substantial house on a particular piece of their land, would seem to be eminently foreseeable and reasonable. From those actions, a promise by the Dows to convey that specific site could be fairly implied. Neither the absence of an explicitly articulated promise, nor the absence of consideration is a bar to enforcing that promise. The Superior Court erred in failing to consider the Dows' actions, in conjunction with their generalized statements, in determining whether the existence of a promissory estoppel is established on these facts. Accordingly, we vacate the judgment and remand the matter to the Superior Court for consideration of the issues identified herein.

The entry is:

Judgment as to count one of the complaint and count one of the counterclaim vacated; remanded for further proceedings on those counts. In all other respects, judgment affirmed.

GREINER V. GREINER
Supreme Court of Kansas
131 Kan. 760 (1930)

Opinion

BURCH, J.

Maggie Greiner commenced an action of forcible detention against her son, Frank Greiner, to recover possession of a quarter section of land, and an additional tract of 80 acres. Frank answered that his mother had given him the 80-acre tract under such circumstances that she not only could not reclaim it, but that she should execute a conveyance to him. The district court ordered plaintiff to execute a deed conveying the 80-acre tract to defendant, and plaintiff appeals.

Peter Greiner died testate, leaving a widow—the plaintiff—and sons and daughters. His sons Henry, Frank, and Nicholas and his daughter, Kate, were disinherited—were given $5 apiece. Henry died in June, 1925, unmarried and intestate, and his mother inherited considerable property from him. She then concluded to place the other two disinherited sons on an equal footing with those who had been favored in the will, and she took active measures to accomplish her purpose. At first she intended to give Frank and Nicholas land, about 90 acres apiece. Later, she entered into a written contract to pay Nicholas $2,000. Frank had gone to Logan county, had homesteaded a quarter section of land, and had lived there sixteen or seventeen years. Mrs. Greiner lived in Mitchell county, and the land in controversy lies in Mitchell county, not far from her home. The brief for plaintiff says she inherited from Henry only a three-sevenths interest in the 80-acre tract. The brief for defendant says she inherited the entire interest, and Mrs. Greiner so testified. In any event, some deeds were to be executed, and in July, 1926, Mrs. Greiner had Nicholas write to Frank and tell Frank to come down, she was going to make settlement with him and Nicholas. Frank came to Mitchell county and had a conversation with his mother. At that time there was a house on the quarter section. In the conversation, Mrs. Greiner told Frank she was going to pay him and Nicholas. Frank told her he did not want money, he wanted a home—a little land for a home. She said all right, she had the land, and she wanted him to move into the house, and they would divide up later. He said that would be all right, and he would move back.

Frank went home, but it seems there was an obstacle to his moving. Louis Greiner, one of the sons favored in the will, testified as follows:

"She called me over in 1926, about Frank's matters; * * * She wanted to know if it could be arranged so she could get that 80 acres there. She told me what she figured on doing; she wanted Frank to move on this eighty, she wanted to give it to him because he was disinherited, and she wanted to equal the thing up for the two boys.

"Q. All right, what did you say to that? A. I said it could be done.

"Q. Yes? A. And the property was divided that way for that purpose.

"Q. Those deeds were made, those deeds that were put in evidence this morning? A. Yes.

"Q. And what if anything was said about Frank and this place? A. Well, some time later she called me, and I came up there, and she told me that she wanted Frank to come back that fall, so he could put out wheat, but he had a mortgage on some horses and mules, and he couldn't come. She gave me some money to go out and pay the mortgage off, and I went out and paid the mortgage off, and they moved right back.

"Q. That released his horses and mules, and he came back? A. Yes, sir."

It appears the mortgage was assigned to Mrs. Greiner, and Frank subsequently paid her.

A. Diebolt, cashier of the Home State Bank of Tipton, prepared the contract between Mrs. Greiner and Nicholas. He testified as follows:

"In the summer or fall of 1926 I had a conversation with Maggie Greiner about Frank coming back to Mitchell county. As near as I can say, it was before wheat sowing time. If I recall correctly, Frank was in the bank with her. The substance of the conversation was that she brought Frank back to Mitchell county, he wasn't doing any good out there, did not have enough to come. I do not know the town, it was in the western part. She said there was plenty of land there; that Frank had been disinherited by his father, and she was going to give him an interest in the land. As I recall, she was going to give him 92 or 97 acres."

Referring to an incident occurring in the fall of 1926, Louis testified as follows:

"At that time I don't remember whether I had a conversation with mother about Frank moving on that eighty, but that was a settled fact at that time, that he was going to move there at that time. Oh, I had several conversations during the year, I was there several times in 1926. I had several conversations with her in the fall of 1926.

"Q. Well, do you remember what she said at any one of those conversations about Frank Greiner? A. Oh, I heard about him moving back, and she gave him that place as his share. * * *

"Q. That eighty acres? A. Yes, sir. * * *

"Q. And did she say why she was going to give him that eighty? A. Yes, sir.

"Q. What did she say? A. Because the rest of us, there were four of them disinherited in the will of my father; he was one of those disinherited."

Frank moved back on September 20, 1926. Mrs. Greiner then determined to move the house from the quarter section to the 80-acre tract, and give that specific tract to Frank. Frank testified as follows:

"Q. You were asked about what was said about this house, moving this house over onto this eighty, was there any conversation about that, when you had this talk with your mother about moving on this place? A. Yes, sir, there was.

"Q. All right now, I don't think you told regarding that; what was that, please? A. Well, she said we would move that house over there, and the buildings, and said, 'That will be a home for you.'"

Albert Greiner, a son favored in the will, testified as follows:

"Q. I will ask you if at any time you heard your mother say that she had made a contract with Frank Greiner, whereby he was to receive that eighty? A. Yes, sir.

"Q. When did you hear her say that? A. I think it was in the fall of '26.

"Q. About what time? A. It must have been the last part of September, somewhere along there.

"Q. That was after he had moved? A. I couldn't say the date exactly.

"Q. What did she say? A. Well, she said she was going to move those buildings over on that eighty for him, for Frank.

"Q. Yes; did she say that she was going to give that place to him, or that she had contracted with him? A. I understood her to say she was going to settle up with Nick and Frank.

"Q. On account of the fact that they had been disinherited by their father? A. Yes, sir."

Flora Greiner, wife of William Greiner, a son favored in the will, testified as follows:

"Maggie Greiner's home is eleven miles from where I live. Until these suits were filed, I saw her often. I had a conversation with her about the time Frank came back in the fall of 1926, regarding this matter. That was at her home.

"Q. What did she say? A. She said Frank's were going to move back here, and said she was going to give him that eighty up there.

"Q. Did she say anything further about it? A. Yes, sir.

"Q. All right, what else? A. She said, 'We are going to move the buildings off of that one hundred sixty, and put them up on that eighty,' and she aimed for Frank to have that for a home."

The buildings were moved from the quarter section to the 80-acre tract, and Frank commenced to occupy the 80-acre tract in the spring of 1927. Mrs. Greiner testified as follows:

"I remember of Frank living in Logan county up to 1926. I remember of his coming back that fall, and at different times. He did not then move on this place. He moved on after we had things arranged and the house fixed. I fixed the house and everything, and had it fixed for him. Then he moved on, and has lived there ever since."

The manner of assuring title to Frank came up. At first a will was contemplated. Louis Greiner testified as follows:

"Q. Now did she say anything about this place, any arrangement, after those deeds were made here, and so on? A. Well, we had fixed a date she was going to make a will to that effect, come to Beloit.

"Q. Yes? A. And in the meantime, she had signed some papers with Diebolt to pay Nick $2,000, and she called me up, and wanted me to come up one morning, and she told me what she had done.

"Q. Yes? A. Said Gustie had been raising so much storm about it, she wanted me to come and see if I couldn't get that paper back, and she would go to Beloit and make a will in favor of Frank and Nick; and so I went to Tipton with her, and we got this paper, and fixed a date to go to Beloit the next week; and the next week came, and I came there, and she absolutely wouldn't go, wouldn't do a thing.

"Q. Did she say why? A. She said Gustie told her if she would make a will they would move her off the place, that if she would make a will, she would be moved off the place at once.

"Q. Then what was done about this place? A. Well, she said that she would let Frank have it the way it was, and she wouldn't make a will."

Later, Mrs. Greiner said she was going to give Frank a deed.

August Greiner, "Gustie," a son favored in the will, lives with his mother. He returned from California a few days after she had made the written contract to pay Nicholas $2,000. The money has not yet been paid. August had a fight with Frank and Albert, and brought an action against them on account of it. He testified he helped move the house from the quarter section to the 80-acre tract, but he testified he never heard that his mother intended to give the 80-acre tract to Frank. A crystal gazer could tell why no deed to Frank has been executed.

An omission is noted in the testimony of Louis Greiner quoted above. Louis testified it was a settled fact that Frank was to move on the eighty, and his mother gave him that place as his share. The matter omitted consisted of a single question and answer as follows: "Q. That she was going to give him that? A. Yes, sir." In that way the learned counsel for plaintiff adroitly turned a settled fact into a matter of future intention, and the appeal is based chiefly on that legal distinction. The contention is that Maggie Greiner was going to settle with the disinherited boys; she was going to give Frank land; she was going to give Frank the 80-acre tract; she was going to move the buildings; she was going to make a will; she was going to give Frank a deed; and these expressions of future intention did not make a contract with Frank that she would give him the 80-acre tract if he would move from Logan county to Mitchell county.

A promise for breach of which the law gives a remedy, or recognizes as creating a legal duty, is a contract. The promise need not be in any crystallized form of words: "I promise," "I agree," etc. Ritual scrupulousness is not required and, generally, any manifestation, by words or conduct or both, which the promisee is justified in understanding as an expression of intention to make a promise, is sufficient. Restatement Law of Contracts, Am. Law Inst., §§ 1, 2, 5. In this instance, there is no doubt whatever respecting the intention of Maggie Greiner, either before or after she first sent for Frank to come to Mitchell county. Indeed, she fulfilled her intention up to the point of the formal matter of executing and delivering a deed. The only question is whether the untutored woman—she could not write—sufficiently expressed a promise to Frank when he came down to see her in response to the letter from Nicholas. The court has no hesitation in saying that Mrs. Greiner did promise to give Frank land for a home if he would move back to Mitchell county. Just at that point the promise was unenforceable because of indefiniteness. No particular land was specified. But the offer was later made perfectly definite. The 80-acre tract was segregated for Frank, Mrs. Greiner fitted it for his occupancy as a home, and she gave him possession of it. Restatement Law of Contracts, Am. Law Inst., § 32, Comment c.

Plaintiff says there was no consideration for Maggie Greiner's promise; she did everything for Frank, and he did nothing for her. Section 90 of the American Law Institute's Restatement of the Law of Contracts reads as follows:

"Section 90. Promise reasonably inducing definite and substantial action is binding. A promise which the promisor should reasonably expect to induce action or forbearance of a definite and substantial character on the part of the promisee and which does induce such action or forbearance, is binding if injustice can be avoided only by enforcement of the promise."

In this instance, Frank did give up his homestead in Logan county, did move to Mitchell county, did establish himself and his family on the 80-acre tract, made some lasting and valuable improvements upon it, and made other expenditures, relying on his mother's promise; and he lived on the land for nearly a year before he was served with notice to quit.

It is not necessary to review the conflicting evidence in detail. The evidence satisfied the district court that Mrs. Greiner should execute a deed to Frank. On the evidence favorable to him, and the inferences derivable from the evidence favorable to him, this court cannot say it would not be unjust to deny him a deed and to put him off, and cannot say a money judgment would afford him adequate relief.

The judgment of the district court is affirmed.

READING ASSIGNMENT 2

RESTATEMENT (SECOND) OF CONTRACTS

§ 2 PROMISE; PROMISOR; PROMISEE; BENEFICIARY

(1) A promise is a manifestation of intention to act or refrain from acting in a specified way, so made as to justify a promisee in understanding that a commitment has been made.

(2) The person manifesting the intention is the promisor.

(3) The person to whom the manifestation is addressed is the promisee.

(4) Where performance will benefit a person other than the promisee, that person is a beneficiary.

Comment:

a. Acts and resulting relations. "Promise" as used in the Restatement of this Subject denotes the act of the promisor. If by virtue of other operative facts there is a legal duty to perform, the promise is a contract; but the word "promise" is not limited to acts having legal effect. Like "contract," however, the word "promise" is commonly and quite properly also used to refer to the complex of human relations which results from the promisor's words or acts of assurance, including the justified expectations of the promisee and any moral or legal duty which arises to make good the assurance by performance. The performance may be specified either in terms describing the action of the promisor or in terms of the result which that action or inaction is to bring about.

b. Manifestation of intention. Many contract disputes arise because different people attach different meanings to the same words and conduct. The phrase "manifestation of intention" adopts an external or objective standard for interpreting conduct; it means the external expression of intention as distinguished from undisclosed intention. A promisor manifests an intention if he believes or has reason to believe that the promisee will infer that intention from his words or conduct. Rules governing cases where the promisee could reasonably draw more than one inference as to the promisor's intention are stated in connection with the acceptance of offers (see §§ 19 and 20), and the scope of contractual obligations (see §§ 201, 219).

c. Promise of action by third person; guaranty. Words are often used which in terms promise action or inaction by a third person, or which promise a result obtainable only by such action. Such words are commonly understood as a promise of conduct by the promisor which will be sufficient to bring about the action or inaction or result, or to answer for harm caused by failure. An example is a guaranty that a third person will perform his promise. Such words constitute a promise as here defined only if they justify a promisee in an expectation of some action or inaction on the part of the promisor.

d. Promise of event beyond human control; warranty. Words which in terms promise that an event not within human control will occur may be interpreted to include a promise to answer for harm caused by the failure of the event to occur. An example is a warranty of an existing or past fact, such as a warranty that a horse is sound, or that a ship arrived in a foreign port some days previously. Such promises are often made when the parties are ignorant of the actual facts regarding which they bargain, and may be dealt with as if the warrantor could cause the fact to be as he asserted. It is then immaterial that the actual condition of affairs may be irrevocably fixed before the promise is made.

Words of warranty, like other conduct, must be interpreted in the light of the circumstances and the reasonable expectations of the parties. In an insurance contract, a "warranty" by the insured is usually not a promise at all; it may be merely a representation of fact, or, more commonly, the fact warranted is a condition of the insurer's duty to pay (see § 225(3)). In the sale of goods, on the other hand, a similar warranty normally also includes a promise to answer for damages (see Uniform Commercial Code § 2–715).

Illustrations:

1.   A, the builder of a house, or the inventor of the material used in part of its construction, says to B, the owner of the house, "I warrant that this house will never burn down." This includes a promise to pay for harm if the house should burn down.

2.   A, by a charter-party, undertakes that the "good ship Dove," having sailed from Marseilles a week ago for New York, shall take on a cargo for B on her arrival in New York. The statement of the quality of the ship and the statement of her time of sailing from Marseilles include promises to pay for harm if the statement is untrue.

e. Illusory promises; mere statements of intention. Words of promise which by their terms make performance entirely optional with the "promisor" whatever may happen, or whatever course of conduct in other respects he may pursue, do not constitute a promise. Although such words are often referred to as forming an illusory promise, they do not fall within the present definition of promise. They may not even manifest any intention on the part of the promisor. Even if a present intention is manifested, the reservation of an option to change that intention means that there can be no promisee who is justified in an expectation of performance.

On the other hand, a promise may be made even though no duty of performance can arise unless some event occurs (see §§ 224, 225(1)). Such a conditional promise is no less a promise because there is small likelihood that any duty of performance will arise, as in the case of a promise to insure against fire a thoroughly fireproof building. There may be a promise in such a case even though the duty to perform depends on a state of mind of the promisor other than his own unfettered wish (see § 228), or on an event within the promisor's control.

Illustration:

3.   A says to B, "I will employ you for a year at a salary of $5,000 if I go into business." This is a promise, even though it is wholly optional with A to go into business or not.

f.   Opinions and predictions. A promise must be distinguished from a statement of opinion or a mere prediction of future events. The distinction is not usually difficult in the case of an informal gratuitous opinion, since there is often no manifestation of intention to act or refrain from acting or to bring about a result, no expectation of performance and no consideration. The problem is frequently presented, however, whether words of a seller of goods amount to a warranty. Under Uniform Commercial Code § 2–313(2) a statement purporting to be merely the seller's opinion does not create a warranty, but the buyer's reliance on the seller's skill and judgment may create an implied warranty that the goods are fit for a particular purpose under Uniform Commercial Code § 2–315. In any case where an expert opinion is paid for, there is likely to be an implied promise that the expert will act with reasonable care and skill.

A promise often refers to future events which are predicted or assumed rather than promised. Thus a promise to render personal service at a particular future time commonly rests on an assumption that the promisor will be alive and well at that time; a promise to paint a building may similarly rest on an assumption that the building will be in existence. Such cases are the subject of Chapter 11. The promisor may of course promise to answer for harm caused by the failure of the future event to occur; if he does not, such a failure may discharge any duty of performance.

Illustration:

4.   A, on seeing a house of thoroughly fireproof construction, says to B, the owner, "This house will never burn down." This is not a promise but merely an opinion or prediction. If A had been paid for his opinion as an expert, there might be an implied promise that he would employ reasonable care and skill in forming and giving his opinion.

g.   Promisee and beneficiary. The word promisee is used repeatedly in discussion of the law of contracts, and it cannot be avoided here. In common usage the promisee is the person to whom the promise is made; as promise is defined here, the promisee might be the person to whom the manifestation of the promisor's intention is communicated. In many situations, however, a promise is complete and binding before the communication is received (see, for example, §§ 63 and 104(1)). To cover such cases, the promisee is defined here as the addressee. As to agents or purported agents of the addressee, see § 52 Comment c.

In the usual situation the promisee also bears other relations to the promisor, and the word promisee is sometimes used to refer to one or more of those relations. Thus, in the simple case of a loan of money, the lender is not only the addressee of the promise but also the person to whom performance is to be rendered, the person who will receive economic benefit, the person who furnished the consideration, and the person to whom the legal duty of the promisor runs. As the word promisee is here defined, none of these relations is essential.

Contractual rights of persons not parties to the contract are the subject of Chapter 14. The promisor and promisee are the "parties" to a promise; a third person who will benefit from performance is a "beneficiary." A beneficiary may or may not have a legal right to performance; like "promisee", the term is neutral with respect to rights and duties. A person who is entitled under the terms of a letter of credit to draw or demand payment is commonly called a beneficiary, but such a person is ordinarily a promisee under the present definition. See Uniform Commercial Code § 5–103.

---

§ 4 HOW A PROMISE MAY BE MADE

A promise may be stated in words either oral or written, or may be inferred wholly or partly from conduct.

Comment:

a. Express and implied contracts. Contracts are often spoken of as express or implied. The distinction involves, however, no difference in legal effect, but lies merely in the mode of manifesting assent. Just as assent may be manifested by words or other conduct, sometimes including silence, so intention to make a promise may be manifested in language or by implication from other circumstances, including course of dealing or usage of trade or course of performance. See Uniform Commercial Code § 1–201(3), defining "agreement."

Illustrations:

1. A telephones to his grocer, "Send me a ten-pound bag of flour." The grocer sends it. A has thereby promised to pay the grocer's current price therefor.

2. A, on passing a market, where he has an account, sees a box of apples marked "25 cts. each." A picks up an apple, holds it up so that a clerk of the establishment sees the act. The clerk nods, and A passes on. A has promised to pay twenty-five cents for the apple.

b. *Quasi-contracts.* Implied contracts are different from quasi-contracts, although in some cases the line between the two is indistinct. See Comment *a* to § 19. Quasi-contracts have often been called implied contracts or contracts implied in law; but, unlike true contracts, quasi-contracts are not based on the apparent intention of the parties to undertake the performances in question, nor are they promises. They are obligations created by law for reasons of justice. Such obligations were ordinarily enforced at common law in the same form of action (assumpsit) that was appropriate to true contracts, and some confusion with reference to the nature of quasi-contracts has been caused thereby. They are dealt with in the Restatement of Restitution. See also §§ 141, 158, 197–99, 272, 370–77.

Illustration:

3. A's wife, B, separates from A for justifiable cause, and, in order to secure necessary clothing and supplies, buys them from C and charges their cost to A. A is bound to pay for them, though he has directed C not to furnish his wife with such supplies; but A's duty is quasi-contractual, not contractual. See Restatement of Restitution § 113.

----

§ 90 PROMISE REASONABLY INDUCING ACTION OR FORBEARANCE

(1) A promise which the promisor should reasonably expect to induce action or forbearance on the part of the promisee or a third person and which does induce such action or forbearance is binding if injustice can be avoided only by enforcement of the promise. The remedy granted for breach may be limited as justice requires.

(2) A charitable subscription or a marriage settlement is binding under Subsection (1) without proof that the promise induced action or forbearance.

Comment:

a.   Relation to other rules. Obligations and remedies based on reliance are
not peculiar to the law of contracts. This Section is often referred to in
terms of "promissory estoppel," a phrase suggesting an extension of the
doctrine of estoppel. Estoppel prevents a person from showing the truth
contrary to a representation of fact made by him after another has relied
on the representation. See Restatement, Second, Agency § 8B;
Restatement, Second, Torts §§ 872, 894. Reliance is also a significant
feature of numerous rules in the law of negligence, deceit and restitution.
See, e.g., Restatement, Second, Agency §§ 354, 378; Restatement, Second,
Torts §§ 323, 537; Restatement of Restitution § 55. In some cases those
rules and this Section overlap; in others they provide analogies useful in
determining the extent to which enforcement is necessary to avoid
injustice.

It is fairly arguable that the enforcement of informal contracts in the action
of assumpsit rested historically on justifiable reliance on a promise.
Certainly reliance is one of the main bases for enforcement of the half-
completed exchange, and the probability of reliance lends support to the
enforcement of the executory exchange. See Comments to §§ 72, 75. This
Section thus states a basic principle which often renders inquiry
unnecessary as to the precise scope of the policy of enforcing bargains.
Sections 87–89 state particular applications of the same principle to
promises ancillary to bargains, and it also applies in a wide variety of non-
commercial situations. See, e.g., § 94.

Illustration:

1.   A, knowing that B is going to college, promises B that A will
give him $5,000 on completion of his course. B goes to college, and
borrows and spends more than $5,000 for college expenses. When
he has nearly completed his course, A notifies him of an intention
to revoke the promise. A's promise is binding and B is entitled to
payment on completion of the course without regard to whether
his performance was "bargained for" under § 71.

b.   Character of reliance protected. The principle of this Section is flexible.
The promisor is affected only by reliance which he does or should foresee,
and enforcement must be necessary to avoid injustice. Satisfaction of the
latter requirement may depend on the reasonableness of the promisee's
reliance, on its definite and substantial character in relation to the remedy
sought, on the formality with which the promise is made, on the extent to
which the evidentiary, cautionary, deterrent and channeling functions of
form are met by the commercial setting or otherwise, and on the extent to
which such other policies as the enforcement of bargains and the
prevention of unjust enrichment are relevant. Compare Comment to § 72.
The force of particular factors varies in different types of cases: thus

reliance need not be of substantial character in charitable subscription cases, but must in cases of firm offers and guaranties. Compare Subsection (2) with §§ 87, 88.

Illustrations:

2. A promises B not to foreclose, for a specified time, a mortgage which A holds on B's land. B thereafter makes improvements on the land. A's promise is binding and may be enforced by denial of foreclosure before the time has elapsed.

3. A sues B in a municipal court for damages for personal injuries caused by B's negligence. After the one year statute of limitations has run, B requests A to discontinue the action and start again in the superior court where the action can be consolidated with other actions against B arising out of the same accident. A does so. B's implied promise that no harm to A will result bars B from asserting the statute of limitations as a defense.

4. A has been employed by B for 40 years. B promises to pay A a pension of $200 per month when A retires. A retires and forbears to work elsewhere for several years while B pays the pension. B's promise is binding.

c.   *Reliance by third persons.* If a promise is made to one party for the benefit of another, it is often foreseeable that the beneficiary will rely on the promise. Enforcement of the promise in such cases rests on the same basis and depends on the same factors as in cases of reliance by the promisee. Justifiable reliance by third persons who are not beneficiaries is less likely, but may sometimes reinforce the claim of the promisee or beneficiary.

Illustrations:

5. A holds a mortgage on B's land. To enable B to obtain a loan, A promises B in writing to release part of the land from the mortgage upon payment of a stated sum. As A contemplated, C lends money to B on a second mortgage, relying on A's promise. The promise is binding and may be enforced by C.

6. A executes and delivers a promissory note to B, a bank, to give B a false appearance of assets, deceive the banking authorities, and enable the bank to continue to operate. After several years B fails and is taken over by C, a representative of B's creditors. A's note is enforceable by C.

7. A and B, husband and wife, are tenants by the entirety of a tract of land. They make an oral promise to B's niece C to give her the tract. B, C and C's husband expend money in building a house

on the tract and C and her husband take possession and live there for several years until B dies. The expenditures by B and by C's husband are treated like those by C in determining whether justice requires enforcement of the promise against A.

d. Partial enforcement. A promise binding under this section is a contract, and full-scale enforcement by normal remedies is often appropriate. But the same factors which bear on whether any relief should be granted also bear on the character and extent of the remedy. In particular, relief may sometimes be limited to restitution or to damages or specific relief measured by the extent of the promisee's reliance rather than by the terms of the promise. See §§ 84, 89; compare Restatement, Second, Torts § 549 on damages for fraud. Unless there is unjust enrichment of the promisor, damages should not put the promisee in a better position than performance of the promise would have put him. See §§ 344, 349. In the case of a promise to make a gift it would rarely be proper to award consequential damages which would place a greater burden on the promisor than performance would have imposed.

Illustrations:

8. A applies to B, a distributor of radios manufactured by C, for a "dealer franchise" to sell C's products. Such franchises are revocable at will. B erroneously informs A that C has accepted the application and will soon award the franchise, that A can proceed to employ salesmen and solicit orders, and that A will receive an initial delivery of at least 30 radios. A expends $1,150 in preparing to do business, but does not receive the franchise or any radios. B is liable to A for the $1,150 but not for the lost profit on 30 radios. Compare Restatement, Second, Agency § 329.

9. The facts being otherwise as stated in Illustration 8, B gives A the erroneous information deliberately and with C's approval and requires A to buy the assets of a deceased former dealer and thus discharge C's "moral obligation" to the widow. C is liable to A not only for A's expenses but also for the lost profit on 30 radios.

10. A, who owns and operates a bakery, desires to go into the grocery business. He approaches B, a franchisor of supermarkets. B states to A that for $18,000 B will establish A in a store. B also advises A to move to another town and buy a small grocery to gain experience. A does so. Later B advises A to sell the grocery, which A does, taking a capital loss and foregoing expected profits from the summer tourist trade. B also advises A to sell his bakery to raise capital for the supermarket franchise, saying "Everything is ready to go. Get your money together and we are set." A sells the bakery taking a capital loss on this sale as well. Still later, B tells A that considerably more than an $18,000 investment will be

needed, and the negotiations between the parties collapse. At the point of collapse many details of the proposed agreement between the parties are unresolved. The assurances from B to A are promises on which B reasonably should have expected A to rely, and A is entitled to his actual losses on the sales of the bakery and grocery and for his moving and temporary living expenses. Since the proposed agreement was never made, however, A is not entitled to lost profits from the sale of the grocery or to his expectation interest in the proposed franchise from B.

11. A is about to buy a house on a hill. Before buying he obtains a promise from B, who owns adjoining land, that B will not build on a particular portion of his lot, where a building would obstruct the view from the house. A then buys the house in reliance on the promise. B's promise is binding, but will be specifically enforced only so long as A and his successors do not permanently terminate the use of the view.

12. A promises to make a gift of a tract of land to B, his son-in-law. B takes possession and lives on the land for 17 years, making valuable improvements. A then dispossesses B, and specific performance is denied because the proof of the terms of the promise is not sufficiently clear and definite. B is entitled to a lien on the land for the value of the improvements, not exceeding their cost.

e. *Gratuitous promises to procure insurance.* This Section is to be applied with caution to promises to procure insurance. The appropriate remedy for breach of such a promise makes the promisor an insurer, and thus may result in a liability which is very large in relation to the value of the promised service. Often the promise is properly to be construed merely as a promise to use reasonable efforts to procure the insurance, and reliance by the promisee may be unjustified or may be justified only for a short time. Or it may be doubtful whether he did in fact rely. Such difficulties may be removed if the proof of the promise and the reliance are clear, or if the promise is made with some formality, or if part performance or a commercial setting or a potential benefit to the promisor provide a substitute for formality.

Illustrations:

13. A, a bank, lends money to B on the security of a mortgage on B's new home. The mortgage requires B to insure the property. At the closing of the transaction A promises to arrange for the required insurance, and in reliance on the promise B fails to insure. Six months later the property, still uninsured, is destroyed by fire. The promise is binding.

14. A sells an airplane to B, retaining title to secure payment of the price. After the closing A promises to keep the airplane covered by insurance until B can obtain insurance. B could obtain insurance in three days but makes no effort to do so, and the airplane is destroyed after six days. A is not subject to liability by virtue of the promise.

f.   Charitable subscriptions, marriage settlements, and other gifts. One of the functions of the doctrine of consideration is to deny enforcement to a promise to make a gift. Such a promise is ordinarily enforced by virtue of the promisee's reliance only if his conduct is foreseeable and reasonable and involves a definite and substantial change of position which would not have occurred if the promise had not been made. In some cases, however, other policies reinforce the promisee's claim. Thus the promisor might be unjustly enriched if he could reclaim the subject of the promised gift after the promisee has improved it.

Subsection (2) identifies two other classes of cases in which the promisee's claim is similarly reinforced. American courts have traditionally favored charitable subscriptions and marriage settlements, and have found consideration in many cases where the element of exchange was doubtful or nonexistent. Where recovery is rested on reliance in such cases, a probability of reliance is enough, and no effort is made to sort out mixed motives or to consider whether partial enforcement would be appropriate.

Illustrations:

15. A promises B $5000, knowing that B desires that sum for the purchase of a parcel of land. Induced thereby, B secures without any payment an option to buy the parcel. A then tells B that he withdraws his promise. A's promise is not binding.

16. A orally promises to give her son B a tract of land to live on. As A intended, B gives up a homestead elsewhere, takes possession of the land, lives there for a year and makes substantial improvements. A's promise is binding.

17. A orally promises to pay B, a university, $100,000 in five annual installments for the purposes of its fund-raising campaign then in progress. The promise is confirmed in writing by A's agent, and two annual installments are paid before A dies. The continuance of the fund-raising campaign by B is sufficient reliance to make the promise binding on A and his estate.

18. A and B are engaged to be married. In anticipation of the marriage A and his father C enter into a formal written agreement by which C promises to leave certain property to A by will. A's subsequent marriage to B is sufficient reliance to make the promise binding on C and his estate.

WRIGHT V. NEWMAN

Supreme Court of Georgia
266 Ga. 519 (1996)

CARLEY, JUSTICE.

Seeking to recover child support for her daughter and her son, Kim Newman filed suit against Bruce Wright. Wright's answer admitted his paternity only as to Newman's daughter and DNA testing subsequently showed that he is not the father of her son. The trial court nevertheless ordered Wright to pay child support for both children. As to Newman's son, the trial court based its order upon Wright's "actions in having himself listed on the child's birth certificate, giving the child his surname and establishing a parent-child relationship. . . ." According to the trial court, Wright had thereby

> allow[ed] the child to consider him his father and in so doing deterr[ed Newman] from seeking to establish the paternity of the child's natural father [,] thus denying the child an opportunity to establish a parent-child relationship with the natural father.

We granted Wright's application for a discretionary appeal so as to review the trial court's order requiring that he pay child support for Newman's son.

Wright does not contest the trial court's factual findings. He asserts only that the trial court erred in its legal conclusion that the facts authorized the imposition of an obligation to provide support for Newman's son. If Wright were the natural father of Newman's son, he would be legally obligated to provide support. OCGA § 19–7–2. Likewise, if Wright had formally adopted Newman's son, he would be legally obligated to provide support. OCGA § 19–8–19(a)(2). However, Wright is neither the natural nor the formally adoptive father of the child and "the theory of 'virtual adoption' is not applicable to a dispute as to who is legally responsible for the support of minor children." Ellison v. Thompson, 240 Ga. 594, 596, 242 S.E.2d 95 (1978).

Although Wright is neither the natural nor the formally adoptive father of Newman's son and the theory of "virtual adoption" is inapplicable, it does not necessarily follow that, as a matter of law, he has no legal obligation for child support. A number of jurisdictions have recognized that a legally enforceable obligation to provide child support can be "based upon parentage or contract. . . ." (Emphasis supplied.) Albert v. Albert, 415 So.2d 818, 819 (Fla.App.1982). See also Anno., 90 A.L.R.2d 583 (1963). Georgia is included among those jurisdictions. Foltz v. Foltz, 238 Ga. 193, 194, 232 S.E.2d 66 (1977). Accordingly, the issue for resolution is whether Wright can be held liable for child support for Newman's son under this state's contract law.

There was no formal written contract whereby Wright agreed to support Newman's son. Compare Foltz v. Foltz, supra. Nevertheless, under this state's contract law,

> [a] promise which the promisor should reasonably expect to induce action or forbearance on the part of the promisee or a third person and which does induce such action or forbearance is binding if injustice can be avoided only by enforcement of the promise. The remedy granted for breach may be limited as justice requires.

OCGA § 13–3–44(a). This statute codifies the principle of promissory estoppel. Insilco Corp. v. First Nat. Bank of Dalton, 248 Ga. 322(1), 283 S.E.2d 262 (1981). In accordance with that principle,

> "[a] party may enter into a contract invalid and unenforceable, and by reason of the covenants therein contained and promises made in connection with the same, wrongfully cause the opposite party to forego a valuable legal right to his detriment, and in this manner by his conduct waive the right to repudiate the contract and become estopped to deny the opposite party any benefits that may accrue to him under the terms of the agreement." [Cits.]

Pepsi Cola Bottling Co. of Dothan, Ala., Inc. v. First Nat. Bank of Columbus, 248 Ga. 114, 116–117(2), 281 S.E.2d 579 (1981).

The evidence authorizes the finding that Wright promised both Newman and her son that he would assume all of the obligations and responsibilities of fatherhood, including that of providing support. As the trial court found, this promise was evidenced by Wright's listing of himself as the father on the child's birth certificate and giving the child his last name. Wright is presumed to know "the legal consequences of his actions. Since parents are legally obligated to support their minor children, [he] accepted this support obligation by acknowledging paternity." Marshall v. Marshall, 386 So.2d 11, 12 (Fla.App.1980). There is no dispute that, at the time he made his commitment, Wright knew that he was not the natural father of the child. Compare NPA v. WBA, 8 Va.App. 246, 380 S.E.2d 178 (1989). Thus, he undertook his commitment knowingly and voluntarily. Moreover, he continued to do so for some 10 years, holding himself out to others as the father of the child and allowing the child to consider him to be the natural father.

The evidence further authorizes the finding that Newman and her son relied upon Wright's promise to their detriment. As the trial court found, Newman refrained from identifying and seeking support from the child's natural father. Had Newman not refrained from doing so, she might now have a source of financial support for the child and the child might now have a natural father who provided emotional, as well as financial, support. If, after 10 years of honoring his voluntary commitment, Wright were now allowed to evade the consequences of his promise, an injustice to Newman and her son would result. Under the evidence, the duty to support which Wright voluntarily assumed 10 years ago remains enforceable under the contractual doctrine of promissory estoppel and the trial court's order which compels Wright to discharge that obligation must be affirmed. See Nygard v. Nygard, 156 Mich.App. 94, 401 N.W.2d 323 (1986); Marshall v. Marshall, supra; In re Marriage of Johnson, 88 Cal.App.3d 848, 152 Cal.Rptr. 121 (1979); Hartford v. Hartford, 53 Ohio App.2d 79, 7 O.O.3d 53, 371 N.E.2d 591 (1977).

Judgment affirmed.

All the Justices concur, except BENHAM, C.J., who dissents.

SEARS, JUSTICE, concurring.

I concur fully with the majority opinion. I write separately only to address the dissenting opinion's misperception that Newman has not relied upon Wright's promise to her detriment.

It is an established principle in Georgia that a promise which the promisor should reasonably expect to induce action or forbearance on the part of the promisee or a third person and which does induce such action or forbearance is binding if injustice can be avoided only by enforcement of the promise. This doctrine, known as "promissory estoppel," prevents a promisor from reneging on a promise, when the promisor should have expected that the promisee would rely upon the promise, and the promisee does in fact rely upon the promise to her detriment. Sufficient consideration to enforce a contractual promise pursuant to promissory estoppel may be found in any benefit accruing to the promisor, or any reliance, loss, trouble, disadvantage, or charge imposed upon the promisee.

Bearing these principles in mind, and as explained very well in the majority opinion, it is clear that Wright's commitment to Newman to assume the obligations of fatherhood as regards her son are enforceable. Specifically, it is abundantly clear that Wright should have known that Newman would rely upon his promise, especially after he undertook for ten years to fulfill the obligations of fatherhood. In this regard, it could hardly have escaped Wright's notice that Newman refrained from seeking to identify and obtain support from the child's biological father while Wright was fulfilling his commitment to her. Moreover, Newman did in fact rely upon Wright's promise, to her detriment when, ten years after he undertook the obligations of fatherhood, Wright reneged on his promise.

Promissory estoppel requires only that the reliance by the injured party be reasonable. In this case, it cannot seriously be argued that Newman's reliance was anything other than reasonable, as she had absolutely no indication that Wright would ever renege, especially after he fulfilled his promise for such a long time. Moreover, contrary to the dissent's implicit assertion, promissory estoppel does not require that the injured party exhaust all other possible means of obtaining the benefit of the promise from any and all sources before being able to enforce the promise against the promisor. In this regard, it is illogical to argue that Newman, after reasonably relying upon Wright's promise for ten years, can now simply seek to determine the identity of the biological father and collect support from him. First, there is nothing in the case law that requires Newman to do so before being entitled to have Wright's promise enforced. Second, this requirement would be an imposing, if not an impossible, burden, and would require Newman not only to identify the father (if possible), but also to locate him, bring a costly legal action against him, and to succeed in that action. Imposing this requirement would effectively penalize Newman for no reasons other than (1) her reasonable reliance upon a promise that was not kept, and (2) for allowing herself to be dissuaded by Wright from seeking the identity of the biological father. As noted, nowhere does the case law support imposing such a requirement, and none of the facts in this case support doing so now.

Finally, there can be no doubt that, unless Wright's promise to Newman is enforced, injustice will result. Given the approximately ten years that have passed since the child's birth, during which time Wright, for all purposes, was the child's father, it likely will be impossible for Newman to establish the identity of the child's biological father, bring a successful paternity action, and obtain support from that individual. Consequently, if Wright is allowed to renege on his obligation, Newman likely will not receive any support to assist in the cost of raising her son, despite having been promised the receipt of such by Wright. Furthermore, an even greater injustice will be inflicted upon the boy himself. A child who has been told by any adult, regardless of the existence of a biological relationship, that he will always be able to depend upon the adult for parenting and sustenance, will suffer a great deal when that commitment is broken. And when a child suffers under those circumstances, society-at-large suffers as well.

Because Wright's promise is capable of being enforced under the law, and because I believe that Wright's promise must be enforced in order to prevent a grave miscarriage of justice, I concur fully in the majority opinion.

BENHAM, CHIEF JUSTICE, dissenting.

I respectfully dissent. While I agree with the majority opinion's statement that liability for child support may be based on promissory estoppel in a case where there is no statutory obligation or express contract, I first note that this issue was not brought by either of the parties. Further, there is a critical element that must be shown for promissory estoppel to apply. In addition to making a showing of expectation and reasonable reliance, a person asserting liability on the theory of promissory estoppel must show that she relied on the promise to her detriment. Nickell v. IAG Federal Credit Union, 213 Ga.App. 516, 445 S.E.2d 335 (1994); Lake Tightsqueeze, Inc. v. Chrysler First Financial Services Corp., 210 Ga.App. 178, 435 S.E.2d 486 (1993). The majority states that Newman and her son incurred detriment by refraining from identifying and seeking support from the child's natural father. However, the record is completely bereft of any evidence that Newman met her burden of proof as to promissory estoppel, and the majority fails to state how she is prevented from now instituting a child support action against the natural father. Newman has not alleged, nor does the record reveal, that she does not know the identity of the natural father, nor does she show that the natural father is dead or unable to be found. Consequently, Newman has not shown that she is now unable to do what she would have had to do ten years ago—seek support from the natural father.

In fact, Wright contends, and Newman does not refute, that Newman severed the relationship and all ties with Wright when the child was approximately three years old. For approximately the next five years, until the child was eight, Newman and Wright did not communicate. Only for the past two years has Wright visited with the child. Importantly, Wright contends that during the past seven years he did not support the child. Thus, taking Wright's undisputed contentions as true, any prejudice incurred by Newman because of the passage of ten years in time is not due to Wright's actions, since, at least for the past seven years, Newman has been in the same situation—receiving no support payments from Wright. Thus, although Wright may be morally obligated to support the ten-year-old child, he is not legally obligated to do so because Newman has failed to show that she or the child incurred any detriment by Wright's failure to fulfill his promise made ten years ago.

For the foregoing reasons, I dissent.

CONRAD V. FIELDS

Court of Appeals of Minnesota
2007 WL 2106302 (2007)
(Unpublished Opinion)

PETERSON, JUDGE.

This appeal is from a judgment and an order denying posttrial motions. The judgment awarded respondent damages in the amount of the cost of her law-school tuition and books based on a determination that the elements of promissory estoppel were proved with respect to appellant's promise to pay for the tuition and books. We affirm the judgment and grant in part and deny in part respondent's motion to strike appellant's brief and appendix.

FACTS

Appellant Walter R. Fields and respondent Marjorie Conrad met and became friends when they were neighbors in an apartment complex in the early 1990's. Appellant started his own business and became a financially successful businessman. Appellant built a $1.2 million house in the Kenwood neighborhood in Minneapolis and leased a Bentley automobile for more than $50,000 a year. Appellant is a philanthropic individual who has sometimes paid education costs for others.

In the fall of 2000, appellant suggested that respondent attend law school, and he offered to pay for her education. Respondent, who had recently paid off an $11,000 medical bill and still owed about $5,000 for undergraduate student loans, did not feel capable of paying for law school on her own. Appellant promised that he would pay tuition and other expenses associated with law school as they became due. Appellant quit her job at Qwest, where she had been earning $45,000 per year, to attend law school. Appellant admitted at trial that before respondent enrolled in law school, he agreed to pay her tuition.

Respondent testified that she enrolled in law school in the summer of 2001 as a result of appellant's "inducement and assurance to pay for [her] education." Appellant made two tuition payments, each in the amount of $1,949.75, in August and October 2001, but he stopped payment on the check for the second payment. At some point, appellant told respondent that his assets had been frozen due to an Internal Revenue Service audit and that payment of her education expenses would be delayed until he got the matter straightened out. In May 2004, appellant and respondent exchanged e-mail messages about respondent's difficulties in managing the debts that she had incurred for law school. In response to one of respondent's messages, appellant wrote, "to be clear and in writing, when you graduate law school and pas[s] your bar exam, I will pay your tuition." Later, appellant told respondent that he would not pay her expenses, and he threatened to get a restraining order against her if she continued attempting to communicate with him.

Respondent brought suit against appellant, alleging that in reliance on appellant's promise to pay her education expenses, she gave up the opportunity to earn income through full-time employment and enrolled in law school. The case was tried to the court, which awarded respondent damages in the amount of $87,314.63 under the doctrine of promissory estoppel. The district court denied appellant's motion for a new trial or amended findings. This appeal followed.

DECISION

I.

The district court's "[f]indings of fact, whether based on oral or documentary evidence, shall not be set aside unless clearly erroneous, and due regard shall be given to the opportunity of the trial court to judge the credibility of the witnesses." Minn. R. Civ. P. 52.01. In applying this rule, "we view the record in the light most favorable to the judgment of the district court." Rogers v. Moore, 603 N.W.2d 650, 656 (Minn.1999). If there is reasonable evidence to support the district court's findings of fact, this court will not disturb those findings. Fletcher v. St. Paul Pioneer Press, 589 N.W.2d 96, 101 (Minn.1999). While the district court's findings of fact are reviewed under the deferential "clearly erroneous" standard, this court reviews questions of law de novo. AFSCME, Council No. 14 v. City of St. Paul, 533 N.W.2d 623, 626 (Minn.App.1995).

"Promissory estoppel implies a contract in law where no contract exists in fact." Deli v. Univ. of Minn., 578 N.W.2d 779, 781 (Minn.App.1998), review denied (Minn. July 16, 1998). "A promise which the promisor should reasonably expect to induce action or forbearance on the part of the promisee or a third person and which does induce such action or forbearance is binding if injustice can be avoided only by enforcement of the promise." Restatement (Second) of Contracts § 90(1) (1981).

The elements of a promissory estoppel claim are (1) a clear and definite promise, (2) the promisor intended to induce reliance by the promisee, and the promisee relied to the promisee's detriment, and (3) the promise must be enforced to prevent injustice. Cohen v. Cowles Media Co., 479 N.W.2d 387, 391 (Minn.1992). Judicial determinations of injustice involve a number of considerations, "including the reasonableness of a promisee's reliance." Faimon v. Winona State Univ., 540 N.W.2d, 879, 883 (Minn.App.1995), review denied (Minn. Feb. 9, 1996).

"Granting equitable relief is within the sound discretion of the trial court. Only a clear abuse of that discretion will result in reversal." Nadeau v. County of Ramsey, 277 N.W.2d 520, 524 (Minn.1979). But [t]he court considers the injustice factor as a matter of law, looking to the reasonableness of the promisee's reliance and weighing public policies (in favor of both enforcing bargains and preventing unjust enrichment). When the facts are taken as true, it is a question of law as to whether they rise to the level of promissory estoppel. Greuling v. Wells Fargo Home Mortgage, Inc., 690 N.W.2d 757, 761 (Minn.App.2005) (citation omitted).

I.

Appellant argues that respondent did not plead or prove the elements of promissory estoppel. Minnesota is a notice-pleading state that does not require absolute specificity in pleading and, instead, requires only information sufficient to fairly notify the opposing party of the claim against it. See Minn. R. Civ. P. 8.01 (requiring pleading to include a "short and plain statement of the claim" showing entitlement to relief); Minn. R. Gen. Pract. 507 (the statement of the claim must "contain a brief statement of the amount and nature of the claim"); Roberge v. Cambridge Coop. Creamery Co., 243 Minn. 230, 232, 67 N.W.2d 400, 402 (1954) (stating that pleadings must be framed so as to give notice of the claim asserted and permit the application of the doctrine of res judicata).

Paragraph 12 of respondent's complaint states, "That as a direct and approximate result of the negligent conduct and breach of contract conduct of [appellant], [respondent] has been damaged. . . ." But the complaint also states:

4.   That in 2000, based on the assurance and inducement of [appellant] to pay for [respondent's] legal education, [respondent] made the decision to enroll in law school at Hamline University School of Law (Hamline) in St. Paul, Minnesota which she did in 2001.

5.   That but for the inducement and assurance of [appellant] to pay for [respondent's] legal education, [respondent] would not have enrolled in law school. [Appellant] was aware of this fact.

Paragraphs four and five of the complaint are sufficient to put appellant on notice of the promissory-estoppel claim.

At a pretrial deposition, respondent testified that negligence and breach of contract were the only two causes of action that she was pleading. Because promissory estoppel is described as a contract implied at law, respondent's deposition testimony can be interpreted to include a promissory-estoppel claim.

In its legal analysis, the district court stated:

The Court finds credible [respondent's] testimony that [appellant] encouraged her to go to law school, knowing that she would not be able to pay for it on her own. He knew that she was short on money, having helped her pay for food and other necessities. He knew that she was working at Qwest and would need to quit her job to go to law school. He offered to pay for the cost of her going to law school, knowing that she had debts from her undergraduate tuition. He made a payment on her law school tuition after she enrolled. [Respondent] knew that [appellant] was a wealthy philanthropist, and that he had offered to pay for the education of strangers he had met in chance encounters. She knew that he had the wealth to pay for her law school education. She knew that [ ] he was established in society, older than she, not married, without children, an owner of a successful company, an owner of an expensive home, and a lessor of an expensive car. Moreover, [appellant] was a friend who had performed many kindnesses for her already, and she trusted him. [Appellant's] promise in fact induced [respondent] to quit her job at Qwest and enroll in law school, which she had not otherwise planned to do. . . .

. . . [T]he circumstances support a finding that it would be unjust not to enforce the promise. Upon reliance on [appellant's] promise, [respondent] quit her job. She attended law school despite a serious health condition that might otherwise have deterred her from going.

These findings are sufficient to show that respondent proved the elements of promissory estoppel.

Appellant argues that because he advised respondent shortly after she enrolled in law school that he would not be paying her law-school expenses as they came due, respondent could not have reasonably relied on his promise to pay her expenses to her detriment after he repudiated the promise. Appellant contends that the only injustice that resulted from his promise involved the original $5,000 in expenses that respondent incurred to enter law school. But appellant's statement that he would not pay the expenses as they came due did not make respondent's reliance unreasonable because appellant also told respondent that his financial problems were temporary and that he would pay her tuition when she graduated and passed the bar exam. This statement made it reasonable for respondent to continue to rely on appellant's promise that he would pay her expenses.

II.

Citing Olson v. Synergistic Techs. Bus. Sys., Inc., 628 N.W.2d 142, 151 (Minn.2001), appellant argues that the doctrine of promissory estoppel is not a substitute for consideration and that respondent had no basis for claiming an enforceable contract given the total lack of consideration. The Olson court stated:

American courts adopted the Chancery court's equitable cause of action based on good-faith reliance to enforce promises unsupported by consideration—not as a consideration substitute, but rather as a doctrine based on reliance that the courts could use to prevent injustice. Eventually, the American courts characterized this line of cases as "promissory estoppel," and identified the key elements of the doctrine of promissory estoppel as (1) a promise, (2) the promisee's right to rely on the promise and the promisor's duty to prevent reliance, and (3) harm suffered in reliance on the promise. Over time, the doctrine of promissory estoppel evolved, and courts began to focus on the promisee's right to rely rather than the promisor's duty to prevent reliance. As the doctrine developed, many courts adopted the Restatement of Contracts § 90 (1932) (setting out the elements of promissory estoppel), but in Minnesota, we limited relief available under Restatement of Contracts § 90 to the extent necessary to prevent injustice. For jurisdictions adopting the Restatement of Contracts § 90, the equitable remedy was not a mechanical calculation, but rather it was determined ad hoc on a case by case basis. In contrast, when a plaintiff pleaded a common-law cause of action based on detrimental reliance as a consideration substitute, the legal remedy consisted of compensating the plaintiff for the full value of the promise.

In Minnesota, we have consistently recognized and applied the equitable aspects of promissory estoppel.

628 N.W.2d at 151 (citations omitted). Read in its entirety, Olson does not indicate that consideration is required for recovery under the promissory-estoppel doctrine.

III.

Appellant argues that because he did not sign a written agreement between the parties and respondent admitted that she intended to take more than one year to complete law school, any contract between the parties is unenforceable under the statute of frauds. Under the statute of frauds, if an agreement "by its terms is not to be performed within one year," no action upon the agreement shall be maintained unless the "agreement, or some note or memorandum thereof, expressing the consideration, is in writing, and subscribed by the party charged therewith[.]" Minn.Stat. § 513.01(1) (2006).

But an agreement "may be taken outside the statute of frauds by ... promissory estoppel." Norwest Bank Minn. v. Midwestern Mach. Co., 481 N.W.2d 875, 880 (1992) (citing Berg v. Carlstrom, 347 N.W.2d 809, 812 (Minn.1984)), review denied (Minn. May 15, 1992). "A promise which the promisor should reasonably expect to induce action or forbearance on the part of the promisee or a third person and which does induce the action or forbearance is enforceable notwithstanding the Statute of Frauds if injustice can be avoided only by enforcement of the promise." Restatement (Second) of Contracts § 139(1) (1981).

Because appellant's expensive home and car and position as a successful business owner made it appear as if he was fully capable of keeping his promise to pay respondent's law-school expenses and because appellant had bestowed his generosity on respondent several times before he promised to pay her law-school expenses, appellant reasonably should have expected his promise to induce action by respondent. The promise did induce action by respondent and left her with a substantial debt when appellant failed to keep his promise. Respondent quit her job and attended law school with the expectation that appellant would pay her law-school expenses and she would not be in debt for these expenses when she graduated. Because it would be unjust to require respondent to pay a debt that she incurred in reliance on appellant's promise to pay the debt, appellant's promise is enforceable notwithstanding the statute of frauds.

IV.

In actions based on promissory estoppel, "[r]elief may be limited to damages measured by the promisee's reliance." Dallum v. Farmers Union Cent. Exchange, Inc., 462 N.W.2d 608, 613 (Minn.App.1990), review denied (Minn. Jan. 14, 1991). "In other words, relief may be limited to the party's out-of-pocket expenses made in reliance on the promise." Id.

Appellant objects to respondent seeking damages for lost income and living expenses, including housing. But the district court awarded respondent damages only for the cost of tuition and books. Appellant argues that respondent sought double recovery for the cost of tuition and the amount of her student loans. But an exhibit prepared by respondent and admitted into evidence shows that tuition totaled $86,462.21 and books cost $2,802.17. The district court awarded respondent $87,314.63 (tuition plus books minus payment made by appellant).

Appellant argues that respondent was obligated to mitigate her damages and she could have avoided all of her damages by dropping out of law school immediately after appellant refused to pay her tuition as it was incurred. But as we explained when addressing the reasonableness of respondent's reliance, appellant told respondent that his financial difficulties were temporary and that he would pay her expenses after graduation. Under these circumstances, respondent was not aware until after she graduated that she would suffer damages, and by the time she graduated, she had already paid for her tuition and books and had no opportunity to mitigate damages.

V.

Appellant argues that because respondent received a valuable law degree, she did not suffer any real detriment by relying on his promise. But receiving a law degree was the expected and intended consequence of appellant's promise, and the essence of appellant's promise was that respondent would receive the law degree without the debt associated with attending law school. Although respondent benefited from attending law school, the debt that she incurred in reliance on appellant's promise is a detriment to her.

VI.

The record on appeal consists of "[t]he papers filed in the trial court, the exhibits, and the transcript of the proceedings[.]" Minn. R. Civ.App. P. 110.01. "An appellate court may not base its decision on matters outside the record on appeal, and may not consider matters not produced and received in evidence [in the district court]." Thiele v. Stich, 425 N.W.2d 580, 582 (Minn.1988).

Respondent argues that appellant's entire brief and appendix should be stricken due to references to deposition transcripts and a tax-lien document. The deposition transcripts were part of the district court record. Appellant's reference to respondent's deposition in his argument relating to the theories pleaded in the complaint is proper, and we deny the motion to strike the entire brief and appendix. Although the deposition is part of the record, because it was not admitted into evidence at trial, it cannot be used to prove facts disputed at trial. Therefore, we grant respondent's motion to strike references to the depositions to support factual allegations.

The tax-lien document was not part of the record before the district court. This court may consider essentially uncontroverted documentary evidence that is not included in the district court file. Franke v. Farm Bureau Mut. Ins. Co., 421 N.W.2d 406, 409 n. 1 (Minn.App.1988), review denied (Minn. May 25, 1988). But the tax lien is evidence of appellant's financial condition, which is a disputed issue in this case. Accordingly, we strike the tax-lien document.

Affirmed; motion granted in part.

COSGROVE V. BARTOLOTTA

Court of Appeals of Minnesota
150 F. 3d 729 (1998)

POSNER, CHIEF JUDGE.

A jury awarded the plaintiff damages of $135,000 in a diversity suit governed by Wisconsin law. The damages were broken down as follows: $117,000 for promissory estoppel, $1,000 for misrepresentation, and $17,000 for unjust enrichment. In response to the defendants' motion under Fed.R.Civ.P. 59(e) to alter or amend the judgment, the judge rendered judgment for the defendants on the promissory estoppel claim on the ground that the plaintiff had failed to prove reliance; but he let the jury's verdict stand with respect to the other claims. Later he denied the plaintiff's motion for costs, on the ground that the plaintiff had failed to recover the minimum amount in controversy fixed in the diversity statute. 28 U.S.C. § 1332(b). Both sides appeal (the plaintiff appeals from the order denying costs as well as from the order amending the judgment). The appeals present issues both of common law and of federal procedure.

The principal defendant is Joseph Bartolotta, but his company—Mary-Bart, LLC—is also named as a defendant; and in a diversity case, whenever there is an unconventional party (that is, someone or something other than either a natural person suing in his own rather than a representative capacity, or a business corporation) a jurisdictional warning flag should go up. In the case of a regular corporation, the owners' state of citizenship is irrelevant to whether there is the required complete diversity; but in the case of a partnership, it is crucial. The citizenship of a partnership is the citizenship of the partners, even if they are limited partners, so that if even one of the partners (general or limited) is a citizen of the same state as the plaintiff, the suit cannot be maintained as a diversity suit. Carden v. Arkoma Associates, 494 U.S. 185, 110 S.Ct. 1015, 108 L.Ed.2d 157 (1990); Northern Trust Co. v. Bunge Corp., 899 F.2d 591, 594 (7th Cir.1990).

Mary-Bart is neither a partnership nor a corporation, but a "limited liability company." Wis. Stat. Chapter 183. This animal is like a limited partnership; the principal difference is that it need have no equivalent to a general partner, that is, an owner who has unlimited personal liability for the debts of the firm. See generally Larry E. Ribstein & Robert R. Keatinge, Ribstein and Keatinge on Limited Liability Companies (1998). Given the resemblance between an LLC and a limited partnership, and what seems to have crystallized as a principle that members of associations are citizens for diversity purposes unless Congress provides otherwise (as it has with respect to corporations, in 28 U.S.C. § 1332(c)(1)), Carden v. Arkoma Associates, supra; United Steelworkers of America v. R.H. Bouligny, Inc., 382 U.S. 145, 152–53, 86 S.Ct. 272, 15 L.Ed.2d 217 (1965); Indiana Gas Co. v. Home Ins. Co., 141 F.3d 314, 317 (7th Cir.1998), we conclude that the citizenship of an LLC for purposes of the diversity jurisdiction is the citizenship of its members. That does not defeat jurisdiction in this case, however, because Mary-Bart, LLC has only one member—Mr. Bartolotta, who is not a citizen of the same state as the plaintiff.

Another threshold issue concerns the scope of our review of the judge's denial of the defendants' motion under Fed.R.Civ.P. Rule 59(e). They had moved for a directed verdict (or as it is now called, "judgment as a matter of law") at the end of the trial, before the jury retired to deliberate. The judge took the motion under advisement and after the jury brought in its verdict he denied the motion and entered judgment for the plaintiff. The defendants filed their Rule 59(e) motion within ten days after the entry of judgment. The ground of the motion was identical to the ground of the defendants' motion for a directed verdict, so that in effect the defendants were asking for reconsideration of the denial of their motion for a directed verdict. The district judge, as we said, granted the motion in part, on the ground that the plaintiff had failed to prove an essential element of his promissory estoppel claim.

Cosgrove argues that the only way the defendants could get such relief was to renew their motion for a directed verdict in the form of a motion under Fed.R.Civ.P. 50(b) for judgment notwithstanding the verdict. That is the standard way, all right. Lambie v. Tibbits, 267 F.2d 902, 903 (7th Cir. 1959); Greer v. United States, 408 F.2d 631, 635 (6th Cir.1969). And the only grounds for a Rule 59(e) motion, as the plaintiff points out, are newly discovered evidence, an intervening change in the controlling law, and manifest error of law. LB Credit Corp. v. Resolution Trust Corp., 49 F.3d 1263, 1267 (7th Cir.1995); Firestone v. Firestone, 76 F.3d 1205, 1208

(D.C.Cir.1996) (per curiam); Hayes v. Douglas Dynamics, Inc., 8 F.3d 88, 91 n. 3 (1st Cir.1993). But the entry of a judgment against the party that was entitled to judgment as a matter of law—the predicate for granting a motion for judgment notwithstanding the verdict—could easily be thought a manifest error. Anyway we cannot believe that any consequences should flow from a mislabeling of the defendants' postjudgment motion, if that is how it should be regarded, as we doubt. The motion was filed within the time limit for a 50(b) motion (which is the same as that for a 59(e) motion— ten days after entry of judgment) and it contained the information required for a 50(b) motion. That was good enough; captions do not control. Cf. Herzog Contracting Corp. v. McGowen Corp., 976 F.2d 1062, 1065 (7th Cir.1992); Kladis v. Brezek, 823 F.2d 1014, 1017 (7th Cir.1987); Scottish Heritable Trust, PLC v. Peat Marwick Main & Co., 81 F.3d 606, 610 (5th Cir.1996).

This brings us to the merits of the appeals. Bartolotta wanted to open a new restaurant in Milwaukee. He asked a family friend—Barry Cosgrove— for help. The help sought was a $100,000 loan from Cosgrove plus Cosgrove's business and legal advice, Cosgrove being an experienced corporate lawyer. Bartolotta promised Cosgrove not only to repay the loan with interest within three years but also to give him a 19 percent ownership interest in the restaurant. Armed with Cosgrove's pledge of the $100,000 loan, Bartolotta was able to obtain the bank financing that he needed for the venture. In reliance on the promise of a share in the ownership of the restaurant, Cosgrove assisted Bartolotta in negotiating the lease of the restaurant premises and the loan from the bank, and it was on Cosgrove's advice that the venture was organized in the form of an LLC. But Cosgrove never actually made the loan and was never given an ownership interest in the restaurant. For after all the arrangements were complete, and though Cosgrove was willing and able to make the loan, Bartolotta obtained alternative financing and cut Cosgrove out of the deal. The restaurant opened and was a success, so the ownership interest that Cosgrove would have gotten had Bartolotta not reneged on his premise has turned out to be worth something; hence this lawsuit.

We have stated the facts as favorably to Cosgrove as the record permits, as we must do in deciding whether it was error for the district judge to take the promissory estoppel case away from the jury. Cosgrove's evidence was vigorously contested, but there was enough to enable a reasonable jury to find the facts that we have summarized. It is true that the jury found against Cosgrove on his breach of contract claim, but this was not inconsistent with its finding promissory estoppel. Cosgrove and Bartolotta never worked out the exact terms under which Cosgrove would receive a share in the restaurant, so the jury could reasonably find that there was no contract even if it believed his testimony about the promise made to him and the services that he performed in reliance on the promise. Promissory estoppel is an alternative basis to breach of contract for seeking damages from the breakdown of a relation. If there is a promise of a kind likely to induce a costly change in position by the promisee in reliance on the promise being carried out, and it does induce such a change, he can enforce the promise even though there was no contract. U.S. Oil Co. v. Midwest Auto Care Services, Inc., 150 Wis.2d 80, 440 N.W.2d 825, 828 (1989); Skycom Corp. v. Telstar Corp., 813 F.2d 810, 817 (7th Cir.1987) (applying Wisconsin law).

Buried in our capsule summary of the law of promissory estoppel is an important qualification: the reliance that makes the promise legally enforceable must be induced by a reasonable expectation that the promise will be carried out. A promise that is vague and hedged about with conditions may nevertheless have a sufficient expected value to induce a reasonable person to invest time and effort in trying to maximize the likelihood that the promise will be carried out. But if he does so knowing that he is investing for a chance, rather than relying on a firm promise that a reasonable person would expect to be carried out, he cannot plead promissory estoppel. See Major Mat Co. v. Monsanto Co., 969 F.2d 579, 583 (7th Cir.1992); Gruen Industries, Inc. v. Biller, 608 F.2d 274, 280–82 (7th Cir.1979); Inter-Mountain Threading, Inc. v. Baker Hughes Tubular Services, Inc., 812 P.2d 555, 559 (Wyo.1991); First Security Savings Bank v. Aitken, 226 Mich.App. 291, 573 N.W.2d 307, 316–18 (1997); Security Bank & Trust Co. v. Bogard, 494 N.E.2d 965, 968–69 (Ind.App.1986). Suppose a father tells his son that he is thinking of promising the son on his next birthday that if he gives up smoking the father will restore him as a beneficiary under his will. In an effort to make sure that he will be able to comply with this condition, the son enrolls in an expensive program for cigarette addicts. His birthday arrives, and the father does not make the promise that the son was hoping for. The son relied, and relied reasonably, on his father's statement, in enrolling in the anti-smoking program; but he was not relying on the carrying out of the promise (not yet made) of being restored as a beneficiary of his father's will, and therefore he has no claim of promissory estoppel. Or suppose a contractor told a subcontractor that it was thinking of hiring him for a job but wouldn't consider him unless the subcontractor had more minority workers in his employ, and the subcontractor goes out and hires some, and, as before, the contractor does not hire him. Again there would be no basis for a claim of promissory estoppel.

The defendants argue that this was such a case. But the jury was entitled to conclude differently. Bartolotta was quite definite in promising Cosgrove an ownership interest in the restaurant, though at first the size of the interest was uncertain. Bartolotta specified no contingencies that might defeat the promise. A reasonable jury could find that Cosgrove invested time and effort in the venture, and pledged to make a $100,000 loan, not because he hoped that this would induce Bartolotta to give him a share in the new company but because he thought he had already been firmly promised a share, contingent only on his honoring his pledge (if called on to do so) and providing business and legal advice as needed—all of which he did or was prepared to do.

A more difficult question is whether Cosgrove actually relied on the promise. It is dangerous to take a legal term in its lay sense. To "rely," in the law of promissory estoppel, is not merely to do something in response to the inducement offered by the promise. There must be a cost to the promisee of doing it. Hoffman v. Red Owl Stores, Inc., 26 Wis.2d 683, 133 N.W.2d 267, 275 (1965); Creative Demos, Inc. v. Wal-Mart Stores, Inc., 142 F.3d 367, 369 (7th Cir.1998). The pledge of $100,000 was not shown to be a cost to Cosgrove. He never actually made the loan, and there is no evidence that the making of the pledge imposed an out-of-pocket cost, as it would have done if, for example, he had had to pay a capital-gains tax in order to obtain cash needed to make the loan if asked to do so. One could not even be certain that the personal services which Cosgrove rendered to Bartolotta cost him something without knowing what the alternative uses of his time were. If he performed these services in his spare time—time for which he had no valuable professional or even leisure use—the cost to him of performing the services for Bartolotta may have been so slight as not to count as reliance for purposes of promissory estoppel doctrine. But this is hardly plausible; Cosgrove was a professional rendering professional services. And, if nothing else, the pledge put Cosgrove at risk, since he would have been bound—by the very doctrine of promissory estoppel that he invokes—had Bartolotta relied, and since, as the subsequent course of events proved, Bartolotta was likely to enforce the pledge only if he couldn't get better terms elsewhere, which would be a sign that the venture might be riskier than it had appeared to be originally.

Since the judge should not have set aside the jury's award of damages on the claim of promissory estoppel, he should not have denied an award of costs to Cosgrove on the ground (28 U.S.C. § 1332(b)) that Cosgrove had failed to recover the statutory minimum amount in controversy; the damages award for promissory estoppel carried Cosgrove well above that level. But for future reference, we point out that the judge erred in thinking that the denial of costs in a case in which the plaintiff fails to recover at least the statutory minimum is mandatory rather than discretionary, Dr. Franklin Perkins School v. Freeman, 741 F.2d 1503, 1525 (7th Cir.1984); Coventry Sewage Associates v. Dworkin Realty Co., 71 F.3d 1, 8 n. 6 (1st Cir.1995); Duchesne v. American Airlines, Inc., 758 F.2d 27, 30 n. 3 (1st Cir.1985)—the statute is clear on that point. Equally clearly, Cosgrove errs in thinking that the award of costs in such a case is mandatory if the suit was brought in good faith. Dr. Franklin Perkins School v. Freeman, supra, 741 F.2d at 1524–25.

The defendants appeal from the part of the judgment that awarded damages for misrepresentation and unjust enrichment. The evidence that Bartolotta misrepresented a present fact—his state of mind when he made the promise—was sufficient to support the jury's verdict. So was the evidence that Cosgrove conferred on Bartolotta a benefit (the pledge of the loan, which was instrumental in enabling Bartolotta to line up bank financing, along with Cosgrove's business and legal advice) for which Cosgrove was entitled to be compensated. When one person confers a benefit on another in circumstances in which the benefactor reasonably believes that he will be paid—that is, when the benefit is not rendered gratuitously, as by an officious intermeddler, or donatively, as by an altruist or friend or relative—then he is entitled to demand the restitution of the market value of the benefit if the recipient refuses to pay. Ramsey v. Ellis, 168 Wis.2d 779, 484 N.W.2d 331, 333–34 (1992); North American Lighting, Inc. v. Hopkins Mfg. Corp., 37 F.3d 1253, 1259 (7th Cir.1994). That describes the present case. The jury could and did find that Cosgrove conferred benefits on Bartolotta in reliance on being compensated by the receipt of an ownership interest in the restaurant.

Where, however, the plaintiff has a good claim for either breach of contract or, as in this case, promissory estoppel, restitution is not really an alternative theory of liability, but an alternative method of computing damages. Should it turn out to be too difficult to value the restaurant business or to determine just how large an ownership interest in it Cosgrove had been promised or even to determine what it cost him in opportunities forgone to render these services, the value of the services that he rendered was available as an alternative measure of damages— alternative to either the opportunity or other costs to Cosgrove of the services that he rendered (the reliance measure of damages) or the value of Bartolotta's promise to him (the expectation measure of damages).

This assumes that you can get an award of expectation damages on a claim of promissory estoppel in Wisconsin, and apparently you can, see Kramer v. Alpine Valley Resort, Inc., 108 Wis.2d 417, 321 N.W.2d 293, 294 (1982), although we said you couldn't in Werner v. Xerox Corp., 732 F.2d 580, 585 (7th Cir.1984). That is of no importance here; what is important is that alternative and cumulative are not synonyms and that it was triple counting for the jury to give Cosgrove the value of the promised interest in the restaurant and the loss that he suffered as a result of Bartolotta's misrepresentation and the value of the services that he rendered to Bartolotta. All that Cosgrove sought was an award of compensatory damages, which is to say an award that would put him in the position that he would have occupied had the defendant not committed wrongful acts. Where Cosgrove would be had Bartolotta carried out his promise would be owning a chunk of Bartolotta's business, a chunk the jury valued at $117,000, presumably taking into account the risk of Cosgrove's losing his

$100,000 loan should the business sour (the restaurant business is highly risky). He would not also have been paid $17,000 for services rendered or $1,000 as a kind of "kill fee" (we don't know what other sense to make of this part of the jury's award), for the ownership share was to be the full compensation for his services. So the damages awarded by the jury were excessive, but as the defendants do not object to the verdict on this ground, the point is waived.

To summarize, the judgment is affirmed in part and reversed in part with directions to reinstate the original judgment and award the plaintiff his costs.

READING ASSIGNMENT 3

MARYLAND NATIONAL BANK V. UNITED JEWISH APPEAL FEDERATION OF GREATER WASHINGTON, INC.

Court of Appeals of Maryland
286 Md. 274 (1979)

ORTH, JUDGE.

The issue in this case is whether a pledge to a charitable institution survives the death of the pledgor and is an enforceable obligation of his estate.

I

Milton Polinger pledged $200,000 to the United Jewish Appeal Federation of Greater Washington, Inc. (UJA) for the year 1975. He died on 20 December 1976. His last will and testament was admitted to probate in the Orphans' Court for Montgomery County and letters were issued to Melvin R. Oksner and Maryland National Bank as personal representatives. At the time of Polinger's death $133,500 was unpaid on his pledge. The personal representatives disallowed the claim for the balance of the pledge. UJA filed a petition praying that the claim be allowed and moved for summary judgment. The personal representatives answered and filed a cross-motion for summary judgment. The court granted UJA's motion for summary judgment, denied the personal representatives' motion for summary judgment, allowed UJA's claim against the estate in the amount of $133,500, and assessed the costs against the personal representatives. The personal representatives noted an appeal to the Court of Special Appeals and petitioned this Court to issue a writ of certiorari to that court before decision by it. We did so.

II

The facts before the court were undisputed in material part. They showed the nature of UJA and its relationship with its beneficiaries. UJA, chartered in the District of Columbia, is a public non-profit corporation. In general, its objective is to solicit, collect and receive funds and property for the support of certain religious, charitable, philanthropic, scientific and educational organizations and institutions, and it enjoys tax exempt status federally and in Maryland, Virginia and the District of Columbia. Based on monies received and pledged, it makes allocations to tax exempt organizations. No formal commitment agreement is executed with respect to the allocations, but UJA undertakes to pay pursuant to the allocation and the beneficiary organizations "go ahead to act as though they are going to have the money and they spend it." In other words, UJA makes allocations to various beneficiary organizations based upon pledges made to it, and the beneficiary organizations incur liabilities based on the allocations. Historically 95% Of the pledges are collected over a three year period, and allowance for the 5% Which may be uncollected is made in determining the amount of the allocations. So, according to Meyer Brissman, Executive Vice-President Emeritus of UJA: "We always pay (the allocated amount). I don't know of any case where we haven't paid." Pledges to "emergency funds" are not paid on the basis of an allocation by UJA. All monies actually collected on those pledges are paid to the emergency funds.

The facts before the court showed the circumstances surrounding the pledge of Polinger with which we are here concerned. It was evidenced by a card signed by Polinger under date of 9 November 1974. It recited:

In consideration of the obligation incurred based upon this pledge, I hereby promise to pay to the United Jewish Appeal the amount indicated on this card.

The amount indicated as his "1975 pledge" was $100,000 for "UJA including local national and overseas," and $100,000 for "Israel Emergency Fund."

[Polinger's Pledge was made during a mission to Israel in 1974. The mission was key to a fundraising effort seeking large pledges from wealthy donors. The mission occurred a year after the 1973 Arab-Israeli War (also known as the Yom Kippur War, the Ramadan War, and the October War) and during the 1974 Israel missile crisis. During the mission, prospective donors met high-level government leaders and citizens who had been in such wars. After a few weeks, the prospective donors participated in a fundraising "caucus," which was designed to encourage donors to make public pledges that encouraged the other participants to make pledges. Mr. Milton, well known for his philanthropy, was used to set the pace for donations by others.]

> * * *

III

We find that the law of Maryland with regard to the enforcement of pledges or subscriptions to charitable organizations is the rule thus expressed in the Restatement of Contracts s 90 (1932):

> A promise which the promisor should reasonably expect to induce action or forbearance of a definite and substantial character on the part of the promisee and which does induce such action or forbearance is binding if injustice can be avoided only by enforcement of the promise.

We reach this conclusion through opinions of this Court in four cases, Gittings v. Mayhew, 6 Md. 113 (1854); Erdman v. Trustees Eutaw M. P. Ch., 129 Md. 595, 99 A. 793 (1917); Sterling v. Cushwa & Sons, 170 Md.

226, 183 A. 593 (1936); and American University v. Collings, 190 Md. 688, 59 A.2d 333 (1948).

Gittings concerned the building of an Atheneum. The subscription contract authorized the calling of payment of installments by the subscribers when a certain amount had been pledged. The amount was reached, installments were called for and paid, contracts to erect the building were made and the Antheneum was completed. It was in these circumstances that the Court said:

> In whatever uncertainty the law concerning voluntary subscriptions of this character may be at this time, in consequence of the numerous decisions pronounced upon the subject, it appears to be settled, that where advances have been made, or expenses or liabilities incurred by others, in consequence of such subscriptions, before notice of withdrawal, this should, on general principles, be deemed sufficient to make them obligatory, provided the advances were authorized by a fair and reasonable dependence on the subscriptions. . . . The doctrine is not only reasonable and just, but consistent with the analogies of the law. (6 Md. at 131–132.)

This statement of the law appeared to be Obiter dictum in Gittings, but if it were, it became the law in Erdman.

Erdman dealt with a suit on a promissory note whereby there was a promise to pay the Eutaw Methodist Protestant Church the sum of $500 four years after date with interest. The consideration for the note was a subscription contract made with the trustees of the church for the purpose of paying off a building debt, which had been incurred for the erection of a new church building. It had been entered on the books of the church, the trustees had subsequently borrowed $2,000 on that subscription and other subscriptions to pay off the indebtedness for the erection of the church building. The Court held that in such circumstances the subscription contract was a valid and binding one and constituted a sufficient consideration to support the note, Id. 129 Md. at 602, 99 A. 793, observing that "(t)he policy of the law, to sustain subscription contracts of the character of the one here in question, is clearly stated by this court, and by other appellate courts, in a number of cases," Id. at 600, 99 A. at 795. The only Maryland case cited was Gittings. The holding in Gittings was said to be "that as the party had authorized others by the subscription to enter into engagements for the accomplishment of the enterprise, the law requires that he should save them harmless to the extent of his subscription." Erdman, 129 Md. at 601, 99 A. at 795. One case in another appellate court was discussed, Trustees v. Garvey, 53 Ill. 401 (1870) and two cited as to like effect, McClure v. Wilson, 43 Ill. 356 (1867) and United Presbyterian Church v. Baird, 60 Iowa 237, 14 N.W. 303 (1882). In Garvey the court noted that "(a)s a matter of public policy, courts have been desirous of sustaining the legal obligation of subscriptions of this character, and in some cases ... have found a sufficient consideration in the mutuality of the promises, where no fraud or deception has been practiced." Id. at 403. "But," the court continued, "while we might be unwilling to go to that extent, and might hold that a subscription could be withdrawn before money had been expended or liability incurred, or work performed on the strength of the subscriptions, and in furtherance of the enterprise," the church trustees had, on the faith of the subscriptions, borrowed money, relying on the subscription as a means of payment and incurred a specific liability. Id. Thus, it seems that Erdman made law of the dictum in Gittings, but that law was that charitable subscriptions to be enforceable require reliance on the subscriptions by the charity which would lead to direct loss to the organization or its officers if the subscriptions were not enforced.

This principle of the law was applied in Sterling. In that case pledges were made to support a failing bank, to restore confidence in it and protect its depositors and creditors, to comply with demands of the bank commissioner so as to keep the bank open and to prevent impairment of its capital. There were, therefore, substantial considerations for the subscriptions. "Not only was every subscription expressly made in consideration of the agreement of other subscribers, who have fulfilled their pledges, but a prior subscription agreement was to be, and was, in fact, released to the specified extent, when the new one became binding, and consent of the bank commissioner to the continued functioning of the bank was thereby induced." Id. at 236, 183 A. at 597. In such circumstances, the Court declared: "The sufficiency of such considerations cannot be doubted." Id., citing Gittings and Erdman.

Gittings and Erdman were referred to in American University v. Collings, 190 Md. 688, 59 A.2d 333 (1948), as cases "which hold that where one has made a subscription and thereby authorized the entering into engagements to accomplish the purpose for which the subscription was made, the subscription was upon a valuable consideration." Id. at 691, 59 A.2d at 334. The Court carefully pointed out that "(in those) cases, however, the promisee had actually incurred obligations relying upon the promises," but that in the case it was considering there was no claim "that any such obligations had been entered into." Id. The case turned on the finding that the pledge was testamentary in nature. Id. at 692, 59 A.2d 333. Compare the dissenting opinion of Delaplaine, J., 190 Md. at 694–697, 59 A.2d 333.

In summary, the rule announced in Gittings, referred to in Collings and applied in Erdman and Sterling, is in substance the rule set out in s 90 of the Restatement of Contracts (1932). It is the settled law of this State.

IV

* * *

In Collings the Court noted that American University had cited a number of cases from other jurisdictions which, the educational institution stated, "represents the general trend of judicial authority, and it is in accordance with the better reasoned opinion, that contracts for subscriptions or donations to churches or charitable or kindred institutions which have been duly accepted are based upon a valid consideration because of the mutual obligations of other subscribers." Id., 190 Md. at 692, 59 A.2d at 334. But the Court also observed Professor Williston's criticism of this view, citing "1 Williston on Contracts, Rev.Ed. s 116." Id. In any event, as we have indicated, the Court had no occasion to decide whether the pledge involved in Collings was given for a valid consideration.

Restatement (Second) of Contracts (Tent. Draft No. 2, 1965) proposes changes in s 90. It would read:

> A promise which the promisor should reasonably expect to induce action or forbearance on the part of the promisee or a third person and which does induce such action or forbearance is binding if injustice can be avoided only by enforcement of the promise. The remedy granted for breach may be limited as justice requires.

This deletes from the existing section the qualification "of a definite and substantial character" with regard to the inducement of action or forbearance and has the inducement of forbearance apply to "a third person" as well as the promisee. It also adds the discretionary limitation as to the remedy. Comment c to the proposed Section concerns "(c)haritable subscriptions, marriage settlements, and other gifts." It begins:

> One of the functions of the doctrine of consideration is to deny enforcement to a promise to make a gift. Such a promise is ordinarily enforced by virtue of the promisee's reliance only if his conduct is foreseeable and reasonable and involves a definite and substantial change of position which would not have occurred if the promise had not been made.

This reflects the previous section and the Maryland rule. The comment then notes that "(i)n some cases, however, other policies reinforce the promisee's claim." It states:

> American courts have traditionally favored charitable subscriptions and marriage settlements, and have found consideration in many cases where the element of exchange was doubtful or nonexistent. Where recovery is rested on reliance in such cases, a probability of reliance is likely to be enough, and no effort is made to sort out mixed motives or to consider whether partial enforcement would be appropriate.

Illustration 7 is of a charitable subscription:

> A orally promises to pay B, a university, $100,000 in five annual
> installments for the purposes of its fund-raising campaign then in
> progress. The promise is confirmed in writing by A's agent, and
> two annual installments are paid before A dies. The continuance
> of the fund-raising campaign by B is sufficient reliance to make
> the promise binding on A and his estate.

Section 90 of the tentative draft No. 2 of the Restatement (Second) of
Contracts, 1965, has not been adopted by the American Law Institute, and
we are not persuaded to follow it.

"Cases throughout the country clearly reflect a conflict between the desired
goal of enforcing charitable subscriptions and the realities of contract law.
The result has been strained reasoning which has been the subject of
considerable criticism." Salsbury v. Northwestern Bell Telephone
Company, 221 N.W.2d 609, 611–612 (Iowa, 1974). When charitable
subscriptions, even though clearly gratuitous promises, have been held
either contracts or offers to contract, the "decisions are based on such a
great variety of reasoning as to show the lack of any really sufficient
consideration." Williston on Contracts, s 116 (3d ed. 1957) (footnotes
omitted). "Very likely, conceptions of public policy have shaped, more or
less subconsciously, the rulings thus made. Judges have been affected by
the thought that 'defenses of (the) character (of lack of consideration are)
breaches of faith towards the public, and especially towards those engaged
in the same enterprise, and an unwarrantable disappointment of the
reasonable expectations of those interested.'" Allegheny College v.
National Chautauqua County Bank, 246 N.Y. 369, 159 N.E. 173, 175
(1927). Therefore, "(c)ourts have . . . purported to find consideration on
various tenuous theories. . . . (The) wide variation in reasoning indicates
the difficulty of enforcing a charitable subscription on grounds of
consideration. Yet, the courts have generally striven to find grounds for
enforcement, indicating the depth of feeling in this country that private
philanthropy serves a highly important function in our society." J.
Calamari & J. Perillo, The Law of Contracts, s 6–5 (1977) (footnotes
omitted). Some courts have forthrightly discarded the facade of
consideration and admittedly held a charitable subscription enforceable
only in respect of what they conceive to be the public policy. See, for
example, Salsbury v. Northwestern Bell Telephone Company, supra; More
Game Birds in America, Inc. v. Boettger, 125 N.J.L. 97, 14 A.2d 778, 780–
781 (1940).

We are not convinced that such departure from the settled law of contracts
is in the public interest. A charitable subscription must be a contract to be
enforceable, unless we characterize it as some other type of agreement,
unknown to established contract law, for which a valid consideration is not

essential. We said in Broaddus v. First Nat. Bank, 161 Md. 116, 155 A. 309 (1931):

It is unnecessary at this time to cite authorities in this state and elsewhere to the effect that every contract must be supported by a consideration; and this must be regarded as one of the elementary principles of the law of contract. (Id. at 121, 155 A.2d 311.)

And, we recently cited Broaddus in Peer v. First Fed. S. & L. Ass'n, 273 Md. 610, 614, 331 A.2d 299, 301 (1975) in asserting, after noting several other requirements of a valid contract: "Finally, the agreement must be supported by sufficient consideration." We abide by that principle in determining the validity of the charitable subscriptions.

V

When the facts concerning the charitable subscription of Polinger are viewed in light of the Maryland law, it is manifest that his promise was not legally enforceable. There was no consideration as required by contract law. The incidents on which Gittings indicated a charitable pledge was enforceable, and on which Erdman and Sterling held the subscriptions in those cases were enforceable are not present here. The consideration recited by the pledge card was "the obligation incurred based upon this pledge. . . ." But there was no legal obligation incurred in the circumstances. Polinger's pledge was not made in consideration of the pledges of others, and there was no evidence that others in fact made pledges in consideration of Polinger's pledge. No release was given or binding agreement made by the UJA on the strength of Polinger's pledge. The pledge was not for a specific enterprise; it was to the UJA generally and to the Israel Emergency Fund. With respect to the former, no allocation by UJA to its beneficiary organization was threatened or thwarted by the failure to collect the Polinger pledge in its entirety, and, with respect to the latter, UJA practice was to pay over to the Fund only what it actually collected, not what was pledged. UJA borrowed no money on the faith and credit of the pledge. The pledge prompted no "action or forbearance of a definite and substantial character" on the part of UJA. No action was taken by UJA on the strength of the pledge that could reasonably be termed "definite and substantial" from which it should be held harmless. There was no change shown in the position of UJA made in reliance on the subscription which resulted in an economic loss, and, in fact, there was no such loss demonstrated. UJA was able to fulfill all of its allocations. Polinger's pledge was utilized as a means to obtain substantial pledges from others. But this was a technique employed to raise money. It did not supply a legal consideration to Polinger's pledge. On the facts of this case, it does not appear that injustice can be avoided only by enforcement of the promise.

To summarize, there was no specific goal prompting the pledge such as existed in Gittings, Erdman and Sterling with a mutual awareness of future reliance on the subscription. UJA did not enter into binding contracts, incur expenses or suffer liabilities in reliance on the pledge. UJA's function was to serve as a conduit or clearinghouse to collect gifts of money from many sources and to funnel them into various charitable organizations. It did, of course, plan for the future, in that it estimated the rate of cash flow based on the pledges it received and told its beneficiaries to expect certain amounts. In so doing, however, it expressly did not incur liabilities in reliance on specific pledges. It seems that none of the organizations to which it allocated money would have legal rights against UJA in the event of failure to pay the allocation, and, in any event, UJA, cognizant of the past history of collections, made due allowance for the fact that a certain percentage of the pledges would not be paid.

We hold that Polinger's pledge to UJA was a gratuitous promise. It had no legal consideration, and under the law of this State was unenforceable. The Orphans' Court for Montgomery County erred in allowing the claim for the unpaid balance of the subscription, and its order of 5 January 1979 is vacated with direction to enter an order disallowing the claim filed by UJA.

ORDER OF 5 JANUARY 1979 OF THE ORPHANS' COURT FOR MONTGOMERY COUNTY VACATED;

CASE REMANDED TO THAT COURT WITH DIRECTION TO ENTER AN ORDER DISALLOWING THE CLAIM FILED BY THE UNITED JEWISH APPEAL FEDERATION OF GREATER WASHINGTON, INC.;

COSTS TO BE PAID BY APPELLEE.

IN RE MORTON SHOE COMPANY, INC.

United States Bankruptcy Court, D. Massachusetts
40 B.R. 948 (1984)

The Debtor's Objection to the Claim of Combined Jewish Philanthropies of Greater Boston ("CJP") came before the Court1 for hearing on March 21, 1984. The parties agreed to the relevant facts and submitted the case to me on oral argument and Memoranda of Law. Based upon the agreed-upon facts and a review of the Memoranda and applicable law, I find and rule as follows.

In 1979 and in 1980 Morton Shoe Company Inc. ("the debtor" or "Morton Shoe") pledged $10,000 per year to CJP during a campaign drive. In 1976, 1977 and 1978 Morton Shoe had made contributions in the same amount, all of which were paid. The 1979 and 1980 pledges totalling $20,000 remain unpaid. CJP has filed a proof of claim for $20,000 to which the debtor timely objected.

CJP solicits pledges by sending campaign workers to address potential corporate contributors at meetings convened for such a purpose. The solicitor describes the purpose and needs of the charity. A pledge card is executed by the subscriber. The card states that the subscription is in consideration of the pledges of others. After the pledge drive, CJP establishes an operating budget, determines the amount of and recipients of distributions, and hires personnel. In addition, based on the estimated amount of subscriptions, CJP borrows money from banks so that it can make immediate distributions to recipients before obtaining the actual pledge amount. The debtor objects to the claim of CJP, asserting that it is unenforceable for lack of consideration.

Traditional legal principles require that consideration support a promise. Corbin, 1 Corbin on Contracts, Section 109 (2d ed. 1963); Jaeger, 1 Williston on Contracts, Section 99 (3d ed. 1977). Consideration is defined as ". . . a benefit to the maker of the promise, or a loss, trouble or inconvenience to, or a charge or obligation resting upon the party to whom the promise is made." Cottage Street Methodist Episcopal Church v. Kendall, 121 Mass. 528, 529–30 (1877).

The debtor objects to this claim asserting that the charitable pledge is unenforceable as it was a promise unsupported by consideration.

The allowability of claims is to be determined under state law. See L. King, 3 Collier on Bankruptcy, Par. 502.02, at 502.24 (15th ed. Supp.1983). Early Massachusetts decisions had ruled that "gratuitious or benevolent proposals prompted by charitable or religious motives . . . will not require a performance." See, e.g., Cottage Street Methodist Church v. Kendall, 121 Mass. 528 (1877); Limerick Academy v. Davis, 11 Mass. 113 (1814). The trend of judicial decisions during the last century, however, has been toward enforcement of charitable pledges as a means of encouraging philanthropy and of promoting religious, educational and social enterprises. See 73 AmJur2d, Subscriptions, Section 2, at 694–95 (Supp.1983). Courts, including those of Massachusetts, have striven to find grounds for enforcing charitable subscriptions, not without engaging in difficult legal reasoning. See J. Calamari and J. Perrillo, Contracts, Section 6–5, at 208–09 (1978).

A review of the Massachusetts case law reveals two rationales the courts have employed to justify enforcement of charitable subscriptions. A series of decisions has found legal consideration in the traditional sense in the charity's agreement to appropriate funds in accordance with the terms of the subscription. E.g., Ladies Collegiate Institute v. French, 82 Mass. 196 (1860), Ives v. Sterling, 47 Mass. 310 (1843). In the French decision, the court enforced a charitable pledge to establish a college, stating:

"It is held that by accepting such a subscription the promisee agrees on his part with the subscribers, that he will hold and appropriate the funds subscribed in conformity with the terms and the objects of the subscription, and thus mutual and independent promises are made, which constitute a legal and sufficient consideration for each other." Id. at 201.

Similarly, in Robinson v. Nutt, 185 Mass. 345, 70 N.E. 198 (1908), the court enforced a promise to make a monthly contribution to a parish, which subscription was conditioned on the parish's raising the full amount by similar contributions. The court enforced the promise against the donor's estate, holding:

Testatrix's subscription was really made in the form of a formal offer which, being accepted by the plaintiffs, became an agreement under which they entered upon the performance of the contemplated plan, by obtaining additional subscriptions from others, and as a result the combined pledges made up the full amount required. When applied the money received from time to time in reduction of the debt of the parish, the object upon which her promise depended had been accomplished.

Id. at 348, 70 N.E. 198. Accord, Estate of Wardwell v. Commissioner, 301 F.2d 632 (8th Cir.1962).

A second rationale adopted by Massachusetts case law for enforcing charitable subscriptions does not attempt to discover consideration, but rather, enforces the pledge because of the charity's reliance on the promise, such as its expenditure of money, labor, and time in furtherance of obtaining the subscription. E.g., Trustees of Amherst Academy v. Cowls, 23 Mass. 427 (1828); Farmington Academy v. Allen, 14 Mass. 171 (1817). Accord, I & I Holding Corp. v. Gainsburg, 276 N.Y. 427, 12 N.E.2d 532 (1938). In the Farmington Academy decision the court utilized the pledgor's knowledge and the town's reliance to enforce the pledge, reasoning:

". . . he was an inhabitant of the town, and must have known of the erection of the building; and he actually advanced some part of the materials, excusing himself from paying the whole subscription only on the ground of his inability at the time. This was sufficient to justify the trustees in proceeding to incur expense, on the faith of the defendant's subscription;"

Id. at 175. Similarly, in Robinson v. Nutt, 185 Mass. 345, 70 N.E. 198 (1908) the court also found that the church relied upon the promised pledge, in addition to finding legal consideration in the additional pledges of others.

Based upon these principles, I believe it is firmly established Massachusetts law that an action to enforce a charitable subscription is enforceable based on a consideration or reliance theory. As in Massachusetts, most courts have enforced charitable subscriptions by struggling to find reliance or consideration. It may be more expeditious and appropriate to eliminate the technical requirements and simply enforce pledges as a desirable social policy. In this vein, the Restatement of Contracts, Section 90, provides that a charitable subscription is enforceable without proof of reliance. Although the Restatement position is an improvement over the current need to satisfy the technical requirement, Massachusetts has not adopted this provision of the Restatement as law of this state, and it is necessary to apply current legal principles to the facts of the present case.

Whether viewed in terms of consideration or reliance, the charitable subscriptions made by Morton Shoe to CJP are enforceable under Massachusetts law, and, therefore are allowable claims in bankruptcy. The pledge document executed by Morton Shoe clearly indicates that by accepting the subscription CJP agrees to apply the pledged amounts in accordance with the charitable purposes set forth in its charter. This is sufficient consideration to support the promise. Moreover, it is clear that CJP substantially relies on the amount of pledged subscriptions in developing operating budgets, in making commitments to beneficiaries, and in borrowing funds to make payments to recipients—all in reliance on the expected payment of outstanding pledges.

For these reasons, the claim of CJP in the amount of $20,000 is allowed.

KING V. TRUSTEES OF BOSTON UNIVERSITY

Supreme Judicial Court of Massachusetts
420 Mass. 52 (1995)

ABRAMS, JUSTICE.

A jury determined that Dr. Martin Luther King, Jr., made a charitable pledge to Boston University (BU) of certain papers he had deposited with BU. The plaintiff, Coretta Scott King, in her capacity as administratrix of the estate of her late husband, and in her individual capacity, appeals from that judgment. The plaintiff sued BU for conversion, alleging that the estate and not BU held title to Dr. King's papers, which have been housed in BU's library's special collection since they were delivered to BU at Dr. King's request in July, 1964.

The case was submitted to the jury on theories of contract, charitable pledge, statute of limitations, and laches. In response to special questions the jury determined that Dr. King made a promise to give absolute title to his papers to BU in a letter signed by him and dated July 16, 1964, and that the promise to give the papers was enforceable as a charitable pledge supported by consideration or reliance. The jury also determined that the letter promising the papers was not a contract. The jury accordingly did not reach BU's additional statute of limitations and laches defenses. The trial judge denied the plaintiff's motion for judgment notwithstanding the verdict or for a new trial. The plaintiff appealed. We granted the plaintiff's application for direct appellate review. We affirm.

I.   Facts. In reviewing the judge's denial of the plaintiff's motion for directed verdict on the affirmative defense of charitable pledge, we summarize the evidence in a light favorable to the nonmoving party, BU. *Young v. Atlantic Richfield Co.*, 400 Mass. 837, 841, 512 N.E.2d 272 (1987). In 1963, BU commenced plans to expand its library's special collections. Once plans for construction of a library to house new holdings were firm, the newly appointed director of special collections, Dr. Howard Gotlieb, began his efforts to obtain Dr. King's papers. Dr. King, an alumnus of BU's graduate school program, was one of the first individuals BU officials sought to induce to deposit documents in the archives.

Around the same time, Dr. King was approached regarding his papers by other universities, including his undergraduate alma mater, Morehouse College. Mrs. King testified that, although her late husband thought "Boston seemed to be the only place, the best place, for safety," he was concerned that depositing his papers with BU would evoke criticism that he was "taking them away from a black institution in the South." However, the volatile circumstances during the 1960s in the South led Dr. King to deposit some of his papers with BU pursuant to a letter, which is the centerpiece of this litigation and is set forth herewith:

"563 Johnson Ave. NE

Atlanta, Georgia

July 16, 1964

"Boston University Library

725 Commonwealth Ave.

Boston 15, Massachusetts

"Dear Sirs:

"On this 16th day of July, 1964, I name the Boston University Library the Repository of my correspondence, manuscripts and other papers, along with a few of my awards and other materials which may come to be of interest in historical or other research.

"In accordance with this action I have authorized the removal of most of the above-mentioned papers and other objects to Boston University, including most correspondence through 1961, at once. It is my intention that after the end of each calendar year, similar files of materials for an additional year should be sent to Boston University.

"All papers and other objects which thus pass into the custody of Boston University remain my legal property until otherwise indicated, according to the statements below. However, if, despite scrupulous care, any such materials are damaged or lost while in custody of Boston University, I absolve Boston University of responsibility to me for such damage or loss.

"I intend each year to indicate a portion of the materials deposited with Boston University to become the absolute property of Boston University as an outright gift from me, until all shall have been thus given to the University. In the event of my death, all such materials deposited with the University shall become from that date the absolute property of Boston University."

"Sincerely yours,

"Martin Luther King, Jr. /s/"

At issue is whether the evidence at trial was sufficient to submit the question of charitable pledge to the jury. BU asserts that the evidence was sufficient to raise a question of fact for the jury as to whether there was a promise by Dr. King to transfer title to his papers to BU and whether any such promise was supported by consideration or reliance by BU. We agree.

II.   Evidence of an enforceable charitable pledge. Because the jury found that BU had acquired rightful ownership of the papers via a charitable pledge, but not a contract, we review the case on that basis. We note at the outset that there is scant Massachusetts case law in the area of charitable pledges and subscriptions.

A charitable subscription is "an oral or written promise to do certain acts or to give real or personal property to a charity or for a charitable purpose." See generally E.L. Fisch, D.J. Freed, & E.R. Schacter, Charities and Charitable Foundations § 63, at 77 (1974). To enforce a charitable subscription or a charitable pledge in Massachusetts, a party must establish that there was a promise to give some property to a charitable institution and that the promise was supported by consideration or reliance. Congregation Kadimah Toras-Moshe v. DeLeo, 405 Mass. 365, 367 & n. 3, 540 N.E.2d 691 (1989), and cases cited therein. See In re Morton Shoe Co., 40 B.R. 948 (Bankr.D.Mass.1984) (discussing Massachusetts law of charitable subscriptions).

The jurors were asked two special questions regarding BU's affirmative defense of rightful ownership by way of a charitable pledge: (1) "Does the letter, dated July 16, 1964, from Martin Luther King, Jr., to [BU], set forth a promise by Dr. King to transfer ownership of his papers to [BU]?"; and (2) "Did [BU] take action in reliance on that promise or was that promise supported by consideration?" In determining whether the case properly was submitted to the jury, we consider first, whether the evidence was sufficient to sustain a conclusion that the letter contained a promise to make a gift and second, whether the evidence was sufficient to support a determination that any promise found was supported by consideration or reliance.

III(A).   Evidence of a promise to make a gift. The plaintiff argues that the terms of the letter promising "to indicate a portion of the materials deposited with [BU] to become the absolute property of [BU] as an outright gift . . . until all shall have been thus given to [BU]," could not as a matter of basic contract law constitute a promise sufficient to establish an inter vivos charitable pledge because there is no indication of a bargained for exchange which would have bound Dr. King to his promise. The plaintiff asserts that the above-quoted excerpt (hereinafter "first statement") from the letter merely described an unenforceable "unilateral and gratuitous mechanism by which he might" make a gift of the papers in the future but by which he was not bound. In support of her position that Dr. King did not intend to bind himself to his statement of intent to make a gift of the papers he deposited with BU, the plaintiff points to the language which appears above the promise to make gifts of the deposited papers that "[a]ll papers and other objects which thus pass into the custody of [BU] remain my legal property until otherwise indicated, according to the statements below." According to the plaintiff, because of Dr. King's initial retention of legal ownership, BU could not reasonably rely on the letter's statements of intent to make a gift of the papers. We do not agree.

The letter contains two sentences which might reasonably be construed as a promise to give personal property to a charity or for a charitable purpose. The first statement, quoted above, is that Dr. King intended in subsequent installments to transfer title to portions of the papers in BU's custody until all the papers in its custody became its property. The second statement immediately follows the first, expressing an intent that "[i]n the event of [Dr. King's] death, all . . . materials deposited with [BU] shall become from that date the absolute property of [BU]" (hereinafter "second statement"). BU claims that these two sentences should be read together as a promise to make a gift of all of the papers deposited with it at some point between the first day of deposit and at the very latest, on Dr. King's death.

Before analyzing the first and second statements, we note the considerations governing our review. A primary concern in enforcing charitable subscriptions, as with enforcement of other gratuitous transfers such as gifts and trusts, is ascertaining the intention of the donor. See, e.g., Fuss v. Fuss (No. 2), 373 Mass. 445, 449, 368 N.E.2d 276 (1977) ("The effect of a purported transfer will be determined by the design of the original transaction as understood by the principal actors"); Stryker v. Kennard, 339 Mass. 373, 377, 159 N.E.2d 71 (1959) ("It is familiar law that in construing a trust instrument the intention of the settlor must be ascertained from the entire instrument, giving due weight to all its language, considered in the light of the attendant circumstances known to the settlor at the time of execution. The intent ascertained in this manner must prevail unless a positive rule of law forbids"). If donative intent is sufficiently clear, we shall give effect to that intent to the extent possible without abandoning basic contractual principles, such as specificity of the donor's promise, consideration, and reasonableness of the charity's reliance. DeLeo, supra 405 Mass. at 368 n. 5, 540 N.E.2d 691. In determining the intention of Dr. King as expressed in the letter and the understanding BU had of that letter, we look first to the language of the letter, in its entirety, but also consider the circumstances and relationship of the parties with respect to the papers.

III(A)(1).First statement. Regarding the first statement, the plaintiff contends that it is not a promise but a mere statement of intent to do something in the future. See, e.g., Phoenix Spring Beverage Co. v. Harvard Brewing Co., 312 Mass. 501, 506, 45 N.E.2d 473 (1942) ("A promise made with an understood intention that it is to be not legally binding, but only expressive of a present intention is not a contract"). We might agree that the first statement could induce nothing more than a "hope or mere expectation" on BU's part, if the statement were considered in a vacuum. Cf. Pappas v. Bever, 219 N.W.2d 720, 722 (Iowa 1974) ("The language of the pledge form in this case, standing alone, shows nothing more than a statement of intention. There is no evidence the pledge was intended to be obligatory" [emphasis added]). However, our interpretation of that first statement is strongly influenced by the bailor-bailee relationship the letter unequivocally establishes between Dr. King and BU.

A bailment is established by "delivery of personalty for some particular purpose, or on mere deposit, upon a contract, express or implied, that after the purpose has been fulfilled it shall be redelivered to the person who delivered it, or otherwise dealt with according to his directions, or kept until he reclaims it, as the case may be." 9 S. Williston, Contracts § 1030 (3d ed. 1967), quoting State v. Warwick, 48 Del. 568, 576, 108 A.2d 85 (1954). See Stuart v. D.N. Kelley & Son, 331 Mass. 76, 77–78, 117 N.E.2d 160 (1954), quoting D.A. Schulte, Inc. v. North Terminal Garage Co., 291 Mass. 251, 256, 197 N.E. 16 (1935) ("A bailment is essentially a consensual transaction arising out of a contract express or implied . . . and there must be an acceptance by the bailee of the goods forming the subject matter of the bailment before there can be any bailment"). The terms of the letter establish a bailment in which certain "correspondence, manuscripts and other papers, along with a few of [Dr. King's] awards" were placed in "the custody of [BU]." The bailed papers were to "remain [Dr. King's] legal property until otherwise indicated." By accepting delivery of the papers, BU assumed the duty of care as bailee set forth in the letter, that of "scrupulous care." Stuart, supra 331 Mass. at 78, 117 N.E.2d 160, quoting D.A. Schulte, Inc., supra ("It is plain the law does not thrust upon one the liabilities of a bailee without his knowledge or consent, and equally obvious that while an acceptance may be implied the law will not infer such until there is something to show notice or knowledge of the alleged bailee that the goods are in fact in his possession").

Generally there will be a case for the jury as to donative intent if property allegedly promised to a charity or other eleemosynary institution is placed by the donor in the custody of the donee. The bailor-bailee relationship established in the letter could be viewed by a rational factfinder as a security for the promise to give a gift in the future of the bailed property, and thus as evidence in addition to the statement in the letter of an intent of the donor to be bound. Furthermore, while we have been unwilling to abandon fundamental principles of contract law in determining the enforceability of charitable subscriptions, see DeLeo, supra 405 Mass. at 368 n. 4, 540 N.E.2d 691, second par. (declining to adopt Restatement [Second] of Contracts rule that charitable subscriptions enforceable without consideration or reliance where justice so requires), we do recognize that the "meeting of minds" between a donor and a charitable institution differs from the understanding we require in the context of enforceable arm's-length commercial agreements. Charities depend on donations for their existence, whereas their donors may give personal property on conditions they choose, with or without imposing conditions or demanding consideration. In re Field's Will, 15 Misc.2d 950, 951, 181 N.Y.S.2d 922 (1959), modified, 11 A.D.2d 774, 204 N.Y.S.2d 947 (1960) ("Charitable subscription agreements can rarely be regarded as part of a bargaining agreement that provide for a quid pro quo"). In combination with the letter and in the context of a disputed pledge to a charity, the bailment of Dr. King's letters provided sufficient evidence of donative intent to submit to the jury the questions whether there was a promise to transfer ownership of the bailed property and whether there was consideration or reliance on that promise.

III(A)(2).Second statement. The parties agree that a testamentary transfer of the papers by means of the July 16, 1964, letter would be invalid because the letter did not comply with the Statute of Wills. G.L. c. 191, § 1 (1992 ed.) (requiring testamentary dispositions to be subscribed by two or more competent witnesses). However, "[t]he statute of wills . . . does not prevent an owner of property from stipulating by contract for the disposition of his property at the time of his death." Hale v. Wilmarth, 274 Mass. 186, 189, 174 N.E. 232 (1931). See Roberts v. Roberts, 419 Mass. 685, 690 n. 7, 646 N.E.2d 1061 (1995), quoting National Shawmut Bank v. Joy, 315 Mass. 457, 471, 53 N.E.2d 113 (1944). The parties dispute whether the statement of intent to transfer title on Dr. King's death comports with the Statute of Frauds for contracts to make testamentary dispositions. G.L. c. 259, § 5 (1992 ed.). General Laws c. 259, § 5, provides in relevant part: "No agreement to make a will of real or personal property or to give a legacy or make a devise shall be binding unless such agreement is in writing signed by the person whose executor or administrator is sought to be charged, or by some person by him duly authorized."

The plaintiff contends that the intent that BU have absolute title to the papers in its possession from Dr. King's death forward was a disposition effective on death of the donor and was invalid because it was not in conformity with the strict formalities imposed on contracts to make testamentary dispositions under G.L. c. 259, § 5. Although the letter was a writing signed by Dr. King, the plaintiff asserts that the second statement does not satisfy the Statute of Frauds because it did not contain all the terms of an enforceable agreement. We do not agree. The Statute of Frauds was not applicable because the letter was not a contract to make a will, but rather was a promise to give BU absolute title to all papers in its possession either at some future point in Dr. King's life or on his death.

BU argues that, even if the Statute of Frauds were to apply, the letter was a writing signed by the promisor and the evidence was sufficient to assure that the risk of fraud or deceit would not increase by enforcing the agreement. As we noted above, the first statement of intent to make gifts during his lifetime of the bailed papers could have been interpreted by the jury as a promise to give gifts on which BU reasonably relied or for which BU rendered consideration. The second statement that papers not yet transferred to BU but in its custody at the time of Dr. King's death could have been interpreted by the jury as a statement of the latest date on which Dr. King intended to make a gift to BU of the bailed property. Such an interpretation states all terms of an enforceable agreement. Thus, the Statute of Frauds governing contracts to make testamentary dispositions would be satisfied.

III(B). Evidence of consideration or reliance. The judge did not err in submitting the second question on charitable pledge, regarding whether there was consideration for or reliance on the promise, to the jury. "It may be found somewhat difficult to reconcile all the views which have been taken, in the various cases that have arisen upon the validity of promises, where the ground of defence has been that they were gratuitous and without consideration." Ives v. Sterling, 6 Met. 310, 315 (1843). There was evidence that BU undertook indexing of the papers, made the papers available to researchers, and provided trained staff to care for the papers and assist researchers. BU held a convocation to commemorate receipt of the papers. Dr. King spoke at the convocation. In a speech at that time, he explained why he chose BU as the repository for his papers.

As we explained above, the letter established that so long as BU, as bailee, attended the papers with "scrupulous care," Dr. King, as bailor, would release them from liability for "any such materials . . . damaged or lost while in [its] custody." The jury could conclude that certain actions of BU, including indexing of the papers, went beyond the obligations BU assumed as a bailee to attend the papers with "scrupulous care" and constituted reliance or consideration for the promises Dr. King included in the letter to transfer ownership of all bailed papers to BU at some future date or at his death. Trustees of Amherst Academy v. Cowls, 6 Pick. 427, 431 (1828) ("It seems that an actual benefit to the promisor, or an actual loss or disadvantage to the promisee, will be a sufficient consideration to uphold a promise deliberately made. Whether the consideration received is equal in value to the sum promised to be paid, seems not to be material to the validity of a note . . ."); Ives, supra at 317–319; Ladies' Collegiate Inst. v. French, 16 Gray 196, 202 (1860).

The issue before us is not whether we agree with the jury's verdict but whether the case was properly submitted to the jury. We conclude that the letter could have been read to contain a promise supported by consideration or reliance; "[t]he issue [of whether transfer of ownership to BU was transferred by way of a charitable pledge by Dr. King] was, therefore, properly submitted to the jury, and their verdicts, unless otherwise untenable, must stand." Carr v. Arthur D. Little, Inc., 348 Mass. 469, 474, 204 N.E.2d 466 (1965) (evidence sufficient as matter of contract law to raise question of fact for jury as to existence of common employment).

IV. Jury instructions. In reviewing the instructions to a jury in a civil case, we are mindful of the purpose of the charge: "The primary purpose of instructions to a jury is to assist them in the discharge of their responsibility for finding the facts in issue and then in applying to the facts found the applicable rules of law to enable them to render a proper verdict. The instructions should be full, fair and clear as to the issues to be decided by the jury, the rules to be followed by the jury in deciding the facts, and the law they are to apply to the facts found. Instructions are not addressed to the lawyers in the case but to the jurors who are persons of varying degrees of education and experience, drawn at random from the community and from all walks of life, but who are not trained in the field of law. The language used in instructing the jury must be appropriately chosen to be helpful to such a group." Pfeiffer v. Salas, 360 Mass. 93, 100–101, 271 N.E.2d 750 (1971).

The judge instructed the jury on the elements of a charitable pledge as follows: "A charitable pledge is really another form of a contract. It is a promise by a person who is called the 'pledgor,' to give a specified sum of money or a specified property to a charitable institution or organization, called the 'pledgee.' Now that promise must be supported either by consideration by the pledgee, that is the charitable organization, or by reliance on the part of the pledgee." The trial judge also instructed the jury on BU's burden of persuasion on its affirmative defense of charitable pledge: "Boston University must prove by a fair preponderance, first that Dr. King promised to transfer ownership of the Papers to [BU] and that [second], [BU] either relied on that promise of transfer of ownership or that

[BU] supplied some consideration for that promise of transfer of ownership." Further, the jurors were instructed that "with respect to whether Dr. King promised to transfer ownership of his Papers to [BU], keep in mind that with respect to this legal theory, any promise made must be sufficiently specific, and it must be sufficiently specific so that any consideration given by the person to whom the promise is made, in this case, [BU], can specifically undertake to respond to that promise. The promise here is the transfer of ownership of his Papers to [BU]."

The plaintiff raises two challenges to the instructions on charitable pledge. The plaintiff argues that the judge erred in defining "promise" for the jury. According to the plaintiff, the judge's instruction, in response to the jury's request for a clarification of the difference between a statement of intention and a promise, that "a statement of intention without more is not a promise, but a statement of intention which binds the person who makes it to forbear from doing something or to do a certain specific thing, and which gives the person to whom the promise is made a right to expect or to claim the performance of some particular thing or act," improperly blurred the line between a statement of intent and a binding promise. We disagree. When we consider the instructions in their entirety, we think that the judge made clear, in language understandable to "persons of varying degrees of education and experience, drawn at random from the community and from all walks of life, but who are not trained in the field of law," Pfeiffer, supra, that "[a] promise made with an understood intention that it is to be not legally binding, but only expressive of a present intention, is not a contract," Phoenix Spring Beverage Co., 312 Mass. 501, 506, 45 N.E.2d 473 (1942). The instructions defining a promise were not legally incorrect.

The plaintiff argues that the judge should have instructed the jury on certain specific facts of the case, i.e., to point to and characterize particular passages of the letter. The parties dispute whether the plaintiff's challenge on appeal to the trial judge's failure to instruct the jury on a specific passage in the letter (All papers and other objects which thus pass into the custody of [BU] remain my legal property . . .) properly was preserved by plaintiff at trial. Because we agree that the plaintiff did not object to this aspect of the charge, we simply note that "[a] judge presiding over a trial by jury is not permitted to charge the jury with respect to matters of fact. . . ." Pfeiffer, supra at 99, 271 N.E.2d 750.

Judgment affirmed.

ACEVES V. U.S. BANK, N.A.

California Court of Appeals
192 Cal.App.4th 218 (2011)

MALLANO, P. J.

* * *

I

BACKGROUND

The facts of this case are taken from the allegations of the operative complaint, which we accept as true. (See Hensler v. City of Glendale (1994) 8 Cal.4th 1, 8, fn. 3, 32 Cal.Rptr.2d 244, 876 P.2d 1043.)

A. Complaint

This action was filed on April 1, 2009. Two months later, a first amended complaint was filed. On August 17, 2009, after the sustaining of a demurrer, a second amended complaint (complaint) was filed. The complaint alleged as follows.

Plaintiff Claudia Aceves, a married woman, obtained a loan from Option One Mortgage Corporation (Option One) on April 20, 2006. The loan was evidenced by a note secured by a deed of trust on Aceves's residence. Aceves borrowed $845,000 at an initial rate of 6.35 percent. After two years, the rate became adjustable. The term of the loan was 30 years. Aceves's initial monthly payments were $4,857.09.

On March 25, 2008, Option One, the mortgagee, transferred its entire interest under the deed of trust to defendant U.S. Bank, National Association, as the "Trustee for the Certificateholders of Asset Backed Securities Corporation Home Equity Loan Trust, Series OOMC 2006-HE5" (U.S. Bank). * * *

In January 2008, Aceves could no longer afford the monthly payments on the loan. On March 26, 2008, Quality Loan Service recorded a "Notice of Default and Election to Sell Under Deed of Trust." (See Civ.Code, § 2924.) Shortly thereafter, Aceves filed for bankruptcy protection under chapter 7 of the Bankruptcy Code (11 U.S.C. §§ 701–784), imposing an automatic stay on the foreclosure proceedings (see 11 U.S.C. § 362(a)). Aceves contacted U.S. Bank and was told that, once her loan was out of bankruptcy, the bank "would work with her on a mortgage reinstatement and loan modification." She was asked to submit documents to U.S. Bank for its consideration.

Aceves intended to convert her chapter 7 bankruptcy case to a chapter 13 case (see 11 U.S.C. §§ 1301–1330) and to rely on the financial resources of her husband "to save her home" under chapter 13. In general, chapter 7, entitled "Liquidation," permits a debtor to discharge unpaid debts, but a debtor who discharges an unpaid home loan cannot keep the home; chapter

13, entitled "Adjustment of Debts of an Individual with Regular Income," allows a homeowner in default to reinstate the original loan payments, pay the arrearages over time, avoid foreclosure, and retain the home. (See 1 Collier on Bankruptcy (16th ed. 2010) ¶¶ 1.07[1][a] to 1.07[1][g], 1.07[5][a] to 1.07 [5][e], pp. 1–25 to 1–30, 1–43 to 1–45.)

U.S. Bank filed a motion in the bankruptcy court to lift the stay so it could proceed with a nonjudicial foreclosure.

On or about November 12, 2008, Aceves's bankruptcy attorney received a letter from counsel for the company servicing the loan, American Home Mortgage Servicing, Inc. (American Home). The letter requested that Aceves's attorney agree in writing to allow American Home to contact Aceves directly to "explore Loss Mitigation possibilities." Thereafter, Aceves contacted American Home's counsel and was told they could not speak to her before the motion to lift the bankruptcy stay had been granted.

In reliance on U.S. Bank's promise to work with her to reinstate and modify the loan, Aceves did not oppose the motion to lift the bankruptcy stay and decided not to seek bankruptcy relief under chapter 13. On December 4, 2008, the bankruptcy court lifted the stay. On December 9, 2008, although neither U.S. Bank nor American Home had contacted Aceves to discuss the reinstatement and modification of the loan, U.S. Bank scheduled Aceves's home for public auction on January 9, 2009.

On December 10, 2008, Aceves sent documents to American Home related to reinstating and modifying the loan. On December 23, 2008, American Home informed Aceves that a "negotiator" would contact her on or before January 13, 2009—four days after the auction of her residence. On December 29, 2008, Aceves received a telephone call from "Samantha," a negotiator from American Home. Samantha said to forget about any assistance in avoiding foreclosure because the "file" had been "discharged" in bankruptcy. On January 2, 2009, Samantha contacted Aceves again, saying that American Home had mistakenly decided not to offer her any assistance: American Home incorrectly thought Aceves's loan had been discharged in bankruptcy; instead, Aceves had merely filed for bankruptcy. Samantha said that, as a result of American Home's mistake, it would reconsider a loss mitigation proposal. On January 8, 2009, the day before the auction, Samantha called Aceves's bankruptcy attorney and stated that the new balance on the loan was $965,926.22; the new monthly payment would be more than $7,200; and a $6,500 deposit was due immediately via Western Union. Samantha refused to put any of those terms in writing. Aceves did not accept the offer.

On January 9, 2009, Aceves's home was sold at a trustee's sale to U.S. Bank. On February 11, 2009, U.S. Bank served Aceves with a three-day notice to vacate the premises and, a month later, filed an unlawful detainer action against her and her husband (U.S. Bank, N.A. v. Aceves

(Super.Ct.L.A.County, 2009, No. 09H00857)). Apparently, Aceves and her husband vacated the premises during the eviction proceedings.

U.S. Bank never intended to work with Aceves to reinstate and modify the loan. The bank so promised only to convince Aceves to forgo further bankruptcy proceedings, thereby permitting the bank to lift the automatic stay and foreclose on the property.

* * *

B. Demurrer

U.S. Bank filed a demurrer separately attacking each cause of action and the requested remedies. Aceves filed opposition.

At the hearing on the demurrer, Aceves's attorney argued that Aceves and her husband "could have saved their house through bankruptcy," but "due to the promises of the bank, they didn't go those routes to save their house. [¶] . . . [¶] . . . [T]hat's the whole essence of promissory estoppel. [¶] . . . [¶] Prior to [American Home's November 12, 2008] letter, there's numerous phone contacts and conversations with [American Home], which was the agent for U.S. Bank, regarding, 'Yes, once we get leave, we will work with you, . . . and they did not work with her at all.' " The trial court replied: "The foreclosure took place. There's no promissory fraud or anything that deluded [Aceves] under the circumstances."

On October 29, 2009, the trial court entered an order sustaining the demurrer without leave to amend and a judgment in favor of U.S. Bank. Aceves filed this appeal.

II

DISCUSSION

Aceves focuses primarily on her claim for promissory estoppel, arguing it is adequately pleaded. She also contends her other claims should have survived the demurrer. U.S. Bank counters that the trial court properly dismissed the case.

* * *

A. Promissory Estoppel

" 'The elements of a promissory estoppel claim are "(1) a promise clear and unambiguous in its terms; (2) reliance by the party to whom the promise is made; (3) [the] reliance must be both reasonable and foreseeable; and (4) the party asserting the estoppel must be injured by his reliance." ' " (Advanced Choices, Inc. v. State Dept. of Health Services (2010) 182 Cal.App.4th 1661, 1672, 107 Cal.Rptr.3d 470.)

1.   Clear and Unambiguous Promise

" '[A] promise is an indispensable element of the doctrine of promissory estoppel. The cases are uniform in holding that this doctrine cannot be invoked and must be held inapplicable in the absence of a showing that a promise had been made upon which the complaining party relied to his prejudice. . . .' . . . The promise must, in addition, be 'clear and unambiguous in its terms.' " (Garcia v. World Savings, FSB (2010) 183 Cal.App.4th 1031, 1044, 107 Cal.Rptr.3d 683, citation omitted.) "To be enforceable, a promise need only be " 'definite enough that a court can determine the scope of the duty[,] and the limits of performance must be sufficiently defined to provide a rational basis for the assessment of damages.' " . . . It is only where " 'a supposed 'contract' does not provide a basis for determining what obligations the parties have agreed to, and hence does not make possible a determination of whether those agreed obligations have been breached, [that] there is no contract." ' " (Id. at p. 1045, 107 Cal.Rptr.3d 683, citation omitted.) "[T]hat a promise is conditional does not render it unenforceable or ambiguous." (Ibid.)

U.S. Bank agreed to "work with [Aceves] on a mortgage reinstatement and loan modification" if she no longer pursued relief in the bankruptcy court. This is a clear and unambiguous promise. It indicates that U.S. Bank would not foreclose on Aceves's home without first engaging in negotiations with her to reinstate and modify the loan on mutually agreeable terms.

U.S. Bank's discussion of Laks v. Coast Fed. Sav. & Loan Assn. (1976) 60 Cal.App.3d 885, 131 Cal.Rptr. 836 misses the mark. There, the plaintiffs applied for a loan and relied on promissory estoppel in arguing that the lender was bound to make the loan. The Court of Appeal affirmed the dismissal of the case on demurrer, explaining that the alleged promise to make a loan was unclear and ambiguous because it did not include all of the essential terms of a loan, including the identity of the borrower and the security for the loan. In contrast, Aceves contends U.S. Bank promised but failed to engage in negotiations toward a solution of her loan problems. Thus, the question here is simply whether U.S. Bank made and kept a promise to negotiate with Aceves, not whether, as in Laks, the bank promised to make a loan or, more precisely, to modify a loan. Aceves does not, and could not, assert she relied on the terms of a modified loan agreement in forgoing bankruptcy relief. She acknowledges that the parties never got that far because U.S. Bank broke its promise to negotiate with her toward a mutually agreeable modification. While Laks turned on the sufficiency of the terms of a loan, Aceves's claim rests on whether U.S. Bank engaged in the promised negotiations. The bank either did or did not negotiate.

Further, U.S. Bank asserts that it offered Aceves a loan modification, referring to the offer it made the day before the auction. That assertion, however, is of no avail. Aceves's promissory estoppel claim is not based on a promise to make a unilateral offer but on a promise to negotiate in an attempt to reach a mutually agreeable loan modification. And, even assuming this case involved a mere promise to make a unilateral offer, we cannot say the bank's offer satisfied such a promise in light of the offer's terms and the circumstances under which it was made.

2. Reliance on the Promise

Aceves relied on U.S. Bank's promise by declining to convert her chapter 7 bankruptcy proceeding to a chapter 13 proceeding, by not relying on her husband's financial assistance in developing a chapter 13 plan, and by not opposing U.S. Bank's motion to lift the bankruptcy stay.

3. Reasonable and Foreseeable Reliance

" 'Promissory estoppel applies whenever a "promise which the promissor should reasonably expect to induce action or forbearance on the part of the promisee or a third person and which does induce such action or forbearance" would result in an "injustice" if the promise were not enforced. . . .' " (Advanced Choices, Inc. v. State Dept. of Health Services, supra, 182 Cal.App.4th at pp. 1671–1672, 107 Cal.Rptr.3d 470, citation omitted, italics added.)

"[A] party plaintiff's misguided belief or guileless action in relying on a statement on which no reasonable person would rely is not justifiable reliance. . . . 'If the conduct of the plaintiff in the light of his own intelligence and information was manifestly unreasonable, . . . he will be denied a recovery.' " (Kruse v. Bank of America (1988) 202 Cal.App.3d 38, 54, 248 Cal.Rptr. 217, citation omitted.) A mere "hopeful expectation [ ] cannot be equated with the necessary justifiable reliance." (Id. at p. 55, 248 Cal.Rptr. 217.)

We conclude Aceves reasonably relied on U.S. Bank's promise; U.S. Bank reasonably expected her to so rely; and it was foreseeable she would do so. U.S. Bank promised to work with Aceves to reinstate and modify the loan. That would have been more beneficial to Aceves than the relief she could have obtained under chapter 13. The bankruptcy court could have reinstated the loan—permitted Aceves to cure the default, pay the arrearages, and resume regular loan payments—but it could not have modified the terms of the loan, for example, by reducing the amount of the regular monthly payments or extending the life of the loan. (See 11 U.S.C. § 1322(b)(2), (3), (5), (c)(1); 8 Collier on Bankruptcy, supra, ¶¶ 1322.06[1], 1322.07[2], 1322.09 [1]-[6], 1322.16 & fn. 5, pp. 23–24, 31–32, 34–42, 55–56.) By promising to work with Aceves to modify the loan in addition to reinstating it, U.S. Bank presented Aceves with a compelling reason to opt for negotiations with the bank instead of seeking bankruptcy relief. (See Garcia v. World Savings, FSB, supra, 183 Cal.App.4th at pp. 1041–1042, 107 Cal.Rptr.3d 683 [discussing justifiable reliance].)

We emphasize that this case involves a long-term loan secured by a deed of trust, one in which the last payment under the loan schedule would be due after the final payment under a bankruptcy plan. (See 11 U.S.C. § 1322(b)(5).) Aceves had more than 28 years left on the loan, and a bankruptcy plan could not have exceeded five years. In contrast, if a case involves a short-term loan, where the last payment under the original loan schedule is due before the final payment under the bankruptcy plan, the bankruptcy court has the authority to modify the terms of the loan. (See 11 U.S.C. § 1322(c)(2); In re Paschen (11th Cir.2002) 296 F.3d 1203, 1205–1209; 8 Collier on Bankruptcy, supra, ¶ 1322.17, pp. 57–58; March et al., Cal. Practice Guide: Bankruptcy (The Rutter Group 2010) ¶ 13:396, p. 13–45; compare id. ¶¶ 13:385 to 13:419, pp. 13–42 to 13–48 [discussing short-term debts] with id. ¶¶ 13:440 to 13:484, pp. 13–49 to 13–54 [discussing long-term debts].) The modification of a short-term loan may include "lienstripping," that is, the bifurcation of the loan into secured and unsecured components based on the value of the home, with the unsecured component subject to a "cramdown." (See In re Paschen, supra, 296 F.3d at pp. 1205–1209; 8 Collier on Bankruptcy, supra, ¶ 1322.17, pp. 57–58; see also March et al., Cal. Practice Guide: Bankruptcy, supra, ¶¶ 13:370 to 13:371.1, p. 13–41 [discussing lienstripping].) If a lien is "stripped down," the lender is "only assured of receiving full [payment] for the secured portion of the [bankruptcy] claim." (In re Paschen, supra, 296 F.3d at p. 1206.)

4. Detriment

U.S. Bank makes no attempt to hide its disdain for the protections offered homeowners by chapter 13, referring disparagingly to Aceves's bankruptcy case as "bad faith." But "Chapter 13's greatest significance for debtors is its use as a weapon to avoid foreclosure on their homes. Restricting initial . . . access to Chapter 13 protection will increase foreclosure rates for financially distressed homeowners. Loss of homes hurts not only the individual homeowner but also the family, the neighborhood and the community at large. Preserving access to Chapter 13 will reduce this harm.

"Chapter 13 bankruptcies do not result in destruction of the interests of traditional mortgage lenders. Under Chapter 13, a debtor cannot discharge a mortgage debt and keep her home. Rather, a Chapter 13 bankruptcy offers the debtor an opportunity to cure a mortgage delinquency over time—in essence it is a statutorily mandated payment plan—but one that requires the debtor to pay precisely the amount she would have to pay to the lender outside of bankruptcy. Under Chapter 13, the plan must provide the amount necessary to cure the mortgage default, which includes the fees and costs allowed by the mortgage agreement and by state law. Mortgage lenders who are secured only by an interest in the debtor's residence enjoy even greater protection under 11 U.S.C. § 1322(b)(2). . . . Known as the 'anti-modification provision,' [section] 1322(b)(2) bars a debtor from modifying any rights of such a lender—including the payment schedule provided for under the loan contract. . . . [Cf. 11 U.S.C. § 1322(c)(2) [bankruptcy court has authority to modify rights of lender, including payment schedule, in cases involving short-term mortgages]; see pt. II.A.3, ante.]

"Even though a debtor must, through reinstatement of her delinquent mortgage by a Chapter 13 repayment plan . . ., pay her full obligation to the lender, Chapter 13 remains the only viable way for most mortgage debtors to cure defaults and save their homes. Mortgage lenders are extraordinarily unwilling to accept repayment schedules outside of bankruptcy. . . . There is no history to support any claim that lenders will accommodate the need for extended workouts without the pressure of bankruptcy as an option for consumer debtors. Reducing the availability of [C]hapter 13 protection to mortgage debtors is most likely to result in higher foreclosure rates, not in greater flexibility by lenders." (DeJarnatt, Once Is Not Enough: Preserving Consumers' Rights To Bankruptcy Protection (Spring 1999) Ind. L.J. 455, 495–496, fn. omitted.)

"It is unrealistic to think mortgage companies will do workouts without the threat of the debtor's access to Chapter 13 protection. The bankruptcy process is still very protective of the mortgage industry. To the extent that the existence of Chapter 13 protections increases the costs of mortgage financing to all consumers, it can and should be viewed as an essential form of consumer insurance. . . ." (DeJarnatt, Once Is Not Enough: Preserving Consumers' Rights To Bankruptcy Protection, supra, Ind. L.J. at p. 499, fn. omitted.)

We mention just a few of the rights Aceves sacrificed by deciding to forgo a chapter 13 proceeding. First, although Aceves initially filed a chapter 7 proceeding, "a chapter 7 debtor may convert to a case[ ] under [chapter 13] at any time without court approval, so long as the debtor is eligible for relief under the new chapter." (1 Collier on Bankruptcy, supra, ¶ 1.06, p. 24, italics added; accord, March et al., Cal. Practice Guide: Bankruptcy, supra, ¶¶ 5:1700 to 5:1701, 5:1715 to 5:1731, pp. 5(II)–1, 5(II)–3 to 5(II)–5; see 11 U.S.C. § 706(a).) In addition, Aceves could have "cured" the default, reinstating the loan to predefault conditions. (See In re Frazer (9th Cir. BAP 2007) 377 B.R. 621, 628; In re Taddeo (2d Cir.1982) 685 F.2d 24, 26– 28; 11 U.S.C. § 1322(b)(5); March et al., Cal. Practice Guide: Bankruptcy, supra, ¶ 13:450, p. 13–50.) She also would have had a "reasonable time"— a maximum of five years—to make up the arrearages. (See 11 U.S.C. § 1322(b)(5), (d); 8 Collier on Bankruptcy, supra, ¶ 1322.09[5], pp. 39–40; March et al., Cal. Practice Guide: Bankruptcy, supra, ¶ 13:443, p. 13–49.) And, by complying with a bankruptcy plan, Aceves could have prevented U.S. Bank from foreclosing on the property. (See 8 Collier on Bankruptcy, supra, ¶¶ 1322.09[1] to 1322.09[3], 1322.16, pp. 34–37, 55–56.) " ' "Indeed, the bottom line of most Chapter 13 cases is to preserve and avoid foreclosure of the family house." ' " (In re King (Bankr.N.D.Fla.1991) 131 B.R. 207, 211; see also March et al., Cal. Practice Guide: Bankruptcy, supra, ¶¶ 8:1050, 8:1375 to 8:1411, pp. 8(II)–1, 8(II)–42 to 8(II)–47 [discussing automatic stay]; In re Hoggle (11th Cir.1994) 12 F.3d 1008, 1008–1012 [affirming district court order denying lender's motion for relief from automatic stay]; Lamarche v. Miles (E.D.N.Y.2009) 416 B.R. 53, 55–62 [affirming bankruptcy court order denying landlord's motion to set aside automatic stay]; In re Gatlin (Bankr.W.D.Ark.2006) 357 B.R. 519, 520–523 [denying lender's motion for relief from automatic stay].)

U.S. Bank maintains that even if Aceves had pursued relief under chapter 13, she could not have afforded the payments under a bankruptcy plan. But the complaint alleged that, with the financial assistance of her husband, Aceves could have saved her home under chapter 13. We accept the truth of Aceves's allegations over U.S. Bank's speculation. (See Hensler v. City of Glendale, supra, 8 Cal.4th at p. 8, fn. 3, 32 Cal.Rptr.2d 244, 876 P.2d 1043.) * * *

III

DISPOSITION

The order and the judgment are reversed to the extent they dismissed the claims for promissory estoppel and fraud. In all other respects, the order and judgment are affirmed. Appellant is entitled to costs on appeal.

SHOEMAKER V. COMMONWEALTH BANK

Superior Court of Pennsylvania
700 A.2d 1003

JOHNSON, JUDGE:

We are asked to determine whether a mortgagor who is obligated by a mortgage to maintain insurance on the mortgaged property can establish a cause of action in promissory estoppel based upon an oral promise made by the mortgagee to obtain insurance. We find no merit in those portions of the instant case sounding in fraud and breach of contract. We conclude, nevertheless, that a mortgagee's promise to obtain insurance can be actionable on a theory of promissory estoppel. Accordingly, on this appeal from the order granting summary judgment to the mortgagee, we affirm in part, reverse in part and remand for further proceedings.

Lorraine and Robert S. Shoemaker obtained a $25,000 mortgage on their home from Commonwealth Bank (Commonwealth). The mortgage agreement provided that the Shoemakers were required to "carry insurance" on the property. By January 1994, the Shoemakers had allowed the home-owners' insurance policy covering their home to expire. In 1995, the Shoemakers' home, still uninsured, was destroyed by fire. The parties disagree as to the series of events that occurred after the insurance had lapsed.

The Shoemakers allege that Commonwealth sent a letter to them, dated January 20, 1994, that informed them that their insurance had been cancelled and that if they did not purchase a new insurance policy, Commonwealth might "be forced to purchase [insurance] and add the premium to [their] loan balance." The Shoemakers further allege that Mrs. Shoemaker received a telephone call from a representative of Commonwealth in which the representative informed her that if the Shoemakers did not obtain insurance, Commonwealth would do so and would add the cost of the premium to the balance of the mortgage. The Shoemakers assert that they assumed, based on the letter and phone conversation, that Commonwealth had obtained insurance on their home. They also contend that they received no further contact from Commonwealth regarding the insurance and that they continued to pay premiums as a part of their loan payments. Only after the house burned, the Shoemakers allege, did they learn that the house was uninsured.

Commonwealth, on the other hand, admits that it sent the letter of January 20, but denies the Shoemakers' allegations regarding the contents of the alleged conversation between its representative and Mrs. Shoemaker. Commonwealth further claims that it obtained insurance coverage for the Shoemakers' home and notified them of this fact by a letter dated February 4, 1994. Commonwealth also asserts that it elected to allow this coverage to expire on December 1, 1994, and that, by the letter dated October 25, 1994, it informed the Shoemakers of this fact and reminded them of their obligation under the mortgage to carry insurance on the property. The Shoemakers deny receiving any letter from Commonwealth regarding the insurance other than the letter dated January 20, 1994, that informed them that their policy had expired.

After the house burned down, Mrs. Shoemaker sued Commonwealth, alleging causes of action in fraud, promissory estoppel and breach of contract; the basis for all three causes of action was Commonwealth's alleged failure to obtain insurance coverage for the Shoemaker home. By order of the court, Mr. Shoemaker was joined as an involuntary plaintiff. Commonwealth then filed a motion for summary judgment.

The trial court granted Commonwealth's motion. The court noted that, even if Commonwealth had promised to obtain insurance on the Shoemakers' home, it made no representation regarding the duration of that coverage. The court concluded that because Commonwealth had actually obtained insurance, even though the policy later expired, it had fulfilled its promise to the Shoemakers. Thus, the court reasoned that because Commonwealth had made no misrepresentation and breached no promise, the Shoemakers could not prevail on any of their causes of action. Mrs. Shoemaker now appeals.

Pennsylvania Rule of Civil Procedure 1035.2 provides that:

After the relevant pleadings are closed, but within such time as not to unreasonably delay trial, any party may move for summary judgment in whole or part as a matter of law

(1) whenever there is no genuine issue of any material fact as to a necessary element of the cause of action or defense which could be established by additional discovery or expert report, or

(2) if, after the completion of discovery relevant to the motion, including the production of expert reports, an adverse party who will bear the burden of proof at trial has failed to produce evidence of facts essential to the cause of action or defense which in a jury trial would require the issues to be submitted to a jury.

Pa.R.C.P. 1035.2. Thus, the court must enter summary judgment when there is no genuine issue of material fact and the moving party is entitled to judgment as a matter of law. Coleman v. Coleman, 444 Pa.Super. 196, 199, 663 A.2d 741, 743 (1995), appeal denied, 543 Pa. 722, 673 A.2d 330 (1996). When considering a motion for summary judgment, the court must view the evidence in the light most favorable to the nonmoving party. Hunger v. Grand Central Sanitation, 447 Pa.Super. 575, 578, 670 A.2d 173, 174, appeal denied, 545 Pa. 664, 681 A.2d 178 (1996). We will reverse the grant of a motion for summary judgment only where the court has committed an error of law. Coleman, supra, at 199, 663 A.2d at 743.

On appeal, Mrs. Shoemaker argues that the trial court erred by entering summary judgment on their fraud and promissory estoppel claims. To prevail on a fraud cause of action, a plaintiff must prove that: (1) the defendant made a misrepresentation that is material to the transaction at hand; (2) the misrepresentation was made with knowledge of the statement's falsity or with reckless disregard as to whether it was true or false; (3) the defendant made the misrepresentation with the intent of inducing reliance; (4) the plaintiff justifiably relied upon the misrepresentation; and (5) the resulting injury was proximately caused by the reliance. Gibbs v. Ernst, 538 Pa. 193, 207, 647 A.2d 882, 889 (1994).

Mrs. Shoemaker argues that Commonwealth made a misrepresentation to her when its representative, in a telephone conversation, stated that Commonwealth would purchase insurance coverage and add the cost of the premium to the cost of her and her husband's loan. Mrs. Shoemaker directs our attention to her deposition testimony:

Q: So you've spoken to a Commonwealth Bank representative on the issue of insurance on your home once and only once; is that correct.

A: Correct.

. . . .

Q: What do you believe [the representative] said?

A: He mentioned that there had been a letter sent to me that the insurance had expired. I didn't recall receiving the letter. He also mentioned that as far as the loan was concerned I was required to have insurance on the property. He basically said that they would acquire insurance for me. I told them go ahead and do so because at that point I was in no financial situation to so on my own.

. . . .

Q: So basically this person from Commonwealth Bank was telling you that because they, Commonwealth Bank, got a notice that the insurance was being terminated that they, the bank, were going to put insurance on the property and they were going to add the cost of doing so to your mortgage; and you told them, go right ahead?

A: Yes.

N.T., deposition of Lorraine Shoemaker, September 9, 1996, at 17–19; R.R. at 38a–39a (emphasis added). Thus, Mrs. Shoemaker claims that the misrepresentation that forms the basis of her and her husband's fraud claim was Commonwealth's promise to obtain insurance for their home.

It is well-established that the breach of a promise to do something in the future is not actionable in fraud. Krause v. Great Lakes Holdings, Inc., 387 Pa.Super. 56, 67, 563 A.2d 1182, 1187 (1989); Edelstein v. Carole House Apartments, Inc., 220 Pa.Super. 298, 303, 286 A.2d 658, 661 (1971). The Shoemakers base their fraud claim on Commonwealth's alleged promise that it would obtain an insurance policy for their home if they failed to do so. Commonwealth was, therefore, promising to take future action. Thus, Commonwealth's promise cannot form the basis of a cause of action in fraud. See Krause, supra, at 67, 563 A.2d at 1187 (an oral representation that a party would assume a debt obligation in exchange for the forbearance from legal action was not actionable in fraud because the representation was a promise to do something in the future); Edelstein, supra, at 304, 286 A.2d at 661 (a promise to relieve person of liability if certain condition was met is not actionable in fraud because representation was promise to do something in the future). We therefore hold that the trial court properly granted summary judgment on the fraud claim.

Mrs. Shoemaker next argues that the trial court erred by granting summary judgment on their promissory estoppel claim. The doctrine of promissory estoppel allows a party, under certain circumstances, to enforce a promise even though that promise is not supported by consideration. See Thatcher's Drug Store of West Goshen, Inc., v. Consolidated Supermarkets, Inc., 535 Pa. 469, 476, 636 A.2d 156, 160 (1994); Restatement (Second) of Contracts § 90. To establish a promissory estoppel cause of action, a party must prove that: (1) the promisor made a promise that he should have reasonably expected would induce action or forbearance on the part of the promisee; (2) the promisee actually took action or refrained from taking action in reliance on the promise; and (3) injustice can be avoided only by enforcing the promise. Holewinski v. Children's Hospital of Pittsburgh, 437 Pa.Super. 174, 178, 649 A.2d 712, 714 (1994), appeal denied, 540 Pa. 641, 659 A.2d 560 (1995); Cardamone v. University of Pittsburgh, 253 Pa.Super. 65, 74, 384 A.2d 1228, 1233 (1978).

In their complaint, the Shoemakers allege that Commonwealth promised that it would purchase "adequate insurance" and add the cost of the premium to the cost of their loan. They further allege that they relied on this promise by not purchasing the insurance on their own and that injustice can be avoided only by enforcing Commonwealth's promise. Commonwealth, on the other hand, argues that the Shoemakers cannot enforce their claim through promissory estoppel because of the Shoemakers' contractual obligation to maintain insurance under the mortgage. Further, Commonwealth argues that even if such a promise was actionable, the facts alleged by the Shoemakers are insufficient to support their claim because they have not alleged that Commonwealth promised to maintain such insurance for a particular duration.

Our research has not discovered any Pennsylvania cases that have addressed the question of whether a mortgagor who is obligated by a mortgage to maintain insurance on their property can establish a cause of action in promissory estoppel based upon an oral promise made by the mortgagee to obtain insurance. We have, however, discovered cases from other jurisdictions that have addressed this question, and the weight of this authority holds that such promises are actionable.

In Graddon v. Knight, 138 Cal.App.2d 577, 292 P.2d 632 (1956), a California appellate court considered whether homeowners, who were obligated under a deed of trust to procure and maintain fire insurance on their home, could establish a cause of action based upon an oral promise by a bank to obtain the insurance on the homeowners' behalf. The court first considered whether the bank's promise to obtain fire insurance was inconsistent with the term of the deed of trust that required the homeowners to concluded that the bank's promise was not inconsistent with the homeowners' obligation under the deed of trust because the deed required only that the homeowners procure and maintain insurance; the deed did not bar them from making a separate agreement under which another party would procure the insurance on their behalf. Id. at 635–36.

The court then held that the evidence presented by the plaintiffs was sufficient to establish a cause of action in promissory estoppel because the plaintiffs relied to their detriment on the bank's promise to obtain insurance. Id. at 636–37; cf. Franklin Investment Co., Inc. v. Huffman, 393 A.2d 119, 122 (D.C.1978) (a gratuitous promise to procure insurance on an automobile obligated the promisor under an estoppel theory to fulfill the promise and obtain insurance); East Providence Credit Union v. Geremia, 103 R.I. 597, 239 A.2d 725, 727–28 (1968) (an owner of chattels could recover based on a theory of promissory estoppel where a loan agreement obligated the owner to maintain insurance on the property; the owner relied on the lender's promise to obtain such insurance, the lender failed to do so and property destroyed) (dicta); Estes v. Lloyd Hammerstad, Inc., 8 Wash.App. 22, 503 P.2d 1149, 1152 (1972) (a gratuitous promise to obtain insurance was enforceable under an estoppel theory). In accord with these cases, illustration 13 to comment e of section 90 of the Restatement (Second) of Contracts provides:

A, a bank, lends money to B on the security of a mortgage on B's new home. The mortgage requires B to insure the property. At the closing of the transaction A promises to arrange for the required insurance, and in reliance on the promise B fails to insure. Six months later the property, still uninsured, is destroyed by fire. The promise is binding.

Restatement (Second) of Contracts § 90, cmt. e, illus. 13. See also Murphy v. Burke, 454 Pa. 391, 398, 311 A.2d 904, 908 (1973) (adopting section 90 as Pennsylvania law). We find this authority persuasive and thus we reject Commonwealth's claim that the Shoemakers cannot maintain a cause of action because of their obligation under the mortgage to maintain insurance on the property.

[7]   We must next determine whether the Shoemakers' allegations and the evidence that they have presented are sufficient to create genuine issues of material fact with regard to each element of a promissory estoppel cause of action and thus survive Commonwealth's motion for summary judgment. The first element of a promissory estoppel cause of action is that the promisor made a promise that he should reasonably have expected to induce action or forbearance on the part of the promisee. Holewinski, supra, at 178, 649 A.2d at 714. The Shoemakers have alleged that the bank promised to obtain insurance on their behalf and that it would add this cost to their mortgage payment. Mrs. Shoemaker testified in her deposition and swore in an affidavit that a representative from Commonwealth stated that the bank would acquire insurance if she did not and that she instructed the representative to take that action. Because the Shoemakers claim that Commonwealth's promise to obtain insurance was, essentially, conditioned upon the Shoemakers course of conduct, i.e., that Commonwealth would obtain insurance if they did not, we conclude that this evidence, if believed, would be sufficient to allow a jury to find that Commonwealth made a

promise upon which it reasonably should have expected the Shoemakers to rely. See Holewinski, supra.

The second element of a promissory estoppel cause of action is that the promisee actually relied upon the promise. Id. at 178, 649 A.2d at 714. The Shoemakers allege that they actually relied upon Commonwealth's promise and, thus, failed to obtain insurance. In support of this allegation, Mrs. Shoemaker testified in her deposition and swore in her affidavit that she instructed Commonwealth's representative to acquire insurance on her behalf. We conclude that this evidence, if believed, would be sufficient to allow a jury to find that the Shoemakers relied upon Commonwealth's promise to obtain insurance. See Holewinski, supra.

The final element of a promissory estoppel cause of action is that injustice can be avoided only by enforcement of the promise. Id. at 178, 649 A.2d at 714. One of the factors that a court may consider in determining whether a promisee has satisfied this element is "'the reasonableness of the promisee's reliance.'" Thatcher's Drug Store, supra, at 477, 636 A.2d at 160, quoting Restatement (Second) of Contracts § 90, cmt. b. Mrs. Shoemaker testified that she and her husband received no communication from Commonwealth regarding their insurance after her conversation with a Commonwealth representative in early 1994. Commonwealth, on the other hand, asserts that it sent the Shoemakers letters informing them that their house would be uninsured after December 1, 1994. We conclude that this evidence is sufficient to create a genuine issue of material fact regarding the reasonableness of the Shoemakers' reliance. Accordingly, we hold that the trial court erred by granting summary judgment on the Shoemakers' promissory estoppel claim.

Finally, the Shoemakers also allege a breach of contract cause of action in their complaint. The trial court granted summary judgment on that claim. Mrs. Shoemaker has made no argument in regard to the contract claim in her brief to this Court. Accordingly, we conclude that she has waived any argument that the trial court erred by granting summary judgment on the contract claim. Olmo v. Matos, 439 Pa.Super. 1, 9, 653 A.2d 1, 5 (1994), appeal denied, 541 Pa. 652, 664 A.2d 542 (1995) (failure to develop argument in the brief results in waiver of the issue).

We therefore reverse that portion of the trial court's order that granted summary judgment on the Shoemakers' promissory estoppel claim and remand for trial on that claim. We affirm the grant of summary judgment on the Shoemakers' fraud and breach of contract claims.

Order AFFIRMED in part, REVERSED in part. Case REMANDED for further proceedings consistent with this Opinion. Jurisdiction RELINQUISHED.

READING ASSIGNMENT 4

HOFFMAN V. RED OWL STORES, INC.
Supreme Court of Wisconsin
26 Wis.2d 683 (1965)

Action for damages. The Circuit Court for Outagamie County, A. W. Parnell, J., entered judgment approving all portions of verdict except for damages as to one item and the defendants appealed and the plaintiffs cross-appealed. The Supreme Court, Currie, C. J., held that court concluded that injustice would result if plaintiffs were not granted damages because of failure of corporation to keep promises made concerning operation of franchise agency store by plaintiffs who had been induced to act to their detriment by those promises.

Order affirmed.

Action by Joseph Hoffman (hereinafter 'Hoffman') and wife, plaintiffs, against defendants Red Owl Stores, Inc. (hereinafter 'Red Owl') and Edward Lukowitz.

The complaint alleged that Lukowitz, as agent for Red Owl, represented to and agreed with plaintiffs that Red Owl would build a store building in Chilton and stock it with merchandise for Hoffman to operate in return for which plaintiffs were to put up and invest a total sum of $18,000; that in reliance upon the above mentioned agreement and representations plaintiffs sold their bakery building and business and their grocery store and business; also in reliance on the agreement and representations Hoffman purchased the building site in Chilton and rented a residence for himself and his family in Chilton; plaintiffs' actions in reliance on the representations and agreement disrupted their personal and business life; plaintiffs lost substantial amounts of income and expended large sums of money as expenses. Plaintiffs demanded recovery of damages for the breach of defendants' representations and agreements.

The action was tried to a court and jury. The facts hereafter stated are taken from the evidence adduced at the trial. Where there was a conflict in the evidence the version favorable to plaintiffs has been accepted since the verdict rendered was in favor of plaintiffs.

Hoffman assisted by his wife operated a bakery at Wautoma from 1956 until sale of the building late in 1961. The building was owned in joint tenancy by him and his wife. Red Owl is a Minnesota corporation having its home office at Hopkins, Minnesota. It owns and operates a number of grocery supermarket stores and also extends franchises to agency stores which are owned by individuals, partnerships and corporations. Lukowitz resides at Green Bay and since September, 1960, has been divisional manager for Red Owl in a territory comprising Upper Michigan and most of Wisconsin in charge of 84 stores. Prior to September, 1960, he was district manager having charge of approximately 20 stores.

In November, 1959, Hoffman was desirous of expanding his operations by establishing a grocery store and contacted a Red Owl representative by the name of Jansen, now deceased. Numerous conversations were had in 1960 with the idea of establishing a Red Owl franchise store in Wautoma. In September, 1960, Lukowitz succeeded Jansen as Red Owl's representative in the negotiations. Hoffman mentioned that $18,000 was all the capital he had available to invest and he was repeatedly assured that this would be sufficient to set him up in business as a Red Owl store. About Christmastime, 1960, Hoffman thought it would be a good idea if he bought a small grocery store in Wautoma and operated it in order that he gain experience in the grocery business prior to operating a Red Owl store in some larger community. On February 6, 1961, on the advice of Lukowitz and Sykes, who had succeeded Lukowitz as Red Owl's district manager, Hoffman bought the inventory and fixtures of a small grocery store in Wautoma and leased the building in which it was operated.

After three months of operating this Wautoma store, the Red Owl representatives came in and took inventory and checked the operations and found the store was operating at a profit. Lukowitz advised Hoffman to sell the store to his manager, and assured him that Red Owl would find a larger store from him elsewhere. Acting on this advice and assurance, Hoffman sold the fixtures and inventory to his manager on June 6, 1961. Hoffman was reluctant to sell at that time because it meant losing the summer tourist business, but he sold on the assurance that he would be operating in a new location by fall and that he must sell this store if he wanted a bigger one. Before selling, Hoffman told the Red Owl representatives that he had $18,000 for 'getting set up in business' and they assured him that there would be no problems in establishing him in a bigger operation. The makeup of the $18,000 was not discussed; it was understood plaintiff's father-in-law would furnish part of it. By June, 1961, the towns for the new grocery store had been narrowed down to two, kewaunee and Chilton. In Kewaunee, Red Owl had an option on a building site. In Chilton, Red Owl had nothing under option, but it did select a site to which plaintiff obtained an option at Red Owl's suggestion. The option stipulated a purchase price of $6,000 with $1,000 to be paid on election to purchase and the balance to be paid within 30 days. On Lukowitz's assurance that everything was all set plaintiff paid $1,000 down on the lot on September 15th.

On September 27, 1961, plaintiff met at Chilton with Lukowitz and Mr. Reymund and Mr. Carlson from the home office who prepared a projected financial statement. Part of the funds plaintiffs were to supply as their investment in the venture were to be obtained by sale of their Wautoma bakery building.

On the basis of this meeting Lukowitz assured Hoffman: '* * * [E]verything is ready to go. Get your money together and we are set.' Shortly after this meeting Lukowitz told plaintiffs that they would have to sell their bakery business and bakery building, and that their retaining this property was the only 'hitch' in the entire plan. On November 6, 1961, plaintiffs sold their bakery building for $10,000. Hoffman was to retain the bakery equipment as he contemplated using it to operate a bakery in connection with his Red Owl store. After sale of the bakery Hoffman obtained employment on the night shift at an Appleton bakery.

The record contains different exhibits which were prepared in September and October, some of which were projections of the fiscal operation of the business and others were proposed building and floor plans. Red Owl was to procure some third party to buy the Chilton lot from Hoffman, construct the building, and then lease it to Hoffman. No final plans were ever made, nor were bids let or a construction contract entered. Some time prior to November 20, 1961, certain of the terms of the lease under which the building was to be rented by Hoffman were understood between him and Lukowitz. The lease was to be for 10 years with a rental approximating $550 a month calculated on the basis of 1 percent per month on the building cost, plus 6 percent of the land cost divided on a monthly basis. At the end of the 10-year term he was to have an option to renew the lease for an additional 10-year period or to buy the property at cost on an instalment basis. There was no discussion as to what the instalments would be or with respect to repairs and maintenance.

On November 22nd or 23rd, Lukowitz and plaintiffs met in Minneapolis with Red Owl's credit manager to confer on Hoffman's financial standing and on financing the agency. Another projected financial statement was there drawn up entitled, 'Proposed Financing For An Agency Store.' This showed Hoffman contributing $24,100 of cash capital of which only $4,600 was to be cash possessed by plaintiffs. Eight thousand was to be procured as a loan from a Chilton bank secured by a mortgage on the bakery fixtures, $7,500 was to be obtained on a 5 percent loan from the father-in-law, and $4,000 was to be obtained by sale of the lot to the lessor at a profit.

A week or two after the Minneapolis meeting Lukowitz showed Hoffman a telegram from the home office to the effect that if plaintiff could get another $2,000 for promotional purposes the deal could go through for $26,000. Hoffman stated he would have to find out if he could get another $2,000. He met with his father-in-law, who agreed to put $13,000 into the business provided he could come into the business as a partner. Lukowitz told Hoffman the partnership arrangement 'sounds fine' and that Hoffman should not go into the partnership arrangement with the 'front office.' On January 16, 1962, the Red Owl credit manager teletyped Lukowitz that the father-in-law would have to sign an agreement that the $13,000 was either a gift or a loan subordinate to all general creditors and that he would prepare the agreement. On January 31, 1962, Lukowitz teletyped the home office that the father-in-law would sign one or other of the agreements. However, Hoffman testified that it was not until the final meeting some time between January 26th and February 2nd, 1962, that he was told that his father-in-law was expected to sign an agreement that the $13,000 he was advancing was to be an outright gift. No mention was then made by the Red Wol representatives of the alternative of the father-in-law signing a subordination agreement. At this meeting the Red Owl agents presented Hoffman with the following projected financial statement:

"Capital required in operation:

"Cash	$ 5,000.00	
"Merchandise	20,000.00	
"Bakery	18,000.00	
"Fixtures	17,500.00	
"Promotional Funds	1,500.00	
"TOTAL:		$62,000.00

"Source of funds:

"Red Owl 7-day terms	$ 5,000.00	
"Red Owl Fixture contract (Term 5 years)	14,000.00	
"Bank loans (Term 9 years Union State Bank of Chilton (Secured by Bakery Equipment)	8,000.00	
"Other loans (Term No-pay) No interest "Father-in-law "(Secured by None)	13,000.00	
"(Secured by Mortgage on Wautoma Bakery Bldg.)	$ 2,000.00	
"Resale of land:	6,000.00	
"Equity Capital:	$ 5,000.00 Cash 17,500.00-Bakery Equip.	
"Amount owner has to invest:	22,500.00	
"TOTAL:		$70,000.00

Hoffman interpreted the above statement to require of plaintiffs a total of $34,000 cash made up of $13,000 gift from his father-in-law, $2,000 on mortgage, $8,000 on Chilton bank loan, $5,000 in cash from plaintiff, and $6,000 on the resale of the Chilton lot. Red Owl claims $18,000 is the total of the unborrowed or unencumbered cash, that is, $13,000 from the father-in-law and $5,000 cash from Hoffman himself. Hoffman informed Red Owl he could not go along with this proposal, and particularly objected to the requirement that his father-in-law sign an agreement that his $13,000 advancement was an absolute gift. This terminated the negotiations between the parties.

The case was submitted to the jury on a special verdict with the first two questions answered by the court. This verdict, as returned by the jury, was as follows:

'Question No. 1: Did the Red Owl Stores, Inc. and Joseph Hoffman on or about mid-May of 1961 initiate negotiations looking to the establishment of Joseph Hoffman as a franchise operator of a Red Owl Store in Chilton? Answer: Yes. (Answered by the Court.)

'Question No. 2: Did the parties mutually agree on all of the details of the proposal so as to reach a final agreement thereon? Answer: No. (Answered by the Court.)

'Question No. 3: Did the Red Owl Stores, Inc., in the course of said negotiations, make representations to Joseph Hoffman that if he fulfilled certain conditions that they would establish him as franchise operator of a Red Owl Store in Chilton? Answer: Yes.

'Question No. 4: If you have answered Question No. 3 'Yes,' then answer this question: Did Joseph Hoffman rely on said representations and was he induced to act thereon? Answer: Yes.

'Question No. 5: If you have answered Question No. 4 'Yes,' then answer this question: Ought Joseph Hoffman, in the exercise of ordinary care, to have relied on said representations? Answer: Yes.

'Question No. 6: If you have answered Question No. 3 'Yes' then answer this question: Did Joseph Hoffman fulfill all the conditions he was required to fulfill by the terms of the negotiations between the parties up to January 26, 1962? Answer: Yes.

'Question No. 7: What sum of money will reasonably compensate the plaintiffs for such damages as they sustained by reason of:

'(a) The sale of the Wautoma store fixtures and inventory?

'Answer: $16,735.00.

'(b) The sale of the bakery building?

'Answer: $2,000.00.

'(c) Taking up the option on the Chilton lot?

'Answer: $1,000.00.

'(d) Expenses of moving his family to Neenah?

'Answer: $140.00.

'(e) House rental in Chilton?

'Answer: $125.00.'

Plaintiffs moved for judgment on the verdict while defendants moved to change the answers to Questions 3, 4, 5, and 6 from 'Yes' to 'No', and in the alternative for relief from the answers to the subdivisions of Question 7 or new trial. On March 31, 1964, the circuit court entered the following order:

'IT IS ORDERED in accordance with said decision on motions after verdict hereby incorporated herein by reference:

'1. That the answer of the jury to Question No. 7(a) be and the same is hereby vacated and set aside and that a new trial be had on the sole issue of the damages for loss, if any, on the sale of the Wautoma store, fixtures and inventory.

'2. That all other portions of the verdict of the jury be and hereby are approved and confirmed and all afterverdict motions of the parties inconsistent with this order are hereby denied.'

Defendants have appealed from this order and plaintiffs have cross-appealed from paragraph 1. thereof.

* * *

Opinion

CURRIE, CHIEF JUSTICE.

The instant appeal and cross-appeal present these questions:

(1) Whether this court should recognize causes of action grounded on promissory estoppel as exemplified by sec. 90 of Restatement, 1 Contracts?

(2) Do the facts in this case make out a cause of action for promissory estoppel?

(3) Are the jury's findings with respect to damages sustained by the evidence?

Recognition of a Cause of Action Grounded on Promissory Estoppel

Sec. 90 of Restatement, 1 Contracts, provides (at p. 110):

'A promise which the promisor should reasonably expect to induce action or forbearance of a definite and substantial character on the part of the promisee and which does induce such action of forbearance is binding if injustice can be avoided only by enforcement of the promise.'

The Wisconsin Annotations to Restatement, Contracts, prepared under the direction of the late Professor William H. Page and issued in 1933, stated (at p. 53, sec. 90):

'The Wisconsin cases do not seem to be in accord with this section of the Restatement. It is certain that no such proposition has ever been announced by the Wisconsin court and it is at least doubtful if it would be approved by the court.'

Since 1933, the closest approach this court has made to adopting the rule of the Restatement occurred in the recent case of Lazarus v. American Motors Corp. (1963), 21 Wis.2d 76, 85, 123 N.W.2d 548, 553, wherein the court stated:

'We recognize that upon different facts it would be possible for a seller of steel to have altered his position so as to effectuate the equitable considerations inherent in sec. 90 of the Restatement.'

While it was not necessary to the disposition of the Lazarus Case to adopt the promissory estoppel rule of the Restatement, we are squarely faced in the instant case with that issue. Not only did the trial court frame the special verdict on the theory of sec. 90 of Restatement, 1 Contracts, but no other possible theory has been presented to or discovered by this court which would permit plaintiffs to recover. Of other remedies considered that of an action for fraud and deceit seemed to be the most comparable. An action at law for fraud, however, cannot be predicated on unfulfilled promises unless the promisor possessed the present intent not to perform. Suskey v. Davidoff (1958), 2 Wis.2d 503, 507, 87 N.W.2d 306, and cases cited. Here, there is no evidence that would support a finding that Lukowitz made any of the promises, upon which plaintiffs' complaint is predicated, in had faith with any present intent that they would not be fulfilled by Red Owl.

Many courts of other jurisdictions have seen fit over the years to adopt the principle of promissory estoppel, and the tendency in that direction continues. As Mr. Justice McFADDIN, speaking in behalf of the Arkansas court, well stated, that the development of the law of promissory estoppel 'is an attempt by the courts to keep remedies abreast of increased moral consciousness of honesty and fair representations in all business dealings.' Peoples National Bank of Little Rock v. Linebarger Construction Company (1951), 219 Ark. 11, 17, 240 S.W.2d 12, 16. For a further discussion of the doctrine of promissory estoppel, see 1A Corbin, Contracts, pp. 187, et seq., secs. 193–209; 3 Pomeroy's Equity Jurisprudence (5th ed.), pp. 211, et seq., sec. 808b; 1 Williston, Contracts (Jaeger's 3d ed.), pp. 607, et seq., sec. 140; Boyer, Promissory Estoppel: Requirements and Limitations of the Doctrine 98 University of Pennsylvania Law Review (1950), 459; Seavey Reliance

Upon Gratuitous Promises or Other Conduct, 64 Harvard Law Review (1951), 913; Annos. 115 A.L.R. 152, and 48 A.L.R.2d 1069.

The Restatement avoids use of the term 'promissory estoppel,' and there has been criticism of it as an inaccurate term. See 1A Corbin, Contracts, p. 232, et seq., sec. 204. On the other hand, Williston advocated the use of this term or something equivalent. 1 Williston, Contracts (1st ed.), p. 308, sec. 139. Use of the word 'estoppel' to describe a doctrine upon which a party to a lawsuit may obtain affirmative relief offends the traditional concept that estoppel merely serves as a shield and cannot serve as a sword to create a cause of action. See Utschig v. McClone (1962), 16 Wis.2d 506, 509, 114 N.W.2d 854. 'Attractive nuisance' is also a much criticized term. See concurring opinion, Flamingo v. City of Waukesha (1952), 262 Wis. 219, 227, 55 N.W.2d 24. However, the latter term is still in almost universal use by the courts because of the lack of the better substitute. The same is also true of the wide use of the term 'promissory estoppel.' We have employed its use in this opinion not only because of its extensive use by other courts but also since a more accurate equivalent has not been devised.

Because we deem the doctrine of promissory estoppel, as stated in sec. 90 of Restatement, 1 Contracts, is one which supplies a needed tool which courts may employ in a proper case to prevent injustice, we endorse and adopt it.

Applicability of Doctrine to Facts of this Case

The record here discloses a number of promises and assurances given to Hoffman by Lukowitz in behalf of Red Owl upon which plaintiffs relied and acted upon to their detriment.

Foremost were the promises that for the sum of $18,000 Red Owl would establish Hoffman in a store. After Hoffman had sold his grocery store and paid the $1,000 on the Chilton lot, the $18,000 figure was changed to $24,100. Then in November, 1961, Hoffman was assured that if the $24,100 figure were increased by $2,000 the deal would go through. Hoffman was induced to sell his grocery store fixtures and inventory in June, 1961, on the promise that he would be in his new store by fall. In November, plaintiffs sold their bakery building on the urging of defendants and on the assurance that this was the last step necessary to have the deal with Red Wol go through.

We determine that there was ample evidence to sustain the answers of the jury to the questions of the verdict with respect to the promissory representations made by Red Owl, Hoffman's reliance thereon in the exercise of ordinary care, and his fulfillment of the conditions required of him by the terms of the negotiations had with Red Owl.

There remains for consideration the question of law raised by defendants that agreement was never reached on essential factors necessary to establish a contract between Hoffman and Red Owl. Among these were the size, cost, design, and layout of the store building; and the terms of the lease with respect to rent, maintenance, renewal, and purchase options. This poses the question of whether the promise necessary to sustain a cause of action for promissory estoppel must embrace all essential details of a proposed transaction between promisor and promisee so as to be the equivalent of an offer that would result in a binding contract between the parties if the promisee were to accept the same.

Originally the doctrine of promissory estoppel was invoked as a substitute for consideration rendering a gratuitous promise enforceable as a contract. See Williston, Contracts (1st ed.), p. 307, sec. 139. In other words, the acts of reliance by the promisee to his detriment provided a substitute for consideration. If promissory estoppel were to be limited to only those situations where the promise giving rise to the cause of action must be so definite with respect to all details that a contract would result were the promise supported by consideration, then the defendants' instant promises to Hoffman would not meet this test. However, see. 90 of Restatement, 1 Contracts, does not impose the requirement that the promise giving rise to the cause of action must be so comprehensive in scope as to meet the requirements of an offer that would ripen into a contract if accepted by the promisee. Rather the conditions imposed are:

    (1) Was the promise one which the promisor should reasonably expect to induce action or forbearance of a definite and substantial character on the part of the promisee?

    (2) Did the promise induce such action or forbearance?

    (3) Can injustice be avoided only by enforcement of the promise?

We deem it would be a mistake to regard an action grounded on promissory estoppel as the equivalent of a breach of contract action. As Dean Boyer points out, it is desirable that fluidity in the application of the concept be maintained. 98 University of Pennsylvania Law Review (1950), 459, at page 497. While the first two of the above listed three requirements of promissory estoppel present issues of fact which ordinarily will be resolved by a jury, the third requirement, that the remedy can only be invoked where necessary to avoid injustice, is one that involves a policy decision by the court. Such a policy decision necessarily embraces an element of discretion.

We conclude that injustice would result here if plaintiffs were not granted some relief because of the failure of defendants to keep their promises which induced plaintiffs to act to their detriment.

Damages

Defendants attack all the items of damages awarded by the jury.

The bakery building at Wautoma was sold at defendants' instigation in order that Hoffman might have the net proceeds available as part of the cash capital he was to invest in the Chilton store venture. The evidence clearly establishes that it was sold at a loss of $2,000. Defendants contend that half of this loss was sustained by Mrs. Hoffman because title stood in joint tenancy. They point out that no dealings took place between her and defendants as all negotiations were had with her husband. Ordinarily only the promisee and not third persons are entitled to enforce the remedy of promissory estoppel against the promisor. However, if the promisor actually foresees, or has reason to foresee, action by a third person in reliance on the promise, it may be quite unjust to refuse to perform the promise. 1A Corbin, Contracts, p. 220, sec. 200. Here not only did defendants foresee that it would be necessary for Mrs. Hoffman to sell her joint interest in the bakery building, but defendants actually requested that this be done. We approve the jury's award of $2,000 damages for the loss incurred by both plaintiffs in this sale.

Defendants attack on two grounds the $1,000 awarded because of Hoffman's payment of that amount on the purchase price of the Chilton lot. The first is that this $1,000 had already been lost at the time the final negotiations with Red Owl fell through in January, 1962, because the remaining $5,000 of purchase price had been due on October 15, 1961. The record does not disclose that the lot owner had foreclosed Hoffman's interest in the lot for failure to pay this $5,000. The $1,000 was not paid for the option, but had been paid as part of the purchase price at the time Hoffman elected to exercise the option. This gave him an equity in the lot which could not be legally foreclosed without affording Hoffman an opportunity to pay the balance. The second ground of attack is that the lot may have had a fair market value of $6,000, and Hoffman should have paid the remaining $5,000 of purchase price. We determine that it would be unreasonable to require Hoffman to have invested an additional $5,000 in order to protect the $1,000 he had paid. Therefore, we find no merit to defendants' attack upon this item of damages.

We also determine it was reasonable for Hoffman to have paid $125 for one month's rent of a home in Chilton after defendants assured him everything would be set when plaintiff sold the bakery building. This was a proper item of damage.

Plaintiffs never moved to Chilton because defendants suggested that Hoffman get some experience by working in a Red Owl store in the Fox River Valley. Plaintiffs, therefore, moved to Neenah instead of Chilton. After moving, Hoffman worked at night in an Appleton bakery but held himself available for work in a Red Owl store. The $140 moving expense would not have been incurred if plaintiffs had not sold their bakery building in Wautoma in reliance upon defendants' promises. We consider the $140 moving expense to be a proper item of damage.

We turn now to the damage item with respect to which the trial court granted a new trial, i. e., that arising from the sale of the Wautoma grocery store fixtures and inventory for which the jury awarded $16,735. The trial court ruled that Hoffman could not recover for any loss of future profits for the summer months following the sale on June 6, 1961, but that damages would be limited to the difference between the sales price received and fair market value of the assets sold, giving consideration to any goodwill attaching thereto by reason of the transfer of a going business. There was no direct evidence presented as to what this fair market value was on June 6, 1961. The evidence did disclose that Hoffman paid $9,000 for the inventory, added $1,500 to it and sold it for $10,000 or a loss of $500. His 1961 federal income tax return showed that the grocery equipment had been purchased for $7,000 and sold for $7,955.96. Plaintiffs introduced evidence of the buyer that during the first eleven weeks of operation of the grocery store his gross sales were $44,000 and his profit was $6,000 or roughly 15 percent. On cross-examination he admitted that this was gross and not net profit. Plaintiffs contend that in a breach of contract action damages may include loss of profits. However, this is not a breach of contract action.

The only relevancy of evidence relating to profits would be with respect to proving the element of goodwill in establishing the fair market value of the grocery inventory and fixtures sold. Therefore, evidence of profits would be admissible to afford a foundation for expert opinion as to fair market value.

Where damages are awarded in promissory estoppel instead of specifically enforcing the promisor's promise, they should be only such as in the opinion of the court are necessary to prevent injustice. Mechanical or rule of thumb approaches to the damage problem should be avoided. In discussing remedies to be applied by courts in promissory estoppel we quote the following views of writers on the subject:

'Enforcement of a promise does not necessarily mean Specific Performance. It does not necessarily mean Damages for breach. Moreover the amount allowed as Damages may be determined by the plaintiff's expenditures or change of position in reliance as well as by the value to him of the promised performance. Restitution is also an 'enforcing' remedy, although it is often said to be based upon some kind of a rescission. In determining what justice requires, the court must remember all of its powers, derived from equity, law merchant, and other sources, as well as the common law. Its decree should be molded accordingly.' 1A Corbin, Contracts, p. 221, sec. 200.

'The wrong is not primarily in depriving the plaintiff of the promised reward but in causing the plaintiff to change position to his detriment. It would follow that the damages should not exceed the loss caused by the change of position, which would never be more in amount, but might be less, than the promised reward.' Seavey, Reliance on Gratuitous Promises or Other Conduct, 64 Harvard Law Review (1951), 913, 926.

'There likewise seems to be no positive legal requirement, and certainly no legal policy, which dictates the allowance of contract damages in every case where the defendant's duty is consensual.' Shattuck, Gratuitous Promises- A New Writ?, 35 Michigan Law Review (1936), 908, 912.

At the time Hoffman bought the equipment and inventory of the small grocery store at Wautoma he did so in order to gain experience in the grocery store business. At that time discussion had already been had with Red Owl representatives that Wautoma might be too small for a Red Owl operation and that a larger city might be more desirable. Thus Hoffman made this purchase more or less as a temporary experiment. Justice does not require that the damages awarded him, because of selling these assets at the behest of defendants, should exceed any actual loss sustained measured by the difference between the sales price and the fair market value.

Since the evidence does not sustain the large award of damages arising from the sale of the Wautoma grocery business, the trial court properly ordered a new trial on this issue.

Order affirmed. Because of the cross-appeal, plaintiffs shall be limited to taxing but two-thirds of their costs.

POP'S CONES, INC. V. RESORTS INTERNATIONAL HOTEL, INC.
Superior Court of New Jersey, Appellate Division
704 A. 2d 1321 (1998)

KLEINER, J.A.D.

Plaintiff, Pop's Cones, Inc., t/a TCBY Yogurt, ("Pop's"), appeals from an order of the Law Division granting defendant, Resorts International, Inc. ("Resorts"), summary judgment and dismissing its complaint seeking damages predicated on a theory of promissory estoppel. Affording all favorable inferences to plaintiff's contentions, Brill v. Guardian Life Ins. Co. of America, 142 N.J. 520, 536, 666 A.2d 146 (1995), we conclude that Pop's presented a prima facie claim sufficient to withstand summary dismissal of its complaint. See R. 4:46-2; Brill, supra, 142 N.J. at 540, 666 A.2d 146. In reversing summary judgment, we rely upon principles of promissory estoppel enunciated in Section 90 of the Restatement (Second) of Contracts, and recent cases which, in order to avoid injustice, seemingly relax the strict requirement of "a clear and definite promise" in making a prima facie case of promissory estoppel.

I

Pop's is an authorized franchisee of TCBY Systems, Inc. ("TCBY"), a national franchisor of frozen yogurt products. Resorts is a casino hotel in Atlantic City that leases retail space along "prime Boardwalk frontage," among other business ventures.

From June of 1991 to September 1994, Pop's operated a TCBY franchise in Margate, New Jersey. Sometime during the months of May or June 1994, Brenda Taube ("Taube"), President of Pop's, had "a number of discussions" with Marlon Phoenix ("Phoenix"), the Executive Director of Business Development and Sales for Resorts, about the possible relocation of Pop's business to space owned by Resorts. During these discussions, Phoenix showed Taube one location for a TCBY vending cart within Resorts Hotel and "three specific locations for the operation of a full service TCBY store."

According to Taube, she and Phoenix specifically discussed the boardwalk property occupied at that time by a business trading as "The Players Club." These discussions included Taube's concerns with the then-current rental fees and Phoenix's indication that Resorts management and Merv Griffin personally2 were "very anxious to have Pop's as a tenant" and that "financial issues . . . could easily be resolved, such as through a percentage of gross revenue." In order to allay both Taube's and Phoenix's concerns about whether a TCBY franchise at The Players Club location would be successful, Phoenix offered to permit Pop's to operate a vending cart within Resorts free of charge during the summer of 1994 so as to "test the traffic flow." This offer was considered and approved by Paul Ryan, Vice President for Hotel Operations at Resorts.

These discussions led to further meetings with Phoenix about the Players Club location, and Taube contacted TCBY's corporate headquarters about a possible franchise site change. During the weekend of July 4, 1994, Pop's opened the TCBY cart for business at Resorts pursuant to the above stated offer. On July 6, 1994, TCBY gave Taupe initial approval for Pop's change in franchise site. In late July or early August of 1994, representatives of TCBY personally visited the Players Club location, with Taube and Phoenix present.

Based on Pop's marketing assessment of the Resorts location, Taube drafted a written proposal dated August 18, 1994, addressing the leasing of Resorts' Players Club location and hand-delivered it to Phoenix. Taube's proposal offered Resorts "7% of net monthly sales (gross less sales tax) for the duration of the [Player's Club] lease . . . [and][i]f this proposal is acceptable, I'd need a 6 year lease, and a renewable option for another 6 years."

In mid-September 1994, Taube spoke with Phoenix about the status of Pop's lease proposal and "pressed [him] to advise [her] of Resorts' position. [Taube] specifically advised [Phoenix] that Pop's had an option to renew the lease for its Margate location and then needed to give notice to its landlord of whether it would be staying at that location no later than October 1, 1994." Another conversation about this topic occurred in late September when Taube "asked Phoenix if [Pop's] proposal was in the ballpark of what Resorts was looking for." He responded that it was and that "we are 95% there, we just need Belisle's3 signature on the deal." Taube admits to having been advised that Belisle had "ultimate responsibility for signing off on the deal" but that Phoenix "assured [her] that Mr. Belisle would follow his recommendation, which was to approve the deal, and that [Phoenix] did not anticipate any difficulties." During this conversation, Taube again mentioned to Phoenix that she had to inform her landlord by October 1, 1994, about whether or not Pop's would renew its lease with them. Taube stated: "Mr. Phoenix assured me that we would have little difficulty in concluding an agreement and advised [Taube] to give notice that [Pop's] would not be extending [its] Margate lease and 'to pack up the Margate store and plan on moving.'"

Relying upon Phoenix's "advice and assurances," Taube notified Pop's landlord in late-September 1994 that it would not be renewing the lease for the Margate location.

In early October, Pop's moved its equipment out of the Margate location and placed it in temporary storage. Taube then commenced a number of new site preparations including: (1) sending designs for the new store to TCBY in October 1994; and (2) retaining an attorney to represent Pop's in finalizing the terms of the lease with Resorts.

By letter dated November 1, 1994, General Counsel for Resorts forwarded a proposed form of lease for The Players Club location to Pop's attorney. The letter provided:

Per our conversation, enclosed please find the form of lease utilized for retail outlets leasing space in Resorts Hotel. You will note that there are a number of alternative sections depending upon the terms of the deal. As I advised, I will contact you . . . to inform you of our decision regarding TCBY. . . .

By letter dated December 1, 1994, General Counsel for Resorts forwarded to Pop's attorney a written offer of the terms upon which Resorts was proposing to lease the Players Club space to Pop's. The terms provided:

[Resorts is] willing to offer the space for an initial three (3) year term with a rent calculated at the greater of 7% of gross revenues or: $50,000 in year one; $60,000 in year two; and $70,000 in year three . . . [with] a three (3) year option to renew after the initial term . . .

The letter also addressed a "boilerplate lease agreement" provision and a proposed addition to the form lease. The letter concluded by stating:

This letter is not intended to be binding upon Resorts. It is intended to set forth the basic terms and conditions upon which Resorts would be willing to negotiate a lease and is subject to those negotiations and the execution of a definitive agreement

. . . [W]e think TCBY will be successful at the Boardwalk location based upon the terms we propose. We look forward to having your client as part of . . . Resorts family of customer service providers and believe TCBY will benefit greatly from some of the dynamic changes we plan.

. . . [W]e would be pleased . . . to discuss this proposal in greater detail. (emphasis added).

In early-December 1994, Taube and her attorney met with William Murtha, General Counsel of Resorts, and Paul Ryan to finalize the proposed lease. After a number of discussions about the lease, Murtha and Ryan informed Taube that they desired to reschedule the meeting to finalize the lease until after the first of the year because of a public announcement they intended to make about another unrelated business venture that Resorts was about to commence. Ryan again assured Taube that rent for the Players Club space was not an issue and that the lease terms would be worked out. "He also assured [Taube] that Resorts wanted TCBY . . . on the boardwalk for the following season."

Several attempts were made in January 1995 to contact Resorts' representatives and confirm that matters were proceeding. On January 30, 1995, Taube's attorney received a letter stating: "This letter is to confirm our conversation of this date wherein I advised that Resorts is withdrawing its December 1, 1994 offer to lease space to your client, TCBY."

According to Taube's certification, "As soon as [Pop's] heard that Resorts was withdrawing its offer, we undertook extensive efforts to reopen [the] franchise at a different location. Because the Margate location had been re-let, it was not available." Ultimately, Pop's found a suitable location but did not reopen for business until July 5, 1996.

On July 17, 1995, Pop's filed a complaint against Resorts seeking damages. The complaint alleged that Pop's "reasonably relied to its detriment on the promises and assurances of Resorts that it would be permitted to relocate its operation to [Resorts'] Boardwalk location. . . ."

After substantial pre-trial discovery, defendant moved for summary judgment. After oral argument, the motion judge, citing Malaker Corp. Stockholders Protective Comm. v. First Jersey Nat. Bank, 163 N.J.Super. 463, 395 A.2d 222 (App.Div.1978), certif. denied, 79 N.J. 488, 401 A.2d 243 (1979), rendered a detailed oral opinion in which he concluded, in part:

> The primary argument of the defendant is that the plaintiff is unable to meet the requirements for a claim of Promissory Estoppel as there was no clear and definite promise ever made to

plaintiff; and, therefore, any reliance on the part of plaintiff upon the statements of the Resorts agent were not reasonable.

. . .

. . . I think that even if a jury would find that a lease was promised, there was lack of specificity in its terms so as to not rise to the level of what is necessary to meet the first element for Promissory Estoppel.

There was no specificity as to the term of this lease. There was no specificity as to the starting date of this lease. There was no specificity as to the rent, although it was represented that rent would not be a problem. Rent had not been agreed upon, and it is not certified that it had been agreed upon. When they left that meeting, according to . . . plaintiff's own facts, they didn't have a lease; they would still have to work out the terms of the lease. It was not in existence at the time.

. . .

. . . We don't have facts in dispute. Neither side, neither the defendant nor the plaintiff, can attest to the terms of the lease, of the essential terms of the lease or still not agreed upon at the time of that the meeting was over in December of 1994.

Based on Brill, supra, 142 N.J. at 540, 666 A.2d 146, the judge concluded that the evidence was so one-sided that defendant was entitled to prevail as a matter of law.

It is quite apparent from the motion judge's reasons that he viewed plaintiff's complaint as seeking enforcement of a lease which had not yet been fully negotiated. If that were plaintiff's intended remedy, we would agree with the judge's conclusion. However, plaintiff's complaint, after reciting the facts from the inception of Taube's initial contact with defendant until January 30, 1995, stated:

19. As a result of its reasonable reliance on the promises and assurances made to it by Resorts, Pop's has been significantly prejudiced and has suffered significant damages, including the following:

a. the loss of its Margate location and its ability to earn profits during the 1995 summer season;

b. out-of-pocket expenses, including attorney's fees; and

c. out-of-pocket expenses in attempting to locate an alternate location.

Wherefore, Pop's demands judgment against defendant, Resorts International Hotel, Inc., for damages, costs of suit and for other and further legal and equitable relief as the Court may deem just and proper.

It seems quite clear from plaintiff's complaint that plaintiff was not seeking damages relating to a lease of the boardwalk property, but rather was seeking damages flowing from its reliance upon promises made to it prior to October 1, 1994, when it failed to renew its lease for its Margate location. Thus, plaintiff's claim was predicated upon the concept of promissory estoppel and was not a traditional breach of contract claim.

The doctrine of promissory estoppel is well-established in New Jersey. Malaker, supra, 163 N.J.Super. at 479, 395 A.2d 222 ("Suffice it to say that given an appropriate case, the doctrine [of promissory estoppel] will be enforced."). A promissory estoppel claim will be justified if the plaintiff satisfies its burden of demonstrating the existence of, or for purposes of summary judgment, a dispute as to a material fact with regard to, four separate elements which include:

(1) a clear and definite promise by the promisor; (2) the promise must be made with the expectation that the promisee will rely thereon; (3) the promisee must in fact reasonably rely on the promise, and (4) detriment of a definite and substantial nature must be incurred in reliance on the promise.

[Ibid.]

The essential justification for the promissory estoppel doctrine is to avoid the substantial hardship or injustice which would result if such a promise were not enforced. Id. at 484, 395 A.2d 222.

In Malaker, the court determined that an implied promise to lend an unspecified amount of money was not "a clear and definite promise" justifying application of the promissory estoppel doctrine. Id. at 478–81, 395 A.2d 222. Specifically, the court concluded that the promisor-bank's oral promise in October 1970 to lend $150,000 for January, February and March of 1971 was not "clear and definite promise" because it did not describe a promise of "sufficient definition." Id. at 479, 395 A.2d 222.

It should be noted that the court in Malaker seems to have heightened the amount of proof required to establish a "clear and definite promise" by searching for "an express promise of a 'clear and definite' nature." Id. at 484, 395 A.2d 222 (emphasis added). This sort of language might suggest that New Jersey Courts expect proof of most, if not all, of the essential legal elements of a promise before finding it to be "clear and definite."

Although earlier New Jersey decisions discussing promissory estoppel seem to greatly scrutinize a party's proofs regarding an alleged "clear and definite promise by the promisor," see, e.g., id. at 479, 484, 395 A.2d 222, as a prelude to considering the remaining three elements of a promissory estoppel claim, more recent decisions have tended to relax the strict adherence to the Malaker formula for determining whether a prima facie case of promissory estoppel exists. This is particularly true where, as here, a plaintiff does not seek to enforce a contract not fully negotiated, but instead seeks damages resulting from its detrimental reliance upon promises made during contract negotiations despite the ultimate failure of those negotiations.

In Peck v. Imedia, Inc., 293 N.J.Super. 151, 679 A.2d 745 (App.Div.) certif. denied, 147 N.J. 262, 686 A.2d 763 (1996), we determined that an at-will employment contract offer was a "clear and definite promise" for purposes of promissory estoppel. See id. at 165–68, 679 A.2d 745. The employment contract offer letter contained the position title, a "detailed position description . . . as well as information on . . . benefits" and an annual salary. Id. at 156, 679 A.2d 745. We recognized that even though an employer can terminate the employment relationship at any time, there may be losses incident to reliance upon the job offer itself. Id. at 167–68, 679 A.2d 745. See also Mahoney v. Delaware McDonald's Corp., 770 F.2d 123, 127 (8th Cir.1985) (holding that plaintiff's purchase of property for lease to defendant in reliance upon defendant's representation that "[w]e have a deal" created cause of action for promissory estoppel); Bercoon, Weiner, Glick & Brook v. Manufacturers Hanover Trust Co., 818 F.Supp. 1152, 1161 (N.D.Ill.1993) (holding that defendant's representation that lease was "done deal" and encouragement of plaintiff to terminate existing lease provided plaintiff with cause of action for promissory estoppel).

Further, the Restatement (Second) of Contracts § 90 (1979), "Promise Reasonably Inducing Action or Forbearance," provides, in pertinent part:

(1) A promise which the promisor should reasonably expect to induce action or forbearance on the part of the promisee or a third person and which does induce such action or forbearance is binding if injustice can be avoided only by enforcement of the promise. The remedy granted for breach may be limited as justice requires.

[Ibid. (emphasis added).]

The Restatement approach is best explained by illustration 10 contained within the comments to Section 90, and based upon Hoffman v. Red Owl Stores, Inc., 26 Wis.2d 683, 133 N.W.2d 267 (1965):

> 10. A, who owns and operates a bakery, desires to go into the grocery business. He approaches B, a franchisor of supermarkets. B states to A that for $18,000 B will establish A in a store. B also advises A to move to another town and buy a small grocery to gain experience. A does so. Later B advises A to sell the grocery, which A does, taking a capital loss and foregoing expected profits from the summer tourist trade. B also advises A to sell his bakery to raise capital for the supermarket franchise, saying "Everything is

ready to go. Get your money together and we are set." A sells the bakery taking a capital loss on this sale as well. Still later, B tells A that considerably more than an $18,000 investment will be needed, and the negotiations between the parties collapse. At the point of collapse many details of the proposed agreement between the parties are unresolved. The assurances from B to A are promises on which B reasonably should have expected A to rely, and A is entitled to his actual losses on the sales of the bakery and grocery and for his moving and temporary living expenses. Since the proposed agreement was never made, however, A is not entitled to lost profits from the sale of the grocery or to his expectation interest in the proposed franchise from B.

[Restatement (Second) of Contracts § 90 cmt. d, illus. 10 (1979).]

We particularly note our recent discussion in Mazza v. Scoleri, 304 N.J.Super. 555, 701 A.2d 723 (App.Div.1997). Although Mazza did not focus on the issue of promissory estoppel, it expressly adopted the exception to the Statute of Frauds enunciated in Restatement (Second) of Contracts, § 139(1) (1979). Mazza, supra, 304 N.J.Super. at 560, 701 A.2d 723. That section provides:

A promise which the promisor should reasonably expect to induce action or forbearance on the part of the promisee or a third person and which does induce the action or forbearance is enforceable notwithstanding the Statute of Frauds if injustice can be avoided only by enforcement of the promise. The remedy granted for breach is limited as justice requires.

[Restatement (Second) of Contracts § 139(1) (1979).]

Mazza also instructs, citing Citibank v. Estate of Simpson, 290 N.J.Super. 519, 530, 676 A.2d 172 (App.Div.1996), that "New Jersey typically gives considerable weight to Restatement views, and has, on occasion, adopted those views as the law of this State when they speak to an issue our courts have not yet considered." Mazza, 304 N.J.Super. at 560, 701 A.2d 723 (citations omitted).

It is thus quite clear that Section 90 of the Restatement complements the exception to the Statute of Frauds discussed in Section 139(1).

As we read the Restatement, the strict adherence to proof of a "clear and definite promise" as discussed in Malaker is being eroded by a more equitable analysis designed to avoid injustice. This is the very approach we adopted in Peck, supra, wherein even in the absence of a clear and definite contract of employment, we permitted the plaintiff to proceed with a cause of action for damages flowing from plaintiff's losses based on her detrimental reliance on the promise of employment. 293 N.J.Super. at 168, 679 A.2d 745.

The facts as presented by plaintiff by way of its pleadings and certifications filed by Taube, which were not refuted or contradicted by defendant before the motion judge or on appeal, clearly show that when Taube informed Phoenix that Pop's option to renew its lease at its Margate location had to be exercised by October 1, 1994, Phoenix instructed Taube to give notice that it would not be extending the lease. According to Phoenix, virtually nothing remained to be resolved between the parties. Phoenix indicated that the parties were "95% there" and that all that was required for completion of the deal was the signature of John Belisle. Phoenix assured Taube that he had recommended the deal to Belisle, and that Belisle would follow the recommendation. Phoenix also advised Pop's to "pack up the Margate store and plan on moving."

It is also uncontradicted that based upon those representations that Pop's, in fact, did not renew its lease. It vacated its Margate location, placed its equipment and personalty into temporary storage, retained the services of an attorney to finalize the lease with defendant, and engaged in planning the relocation to defendant's property. Ultimately, it incurred the expense of relocating to its present location. That plaintiff, like the plaintiff in Peck, relied to its detriment on defendant's assurances seems unquestionable; the facts clearly at least raise a jury question. Additionally, whether plaintiff's reliance upon defendant's assurances was reasonable is also a question for the jury.

Conversely, following the Section 90 approach, a jury could conclude that Phoenix, as promisor, should reasonably have expected to induce action or forbearance on the part of plaintiff to his precise instruction "not to renew the lease" and to "pack up the Margate store and plan on moving." In discussing the "character of reliance protected" under Section 90, comment b states:

The principle of this Section is flexible. The promisor is affected only by reliance which he does or should foresee, and enforcement must be necessary to avoid injustice. Satisfaction of the latter requirement may depend on the reasonableness of the promisee's reliance, on its definite and substantial character in relation to the remedy sought, on the formality with which the promise is made, on the extent to which evidentiary, cautionary, deterrent and channeling functions of form are met by the commercial setting or otherwise, and on the extent to which such other policies as the enforcement of bargains and the prevention of unjust enrichment are relevant. . . .

[Restatement (Second) of Contracts § 90 cmt. b (1979) (citations omitted).]

Plaintiff's complaint neither seeks enforcement of the lease nor speculative lost profits which it might have earned had the lease been fully and successfully negotiated. Plaintiff merely seeks to recoup damages it incurred, including the loss of its Margate leasehold, in reasonably relying to its detriment upon defendant's promise. Affording plaintiff all favorable inferences, its equitable claim raised a jury question. See Brill, supra, 142 N.J. at 540, 666 A.2d 146. Plaintiff's complaint, therefore, should not have been summarily dismissed.

Reversed and remanded for further appropriate proceedings.

TOUR COSTA RICA V. COUNTRY WALKERS, INC.

Supreme Court of Vermont
171 Vt. 116 (2000)

SKOGLUND, J.

Defendants Country Walkers, Inc. (CW) and Robert Maynard (Maynard)1 appeal from the superior court's denial of their V.R.C.P. 50(b) motion for judgment as a matter of law, following a jury verdict for plaintiff, Tour Costa Rica (TCR), on its promissory estoppel claim. The jury awarded plaintiff, a company that runs tours in Costa Rica, damages after finding that defendant had breached a promise of a two-year commitment to use TCR to develop, organize and operate Costa Rican walking tours for defendant during that period. We affirm.

Because this is an appeal from a denial of a motion for judgment as a matter of law, we view the evidence in the light most favorable to plaintiff. See Brueckner v. Norwich Univ., 169 Vt. 118, 120–21, 730 A.2d 1086, 1089 (1999).

CW is a Vermont business, owned by Maynard and his wife, that sells guided tours at locations around the world. In 1994, Leigh Monahan, owner of TCR, contacted Maynard and offered to design, arrange and lead walking tours in Costa Rica for defendant. During negotiations, Monahan explained to Maynard that she had just incorporated the tour company and, because the company had limited resources, she could not afford to develop specialized tours for defendant unless she had a two-year commitment from CW to run its Costa Rican tours through TCR. In the summer of 1994, the parties entered into a verbal agreement under which plaintiff was to design, arrange and lead customized walking tours in Costa Rica for CW from 1995 through 1997. Pursuant to this agreement, Monahan designed a customized tour for CW, a task that included investigating and testing walking tours, investigating and booking hotels, making transportation arrangements, conducting research, checking medical facilities, writing and editing copy for CW's brochures and drafting itineraries for clients.

In March and April 1995, plaintiff conducted two walking tours for CW. Although other tours had been scheduled for 1995, both defendant and plaintiff canceled some for various reasons. Between the end of April and June of 1995, the parties discussed the details of, and scheduled the dates for, approximately eighteen walking tours for 1996 and 1997. Due to limited resources, plaintiff could not conduct tours for anyone else while working with defendant and, therefore, stopped advertising and promoting its business, did not pursue other business opportunities and, in fact, turned down other business during this period.

In August 1995, a few weeks before the next tour was to occur, defendant informed plaintiff that it would be using another company for all of its future tours in Costa Rica. When challenged by plaintiff with its promised commitment, Maynard responded: "If I did and I certainly may have promised you a two year commitment, I apologize for not honoring it." Notwithstanding this apology, defendant went on to operate tours in Costa Rica using a rival company. Plaintiff was forced to cancel transportation arrangements and hotel and restaurant reservations it had made on defendant's behalf. Due to the suddenness of the break with CW, plaintiff was left without tours to run during a prime tourist season, and without sufficient time to market any new tours of its own.

Plaintiff filed suit against defendant, alleging breach of contract, promissory estoppel, unjust enrichment, conversion, fraud, and breach of covenant of good faith and fair dealing. Plaintiff dismissed the conversion count at the beginning of trial. At the close of plaintiff's evidence, defendant moved for a directed verdict on the remaining counts. The court granted defendant's motion with respect to the fraud claim, but denied it with respect to the other claims. Defendant renewed its motion at the close of all the evidence, and the court denied it. At that time, defendant also requested a directed verdict with regard to damages, arguing that there was insufficient evidence to support a damage award. The court denied this motion, as well. Subsequently, the court presented the parties with its proposed jury instructions, which included the following: "As to the claims of breach of contract and promissory estoppel, plaintiff would be entitled to damages which would put it in the same position as if the contract or promise had been fulfilled by Country Walkers." The court then held a jury charge conference, during which both plaintiff and defendant objected to portions of the court's proposed instructions. Defendant, however, did not object to the above-quoted portion.

The case went to the jury, and the jury found for defendant on the breach of contract, unjust enrichment, and breach of covenant of good faith and fair dealing claims, but found for plaintiff on the promissory estoppel claim, and awarded expectation damages in the amount of $22,520.00. Defendant then filed a motion for judgment as a matter of law, alleging, as it had in its previous motions, that plaintiff had failed to prove promissory estoppel and that there was insufficient evidence to support the jury's damage award. Defendant also argued, for the first time, that, as a matter of law, expectation damages are not available in a promissory estoppel action. The court denied defendant's motion. This appeal followed.

Pursuant to V.R.C.P. 50, a court may grant judgment as a matter of law where "there is no legally sufficient evidentiary basis for a reasonable jury to find for [the nonmoving] party." V.R.C.P. 50(a)(1). When reviewing a motion for judgment as a matter of law, we view the evidence in the light most favorable to the nonmoving party, excluding the effect of any modifying evidence, in order to determine whether the result reached by the jury is sound in law on the evidence produced. See Haynes v. Golub Corp., 166 Vt. 228, 233, 692 A.2d 377, 380 (1997); Foote v. Simmonds Precision Prods. Co., 158 Vt. 566, 570, 613 A.2d 1277, 1279 (1992). The trial court's denial of such motion will be upheld "if any evidence fairly or reasonably supports a lawful theory of the plaintiff." Haynes, 166 Vt. at 233, 692 A.2d at 380. In this case, there was substantial evidence supporting plaintiff's claims, and the trial court did not err in denying defendant's motion for judgment as a matter of law.

I.

Defendant first argues that plaintiff failed to make out a prima facie case of promissory estoppel. Under the doctrine of promissory estoppel:

"A promise which the promisor should reasonably expect to induce action or forbearance on the part of the promisee or a third person and which does induce such action or forbearance is binding if injustice can be avoided only by enforcement of the promise."

Foote, 158 Vt. at 573, 613 A.2d at 1281 (quoting Restatement (Second) of Contracts § 90(1) (1981)). The action or inaction taken in reliance on the promise must be " 'of a definite and substantial character.' " Ragosta v. Wilder, 156 Vt. 390, 396, 592 A.2d 367, 371 (1991) (quoting Stacy v. Merchants Bank, 144 Vt. 515, 521, 482 A.2d 61, 64 (1984)). In other words, the promisee must have detrimentally relied on the promise. See Larose v. Agway, Inc., 147 Vt. 1, 4, 508 A.2d 1364, 1366 (1986), overruled on other grounds by Taylor v. National Life Ins. Co., 161 Vt. 457, 652 A.2d 466 (1993). Defendant does not seriously dispute that there was a promise or that plaintiff did take action based on the promise. Rather, defendant argues that plaintiff's reliance was not reasonable or detrimental, and that this is not a case where injustice can be avoided only by enforcement of the promise. We first address defendant's argument that plaintiff's reliance was not reasonable.

A.

In determining whether a plaintiff reasonably relied on a defendant's promise, courts examine the totality of the circumstances. See In re Bonnanzio, 91 F.3d 296, 305 (2d Cir.1996). Here, plaintiff presented evidence that it relied on defendant's promise of a two-year exclusive commitment by (a) ceasing to advertise and promote the business, failing to pursue other business opportunities, and turning down other business; (b) making hotel and restaurant reservations and arranging for transportation for the tours it was to operate for CW; and (c) making purchases related to the tours it was to operate for CW. Plaintiff suggests that this reliance was reasonable because, in negotiations with Maynard, plaintiff made clear that it required a two-year commitment due to its limited resources, the time it would have to devote to develop specialized tours for CW, and the ongoing communication between the parties as to future dates and requirements for tours.

Defendant argues that plaintiff's reliance was not reasonable based solely on standard industry practice that permits the cancellation of tours upon thirty to sixty days' notice.

While there was no dispute that tours could be canceled with appropriate notice, there was evidence that this industry practice did not apply to the parties' two-year commitment. Monahan testified that she and Maynard specifically agreed to the two-year time frame because she wanted a measure of security for her fledgling company. She further testified that it was her understanding, from negotiations with Maynard, that the two-year commitment was unaffected by the possibility that some scheduled tours might be canceled if, for example, too few people signed. This understanding finds support in Maynard's proposed method of handling deposits of people who canceled tour bookings: if guests canceled more than sixty days before the trip, defendant would keep $50.00 of the deposit; if the cancellation was made less than sixty but more than thirty days prior to the trip, defendant and plaintiff would split the deposit; and, if the cancellation was made less than thirty days before the trip, plaintiff would be paid the full amount of the deposit.

Based on the foregoing, we find that plaintiff presented sufficient evidence to enable the jury to conclude that plaintiff's reliance on defendant's promise was reasonable.

B.

Defendant next argues that plaintiff's reliance on defendant's promise was not detrimental. Defendant suggests that the only evidence of detriment offered by plaintiff was Monahan's testimony concerning expenses for a few minor equipment purchases. Plaintiff disagrees.

Plaintiff maintains that its reliance was detrimental because (1) it lost business due to the fact that (a) it stopped advertising and promoting the business, did not pursue other business opportunities, and turned down other business in reliance on the parties' agreement, and (b) after defendant breached the agreement, plaintiff had no money to advertise or conduct other tours; (2) it spent money in preparation for the tours it was to operate for defendant; and (3) its reputation in the industry suffered because it had to cancel two-years' worth of reservations it had made on behalf of defendant.

Defendant does not dispute that plaintiff stopped advertising and promoting the business, did not pursue other business opportunities and turned down other business, or that plaintiff's reputation was harmed. Instead, defendant contends that (1) plaintiff would have had to arrange for transportation and make reservations at hotels and restaurants for any tours it arranged for CW, whether or not the tours were part of an exclusive two-year arrangement, and (2) the money plaintiff spent in preparation for the tours is not, in and of itself, sufficient to show detrimental reliance.

Defendant's first argument is flawed because, as noted above, Monahan testified that she told Maynard that plaintiff could not afford to arrange tours for CW without an exclusive two-year agreement. There was no evidence that plaintiff would have prepared tours for CW if the parties did not have an exclusive two-year agreement. Defendant's second argument is flawed because it overlooks the facts that plaintiff stopped advertising and promoting the business, did not pursue other business opportunities, and in fact turned down other business. In reliance on a two-year commitment, plaintiff stopped soliciting business from other sources and declined other bookings, a substantial change in position for a fledgling tour business. See Ragosta, 156 Vt. at 396, 592 A.2d at 371. Further, plaintiff's reputation in Costa Rica's tourism industry was damaged.

The evidence shows that, as a result of defendant's breach of the parties' agreement, plaintiff suffered significant harm for each of the above-mentioned reasons. Accordingly, the jury could reasonably conclude that plaintiff's reliance on defendant's promise was detrimental.

C.

Whether injustice can be avoided only by enforcement of the promise is a question of law4 informed by several factors, including:

(a) the availability and adequacy of other remedies, particularly cancellation and restitution;

(b) the definite and substantial character of the action or forbearance in relation to the remedy sought;

(c) the extent to which the action or forbearance corroborates evidence of the making and terms of the promise, or the making and terms are otherwise established by clear and convincing evidence;

(d) the reasonableness of the action or forbearance; [and]

(e) the extent to which the action or forbearance was foreseeable by the promisor.

Restatement (Second) of Contracts § 139(2) (1981).

With regard to the availability and adequacy of other remedies, we have previously stated that, "[w]hile a full range of legal damages may be available, promissory estoppel plaintiffs are not necessarily entitled to them as of right." Remes v. Nordic Group, Inc., 169 Vt. 37, 41, 726 A.2d 77, 79–80 (1999). Damages available in a promissory estoppel action depend upon the circumstances of the case. See id. While the jury in the instant case found no contract, an analysis of breach-of-contract remedies is relevant to the determination of whether injustice can be avoided only by enforcement of the promise. We do not, however, intend to suggest "that promissory estoppel damages are coextensive with full contractual remedies." Id. at 40, 726 A.2d at 79.

Expectation damages, which the jury awarded in this case, provide the plaintiff with an amount equal to the benefit of the parties' bargain. One potential component of expectation damages is loss of future profits. The purpose of expectation damages is to "put the non-breaching party in the same position it would have been [in] had the contract been fully performed." McKinley Allsopp, Inc. v. Jetborne Int'l, Inc., No. 89 CIV. 1489(PNL), 1990 WL 138959 at *8 (S.D.N.Y. Sept.19, 1990). Restitution damages seek to compensate the plaintiff for any benefit it conferred upon the defendant as a result of the parties' contract. The purpose of restitution damages is to return the plaintiff to the position it held before the parties' contract. See id. Reliance damages give the plaintiff any reasonably foreseeable costs incurred in reliance on the contract. As with restitution, the purpose of reliance damages is to return the plaintiff to the position it was in prior to the parties' contract. See id.

Restitution damages are inapplicable in the instant case because there is no evidence that plaintiff conferred any benefit on defendant as a result of defendant's promise. Further, cancellation is inapplicable, as defendant had already breached its promise, and cancellation would provide no remedy for plaintiff. Reliance damages are also inappropriate because the majority of the harm plaintiff suffered was not expenditures it made in reliance on defendant's promise, but rather, lost profits from the tours it had scheduled with defendant, lost potential profits because it failed to pursue other business opportunities, and harm to its reputation. Therefore, an award of expectation damages is the only remedy that adequately compensates plaintiff for the harm it suffered.

As to the other factors considered, plaintiff's actions and inactions were of a definite and substantial character. These actions and inactions strongly corroborate both Monahan's and Maynard's testimony, as well as documentary evidence submitted by plaintiff, regarding the making and terms of the promise. As previously discussed, plaintiff's reliance on defendant's promise was reasonable, and plaintiff's actions and inactions were foreseeable by defendant. Defendant expected plaintiff to take specific actions on defendant's behalf and to design and conduct tours to defendant's specifications. Further, defendant was aware that plaintiff was a new company without a lot of capital, and that it was spending much of that capital preparing tours for defendant.

Taking the above factors into consideration, there was sufficient evidence to allow the jury to conclude that, in this case, injustice could be avoided only by enforcement of the promise through an award of monetary damages.

[The court upheld the damages award.]

Affirmed.

JAMES BAIRD CO. v. GIMBEL BROS., INC.
United States Court of Appeals for the Second Circuit
64 F.2d 344 (1933)

L. HAND, CIRCUIT JUDGE.

The plaintiff sued the defendant for breach of a contract to deliver linoleum under a contract of sale; the defendant denied the making of the contract; the parties tried the case to the judge under a written stipulation and he directed judgment for the defendant. The facts as found, bearing on the making of the contract, the only issue necessary to discuss, were as follows: The defendant, a New York merchant, knew that the Department of Highways in Pennsylvania had asked for bids for the construction of a public building. It sent an employee to the office of a contractor in Philadelphia, who had possession of the specifications, and the employee there computed the amount of the linoleum which would be required on the job, underestimating the total yardage by about one-half the proper amount. In ignorance of this mistake, on December twenty-fourth the defendant sent to some twenty or thirty contractors, likely to bid on the job, an offer to supply all the linoleum required by the specifications at two different lump sums, depending upon the quality used. These offers concluded as follows: 'If successful in being awarded this contract, it will be absolutely guaranteed, * * * and * * * we are offering these prices for reasonable' (sic), 'prompt acceptance after the general contract has been awarded.' The plaintiff, a contractor in Washington, got one of these on the twenty-eighth, and on the same day the defendant learned its mistake and telegraphed all the contractors to whom it had sent the offer, that it withdrew it and would substitute a new one at about double the amount of the old. This withdrawal reached the plaintiff at Washington on the afternoon of the same day, but not until after it had put in a bid at Harrisburg at a lump sum, based as to linoleum upon the prices quoted by the defendant. The public authorities accepted the plaintiff's bid on December thirtieth, the defendant having meanwhile written a letter of confirmation of its withdrawal, received on the thirty-first. The plaintiff formally accepted the offer on January second, and, as the defendant persisted in declining to recognize the existence of a contract, sued it for damages on a breach.

Unless there are circumstances to take it out of the ordinary doctrine, since the offer was withdrawn before it was accepted, the acceptance was too late. Restatement of Contracts, § 35. To meet this the plaintiff argues as follows: It was a reasonable implication from the defendant's offer that it should be irrevocable in case the plaintiff acted upon it, that is to say, used the prices quoted in making its bid, thus putting itself in a position from which it could not withdraw without great loss. While it might have withdrawn its bid after receiving the revocation, the time had passed to submit another, and as the item of linoleum was a very trifling part of the cost of the whole building, it would have been an unreasonable hardship to expect it to lose the contract on that account, and probably forfeit its deposit. While it is true that the plaintiff might in advance have secured a contract conditional upon the success of its bid, this was not what the defendant suggested. It understood that the contractors would use its offer in their bids, and would thus in fact commit themselves to supplying the linoleum at the proposed prices. The inevitable implication from all this was that when the contractors acted upon it, they accepted the offer and promised to pay for the linoleum, in case their bid were accepted.

It was of course possible for the parties to make such a contract, and the question is merely as to what they meant; that is, what is to be imputed to the words they used. Whatever plausibility there is in the argument, is in the fact that the defendant must have known the predicament in which the contractors would be put if it withdrew its offer after the bids went in. However, it seems entirely clear that the contractors did not suppose that they accepted the offer merely by putting in their bids. If, for example, the successful one had repudiated the contract with the public authorities after it had been awarded to him, certainly the defendant could not have sued him for a breach. If he had become bankrupt, the defendant could not prove against his estate. It seems plain therefore that there was no contract between them. And if there be any doubt as to this, the language of the offer sets it at rest. The phrase, 'if successful in being awarded this contract,' is scarcely met by the mere use of the prices in the bids. Surely such a use was not an 'award' of the contract to the defendant. Again, the phrase, 'we are offering these prices for * * * prompt acceptance after the general contract has been awarded,' looks to the usual communication of an acceptance, and precludes the idea that the use of the offer in the bidding shall be the equivalent. It may indeed be argued that this last language contemplated no more then an early notice that the offer had been accepted, the actual acceptance being the bid, but that would wrench its natural meaning too far, especially in the light of the preceding phrase. The contractors had a ready escape from their difficulty by insisting upon a contract before they used the figures; and in commercial transactions it does not in the end promote justice to seek strained interpretations in aid of those who do not protect themselves.

But the plaintiff says that even though no bilateral contract was made, the defendant should be held under the doctrine of 'promissory estoppel.' This is to be chiefly found in those cases where persons subscribe to a venture, usually charitable, and are held to their promises after it has been completed. It has been applied much more broadly, however, and has now been generalized in section 90, of the Restatement of Contracts. We may arguendo accept it as it there reads, for it does not apply to the case at bar. Offers are ordinarily made in exchange for a consideration, either a counter-promise or some other act which the promisor wishes to secure. In such cases they propose bargains; they presuppose that each promise or performance is an inducement to the other. Wisconsin, etc., Ry. v. Powers, 191 U. S. 379, 386, 387, 24 S. Ct. 107, 48 L. Ed. 229; Banning Co. v. California, 240 U. S. 142, 152, 153, 36 S. Ct. 338, 60 L. Ed. 569. But a man may make a promise without expecting an equivalent; a donative promise, conditional or absolute. The common law provided for such by sealed instruments, and it is unfortunate that these are no longer generally available. The doctrine of 'promissory estoppel' is to avoid the harsh results of allowing the promisor in such a case to repudiate, when the promisee has acted in reliance upon the promise. Siegel v. Spear & Co., 234 N. Y. 479, 138 N. E. 414, 26 A. L. R. 1205. Cf. Allegheny College v. National Bank, 246 N. Y. 369, 159 N. E. 173, 57 L. R. A. 980. But an offer for an exchange is not meant to become a promise until a consideration has been received, either a counter-promise or whatever else is stipulated. To extend it would be to hold the offeror regardless of the stipulated condition of his offer. In the case at bar the defendant offered to deliver the linoleum in exchange for the plaintiff's acceptance, not for its bid, which was a matter of indifference to it. That offer could become a promise to deliver only when the equivalent was received; that is, when the plaintiff promised to take and pay for it. There is no room in such a situation for the doctrine of 'promissory estoppel.'

Nor can the offer be regarded as of an option, giving the plaintiff the right seasonably to accept the linoleum at the quoted prices if its bid was accepted, but not binding it to take and pay, if it could get a better bargain elsewhere. There is not the least reason to suppose that the defendant meant to subject itself to such one-sided obligation. True, if so construed, the doctrine of 'promissory estoppel' might apply, the plaintiff having acted in reliance upon it, though, so far as we have found, the decisions are otherwise. Ganss v. Guffey Petroleum Co., 125 App. Div. 760, 110 N. Y. S. 176; Comstock v. North, 88 Miss. 754, 41 So. 374. As to that, however, we need not declare ourselves.

Judgment affirmed.

DRENNAN V. STAR PAVING COMPANY

Supreme Court of California
51 Cal.2d 406 (1958)

TRAYNOR, JUSTICE.

Defendant appeals from a judgment for plaintiff in an action to recover damages caused by defendant's refusal to perform certain paving work according to a bid it submitted to plaintiff.

On July 28, 1955, plaintiff, a licensed general contractor, was preparing a bid on the 'Monte Vista School Job' in the Lancaster school district. Bids had to be submitted before 8:00 p. m. Plaintiff testified that it was customary in that area for general contractors to receive the bids of subcontractors by telephone on the day set for bidding and to rely on them in computing their own bids. Thus on that day plaintiff's secretary, Mrs. Johnson, received by telephone between fifty and seventy-five subcontractors' bids for various parts of the school job. As each bid came in, she wrote it on a special form, which she brought into plaintiff's office. He then posted it on a master cost sheet setting forth the names and bids of all subcontractors. His own bid had to include the names of subcontractors who were to perform one-half of one per cent or more of the construction work, and he had also to provide a bidder's bond of ten per cent of his total bid of $317,385 as a guarantee that he would enter the contract if awarded the work.

Late in the afternoon, Mrs. Johnson had a telephone conversation with Kenneth R. Hoon, an estimator for defendant. He gave his name and telephone number and stated that he was bidding for defendant for the paving work at the Monte Vista School according to plans and specifications and that his bid was $7,131.60. At Mrs. Johnson's request he repeated his bid. Plaintiff listened to the bid over an extension telephone in his office and posted it on the master sheet after receiving the bid form from Mrs. Johnson. Defendant's was the lowest bid for the paving. Plaintiff computed his own bid accordingly and submitted it with the name of defendant as the subcontractor for the paving. When the bids were opened on July 28th, plaintiff's proved to be the lowest, and he was awarded the contract.

On his way to Los Angeles the next morning plaintiff stopped at defendant's office. The first person he met was defendant's construction engineer, Mr. Oppenheimer. Plaintiff testified: 'I introduced myself and he immediately told me that they had made a mistake in their bid to me the night before, they couldn't do it for the price they had bid, and I told him I would expect him to carry through with their original bid because I had used it in compiling my bid and the job was being awarded them. And I would have to go and do the job according to my bid and I would expect them to do the same.'

Defendant refused to do the paving work for less than $15,000. Plaintiff testified that he 'got figures from other people' and after trying for several months to get as low a bid as possible engaged L & H Paving Company, a firm in Lancaster, to do the work for $10,948.60.

The trial court found on substantial evidence that defendant made a definite offer to do the paving on the Monte Vista job according to the plans and specifications for $7,131.60, and that plaintiff relied on defendant's bid in computing his own bid for the school job and naming defendant therein as the subcontractor for the paving work. Accordingly, it entered judgment for plaintiff in the amount of $3,817.00 (the difference between defendant's bid and the cost of the paving to plaintiff) plus costs.

Defendant contends that there was no enforceable contract between the parties on the ground that it made a revocable offer and revoked it before plaintiff communicated his acceptance to defendant.

There is no evidence that defendant offered to make its bid irrevocable in exchange for plaintiff's use of its figures in computing his bid. Nor is there evidence that would warrant interpreting plaintiff's use of defendant's bid as the acceptance thereof, binding plaintiff, on condition he received the main contract, to award the subcontract to defendant. In sum, there was neither an option supported by consideration nor a bilateral contract binding on both parties.

Plaintiff contends, however, that he relied to his detriment on defendant's offer and that defendant must therefore answer in damages for its refusal to perform. Thus the question is squarely presented: Did plaintiff's reliance make defendant's offer irrevocable?

Section 90 of the Restatement of Contracts states: 'A promise which the promisor should reasonably expect to induce action or forbearance of a definite and substantial character on the part of the promisee and which does induce such action or forbearance is binding if injustice can be avoided only by enforcement of the promise.' This rule applies in this state. Edmonds v. County of Los Angeles, 40 Cal.2d 642, 255 P.2d 772; Frebank Co. v. White, 152 Cal.App.2d 522, 313 P.2d 633; Wade v. Markwell & Co., 118 Cal.App.2d 410, 258 P.2d 497, 37 A.L.R.2d 1363; West v. Hunt Foods Co., 101 Cal.App.2d 597, 225 P.2d 978; Hunter v. Sparling, 87 Cal.App.2d 711, 197 P.2d 807; see 18 Cal.Jur.2d 407–408; 5 Stan.L.Rev. 783.

Defendant's offer constituted a promise to perform on such conditions as were stated expressly or by implication therein or annexed thereto by operation of law. (See 1 Williston, Contracts (3rd. ed.), s 24A, p. 56, s 61, p. 196.) Defendant had reason to expect that if its bid proved the lowest it would be used by plaintiff. It induced 'action * * * of a definite and substantial character on the part of the promisee.'

Had defendant's bid expressly stated or clearly implied that it was revocable at any time before acceptance we would treat it accordingly. It was silent on revocation, however, and we must therefore determine whether there are conditions to the right of revocation imposed by law or reasonably inferable in fact. In the analogous problem of an offer for a unilateral contract, the theory is now obsolete that the offer is revocable at any time before complete performance. Thus section 45 of the Restatement of Contracts provides: 'If an offer for a unilateral contract is made, and part of the consideration requested in the offer is given or tendered by the offeree in response thereto, the offeror is bound by a contract, the duty of immediate performance of which is conditional on the full consideration being given or tendered within the time stated in the offer, or, if no time is stated therein, within a reasonable time.' In explanation, comment b states that the 'main offer includes as a subsidiary promise, necessarily implied, that if part of the requested performance is given, the offeror will not revoke his offer, and that if tender is made it will be accepted. Part performance or tender may thus furnish consideration for the subsidiary promise. Moreover, merely acting in justifiable reliance on an offer may in some cases serve as sufficient reason for making a promise binding (see s 90).'

Whether implied in fact or law, the subsidiary promise serves to preclude the injustice that would result if the offer could be revoked after the offeree had acted in detrimental reliance thereon. Reasonable reliance resulting in a foreseeable prejudicial change in position affords a compelling basis also for implying a subsidiary promise not to revoke an offer for a bilateral contract.

The absence of consideration is not fatal to the enforcement of such a promise. It is true that in the case of unilateral contracts the Restatement finds consideration for the implied subsidiary promise in the part performance of the bargained-for exchange, but its reference to section 90 makes clear that consideration for such a promise is not always necessary. The very purpose of section 90 is to make a promise binding even though there was no consideration 'in the sense of something that is bargained for and given in exchange.' (See 1 Corbin, Contracts 634 et seq.) Reasonable reliance serves to hold the offeror in lieu of the consideration ordinarily required to make the offer binding. In a case involving similar facts the Supreme Court of South Dakota stated that 'we believe that reason and justice demand that the doctrine (of section 90) be applied to the present facts. We cannot believe that by accepting this doctrine as controlling in the state of facts before us we will abolish the requirement of a consideration in contract cases, in any different sense than an ordinary estoppel abolishes some legal requirement in its application. We are of the opinion, therefore, that the defendants in executing the agreement (which was not supported by consideration) made a promise which they should have reasonably expected would induce the plaintiff to submit a bid based thereon to the Government, that such promise did induce this action, and that injustice can be avoided only by enforcement of the promise.' Northwestern Engineering Co. v. Ellerman, 69 S.D. 397, 408, 10 N.W.2d 879, 884; see also, Robert Gordon, Inc., v. Ingersoll-Rand Co., 7 Cir., 117 F.2d 654, 661; cf. James Baird Co. v. Gimbel Bros., 2 Cir., 64 F.2d 344.

When plaintiff used defendant's offer in computing his own bid, he bound himself to perform in reliance on defendant's terms. Though defendant did not bargain for this use of its bid neither did defendant make it idly, indifferent to whether it would be used or not. On the contrary it is reasonable to suppose that defendant submitted its bid to obtain the subcontract. It was bound to realize the substantial possibility that its bid would be the lowest, and that it would be included by plaintiff in his bid. It was to its own interest that the contractor be awarded the general contract; the lower the subcontract bid, the lower the general contractor's bid was likely to be and the greater its chance of acceptance and hence the greater defendant's chance of getting the paving subcontract. Defendant had reason not only to expect plaintiff to rely on its bid but to want him to. Clearly defendant had a stake in plaintiff's reliance on its bid. Given this interest and the fact that plaintiff is bound by his own bid, it is only fair that plaintiff should have at least an opportunity to accept defendant's bid after the general contract has been awarded to him.

It bears noting that a general contractor is not free to delay acceptance after he has been awarded the general contract in the hope of getting a better price. Nor can he reopen bargaining with the subcontractor and at the same time claim a continuing right to accept the original offer. See, R. J. Daum Const. Co. v. Child, Utah, 247 P.2d 817, 823. In the present case plaintiff promptly informed defendant that plaintiff was being awarded the job and that the subcontract was being awarded to defendant.

Defendant contends, however, that its bid was the result of mistake and that it was therefore entitled to revoke it. It relies on the rescission cases of M. F. Kemper Const. Co. v. City of Los Angeles, 37 Cal.2d 696, 235 P.2d 7, and Brunzell Const. Co. v. G. J. Weisbrod, Inc., 134 Cal.App.2d 278, 285 P.2d 989. See also, Lemoge Electric v. San Mateo County, 46 Cal.2d 659, 662, 297 P.2d 638. In those cases, however, the bidder's mistake was known or should have been known to the offeree, and the offeree could be placed in status quo. Of course, if plaintiff had reason to believe that defendant's bid was in error, he could not justifiably rely on it, and section 90 would afford no basis for enforcing it. Robert Gordon, Inc., v. Ingersoll-Rand, Inc., 7 Cir., 117 F.2d 654, 660. Plaintiff, however, had no reason to know that defendant had made a mistake in submitting its bid, since there was usually a variance of 160 per cent between the highest and lowest bids for paving in the desert around Lancaster. He committed himself to performing the main contract in reliance on defendant's figures. Under these circumstances defendant's mistake, far from relieving it of its obligation, constitutes an additional reason for enforcing it, for it misled plaintiff as to the cost of doing the paving. Even had it been clearly understood that defendant's offer was revocable until accepted, it would not necessarily follow that defendant had no duty to exercise reasonable care in preparing its bid. It presented its bid with knowledge of the substantial possibility that it would be used by plaintiff; it could foresee the harm that would ensue from an erroneous underestimate of the cost. Moreover, it was motivated by its own business interest. Whether or not these considerations alone would justify recovery for negligence had the case been tried on that theory (see Biakanja v. Irving, 49 Cal.2d 647, 650, 320 P.2d 16), they are persuasive that defendant's mistake should not defeat recovery under the rule of section 90 of the Restatement of Contracts. As between the subcontractor who made the bid and the general contractor who reasonably relied on it, the loss resulting from the mistake should fall on the party who caused it.

Leo F. Piazza Paving Co. v. Bebek & Brkich, 141 Cal.App.2d 226, 296 P.2d 368, 371, and Bard v. Kent, 19 Cal.2d 449, 122 P.2d 8, 139 A.L.R. 1032, are not to the contrary. In the Piazza case the court sustained a finding that defendants intended, not to make a firm bid, but only to give the plaintiff 'some kind of an idea to use' in making its bid; there was evidence that the defendants had told plaintiff they were unsure of the significance of the specifications. There was thus no offer, promise, or representation on which the defendants should reasonably have expected the plaintiff to rely. The Bard case held that an option not supported by consideration was revoked by the death of the optionor. The issue of recovery under the rule of section 90 was not pleaded at the trial, and it does not appear that the offeree's reliance was 'of a definite and substantial character' so that injustice could be avoided 'only by the enforcement of the promise.'

There is no merit in defendant's contention that plaintiff failed to state a cause of action, on the ground that the complaint failed to allege that plaintiff attempted to mitigate the damages or that they could not have been mitigated. Plaintiff alleged that after defendant's default, 'plaintiff had to procure the services of the L & H Co. to perform said asphaltic paving for the sum of $10,948.60. Plaintiff's uncontradicted evidence showed that he spent several months trying to get bids from other subcontractors and that he took the lowest bid. Clearly he acted reasonably to mitigate damages. In any event any uncertainty in plaintiff's allegation as to damages could have been raised by special demurrer. Code Civ.Proc. s 430, subd. 9. It was not so raised and was therefore waived. Code Civ.Proc. s 434.

The judgment is affirmed.

In PAVEL ENTERPRISES, INC. v. A.S. JOHNSON COMPANY, INC., 342 Md. 143 (Md. 1996), the Court of Appeals of Maryland considered whether to apply the doctrine of promissory estoppel to a bidding relationship between a general contractor and a subcontractor. The court expertly described the nature of the bidding relationships involved:

> "In such a building project there are basically three parties involved: the letting party, who calls for bids on its job; the general contractor, who makes a bid on the whole project; and the subcontractors, who bid only on that portion of the whole job which involves the field of its specialty. The usual procedure is that when a project is announced, a subcontractor, on his own initiative or at the general contractor's request, prepares an estimate and submits a bid to one or more of the general contractors interested in the project. The general contractor evaluates the bids made by the subcontractors in each field and uses them to compute its total bid to the letting party. After receiving bids from general contractors, the letting party ordinarily awards the contract to the lowest reputable bidder."

Id. (Quoting Maryland Supreme Corp. v. Blake Co., 279 Md. 531, 533–534 (1977).)

Pavel Enterprises, a general contractor, was bidding on a building renovation project for the National Institutes of Health, and it received a subcontractor bid from A.S. Johnson Company to do work on the HVAC system in the building. After Pavel Enterprises submitted its bid to NIH, A.S. Johnson withdrew its bid. The trial court found that Pavel Enterprises relied on A.S. Johnson's bid in order create its own bid for the NIH work. It also found that Pavel Enterprises' solicitation of subcontractor bids made clear "that there was no definite agreement between PEI and Johnson, and that PEI was not relying on Johnson's bid." The trial court concluded that Pavel Enterprises and A.S. Johnson did not form a contract under a detrimental reliance theory because, among other things, there was a "time lapse between the bid opening and award."

The Court of Appeals affirmed the trial court's conclusions. Although Pavel Enterprises had relied on A.S. Johnson's bid to make its initial bid, the Court of Appeals held that the trial court's did not clearly err by concluding that the "subcontractor's expectation that the general contractor [would] rely upon the sub-bid" lapsed in the month between the sub-bid and the bid award.

UNIVERSAL COMPUTER SYSTEMS V.
MEDICAL SERVICES ASSOCIATION

United States Court of Appeals for the Third Circuit
628 F.2d 820 (1980)

OSENN, CIRCUIT JUDGE.

This is a diversity action in which we are asked to consider questions of agency and promissory estoppel under Pennsylvania law. Specifically, we are asked to consider whether a principal is bound under a theory of promissory estoppel when an employee promised to pick up a bid from a potential bidder. We hold that the employee possessed apparent authority to make a binding promise on which the promisee relied to its detriment and accordingly reinstate the verdict of the jury awarding damages for the breach of that promise.

I.

In July of 1975, Medical Services Association of Pennsylvania (Blue Shield) located in Camp Hill, Pennsylvania, solicited bids for the lease of a computer. Pursuant to the bid solicitation, Universal Computer Systems, Inc. (Universal) of Westport, Connecticut, prepared a bid proposal. In order to be considered, the terms of the solicitation required that it be received by Blue Shield at Harrisburg, Pennsylvania, no later than 12:00 Noon on August 18, 1975.

Joel Gebert, an employee of Blue Shield, served as liaison between Blue Shield and prospective bidders on this contract. Shortly before the date of the bidding deadline, most probably on Friday, August 15, Warren Roy Wilson, President of Universal, telephoned Gebert and informed him that Universal could furnish a computer which would meet the required specifications. Being reluctant to entrust the bid to a conventional courier source, Wilson informed Gebert that he expected to transmit the bid via Allegheny Airlines to Harrisburg, Pennsylvania, and asked Gebert if he could arrange to have someone pick up the proposal at the Harrisburg airport on Monday morning. Gebert assured Wilson that the proposal would be picked up at the airport and delivered to Blue Shield in time to meet the bidding deadline.

On the appointed day, Wilson dispatched the bid proposal from La Guardia Airport in New York by Allegheny Airlines PDQ Service on August 18, 1975, at approximately 8:30 A.M. Wilson called Gebert again to give him the necessary information so that the bid could be picked up at Harrisburg as Gebert had agreed and timely delivered to Blue Shield. Gebert, however, informed Wilson that he had changed his mind and could not pick up the proposal. Wilson then unsuccessfully attempted to make other arrangements with Allegheny to have the proposal picked up by courier or other agents and timely delivered to Blue Shield.

Allegheny originally refused to allow anyone to pick up the proposal other than a direct employee of either plaintiff or Blue Shield. Wilson was finally able to contact the supervisors of the airline manager who instructed the manager to release the package to a courier. The bid proposal, however, was released too late to meet the noon deadline. Consequently, Blue Shield rejected the bid as untimely and returned it unopened.

Thereafter, Universal filed a complaint in the United States District Court for the Middle District of Pennsylvania seeking damages for the alleged breach of Blue Shield's promise. The case was tried before a jury which returned a verdict in the amount of $13,000 against Blue Shield. Thereafter Blue Shield filed a motion for judgment non obstante veredicto (n. o. v.) and a motion for a new trial. The district court granted the motion for judgment n. o. v. but denied the motion for a new trial. Universal appealed from the court's entry of judgment n. o. v. and Blue Shield cross-appeals from the denial of its motion for a new trial.

II.

* * *

[W]e believe that the district court erred in ruling that Gebert's promise should not be enforced on principles of promissory estoppel. To create liability on the basis of promissory estoppel, a promise must be of such a nature and made under such circumstances that the promisor should reasonably anticipate that it will induce action or forbearance of a definite and substantial character on the part of the promisee. Further, the promise must actually induce such action or forbearance and the circumstances must be such that injustice can only be avoided by enforcement of the promise. Restatement of Contracts s 90 (1932). The remedy may be limited as justice requires. Restatement of Contracts s 201 (Tent.Draft No. 2, April 30, 1965).

In the case before us, the district court found that, assuming that there had been authority to make a promise, the jury reasonably could have found that there was a promise upon which Universal had relied to its detriment. The court, however, concluded that Universal's reliance was unjustified. As we have already alluded, the court reasoned that Universal should have been aware of the federal procurement regulations and of their prohibition against the kind of service Gebert had agreed to perform for Universal. Thus, the court found Universal's reliance unjustified and declined to enforce the promise on principles of promissory estoppel. For the reasons we have stated above, however, we believe the court erred in concluding that Universal should have been aware of the applicability of federal procurement regulations to Gebert's promise to pick up their bid at the airport.

Nor do we believe that our holding is contrary to Stelmack v. Glen Alden Coal Co., 339 Pa. 410, 14 A.2d 127 (1940), and TMA Fund, Inc. v. Biever, 380 F.Supp. 1248 (E.D.Pa.1974), as urged by Blue Shield.

In Stelmack the defendant coal company requested permission to enter upon the plaintiffs' land and erect supports about their building so as to protect it against damage from defendant's impending subsurface mining operations. Plaintiffs granted permission and the supports were erected. As the mining operations continued, the defendant made repairs to the building from time to time but later refused to restore it to its previous condition. The plaintiffs later brought an action, seeking to recover on various theories of contract and promissory estoppel. In rejecting the promissory estoppel theory, the court stated:

The doctrine of promissory estoppel . . . may be invoked only in those cases where all the elements of a true estoppel are present, for if it is loosely applied any promise, regardless of the complete absence of consideration, would be enforceable.

339 Pa. at 416, 14 A.2d at 129. The court, however, proceeded to analyze the case under section 90 of the Restatement of Contracts. The court stated:

Here no action was taken by plaintiffs in reliance upon the defendant's promise which resulted in disadvantage to them. They did not alter their position adversely or substantially. They have suffered no injustice in being deprived of a gratuitous benefit to which they have no legal or equitable right.

Id., 14 A.2d at 130.

The instant case is different, however. Here it is clear that plaintiff incurred a substantial detriment as a result of relying upon defendant's promise. Plaintiff has suffered an injustice in being deprived of the service promised by Blue Shield's employee, Gebert.

TMA Fund is also distinguishable. There, defendants were induced to sign a promissory note to support a failing business on the false representation that other financing had also been arranged. On an action against defendants to enforce the terms of the note, the court held the note unenforceable for lack of consideration. The court noted that TMA Fund "did not agree to do anything when the agreement and notes were executed in return for the payment on the notes. TMA Fund is to this day not required to do anything or to refrain from doing any act which it had a right to do under the terms of the purported agreement." 380 F.Supp. at 1254. In the instant case, however, Blue Shield promised to pick up the bid and Universal relied upon that promise to its detriment.

Accordingly, we believe that, under Pennsylvania law, the jury could reasonably have found that Gebert possessed apparent authority to make a promise binding upon Blue Shield, that Universal relied upon that promise to its detriment, and that that promise should be enforced on the basis of promissory estoppel.

* * *

The order of the district court denying Blue Shield's motions for judgment n. o. v. and for a new trial (No. 79–2401) will be affirmed. The court's order entering judgment n. o. v. for Blue Shield on the issue of liability (No. 79–2400) will be reversed and the case remanded to the district court with directions to reinstate the jury's verdict. Costs taxed against Blue Shield in both appeals.

BRANCO ENTERPRISES, INC. V. DELTA ROOFING, INC.
Missouri Court of Appeals
886 S.W.2d 157 (1994)

PARRISH, JUDGE.

Branco Enterprises, Inc., (Branco) brought an action against Delta Roofing, Inc., (Delta) to recover damages for Delta's refusal to install a roof on a Consumers Market building renovated by Branco. The trial court determined (a) the parties had a contract that required Delta to install the required roof at a price of $21,545, and (b) Branco was entitled to and did rely on Delta's bid of $21,545 to its detriment. Judgment was entered for Branco in the amount of $18,695.

Delta appeals contending the determination that the parties had a contract was erroneous and there was insufficient evidence for the trial court to have found that Branco was entitled to rely on Delta's bid of $21,545 as the cost for installing the required roof. Appellate review is undertaken in accordance with Rule 73.01(c). The judgment is affirmed.

Branco desired to bid on a proposed renovation of a Consumers Market building in Neosho, Missouri. It undertook to subcontract part of the job. Branco requested bids from subcontractors for installation of a new roof on the Neosho store. The architectural specifications for the job required the new roof to be a modified bitumen roof using Derbigum, a product of Owens-Corning Fiberglass Corporation (Owens-Corning), or an approved substitute of equal quality. Any substitute was required to be approved by the architect. In order to obtain a manufacturer's warranty on a Derbigum roof, the roof had to be installed by a roofer who was certified by Owens-Corning to install the product.

Delta submitted a bid to Branco of $21,545 for installation, plus $1,200 for warranty of the roof. Delta's bid was significantly lower than other bids Branco received.

Branco's president, John Branham, called Delta to confirm its bid. He spoke to Cliff Cook, an estimator for Delta. Mr. Cook told Branham that Delta was seeking approval of alternative roofing from the architect; that if Delta could not get approval for its alternative roofing, Delta could get Owens-Corning certification.

Mr. Branham told Mr. Cook that Branco was relying on Delta's bid in placing its bid as general contractor for the project. Cook answered, "That's fine." Branco's bid was accepted. The contract was signed April 9, 1990.

On April 12, 1990, Branco sent three copies of a written subcontract agreement to Delta, together with a transmittal letter requesting Delta to execute and return all copies of the contract and to provide Branco certificates of insurance evidencing certain insurance coverage. Delta did not execute and return the contracts. It did send Branco a certificate of insurance. James Spears, president of Delta, explained why Delta sent the certificate of insurance to Branco. He testified, "We had intentions of doing the job."

On June 4, 1990, after the work on the project had begun, Mr. Branham had a telephone conversation with Mr. Cook. Cook told Branham, "We're not going to do the job." Cook explained that Delta had not gotten certified by Owens-Corning to apply Derbigum.

Branco then contracted with another roofing company for the work Delta was to have performed. The contract price with the new company was $40,240—$18,565 more than Delta's bid.

The trial court's conclusions of law included:

    1.   That [Delta's] bids to [Branco] on March 6, 1990 were offers to perform.

    2.   That [Branco] conditionally accepted [Delta's] $21,545.00 bid on March 6, 1990, said acceptance being contingent only on the award of the prime contract for renovation of the Consumer's [sic] Market in Neosho, Missouri to [Branco].

    . . . .

    4.   That on March 19, 1990,[1] the oral agreement between [Branco] and [Delta] became final when [Branco] signed said prime contract, creating a contractual obligation in [Delta].

    5.   That [Delta] breached its oral agreement with [Branco] by refusing to perform.

    6.   That in Missouri, detrimental reliance on an oral bid can be enforced under the doctrine of promissory estoppel. . . .

    7.   That [Branco] relied on [Delta's] March 6, 1990 bid to its detriment.

8. That [Delta] knew or should have known that [Branco] was relying on its bid.

9. That [Branco] had the right to rely on [Delta's] repreentations [sic].

10. [Branco's] reliance on [Delta's] bid and [Delta's] breach of agreement resulted in damage to [Branco] in the amount of $18,695.00 and it should have judgment on its petition and against [Delta] in that amount.

Delta presents two points on appeal. Both go to the question of whether there was an offer and acceptance between the parties that was sufficiently specific as to terms of a contract to manifest a common assent by them. If there was, a contract exists. If not, there was no contract. Bare v. Kansas City Federation of Musicians Local 34–627, 755 S.W.2d 442, 444 (Mo.App.1988).

Point I contends the trial court erred in finding that there was a contract because there was "no unequivocal acceptance of Delta's bid by Branco." Point II claims the trial court erred in applying the doctrine of promissory estoppel because "no unequivocal promise had been made by [Delta] in making its bid to [Branco] sufficient to permit [Branco] to unquestionably expect performance and to reasonably rely thereon." The facts relevant to each point are the same. The points will be discussed together.

Clifford Cook, the estimator for Delta who bid the roofing subcontract, testified by deposition. He testified that he had seen the plans or specifications for the job before he submitted Delta's bid. Based on the job requirements, he submitted an initial bid on behalf of Delta and, on the day Branco was compiling its bid, a revised bid. The representative of Branco with whom Mr. Cook talked told Cook that Branco was relying on Delta's bid in formulating its bid for the general contract with the owner.

In Delmo, Inc. v. Maxima Elec. Sales, Inc., 878 S.W.2d 499 (Mo.App.1994), this court held that a contract may be effected between a general contractor and a subcontractor based on the general contractor's reliance on the subcontractor's bid for a component of the project being bid. The decision in Delmo was based on application of the doctrine Missouri courts refer to as promissory estoppel. Id. at 504. The necessary elements for promissory estoppel are "(1) a promise, (2) foreseeable reliance, (3) reliance, and (4) injustice absent enforcement." Id.

Delmo is consistent with Drennan v. Star Paving Co., 51 Cal.2d 409, 333 P.2d 757 (1958), a case with facts similar to those in this appeal. Drennan was a general contractor. He sought bids from subcontractors and relied on them in computing his own bid. On the day bids had to be submitted, he received the bid from Star Paving Co. for paving work Drennan planned to subcontract. Star Paving Co.'s bid was the lowest bid for the paving.

Drennan used it in his calculation of his bid on the general contract. Drennan was awarded the contract.

Star Paving Co. refused to perform the work it had bid. The California court, following the reasoning in Northwestern Engineering Co. v. Ellerman, 69 S.D. 397, 408, 10 N.W.2d 879, 884 (1943), held that Star Paving Co.'s bid became binding upon Drennan being awarded the general contract. The court explained:

When [Drennan] used [Star Paving Co.'s] offer in computing his own bid, he bound himself to perform in reliance on [Star Paving Co.'s] terms. Though [Star Paving Co.] did not bargain for this use of its bid neither did [Star Paving Co.] make it idly, indifferent to whether it would be used or not. On the contrary it is reasonable to suppose that [Star Paving Co.] submitted its bid to obtain the subcontract. It was bound to realize the substantial possibility that its bid would be the lowest, and that it would be included by [Drennan] in his bid. It was to its own interest that the contractor be awarded the general contract; the lower the subcontract bid, the lower the general contractor's bid was likely to be and the greater its chance of acceptance and hence the greater [Star Paving Co.'s] chance of getting the paving subcontract. [Star Paving Co.] had reason not only to expect [Drennan] to rely on its bid but to want him to. Clearly [Star Paving Co.] had a stake in [Drennan's] reliance on its bid. Given this interest and the fact that [Drennan] is bound by his own bid, it is only fair that [Drennan] should have at least an opportunity to accept [Star Paving Co.'s] bid after the general contract has been awarded to him.

333 P.2d at 760.

Clifford Cook, Delta's representative, had seen the specifications for the required work. He knew that the specifications for the roof required use of the Owens-Corning product Derbigum with complete warranty that was available only when the material was installed by a roofer who was certified by Owens-Corning. A variance based on installation of other roofing material of equal quality could be granted only by the architect for the project.

The trial court heard testimony that Cook, knowing these things, told Mr. Branham, Branco's president, that if Delta could not get an alternative product approved, Delta could be certified by Owens-Corning. Branham testified he told Mr. Cook that Branco was relying on Delta's bid in seeking award of the general contract. There was testimony that Mr. Cook agreed on behalf of Delta. Deferring to the trial court's opportunity to judge the credibility of the witnesses, Rule 73.01(c)(2), this court holds the trial court's finding that an oral agreement was made on March 6, 1990, that became final when Branco signed the general contract is not erroneous.

Delta's contention, in Point I, that there was no "unequivocal acceptance of Delta's bid by Branco" fails. The fact that a written subcontract was not tendered to Delta by Branco until after the general contract was signed is of no significance under the facts of this case. As explained by Mr. Branham, "The [written] contract [was] just a confirmation." He further explained, "I had already committed to Delta that I was using them. I committed to them at 2:48 on the day of the bid letting. I specifically said, 'We are using your bid. If we get it, you will get the job.'"

Delta's contention in Point II also fails. Delta argues that Delta's bid did not make an unequivocal promise to Branco "sufficient to permit [Branco] to unquestionably expect performance and to reasonably rely thereon."

There was testimony that Mr. Branham was told that Delta would obtain a variance to permit it to substitute another product for Derbigum or would obtain Owens-Corning certification to permit Delta to apply Derbigum and provide a full warranty; that Delta would perform the roofing task for the amount of its bid. A promise was made by Delta to Branco.

Mr. Branham told Delta that Branco was relying on Delta's bid. Mr. Cook acknowledged that the reliance was acceptable to Delta. It was foreseeable that Branco would rely on Delta's promise to perform at the bid price.

Branco submitted its bid to the owner and included in its calculation Delta's bid for roofing. Branco relied on Delta's promise.

Delta refused to perform in accordance with its promise. Branco was required to expend a greater sum to get the work done than the amount to which Delta had agreed. Absent Branco obtaining reimbursement from Delta, an injustice would occur.

Missouri's doctrine of promissory estoppel applies. This court holds that the trial court's judgment is supported by substantial evidence and is not against the weight of the evidence; that it neither erroneously declares or applies the law. See Thurmond v. Moxley, 879 S.W.2d 709, 710 (Mo.App.1994). Judgment affirmed.

GARRISON, P.J., and CROW, J., concur.

WEITZ COMPANY, LLC V. HANDS, INC.

Supreme Court of Nebraska
294 Neb. 215 (2016)

CONNOLLY, J.

I. SUMMARY

The Weitz Company, LLC (Weitz), a general contractor, received an invitation to bid on a planned nursing facility. Hands, Inc., doing business as H & S Plumbing and Heating (H & S), submitted a bid to Weitz for the plumbing work, as well as the heating, ventilation, and air conditioning

(HVAC) parts of the job. Weitz' bid to the project owner incorporated the amount of H & S' bid. After the owner awarded the project to Weitz, H & S refused to honor its bid. Weitz completed the project with different subcontractors at greater expense.

At trial, Weitz sought to enforce H & S' bid under promissory estoppel. The court determined that Weitz reasonably and foreseeably relied on H & S' bid, and it therefore estopped H & S from reneging. The court measured Weitz' damages as the difference between H & S' bid and the amount Weitz paid to substitute subcontractors. H & S appeals. We affirm the judgment and the amount of damages.

II. BACKGROUND

1. WEITZ IS INVITED TO BID

In 2011, the Evangelical Lutheran Good Samaritan Society (Good Samaritan) invited four "prequalified General Contractors," including Weitz, to bid on a proposed nursing facility in Beatrice, Nebraska. Good Samaritan chose the four prequalified general contractors based on "prior relationships" recommendations from its architect and its own research.

Good Samaritan is a "big player" in the retirement living market. Weitz is a "dominant contractor" in the same market. Alan Kennedy, a Weitz executive, said that Weitz had sought to build a relationship with Good Samaritan that would lead to "negotiated work," meaning that Good Samaritan would work with Weitz without inviting other general contractors to bid. Kennedy testified that negotiated work is "one of the best places to be as a contractor." When Good Samaritan invited Weitz to bid on the Beatrice project, Weitz knew of another potential project with Good Samaritan in Sarpy County, Nebraska.

Good Samaritan's "Invitation to Bid" stated that it would not consider bids received after 2 p.m. on August 30, 2011 (bid day). The invitation incorporated certain "Instructions to Bidders," which provided that Good Samaritan and its architect could object to a general contractor's proposed subcontractors. The invitation stated that "[n]o bids may be withdrawn for a period of 60 days after opening of bids." If a general contractor refused to enter into a contract, the instructions provided to bidders state that the general contractor would forfeit its bid security as liquidated damages. A bid security is a bond that "assures the owner that [it] can rely upon the bids." But Good Samaritan did not ask for bid securities, because it prequalified the general contractors.

2. BID-DAY MADNESS

Before bid day, Weitz assigned "lead person[s]" to the different categories of work on the project, referred to as "tickets." The ticket leaders reviewed the project specifications and created a "scope checklist" that described the work for each ticket. Weitz prepared scope checklists because subcontractors sometimes excluded certain work from their bid.

On bid day, Weitz assembled its people in a conference room to collect and organize the hundreds of bids from subcontractors. Ticket leaders called out the bids after comparing them with the scope checklist. Weitz then added the numbers to a "bid day spreadsheet."

Subcontractors in the mechanical, engineering, and plumbing fields typically submit their bids within 15 minutes of the deadline. As a result, Weitz is often "at the wire turning in [its] number to an owner." Brian Mahlendorf, a project executive for Weitz, oversaw Weitz' bid for the Good Samaritan project. Mahlendorf said that Weitz received H & S' bid "less than 15 minutes or so" before the 2 p.m. deadline.

Kennedy, who had been involved in "well over a hundred bids," testified that it was "customary for general contractors to rely on bids submitted by subcontractors" and that subcontractors submit bids because they want the job. Mahlendorf, who had more than 20 years of experience in the construction industry, testified that it was customary for Weitz to rely on subcontractors' bids, that subcontractors knew that Weitz relied on their bids, and that subcontractors submitted bids because they wanted to procure work. Mahlendorf said it was "very rare" for a subcontractor to refuse to honor its bid.

3.   H & S SUBMITS A BID TO WEITZ

On bid day, H & S sent Weitz a bid for the plumbing and HVAC parts of the project. H & S' base bid was $2,430,600. For alternate duct and radiant heating work, H & S quoted $39,108 and $52,500, respectively. H & S also sent Weitz a "revised" base bid of $2,417,000, but Weitz received the revised bid too late to use in its bid to Good Samaritan.

Kennedy and Mahlendorf would confirm a subcontractor's bid if it looked "funny" or "off," but H & S' bid did not seem unusual to them. Weitz had estimated what each ticket would cost based on historical data, and H & S' bid was above Weitz' estimate. Mahlendorf was also comfortable with H & S because Weitz had worked with H & S before. Furthermore, Mahlendorf assumed that H & S was "actually looking at [its] number" because it sent Weitz a revised bid. Two of the other four prequalified general contractors stated that they planned to use H & S for the plumbing and the HVAC work.

Kennedy and Mahlendorf testified that the market for construction services was weak in 2011. Subcontractors were "aggressively seeking work" and making low bids to "keep their people busy." Kennedy said that subcontractors' bids had "ranges that you hadn't traditionally seen in the marketplace." A difference of 15 percent between the lowest and second-lowest bids was not uncommon.

4. WEITZ SUBMITS ITS BID TO GOOD SAMARITAN

Mahlendorf said that Weitz used H & S' bid in its own bid to Good Samaritan. Weitz chose H & S' bid because it included the "complete scope with the lowest cost." Mahlendorf said that H & S' bid was "comprehensive" and that Weitz was "willing to take it as is." Mahlendorf added H & S' base bid to Weitz' bid-day spreadsheet for the plumbing and HVAC tickets.

On bid day, Weitz sent Good Samaritan a base bid of $9.2 million. Kennedy and Mahlendorf testified that Weitz' base bid of $9.2 million included H & S' $2,430,600 bid. Weitz promised Good Samaritan that it would execute a contract for its base bid if offered the project within 60 days. Weitz' bid to Good Samaritan included a list of "Major Sub-Contractors." For the plumbing subcontractor, Weitz wrote "HEP or H & S." For the HVAC subcontractor, Weitz wrote "Falcon or H & S."

Mahlendorf explained that he used a disjunctive list of major subcontractors because H & S' bid "came in late enough after this form had been basically ready to send out, and we had to add [its] name to those two line items." Mahlendorf said that Weitz did not use the bids of the other plumbing and HVAC subcontractors, "HEP" and Falcon Heating and Air Conditioning (Falcon), to reach its $9.2 million base bid. Even if Weitz could have used HEP and Falcon instead of H & S, Mahlendorf said that Weitz intended to use H & S.

5. GOOD SAMARITAN AWARDS THE PROJECT TO WEITZ

On September 1, 2011, Weitz received "early indications" that Good Samaritan would select its bid. Weitz received "[f]inal notification" on September 2. Mahlendorf called H & S on September 6 and told the head of H & S' engineering department that Weitz had won the bidding and had "carried the H & S number." He said that he told H & S that "we used [its] number in our bid, and we were prepared to enter into a contract with [H & S] and move forward."

Usually, after the owner of a project accepted Weitz' bid, Weitz asked its subcontractors to sign a "subcontract" establishing the "[e]xact contract terms" between Weitz and the subcontractor. Weitz had used a similar subcontract for more than a dozen years. H & S' chief executive officer testified that in the 10 or 15 times that H & S had worked with Weitz, Weitz had always accepted H & S' revisions to the subcontract.

Weitz signed a contract with Good Samaritan for the base bid of $9.2 million plus six additional areas of work not included in the base bid. The opening paragraph of the contract states that it was "made and entered" on, and has an "Effective Date" of, September 7, 2011. But "Date: 9–19–11" appears below the signature of Good Samaritan's representatives.

Under the contract, Good Samaritan and its architect had the right to reject Weitz' proposed subcontractors. But Good Samaritan did not veto H

& S or any of Weitz' other subcontractors. Good Samaritan's architect could not recall having a "conversation of significance" about subcontractors. Despite an owner's reservation of the right to veto subcontractors, Mahlendorf said that "[i]n the real world," a general contractor treats an owner's silence as an approval and that owners are usually silent.

6.   H & S RENEGES ON ITS BID

Hugh Sieck, Jr., H & S' owner and chief executive officer, was fishing in Alaska on bid day. Sieck testified that he told his team of estimators before he left for Alaska not to send a bid to Weitz. He had "bitter feelings" for Weitz because it had a "history of bid shopping," meaning that Weitz would "get a bid, . . . look at it, and [it] will go to another contractor to get a lower number." Sieck said every general contractor "bid shops," but he thought Weitz did more than most.

John Sampson, who worked for one of the other prequalified general contractors, called Sieck on bid day and suggested that Sieck review H & S' bid. Sampson noticed a "considerable difference" between H & S' bid and the other subcontractors' bids, although he did not say what the difference was or whether the scope of the subcontractors' bids differed. Asked what might prompt him to confirm a bid with a subcontractor, Sampson said a difference of 10 or 15 percent between bids might be enough "if I had to pull a number out of the air," but "when it gets 20 or 30 percent then you really start getting concerned."

According to Sieck, he ordered a member of H & S' estimating team to "[p]ull your bid" after Sieck spoke with Sampson. But when Sieck returned to H & S' offices on September 6, 2011, he learned that his employees had, contrary to orders, submitted a bid to Weitz and had failed to withdraw the bid. He "surmised" that H & S' bid contained errors, so he "told [his] team to go out and find a mistake."

Lloyd Ness, the person responsible for preparing the plumbing and piping parts of H & S' bid, said that Sieck was upset after bid day because H & S "left too much money on the table." Ness testified that H & S' estimating team reviewed its bid after Sieck returned but concluded there "was not a hair out of place." So, according to Ness, Sieck told him to "lie to Weitz and tell Weitz that we forgot travel time and we missed showers." Ness refused to lie and resigned because of the incident. Sieck denied asking Ness to lie. Another member of H & S' estimating team, Thomas Santillan, Jr., said that Sieck did not ask him to lie.

Sieck personally took a hand in looking for a mistake and ultimately landed on a miscalculation involving shower units. He told Santillan to inform Weitz of H & S' " 'belief of the mistake.' "

On September 8, 2011, Santillan sent an e-mail with a letter attachment to Mahlendorf stating that H & S had found two errors after "thoroughly reviewing" its bid: (1) a miscalculation of the cost of shower installation and (2) the omission of travel time from the cost of labor. The collective magnitude of the claimed errors exceeded $250,000.

Santillan later took another look at H & S' bid and concluded that the original calculation of the cost for shower installation was, in fact, correct. But Santillan maintained that H & S had underbid travel costs. And Santillan said that H & S eventually unearthed "numerous mistakes" in its bid. Specifically, "the material was just not accurate," "the dollar amount did not appear to be accurate," and "there wasn't enough material."

Mahlendorf came to H & S' offices for a meeting on September 9, 2011. According to Sieck, Mahlendorf mentioned, " 'I've got to get to Beatrice because I haven't got all my shopping done.' " Sieck understood Mahlendorf's statement to mean that "as per usual, they are out shopping the bids."

But Mahlendorf said that Sieck's recollection did not "comport with [Mahlendorf's] memory." Asked if Weitz would ever "carry one number but you continue negotiating and replace it with a different bidder," Mahlendorf said he was "sure that has happened for some reason or another." But he said that Weitz did not intend to shop H & S' bid. H & S' bid was "comprehensive," and Weitz was "willing to take it as is."

Weitz and H & S could not come to terms. The magnitude of H & S' error kept growing and eventually ballooned to more than $430,000. In October 2011, Weitz informed H & S that it would use other subcontractors.

7. WEITZ HONORS ITS BID TO GOOD SAMARITAN

Weitz did not try to withdraw its bid from Good Samaritan because of its dispute with H & S. Instead, it completed the project with other plumbing and HVAC subcontractors. Kennedy and Mahlendorf testified that the bidding documents prohibited Weitz from withdrawing or modifying its bid for 60 days. And the contract between Weitz and Good Samaritan was "already in progress" by the time Weitz learned that H & S would not honor its bid.

Business reasons also prevented Weitz from abandoning the project. Kennedy testified that the "integrity of our bids" was particularly important if the owner selected Weitz as a prequalified general contractor. Mahlendorf explained that backing out would have harmed Weitz' reputation in its industry:

On a project like this where the architect and owner have preselected general contractors, if we wouldn't honor our bid, we would be at risk for future work from the design firm that did it and in addition to the owner group. From a business standpoint, we do a lot of [business with] senior living [clients], and it would be detrimental if we were starting to be excluded from senior living clients like the Good Samaritan Society.

Withdrawal would have also lowered Weitz' standing with Good Samaritan's architect, with which Weitz had an "ongoing business relationship."

8. WEITZ MEASURES ITS LOSSES

After H & S made it clear that it would not stand by its bid, Weitz asked for bids from other subcontractors. Weitz selected the subcontractors Falcon and "MMC" for the plumbing and HVAC portions of the project because their bids had the "lowest cost complete scope that we could obtain." The amount Weitz paid Falcon and MMC under their subcontracts was $1,187,900 and $1,626,800, respectively. The subcontract prices did not include any "change orders," which could have affected the total amount Weitz ultimately paid to the subcontractors. H & S' bid did not include change orders either.

To calculate Weitz' damages, Mahlendorf added Falcon's and MMC's subcontract prices for the sum of $2,814,700. From that sum, Mahlendorf subtracted H & S' base bid of $2,430,600 and its bids of $39,108 and $52,500 on optional work which Good Samaritan ultimately asked Weitz to perform. The difference is $292,492.

9. PROCEDURAL HISTORY

Weitz pleaded two causes of action in its complaint against H & S. First, Weitz alleged that H & S breached a contract formed by Weitz' acceptance of H & S' bid. Second, Weitz argued that promissory estoppel bound H & S to its bid because Weitz reasonably and foreseeably relied on the bid.

A few years after H & S filed its answer—which did not affirmatively allege an election of remedies defense—it moved for an "Order requiring [Weitz] to elect between its claim for breach of contract and promissory estoppel." The court overruled H & S' motion.

After a bench trial, the court determined that the parties had not formed a contract. But it enforced H & S' bid under promissory estoppel. The court awarded Weitz damages of $292,492.

III. ASSIGNMENTS OF ERROR

H & S assigns, restated, that the court erred by (1) entering a judgment for Weitz on its promissory estoppel claim, (2) "awarding breach of contract damages instead of reliance damages for promissory estoppel," and (3) overruling H & S' pretrial motion to require Weitz to elect between its contract and promissory estoppel claims.

IV. STANDARD OF REVIEW

Although a party can raise estoppel claims in both legal and equitable actions, estoppel doctrines have their roots in equity. In reviewing judgments and orders disposing of claims sounding in equity, we decide factual questions de novo on the record and reach independent conclusions on questions of fact and law. But when credible evidence is in conflict on material issues of fact, we consider and may give weight to the fact that the trial court observed the witnesses and accepted one version of the facts over another.

V. ANALYSIS

1. PROMISSORY ESTOPPEL

H & S argues that the court should not have enforced its bid under promissory estoppel. Courts often use promissory estoppel to hold a subcontractor to its bid until the general contractor has had a reasonable length of time to accept the bid after receiving the prime contract. The leading case is Drennan v. Star Paving Co. There, the California Supreme Court held that because the general contractor was bound by its bid, fairness required that the general contractor have an opportunity to accept the subcontractor's bid after receiving the prime contract. Drennan has had a "very broad following."

In Nebraska, a claim of promissory estoppel requires a plaintiff to show: (1) a promise that the promisor should have reasonably expected to induce the plaintiff's action or forbearance, (2) the promise did in fact induce the plaintiff's action or forbearance, and (3) injustice can only be avoided by enforcing the promise. The promise need not be definite enough to support a unilateral contract, but it must be definite enough to show that the plaintiff's reliance on it was reasonable and foreseeable. Here, we start our review of the court's judgment by asking if H & S' bid was a promise on which it should have foreseen reliance.

(a) H & S' Bid Was a Promise on Which Reliance Was Foreseeable

H & S' bid was a promise to perform the work described in the bid. H & S said it was "bidding the Plumbing, Hydronic Piping, & HVAC portion" of the Good Samaritan project and specifically listed the work that it was willing to perform. H & S asked for the general contractors' "consideration" and hoped to "be of service" to them.

And H & S should have foreseen that Weitz would rely on its bid. Kennedy and Mahlendorf testified that subcontractors generally expect (and hope) that general contractors will rely on their bids. Usages of trade are strong evidence of the foreseeability of reliance. Furthermore, Weitz received H & S' bid about 15 minutes before the 2 p.m. deadline. Evidence that a promisee had little time to act on the promise shows that the promisee's reliance was foreseeable. And, as noted, H & S expressly asked Weitz to consider its bid. Having determined that H & S should have expected Weitz to rely on its bid, our next question is whether Weitz in fact relied on the bid and, if so, whether its reliance was reasonable.

(b) Weitz Reasonably Relied on H & S' Bid

Weitz relied on H & S' bid by including the base amount of H & S' bid in Weitz' own bid to Good Samaritan. Mahlendorf testified that he slotted H & S' bid into the plumbing and HVAC tickets, which is reflected in the bid-day spreadsheet. Although Weitz disjunctively listed the major subcontractors in its bid to Good Samaritan, the evidence shows that Weitz actually relied on H & S' bid. Both Kennedy and Mahlendorf testified that Weitz' $9.2 million base bid incorporated H & S' base bid of $2,430,600.

We further conclude that Weitz' reliance on H & S' bid was reasonable. The evidence shows that general contractors customarily rely on subcontractors' bids. Mahlendorf testified that it was "very rare" for a subcontractor to refuse to honor its bid. In particular, Weitz had worked with H & S 10 or 15 times before without incident. Weitz' reliance was also reasonable because it had only 15 minutes to review H & S' bid. Weitz could not independently verify every item in H & S' bid in a quarter of an hour. How could competitive bidding function at all if general contractors did not rely on subcontractors' bids?

H & S marshals a number of arguments why Weitz did not reasonably rely on its bid, which we consolidate into five that merit discussion. First, H & S argues that the bidding documents "absolutely precluded any reliance." Specifically, H & S emphasizes that Good Samaritan had the right to veto subcontractors.

But the bare fact that Good Samaritan could have, in theory, rejected H & S' bid did not make Weitz' reliance on H & S' bid unreasonable. Good Samaritan did not object to any of Weitz' subcontractors. Mahlendorf testified that despite an owner's reservation of the right to veto subcontractors, owners generally do not exercise that right "[i]n the real world." If the chance that Good Samaritan would nix H & S were significant, Weitz' reliance on H & S' bid might not have been reasonable. But the record lacks this evidence.

We similarly reject H & S' second argument, which is that Weitz' reliance was unreasonable because Weitz "did not require any quotation be kept open for any period of time as a precondition to its consideration." General contractors customarily rely on subcontractors' bids, as discussed above, and the record lacks any evidence that prudent general contractors turn away bids that do not have such a provision. We cannot find any authority that conditions promissory estoppel, as a matter of law, on a demand by the general contractor that subcontractors insert such clauses into their bids. The only case that H & S cites is from a jurisdiction that allowed parties to use promissory estoppel only as a defense. That case is an outlier.

H & S' third argument is that Weitz did not reasonably rely on its bid because it could have pulled out of the project without any consequences. H & S notes that, although the invitation to bid required Weitz to hold its bid open for 60 days, Good Samaritan did not ask for a bid security. Furthermore, Weitz knew that H' & S had cold feet before Weitz and Good Samaritan formally signed a contract.

But H & S could not expect Weitz to abandon the project because H & S decided its bid was too low. Weitz promised Good Samaritan that it would hold its bid open for 60 days, and breaking that promise would have sullied Weitz' reputation. In particular, Good Samaritan might have been reluctant to work with Weitz again. Losing Good Samaritan's business would have been a significant loss to Weitz because Weitz and Good Samaritan are both active in the retirement living market. Pulling out of the project would also have jeopardized Weitz' preexisting relationship with the project architect. Good Samaritan selected the prequalified general contractors based, in part, on the architect's recommendations. Weitz did not have to tell Good Samaritan that, as things turned out, it would not build the facility because of a squabble with a plumbing and HVAC subcontractor.

The fourth reason why, according to H & S, Weitz did not reasonably rely on its bid is that Weitz "attempted to accept quotations on materially different terms." H & S argues, restated, that Weitz did not rely on its subcontractors' bids, because it later asked subcontractors to sign a subcontract that did not mirror the terms of the subcontractors' bids. H & S backed out before Weitz could send it a subcontract. But H & S suggests that Weitz would have sent it a subcontract similar to the one that Weitz sent to its other subcontractors and that this hypothetical subcontract would have been materially different from H & S' bid.

A general contractor can reasonably rely on a subcontractor's bid even if the general contractor and subcontractor contemplate signing a formal subcontract with additional standard terms after the bidding process ends. But a general contractor cannot demand that a subcontractor agree to unusual and onerous terms while still holding the subcontractor to its original bid. For example, in Hawkins Constr. Co. v. Reiman Corp., a general contractor demanded that a subcontractor agree to multiple "nonstandard additional conditions which could be considered onerous." After the subcontractor refused to accept the terms, the general contractor tried to enforce the subcontractor's bid under promissory estoppel. We held that the general contractor's reliance was not reasonable because it could not assume that the subcontractor would acquiesce to onerous nonstandard terms.

But differences between a subcontractor's bid and the subcontract do not matter if they are an "afterthought" raised by a subcontractor that wants to avoid its promise for other reasons. Here, H & S reneged because its bid was too low, and it did so before Weitz sent it a subcontract. So, H & S' dispute with the terms of the subcontract is even less than an afterthought:

It is imaginary. Plus, Sieck testified that Weitz had always accepted H & S' revisions to the subcontract.

Finally, we reach H & S' fifth argument as to why Weitz did not reasonably rely on its bid: It was so low that Weitz was on notice that H & S had made mistakes. Differences between the scope of H & S' bid and the scopes of the other bids make a dollar-for-dollar comparison difficult, but H & S asserts that its bid was "considerably lower" than the those of its rivals.

We conclude that H & S' bid was not so low that Weitz' reliance on it was unreasonable. If a bid is so low that a mistake should be apparent, a general contractor cannot reasonably rely on the bid. But H & S' bid was higher than what Weitz had budgeted based on historical data. Furthermore, the market for construction services was weak in 2011 and subcontractors were bidding aggressively. Kennedy and Mahlendorf testified that bids during this period could be unusually low compared to years in which the market was more robust. H & S sent its bid to all four of the prequalified general contractors. Two of the general contractors, including Weitz, chose H & S without first checking to see if H & S had made a mistake.

So, H & S' bid was a promise on which reliance was foreseeable and Weitz reasonably relied on the bid. One question remains: Did the court have to enforce H & S' bid to prevent injustice?

(c)   Enforcement of H & S' Bid Was Necessary to Prevent Injustice

We conclude that the court could avoid injustice only by enforcing H & S' bid. As discussed above, many courts have recognized the unfairness of allowing a subcontractor to renege after the general contractor has relied on the subcontractor's bid in the general contractor's own successful bid to the owner. H & S argues that it is not fair to enforce its bid, because it made mistakes. But Weitz should not have to bear the cost of H & S' errors: "As between the subcontractor who made the bid and the general contractor who reasonably relied on it, the loss resulting from the mistake should fall on the party who caused it."

H & S argues that we should not enforce its bid, because Weitz engaged in the "unethical practice of bid shopping." A general contractor bid shops by taking the lowest subcontractor's bid to other subcontractors and asking them to undercut it. Courts are reluctant to use promissory estoppel if the general contractor bid shopped, either because bid shopping shows that the general contractor did not rely on the bid, or because injustice no longer requires enforcement of the bid, or both.

But the record does not show that Weitz shopped H & S' bid. Sieck testified that he had "bitter feelings" about an earlier project in which Weitz bid shopped. That project, however, involved a bidding process different from the competitive process used by Good Samaritan. The only direct evidence that Weitz bid shopped during the Beatrice project is Sieck's testimony about Mahlendorf's aside about "shopping" in Beatrice. Mahlendorf did not remember making that statement. He testified that Weitz had no intent to shop H & S' bid. In a credibility battle, Mahlendorf has the better of the admittedly bitter Sieck, who candidly testified about "toying with" his memory of the communications between H & S and Weitz.

In conclusion, H & S' bid was a promise on which reliance was foreseeable. Weitz actually and reasonably relied on the bid. And justice required the court to enforce H & S' bid. So the court did not err by entering a judgment for Weitz on its promissory estoppel claim.

2. DAMAGES

H & S does not agree with the amount of damages. It argues that the court erred by "awarding benefit of the bargain / contract damages rather than reliance damages." H & S further contends that Weitz did not prove its damages with reasonable certainty and that its damages are necessarily zero, because Good Samaritan did not ask for a bid security.

No single measure of damages applies in every promissory estoppel case. The commentary to the Restatement (Second) of Contracts explains that the ultimate standard for enforcing the promise—the prevention of injustice—also guides the measurement of damages. The damages that the promisor ought to pay are those that justice requires. In some cases, justice requires only reliance damages.

For example, we approved of reliance damages in Rosnick v. Dinsmore. There, we held that contract law's "definiteness" requirement does not apply to promissory estoppel. To explain this distinction, we stated that promissory estoppel provides for damages as justice requires, rather than damages based on the benefit of the bargain. In the "usual" case, we anticipated that courts would award damages measured by the promisee's reliance. We note that if a promise is indefinite, the theoretical availability of damages measured by the promise's value might be moot.

We did not limit damages to the extent of the promisee's reliance in every promissory estoppel case. As we said in Rosnick, promissory estoppel provides for damages as justice requires. Remedial flexibility is consistent with promissory estoppel's equitable roots. Justice does not require the same measure of damages in every context.

In the construction bidding context, courts have "consistently and uniformly" measured the general contractor's damages as the difference between the reneging subcontractor's bid and the amount the general contractor paid to replacement subcontractors. Here, the court measured Weitz' damages in a consistent manner. It is "plain that justice required this measure of damages."

We reject H & S' argument that Weitz did not prove its damages with enough exactitude. A plaintiff's burden is to prove his or her damages to a reasonable certainty, not beyond all reasonable doubt. Nor were Weitz' damages zero simply because Good Samaritan did not ask for a bid security. As we explained above, H & S could not demand that Weitz walk away from the project because H & S was unhappy with its bid.

3. ELECTION OF REMEDIES

Finally, H & S waived its argument that the court should have required Weitz to elect between its contract and promissory estoppel claims. The election of remedies doctrine is an affirmative defense. A party must specifically plead an affirmative defense for the court to consider it. H & S did not specifically plead election of remedies as a defense, so we will not consider it.

VI. CONCLUSION

We affirm the judgment for Weitz on its promissory estoppel claim. H & S' bid was a promise, and it should have foreseen that Weitz, as was usual in the construction industry, might rely on the bid. Weitz reasonably relied on the bid by incorporating it in Weitz' own bid to the project owner. And the court could avoid injustice only by enforcing H & S' bid. We further conclude that the court correctly measured Weitz' damages.

AFFIRMED.

READING ASSIGNMENT 5

KATZ v. DANNY DARE, INC.

Missouri Court of Appeals, Western District.
610 S.W.2d 121

Opinion

TURNAGE, PRESIDING JUDGE.

I. G. Katz filed three suits in the Associate Division of the Circuit Court seeking pension payments for three separate time periods alleged to be due from Danny Dare, Inc. Two suits resulted in judgment in favor of Katz, but a request for a trial de novo was filed and those causes were assigned to a circuit judge for trial. The other suit pending in the Associate Division was transferred to the same circuit judge and all the cases were consolidated for trial without a jury. Judgment was entered in favor of Dare in all cases. On this appeal Katz contends the promise of pension payments made to him by Dare is binding under the Doctrine of Promissory Estoppel. Reversed and remanded.

There is little or no dispute as to the facts in this case. Katz began work for Dare in 1950 and continued in that employ until his retirement on June 1, 1975. The president of Dare was Harry Shopmaker, who was also the brother of Katz's wife. Katz worked in a variety of positions including executive vice president, sales manager, and a member of the board of directors, although he was not a member of the board at the time of his retirement. In February 1973, Katz was opening a store, operated by Dare, for business and placed a bag of money on the counter next to the cash register. A man walked in, picked up the bag of money and left. When Katz followed him and attempted to retrieve the money, Katz was struck in the head. He was hospitalized and even though he returned to work he conceded he had some difficulties. His walk was impaired and he suffered some memory loss and was not able to function as he had before. Shopmaker and others testified to many mistakes which Katz made after his return at considerable cost to Dare. Shopmaker reached the decision that he would have to work out some agreeable pension to induce Katz to retire because he did not feel he could carry Katz as an employee. At that time Katz's earnings were about $23,000 per year.

Shopmaker began discussions with Katz concerning retirement but Katz insisted that he did not want to retire but wanted to continue working. Katz was 65 at the time of his injury and felt he could continue performing useful work for Dare to justify his remaining as an employee. However, Shopmaker persisted in his assessment that Katz was more of a liability than an asset as an employee and continued negotiating with Katz over a period of about 13 months in an effort to reach an agreement by which Katz would retire with a pension from Dare. Shopmaker first offered Katz

$10,500 per year as a pension but Katz refused. Thereafter, while Katz was on vacation, Shopmaker sent Katz a letter to demonstrate how Katz could actually wind up with more take-home pay by retiring than he could by continuing as an employee. In the letter Shopmaker proposed an annual pension payable by Dare of $13,000, added the Social Security benefit which Katz and his wife would receive after retirement, and added $2,520 per year which Katz could earn for part-time employment, but not necessarily from Dare, to demonstrate that Katz would actually realize about $1,000 per year more in income by retiring with the Dare pension over what he would realize if he continued his employment. Shopmaker testified that he sent this letter in an effort to persuade Katz to retire.

Katz acceded to the offer of a pension of $13,000 per year for life, and on May 22, 1975, the board of directors of Dare unanimously approved the following resolution:

WHEREAS, I. G. Katz has been a loyal employee of Danny Dare, Inc. and its predecessor companies for more than 25 years; and,

WHEREAS, the said I. G. Katz has requested retirement because of failing health; and,

WHEREAS, it has been the custom in the past for the company to retire all executives having loyally served the company for many years with a remuneration in keeping with the sum received during their last five years of employment;

NOW THEN BE IT RESOLVED, That Danny Dare, Inc. pay to I. G. Katz the sum of $500.00 bi-weekly, or a total of $13,000.00 per year, so long as he shall live.

Katz retired on June 1, 1975, at age 67, and Dare began payment of the pension at the rate of $500 every other week. Katz testified that he would not have retired without the pension and relied on the promise of Dare to pay the pension when he made his decision to retire. Shopmaker testified that at the time the board resolution was passed, the board intended for Katz to rely on the resolution and to retire, but he said Katz would have been fired had he not elected to retire.

In the Fall of 1975, Katz began working for another company on 3 to 4 half-days per week. At the end of that year Shopmaker asked Katz if he could do part-time work for Dare and Katz told him he could work one-half day on Wednesdays. For the next two and one-half years Katz continued to work for Dare one-half day per week.

In July, 1978, Dare sent a semi-monthly check for $250 instead of $500. Katz sent the check back and stated he was entitled to the full $500. Thereafter Dare stopped sending any checks. Shopmaker testified that he cut off the checks to Katz because he felt Katz's health had improved to the point that he could work, as demonstrated by the part-time job he held.

Katz testified the decrease was made after Shopmaker told him he would have to work one-half day for five days a week for Dare or his pension would be cut in half. Katz testified, without challenge, that he was not able to work 40 hours per week in 1978 at age 70.

The trial court entered a judgment in which some findings of fact were made. The court found that Katz based his claim on the Doctrine of Promissory Estoppel as applied in Feinberg v. Pfeiffer Company, 322 S.W.2d 163 (Mo.App.1959). The court found that Katz was not in the same situation as Feinberg had been because Katz faced the prospect of being fired if he did not accept the pension offer whereas there was no such evidence in the Feinberg case. The court found the pension from Dare did not require Katz to do anything and he was in fact free to work for another company. The court found Katz did not give up anything to which he was legally entitled when he elected to retire. The court found that since Katz had the choice of accepting retirement and a pension or being fired, that it could not be said that he suffered any detriment or significant change of position when he elected to retire. The court further found that it could not find any injustice resulting to Katz because by the time payments had been terminated, he had received about $40,000 plus a paid vacation for his wife and himself to Hawaii. The court found these were benefits he would not have received had he been fired.

Katz contends he falls within the holding in Feinberg and Dare contends that because Katz faced the alternative of accepting the pension or being fired that he falls without the holding in Feinberg.

At the outset it is interesting to note in view of the argument made by Dare that the court in Feinberg stated at p. 165:

It is clear from the evidence that there was no contract, oral or written, as to plaintiff's length of employment, and that she was free to quit, and the defendant to discharge her, at any time.

In Feinberg the board of directors passed a resolution offering Feinberg the opportunity to retire at any time she would elect with retirement pay of $200 per month for life. Feinberg retired about two and one-half years after the resolution was passed and began to receive the retirement pay. The pay continued for about seven years when the company sent a check for $100 per month, which Feinberg refused and thereafter payments were discontinued.

The court observed that Section 90 of the Restatement of the Law of Contracts had been adopted by the Supreme Court in In Re Jamison's Estate, 202 S.W.2d 879 (Mo.1947). The court noted that one of the illustrations under s 90 was strikingly similar to the facts in Feinberg. The court applied the Doctrine of Promissory Estoppel, as articulated in s 90, and held that Feinberg had relied upon the promise of the pension when she resigned a paying position and elected to accept a lesser amount in pension. The court held it was immaterial as to whether Feinberg became unable to obtain other employment before or after the company discontinued the pension payment. The court held the reliance by Feinberg was in giving up her job in reliance on the promise of a pension. Her subsequent disability went to the prevention of injustice which is part of the Doctrine of Promissory Estoppel.

There are three elements to be satisfied to invoke the Doctrine of Promissory Estoppel. These are: (1) a promise; (2) a detrimental reliance on such promise; and (3) injustice can be avoided only by enforcement of the promise.

This court is not convinced that the alternative Shopmaker gave to Katz of either accepting the pension and retiring or be fired takes this case out of the operation of Promissory Estoppel. The fact remains that Katz was not fired, but instead did voluntarily retire, but only after the board of directors had adopted the resolution promising to pay Katz a pension of $13,000 per year for life. Thus, the same facts are present in this case as were present in Feinberg. When Katz elected to retire and give up earnings of about $23,000 per year to accept a pension of $13,000 per year, he did so as a result of a promise made by Dare and to his detriment by the loss of $10,000 per year in earnings. It is conceded Dare intended that Katz rely on its promise of a pension and Dare does not contend Katz did not in fact rely on such promise. The fact that the payments continued for about three years and that Katz at age 70 could not work full-time was unquestioned. Thus, the element that injustice can be avoided only by enforcement of the promise is present, because Katz cannot now engage in a full-time job to return to the earnings which he gave up in reliance on the pension.

Dare's argument that the threat of being fired removes this case from the operation of Promissory Estoppel is similar to an argument advanced in Trexler's Estate, 27 Pa.Dist. & Co.Rep. 4 (1936), cited with approval in Fried v. Fisher, 328 Pa. 497, 196 A. 39 (1938). In Trexler the depression had forced General Trexler to decide whether to fire several employees who had been with him for many years or place them on a pension. The General decided to promise them a pension of $50 per month and at his death, the employees filed a claim against his estate for the continuation of the payments. The court observed that the General could have summarily discharged the employees, but was loath to do this without making some provision for their old age. This was shown by the numerous conferences which the General had with his executives in considering each employee's financial situation, age and general status. The court said it was clear that the General wanted to reduce overhead and at the same time wanted to give these faithful employees some protection. The court stated it as an open question of what the General would have done if the men had not accepted his offer of a lifetime pension. The court said it would not speculate on that point but it was sufficient to observe that the men accepted the offer and received the pension. The court applied s 90 of the Restatement and held that under the Doctrine of Promissory Estoppel the estate was bound to continue the payments.

The facts in this case are strikingly similar to Trexler. Shopmaker undoubtedly wanted to reduce his overhead by reducing the amount being paid to Katz and it is true that Katz could have been summarily discharged. However, it is also true that Shopmaker refused to fire Katz, but instead patiently negotiated for about 13 months to work out a pension which Katz did agree to accept and voluntarily retired.

While Dare strenuously urges that the threat of firing effectively removed any legitimate choice on the part of Katz, the facts do not bear this out. The fact is that Katz continued in his employment with Dare until he retired and such retirement was voluntary on the part of Katz. Had Shopmaker desired to terminate Katz without any promise of a pension he could have done so and Katz would have had no recourse. However, the fact is that Shopmaker did not discharge Katz but actually made every effort to induce Katz to retire voluntarily on the promise of a pension of $13,000 per year.

Dare appears to have led the trial court into error by relying on Pitts v. McGraw-Edison Co., 329 F.2d 412 (6th Cir. 1964). Pitts was informed that the company had retired him and would pay him a certain percentage of sales thereafter. Thus, the main distinction between this case and Pitts is that Pitts did not elect to retire on the promise of any payment, but was simply informed that he had been retired by the company and the company would make payment to him. There was no promise made to Pitts on which he acted to his detriment. In addition, the court was applying the law of Tennessee and the court stated that Tennessee had not adopted s 90 of the Restatement. The court in Pitts found that Pitts had not given up anything to which he was legally entitled and was not restricted in any way in his activities after being placed in retirement by his company.

The facts in Pitts would not enable Pitts to recover under Promissory Estoppel in Missouri because there was no action taken by Pitts in reliance on a promise. The test to be applied in this case is not whether Katz gave up something to which he was legally entitled, but rather whether Dare made a promise to him on which he acted to his detriment. The legally entitled test could never be met by an employee such as Katz or Feinberg because neither could show any legal obligation on the company to promise a pension. The Doctrine of Promissory Estoppel is designed to protect those to whom a promise is made which is not legally enforcible until the requirements of the doctrine are met. Pitts is not applicable either on the facts or the law.

The trial court misapplied the law when it held that Katz was required to show that he gave up something to which he was legally entitled before he could enforce the promise of a pension made by Dare. The elements of

Promissory Estoppel are present: a promise of a pension to Katz, his detrimental reliance thereon, and injustice can only be avoided by enforcing that promise. The judgment is reversed and the case is remanded with directions to enter judgment in all suits in favor of Katz for the amount of unpaid pension.

All concur.

FEINBERG V. PFEIFFER COMPANY

Circuit Court of the City of St. Louis
322 S.W.2d 163 (Mo. 1959)

DOERNER, COMMISSIONER.

This is a suit brought in the Circuit Court of the City of St. Louis by plaintiff, a former employee of the defendant corporation, on an alleged contract whereby defendant agreed to pay plaintiff the sum of $200 per month for life upon her retirement. A jury being waived, the case was tried by the court alone. Judgment below was for plaintiff for $5,100, the amount of the pension claimed to be due as of the date of the trial, together with interest thereon, and defendant duly appealed.

The parties are in substantial agreement on the essential facts. Plaintiff began working for the defendant, a manufacturer of pharmaceuticals, in 1910, when she was but 17 years of age. By 1947 she had attained the position of bookkeeper, office manager, and assistant treasurer of the defendant, and owned 70 shares of its stock out of a total of 6,503 shares issued and outstanding. Twenty shares had been given to her by the defendant or its then president, she had purchased 20, and the remaining 30 she had acquired by a stock split or stock dividend. Over the years she received substantial dividends on the stock she owned, as did all of the other stockholders. Also, in addition to her salary, plaintiff from 1937 to 1949, inclusive, received each year a bonus varying in amount from $300 in the beginning to $2,000 in the later years.

On December 27, 1947, the annual meeting of the defendant's Board of Directors was held at the Company's offices in St. Louis, presided over by Max Lippman, its then president and largest individual stockholder. The other directors present were George L. Marcus, Sidney Harris, Sol Flammer, and Walter Weinstock, who, with Max Lippman, owned 5,007 of the 6,503 shares then issued and outstanding. At that meeting the Board of Directors adopted the following resolution, which, because it is the crux of the case, we quote in full:

'The Chairman thereupon pointed out that the Assistant Treasurer, Mrs. Anna Sacks Feinberg, has given the corporation many years of long and faithful service. Not only has she served the corporation devotedly, but with exceptional ability and skill. The President pointed out that although all of the officers and directors sincerely hoped and desired that Mrs. Feinberg would continue in her present position for as long as she felt able, nevertheless, in view of the length of service which she has contributed provision should be made to afford her retirement privileges and benefits which should become a firm obligation of the corporation to be available to her whenever she should see fit to retire from active duty, however many years in the future such retirement may become effective. It was, accordingly, proposed that Mrs. Feinberg's salary which is presently $350.00 per month, be increased to $400.00 per month, and that Mrs. Feinberg would be given the privilege of retiring from active duty at any time she may elect to see fit so to do upon a retirement pay of $200.00 per month for life, with the distinct understanding that the retirement plan is merely being adopted at the present time in order to afford Mrs. Feinberg security for the future and in the hope that her active services will continue with the corporation for many years to come. After due discussion and consideration, and upon motion duly made and seconded, it was—

'Resolved, that the salary of Anna Sacks Feinberg be increased from $350.00 to $400.00 per month and that she be afforded the privilege of retiring from active duty in the corporation at any time she may elect to see fit so to do upon retirement pay of $200.00 per month, for the remainder of her life.'

At the request of Mr. Lippman his sons-in-law, Messrs. Harris and Flammer, called upon the plaintiff at her apartment on the same day to advise her of the passage of the resolution. Plaintiff testified on cross-examination that she had no prior information that such a pension plan was contemplated, that it came as a surprise to her, and that she would have continued in her employment whether or not such a resolution had been adopted. It is clear from the evidence that there was no contract, oral or written, as to plaintiff's length of employment, and that she was free to quit, and the defendant to discharge her, at any time.

Plaintiff did continue to work for the defendant through June 30, 1949, on which date she retired. In accordance with the foregoing resolution, the defendant began paying her the sum of $200 on the first of each month. Mr. Lippman died on November 18, 1949, and was succeeded as president of the company by his widow. Because of an illness, she retired from that office and was succeeded in October, 1953, by her son-in-law, Sidney M. Harris. Mr. Harris testified that while Mrs. Lippman had been president she signed the monthly pension check paid plaintiff, but fussed about doing so, and considered the payments as gifts. After his election, he stated, a new accounting firm employed by the defendant questioned the validity of the payments to plaintiff on several occasions, and in the Spring of 1956, upon its recommendation, he consulted the Company's then attorney, Mr. Ralph Kalish. Harris testified that both Ernst and Ernst, the accounting firm, and Kalish told him there was no need of giving plaintiff the money. He also stated that he had concurred in the view that the payments to plaintiff were mere gratuities rather than amounts due under a contractual obligation, and that following his discussion with the Company's attorney plaintiff was sent a check for $100 on April 1, 1956. Plaintiff declined to accept the reduced amount, and this action followed. Additional facts will be referred to later in this opinion.

Appellant's first assignment of error relates to the admission in evidence of plaintiff's testimony over its objection, that at the time of trial she was sixty-five and a half years old, and that she was no longer able to engage in gainful employment because of the removal of a cancer and the performance of a colocholecystostomy operation on November 25, 1957. Its complaint is not so much that such evidence was irrelevant and immaterial, as it is that the trial court erroneously made it one basis for its decision in favor of plaintiff. As defendant concedes, the error (if it was error) in the admission of such evidence would not be a ground for reversal, since, this being a jury-waived case, we are constrained by the statutes to review it upon both the law and the evidence, Sec. 510.310 RSMo 1949, V.A.M.S., and to render such judgment as the court below ought to have given. Section 512.160, Minor v. Lillard, Mo., 289 S.W.2d 1; Thumm v. Lohr, Mo.App., 306 S.W.2d 604. We consider only such evidence as is admissible, and need not pass upon questions of error in the admission and exclusion of evidence. Hussey v. Robinson, Mo., 285 S.W.2d 603. However, in fairness to the trial court it should be stated that while he briefly referred to the state of plaintiff's health as of the time of the trial in his amended findings of fact, it is obvious from his amended grounds for decision and judgment that it was not, as will be seen, the basis for his decision.

Appellant's next complaint is that there was insufficient evidence to support the court's findings that plaintiff would not have quit defendant's employ had she not known and relied upon the promise of defendant to pay her $200 a month for life, and the finding that, from her voluntary retirement until April 1, 1956, plaintiff relied upon the continued receipt of the pension installments. The trial court so found, and, in our opinion, justifiably so. Plaintiff testified, and was corroborated by Harris, defendant's witness, that knowledge of the passage of the resolution was communicated to her on December 27, 1947, the very day it was adopted. She was told at that time by Harris and Flammer, she stated, that she could take the pension as of that day, if she wished. She testified further that she continued to work for another year and a half, through June 30, 1949; that at that time her health was good and she could have continued to work, but that after working for almost forty years she thought she would take a rest. Her testimony continued:

'Q. Now, what was the reason—I'm sorry. Did you then quit the employment of the company after you—after this year and a half? A. Yes.

'Q. What was the reason that you left? A. Well, I thought almost forty years, it was a long time and I thought I would take a little rest.

'Q. Yes. A. And with the pension and what earnings my husband had, we figured we could get along.

'Q. Did you rely upon this pension? A. We certainly did.

'Q. Being paid? A. Very much so. We relied upon it because I was positive that I was going to get it as long as I lived.

'Q. Would you have left the employment of the company at that time had it not been for this pension? A. No.

'Mr. Allen: Just a minute, I object to that as calling for a conclusion and conjecture on the part of this witness.

'The Court: It will be overruled.

'Q. (Mr. Agatstein continuing): Go ahead, now. The question is whether you would have quit the employment of the company at that time had you not relied upon this pension plan? A. No, I wouldn't.

'Q. You would not have. Did you ever seek employment while this pension was being paid to you—A. (interrupting): No.

'Q. Wait a minute, at any time prior—at any other place? A. No, sir.

'Q. Were you able to hold any other employment during that time? A. Yes, I think so.

'Q. Was your health good? A. My health was good.'

It is obvious from the foregoing that there was ample evidence to support the findings of fact made by the court below.

We come, then, to the basic issue in the case. While otherwise defined in defendant's third and fourth assignments of error, it is thus succinctly stated in the argument in its brief: '* * * whether plaintiff has proved that she has a right to recover from defendant based upon a legally binding contractual obligation to pay her $200 per month for life.'

It is defendant's contention, in essence, that the resolution adopted by its Board of Directors was a mere promise to make a gift, and that no contract resulted either thereby, or when plaintiff retired, because there was no consideration given or paid by the plaintiff. It urges that a promise to make a gift is not binding unless supported by a legal consideration; that the only apparent consideration for the adoption of the foregoing resolution was the 'many years of long and faithful service' expressed therein; and that past services are not a valid consideration for a promise. Defendant argues further that there is nothing in the resolution which made its effectiveness conditional upon plaintiff's continued employment, that she was not under contract to work for any length of time but was free to quit whenever she wished, and that she had no contractual right to her position and could have been discharged at any time.

Plaintiff concedes that a promise based upon past services would be without consideration, but contends that there were two other elements which supplied the required element: First, the continuation by plaintiff in the employ of the defendant for the period from December 27, 1947, the date when the resolution was adopted, until the date of her retirement on June 30, 1949. And, second, her change of position, i. e., her retirement, and the abandonment by her of her opportunity to continue in gainful employment, made in reliance on defendant's promise to pay her $200 per month for life.

We must agree with the defendant that the evidence does not support the first of these contentions. There is no language in the resolution predicating plaintiff's right to a pension upon her continued employment. She was not required to work for the defendant for any period of time as a condition to gaining such retirement benefits. She was told that she could quit the day upon which the resolution was adopted, as she herself testified, and it is clear from her own testimony that she made no promise or agreement to continue in the employ of the defendant in return for its promise to pay her a pension. Hence there was lacking that mutuality of obligation which is essential to the validity of a contract. Middleton v. Holecroft, Mo.App., 270 S.W.2d 90; Solace v. T. J. Moss Tie Co., Mo.App., 142 S.W.2d 1079; Aslin v. Stoddard County, 341 Mo. 138, 106 S.W.2d 472; Fuqua v. Lumbermen's Supply Co., 229 Mo.App. 210, 76 S.W.2d 715; Hudson v. Browning, 264 Mo. 58, 174 S.W. 393; Campbell v. American Handle Co., 117 Mo.App. 19, 94 S.W. 815.

But as to the second of these contentions we must agree with plaintiff. By the terms of the resolution defendant promised to pay plaintiff the sum of $200 a month upon her retirement. Consideration for a promise has been defined in the Restatement of the Law of Contracts, Section 75, as:

'(1) Consideration for a promise is

(a) an act other than a promise, or

(b) a forbearance, or

(c) the creation, modification or destruction of a legal relation, or

(d) a return promise, bargained for and given in exchange for the promise.'

As the parties agree, the consideration sufficient to support a contract may be either a benefit to the promisor or a loss or detriment to the promisee. Industrial Bank & Trust Co. v. Hesselberg, Mo., 195 S.W.2d 470; State ex rel. Kansas City v. State Highway Commission, 349 Mo. 865, 163 S.W.2d 948; Duvall v. Duncan, 341 Mo. 1129, 111 S.W.2d 89; Thompson v. McCune, 333 Mo. 758, 63 S.W.2d 41.

Section 90 of the Restatement of the Law of Contracts states that: 'A promise which the promisor should reasonably expect to induce action or forbearance of a definite and substantial character on the part of the promisee and which does induce such action or forbearance is binding if injustice can be avoided only by enforcement of the promise.' This doctrine has been described as that of 'promissory estoppel,' as distinguished from that of equitable estoppel or estoppel in pais, the reason for the differentiation being stated as follows:

'It is generally true that one who has led another to act in reasonable reliance on his representations of fact cannot afterwards in litigation between the two deny the truth of the representations, and some courts have sought to apply this principle to the formation of contracts, where, relying on a gratuitous promise, the promisee has suffered detriment. It is to be noticed, however, that such a case does not come within the ordinary definition of estoppel. If there is any representation of an existing fact, it is only that the promisor at the time of making the promise intends to fulfill it. As to such intention there is usually no misrepresentation and if there is, it is not that which has injured the promisee. In other words, he relies on a promise and not on a misstatement of fact; and the term 'promissory' estoppel or something equivalent should be used to make the distinction.' Williston on Contracts, Rev. Ed., Sec. 139, Vol. 1.

In speaking of this doctrine, Judge Learned Hand said in Porter v. Commissioner of Internal Revenue, 2 Cir., 60 F.2d 673, 675, that '* * * 'promissory estoppel' is now a recognized species of consideration.'

As pointed out by our Supreme Court in In re Jamison's Estate, Mo., 202 S.W.2d 879, 887, it is stated in the Missouri Annotations to the Restatement under Section 90 that:

"There is a variance between the doctrine underlying this section and the theoretical justifications that have been advanced for the Missouri decisions."

That variance, as the authors of the Annotations point out, is that:

'This § 90, when applied with § 85, means that the promise described is a contract without any consideration. In Missouri the same practical result is reached without in theory abandoning the doctrine of consideration. In Missouri three theories have been advanced as ground for the decisions (1) Theory of act for promise. The induced 'action or forbearance' is the consideration for the promise. Underwood Typewriter Co. v. Century Realty Co. (1909) 220 Mo. 522, 119 S.W. 400, 25 L.R.A., N.S., 1173. See § 76. (2) Theory of promissory estoppel. The induced 'action or forbearance' works an estoppel against the promisor. (Citing School District of Kansas City v. Sheidley (1897) 138 Mo. 672, 40 S. W. 656 [37 L.R.A. 406]) * * * (3) Theory of bilateral contract. When the induced 'action or forbearance' is begun, a promise to complete is implied, and we have an enforceable bilateral contract, the implied promise to complete being the consideration for the original promise.' (Citing cases.)

Was there such an act on the part of plaintiff, in reliance upon the promise contained in the resolution, as will estop the defendant, and therefore create an enforceable contract under the doctrine of promissory estoppel? We think there was. One of the illustrations cited under Section 90 of the Restatement is: '2. A promises B to pay him an annuity during B's life. B thereupon resigns a profitable employment, as A expected that he might. B receives the annuity for some years, in the meantime becoming disqualified from again obtaining good employment. A's promise is binding.' This illustration is objected to by defendant as not being applicable to the case at hand. The reason advanced by it is that in the illustration B became 'disqualified' from obtaining other employment before A discontinued the payments, whereas in this case the plaintiff did not discover that she had cancer and thereby became unemployable until after the defendant had discontinued the payments of $200 per month. We think the distinction is immaterial. The only reason for the reference in the illustration to the disqualification of A is in connection with that part of Section 90 regarding the prevention of injustice. The injustice would occur regardless of when the disability occurred. Would defendant contend that the contract would be enforceable if the plaintiff's illness had been discovered on March 31, 1956, the day before it discontinued the payment of the $200 a month, but not if it occurred on April 2nd, the day after? Furthermore, there are more ways to become disqualified for work, or unemployable, than as the result of illness. At the time she retired plaintiff was 57 years of age. At the time the payments were discontinued she was over 63 years of age. It is a matter of common knowledge that it is virtually impossible for a woman of that age to find satisfactory employment, much less a position comparable to that which plaintiff enjoyed at the time of her retirement.

The fact of the matter is that plaintiff's subsequent illness was not the 'action or forbearance' which was induced by the promise contained in the resolution. As the trial court correctly decided, such action on plaintiff's part was her retirement from a lucrative position in reliance upon defendant's promise to pay her an annuity or pension. In a very similar case, Ricketts v. Scothorn, 57 Neb. 51, 77 N.W. 365, 367, 42 L.R.A. 794, the Supreme Court of Nebraska said:

'* * * According to the undisputed proof, as shown by the record before us, the plaintiff was a working girl, holding a position in which she earned a salary of $10 per week. Her grandfather, desiring to put her in a position of independence, gave her the note accompanying it with the remark that his other grandchildren did not work, and that she would not be obliged to work any longer. In effect, he suggested that she might abandon her employment, and rely in the future upon the bounty which he promised. He doubtless desired that she should give up her occupation, but, whether he did or not, it is entirely certain that he contemplated such action on her part as a reasonable and probable consequence of his gift. Having intentionally influenced the plaintiff to alter her position for the worse on the faith of the note being paid when due, it would be grossly inequitable to permit the maker, or his executor, to resist payment on the ground that the promise was given without consideration.'

The Commissioner therefore recommends, for the reasons stated, that the judgment be affirmed.

PER CURIAM.

PITTS V. MCGRAW-EDISON COMPANY
United States Court of Appeals for the Sixth Circuit
329 F.2d 412 (1964)

SHACKELFORD MILLER, JR., CIRCUIT JUDGE.

Plaintiff, L. U. Pitts, brought this action in the District Court to recover damages in the amount of $15,000 for an alleged breach of a retirement contract by the defendant. He also sought a declaration of rights with respect to future payments under the contract. Jurisdiction is based upon diversity of citizenship and the amount involved. Section 1332, Title 28 United States Code. Plaintiff appeals from a judgment dismissing the action.

The facts, which are mostly undisputed, are as follows. Plaintiff was a manufacturer's representative in Memphis, Tennessee, for a period of many years prior to July 1, 1955. For approximately twenty-five years preceding that date, he sold the products of the defendant's predecessor and the defendant, McGraw-Edison Company, on a commission basis in an assigned territory comprising several southern states. In his capacity as a manufacturer's representative he was an independent business man, hiring and firing his own employees, paying his own expenses and overhead, and managing his business as he saw fit. He had no written contract with the defendant and the defendant had no obligation to him except to compensate him on a commission basis for sales made in the assigned territory. The relationship between the parties was independent and was not that of employer and employee. It was terminable at will, without notice by either party at any time. The plaintiff was free to handle any other products he desired, including those of competitors of the defendant, and he did so until early in 1954, when on his own volition and without any requirement by the defendant, he discontinued his representation of other manufacturers.

At no time during the relationship of the parties did the plaintiff make contributions to a pension fund or a retirement fund of any kind.

In April 1955 when the plaintiff was approximately 67 years of age, he accompanied O. Dee Harrison, the sales manager for the defendant, to Little Rock, Arkansas, for a meeting with one Paul Thurman, who had formerly worked for the plaintiff but at the time was working the State of Arkansas as a factory representative for the defendant and others. At that meeting Mr. Harrison told the plaintiff that the defendant was making arrangements for the plaintiff to retire at a time shortly thereafter and for Thurman to take over the plaintiff's territory, with the plaintiff receiving an overwrite commission of 1% From the defendant on all sales made in that territory. Thereafter the plaintiff received a letter dated July 1, 1955, from O. Dee Harrison reading in part as follows:

'Dear Lou:

'Whether you know it or not, you are on retirement effective July 1st. But to make the matter of retirement a little less distasteful, we are going ahead as you and I talked last time we were together by paying each month 1% Of the * * * sales from the Mississippi and Tennessee states. You will get your check each month just as you have been in the habit of getting our check on commissions. Let us hope that there is enough to help keep a few pork chops on the table and a few biscuits in the oven.

'We are going to keep you on the list for bulletins, Lou, so that you will know what is going on. I know that you will help Paul in every way that you can, and I know that your help will be greatly appreciated by Paul.'

There was an error in this letter regarding the territory to which it referred and Mr. Harrison corrected this error in a letter to the plaintiff dated July 20, 1955. In addition, this letter contained the following:

'Now in regard to your 1% Deal, Lou, I have talked with our office in Boonville on this matter. There is a problem of keeping things straight without undue complications, also. So what I am going to do is to give you 1% On Paul's territory, which will enable Dorothy to quickly figure the thing each month. * * * I am sorry I cannot include the rest of the United States, Lou, but I don't think this will be too bad a proposition for you.'

The letter also said in closing:

'We will keep you on the mailing list and any time you can throw a little weight our way we will appreciate any effort you make, Lou. And any time you have any questions, don't be afraid to ask us about them.'

Although plaintiff testified that the arrangements were completed at the April meeting in Little Rock, he unequivocally conceded on his cross-examination that the foregoing two letters contained the entire understanding between him and the defendant, and that there was nothing else either orally or in writing.

The plaintiff received a check from the defendant each month regularly from July 1955 through June 1960 covering the 1% Commission on sales in the specified territory. The amounts received were:

For the last six months of 1955, $ 759.67

For 1956, $ 2,630.23

For 1957, $ 2,696.31

For 1958, $ 2,629.04

For 1959, $ 4,337.38

For first six months of 1960 $ 3,233.46

Under date of July 23, 1960, the plaintiff was advised by letter from the Division Controller of the defendant, reading in part as follows:

'Dear Mr. Pitts:

'I am enclosing our check #50064752 for $238.51 which, according to our records, completes the five year series of payments to be paid after your retirement from the Company.'

Plaintiff wrote the defendant protesting the discontinuance of the payments. Mr. Harrison responded at some length, pointing out that the plaintiff was at no time an employee of the defendant, that he was not eligible for any company pension had there been one available, which there was not, and that in order to make the retirement a little less painful, the Company had voluntarily paid the 1% Commission for a period of five years but was not willing to continue it for an additional period. He pointed out that this was the same position taken by the Company with respect to three other employees who were all retired at the same general period, and that he did not know of any other company which gave any separation pay at all to manufacturer's representatives who represented them.

This action followed. Following a trial to the Court without a jury, the District Judge held that the plaintiff was not entitled to recover any amount whatever and dismissed his complaint.

Plaintiff contends that the negotiations between the Company and him leading to his retirement were in substance an offer on the part of the Company that if he would retire as a manufacturer's representative on July 1, 1955, and turn over to his successor representative all of his customer account records containing valuable information on active and inactive accounts, which had been built up over a period of twenty years or more, the Company would pay him monthly thereafter a 1% Overwrite commission on sales by the defendant in the territory which was at that time allotted to him; that after considering the offer, he accepted it and thereafter carried it out by retiring as a manufacturer's representative and turning over to his successor the stipulated records; and that the defendant breached the contract by refusing to make the payments after July 1, 1960.

Defendant contends that the so-called 'retirement' of the plaintiff was actually not a 'retirement' in that the plaintiff was not an employee of the defendant, but was a termination of defendant's business relations with the plaintiff, made effective by a unilateral act on its part, which it was legally authorized to do; that it was not an offer to the plaintiff on its part and acceptance thereof by the plaintiff; that it imposed no contractual obligation on its part to make any payment to the plaintiff; and that even if construed as a retirement contract between it and the plaintiff, it was void and unenforceable for lack of consideration.

In considering these contentions, it must be kept in mind that the plaintiff was an independent business man, not an employee of the defendant. His relationship with the defendant could be terminated by either party at any time without notice and without liability therefor. The plaintiff in his testimony concedes this, and it was so found as a fact by the District Judge. Unless the plaintiff is able to establish a valid contract obligating the defendant to pay the 'retirement' benefits claimed, he has no cause of action.

Assuming, without so holding, that there was a promise by the defendant to pay the plaintiff the retirement benefits claimed, we are faced with the question of what consideration passed from the plaintiff to the defendant to make this promise enforceable.

Plaintiff vigorously argues that although he did not promise to do anything or to refrain from doing anything, as plainly appears from the two letters, and so conceded by him, consideration nevertheless exists because of the action taken by him at the request of the defendant, namely, his retirement as a manufacturer's representative, including other manufacturers as well as the defendant, and his turning over to the defendant his personal records pertaining to customers and sales over a period of years in the past. There would be merit in this contention if it was supported by the facts. Farabee-Treadwell Co. v. Union & Planters' Bank & Trust Co., 135 Tenn. 208, 216, 186 S.W. 92, L.R.A.1916F, 501; Meurer Steel Barrel Co., Inc. v.

Martin, 1 F.2d 687, C.A.3rd; Messick v. Powell, 314 Ky. 805, 809, 236 S.W.2d 897.

However, these factual contentions of the plaintiff were disputed by the evidence of the defendant. The District Judge made findings of fact that the plaintiff was not required by the terms of the letters, or by any other statements on the part of the defendant, or its agents, to do anything whatsoever; that upon his retirement on July 1, 1955, the plaintiff was free to handle the products of any other manufacturer or competitor if he so desired, to seek other employment, or to do as he pleased; that nothing in the arrangement circumscribed the plaintiff's actions or rights in any manner; and that the plaintiff was not obligated to perform any duties on behalf of the defendant. These findings are fully supported by the evidence. In fact, they were substantially conceded by the plaintiff in the cross-examination of him as a witness, in which he apparently contended that he did certain things for the defendant after his retirement although he was not required to do so.

On the basis of these facts, the District Judge ruled that the payments to the plaintiff over the period of July 1, 1955, to July 1, 1960, were without consideration, were the result of voluntary action on the part of the defendant, and were mere gratuities terminable by the defendant at will.

We concur in the ruling. Combs v. Standard Oil Co., 166 Tenn. 88, 59 S.W.2d 525; Judd v. Wasie, 211 F.2d 826, 832, C.A.8th; Big Cola Corporation v. World Bottling Co., 134 F.2d 718, C.A.6th; Tennessee Enamel Mfg. Co. v. Stoves, Inc., 192 F.2d 863, C.A.6th, cert. denied, 342 U.S. 946, 72 S.Ct. 561, 96 L.Ed. 704.

Plaintiff further contends that although defendant's promise may not be supported by legal consideration, it is nevertheless enforceable under the doctrine of promissory estoppel, which, as explained by the authorities, is different from the well recognized principle of estoppel in pais, based on misrepresentation of fact. Plaintiff relies upon this principle as explained and applied in Ricketts v. Scothorn, 57 Neb. 51, 77 N.W. 365, 42 L.R.A. 794; Sessions v. Southern California Edison Co., 47 Cal.App.2d 611, 118 P.2d 935; and Feinberg v. Pfeiffer Company, (Mo.App.1959) 322 S.W.2d 163.

Promissory estoppel is defined in Restatement, Contracts, Section 90, as follows:

'A promise which the promisor should reasonably expect to induce action or forbearance of a definite and substantial character on the part of the promisee and which does induce such action or forbearance is binding if injustice can be avoided only by enforcement of the promise.'

This principle appears to be of somewhat limited application in the United States. Annotation, 48 A.L.R.2d 1069, 1081, 1085. We are not shown that it has ever been recognized or applied as the law of Tennessee. The indications are to the contrary. Barnes v. Boyd, 18 Tenn.App. 55, 72 S.W.2d 573; Comment, 23 Tenn.Law Review, 423. We construe the ruling in Marsh v. State Bank & Trust Co., 153 Tenn. 400 (see page 406), 284 S.W. 380, 48 A.L.R. 1365, relied upon by plaintiff, to be based upon estoppel in pais, rather than upon promissory estoppel.

Although there may be other facts in the present case which prevent it from coming within the scope of that definition, we believe that an important fact is that the plaintiff in no way altered his position for the worse by reason of defendant's letters of July 1 and July 20, 1955. The District Judge found as a fact that the plaintiff gave up nothing to which he was legally entitled and was restricted in no way in his activities thereafter. Plaintiff gave up nothing in accepting retirement that he would not have lost if he had refused to accept it. We do not find in the present case the injustice required in order to enforce the alleged promise.

In the Nebraska, California and Missouri cases, referred to above and relied on by the plaintiff, the plaintiff in each case relinquished some right to which he or she was entitled in reliance upon the promise of the defendant. They are not applicable here. See also: Insurance Co. v. Mowry, 96 U.S. 544, 547, 24 L.Ed. 674; Faxton v. Faxon, 28 Mich. 159, 161.

The judgment is affirmed.

HAYES V. PLANTATIONS STEEL COMPANY

Supreme Court of Rhode Island
438 A.2d 1091 (1982)

SHEA, JUSTICE.

The defendant employer, Plantations Steel Company (Plantations), appeals from a Superior Court judgment for the plaintiff employee, Edward J. Hayes (Hayes). The trial justice, sitting without a jury, found that Plantations was obligated to Hayes on the basis of an implied-in-fact contract to pay him a yearly pension of $5,000. The award covered three years in which payment had not been made. The trial justice ruled, also, that Hayes had made a sufficient showing of detrimental reliance upon Plantations's promise to pay to give rise to its obligation based on the theory of promissory estoppel. The trial justice, however, found in part for Plantations in ruling that the payments to Hayes were not governed by the Employee Retirement Income Security Act, 29 U.S.C.A. ss 1001–1461 (West 1975), and consequently he was not entitled to attorney's fees under s 1132(g) of that act. Both parties have appealed.

We reverse the findings of the trial justice regarding Plantations's contractual obligation to pay Hayes a pension. Consequently we need not deal with the cross-appeal concerning the award of attorney's fees under the federal statute.

Plantations is a closely held Rhode Island corporation engaged in the manufacture of steel reinforcing rods for use in concrete construction. The company was founded by Hugo R. Mainelli, Sr., and Alexander A. DiMartino. A dispute between their two families in 1976 and 1977 left the DiMartinos in full control of the corporation. Hayes was an employee of the corporation from 1947 until his retirement in 1972 at age of sixty-five. He began with Plantations as an "estimator and draftsman" and ended his career as general manager, a position of considerable responsibility. Starting in January 1973 and continuing until January 1976, Hayes received the annual sum of $5,000 from Plantations. Hayes instituted this action in December 1977, after the then company management refused to make any further payments.

Hayes testified that in January 1972 he announced his intention to retire the following July, after twenty-five years of continuous service. He decided to retire because he had worked continuously for fifty-one years. He stated, however, that he would not have retired had he not expected to receive a pension. After he stopped working for Plantations, he sought no other employment.

Approximately one week before his actual retirement Hayes spoke with Hugo R. Mainelli, Jr., who was then an officer and a stockholder of Plantations. This conversation was the first and only one concerning payments of a pension to Hayes during retirement. Mainelli said that the company "would take care" of him. There was no mention of a sum of money or a percentage of salary that Hayes would receive. There was no formal authorization for payments by Plantations's shareholders and/or board of directors. Indeed, there was never any formal provision for a pension plan for any employee other than for unionized employees, who benefit from an arrangement through their union. The plaintiff was not a union member.

Mr. Mainelli, Jr., testified that his father, Hugo R. Mainelli, Sr., had authorized the first payment "as a token of appreciation for the many years of (Hayes's) service." Furthermore, "it was implied that that check would continue on an annual basis." Mainelli also testified that it was his "personal intention" that the payments would continue for "as long as I was around."

Mainelli testified that after Hayes's retirement, he would visit the premises each year to say hello and renew old acquaintances. During the course of his visits, Hayes would thank Mainelli for the previous check and ask how long it would continue so that he could plan an orderly retirement.

The payments were discontinued after 1976. At that time a succession of several poor business years plus the stockholders' dispute, resulting in the takeover by the DiMartino family, contributed to the decision to stop the payments.

The trial justice ruled that Plantations owed Hayes his annual sum of $5,000 for the years 1977 through 1979. The ruling implied that barring bankruptcy or the cessation of business for any other reason, Hayes had a right to expect continued annual payments.

The trial justice found that Hugo Mainelli, Jr.'s statement that Hayes would be taken care of after his retirement was a promise. Although no sum of money was mentioned in 1972, the four annual payments of $5,000 established that otherwise unspecified term of the contract. The trial justice also found that Hayes supplied consideration for the promise by voluntarily retiring, because he was under no obligation to do so. From the words and conduct of the parties and from the surrounding circumstances, the trial justice concluded that there existed an implied contract obligating the company to pay a pension to Hayes for life. The trial justice made a further finding that even if Hayes had not truly bargained for a pension by voluntarily retiring, he had nevertheless incurred the detriment of foregoing other employment in reliance upon the company's promise. He specifically held that Hayes's retirement was in response to the promise and held also that Hayes refrained from seeking other employment in further reliance thereon.

The findings of fact of a trial justice sitting without a jury are entitled to great weight when reviewed by this court. His findings will not be disturbed unless it can be shown that they are clearly wrong or that the trial justice misconceived or overlooked material evidence. Lisi v. Marra, R.I., 424 A.2d 1052 (1981); Raheb v. Lemenski, 115 R.I. 576, 350 A.2d 397 (1976). After careful review of the record, however, we conclude that the trial justice's findings and conclusions must be reversed.

Assuming for the purpose of this discussion that Plantations in legal effect made a promise to Hayes, we must ask whether Hayes did supply the required consideration that would make the promise binding? And, if Hayes did not supply consideration, was his alleged reliance sufficiently induced by the promise to estop defendant from denying its obligation to him? We answer both questions in the negative.

We turn first to the problem of consideration. The facts at bar do not present the case of an express contract. As the trial justice stated, the existence of a contract in this case must be determined from all the circumstances of the parties' conduct and words. Although words were expressed initially in the remark that Hayes "would be taken care of," any contract in this case would be more in the nature of an implied contract. Certainly the statement of Hugo Mainelli, Jr., standing alone is not an expression of a direct and definite promise to pay Hayes a pension. Though we are analyzing an implied contract, nevertheless we must address the question of consideration.

Contracts implied in fact require the element of consideration to support them as is required in express contracts. The only difference between the two is the manner in which the parties manifest their assent. J. Koury Steel Erectors, Inc. v. San-Vel Concrete Corp., R.I., 387 A.2d 694 (1978); Bailey v. West, 105 R.I. 61, 249 A.2d 414 (1969). In this jurisdiction, consideration consists either in some right, interest, or benefit accruing to one party or some forbearance, detriment, or responsibility given, suffered, or undertaken by the other. See Dockery v. Greenfield, 86 R.I. 464, 136 A.2d 682 (1957); Darcey v. Darcey, 29 R.I. 384, 71 A. 595 (1909). Valid consideration furthermore must be bargained for. It must induce the return act or promise. To be valid, therefore, the purported consideration must not have been delivered before a promise is executed, that is, given without reference to the promise. Plowman v. Indian Refining Co., 20 F.Supp. 1 (E.D.Ill.1937). Consideration is therefore a test of the enforceability of executory promises, Angel v. Murray, 113 R.I. 482, 322 A.2d 630 (1974), and has no legal effect when rendered in the past and apart from an alleged exchange in the present. Zanturjian v. Boornazian, 25 R.I. 151, 55 A. 199 (1903).

In the case before us, Plantations's promise to pay Hayes a pension is quite clearly not supported by any consideration supplied by Hayes. Hayes had announced his intent to retire well in advance of any promise, and therefore the intention to retire was arrived at without regard to any promise by Plantations. Although Hayes may have had in mind the receipt of a pension when he first informed Plantations, his expectation was not based on any statement made to him or on any conduct of the company officer relative to him in January 1972. In deciding to retire, Hayes acted on his own initiative. Hayes's long years of dedicated service also is legally insufficient because his service too was rendered without being induced by Plantations's promise. See Plowman v. Indian Refining Co., supra.

Clearly then this is not a case in which Plantations's promise was meant to induce Hayes to refrain from retiring when he could have chosen to do so in return for further service. 1 Williston on Contracts, s 130B (3d ed., Jaeger 1957). Nor was the promise made to encourage long service from the start of his employment. Weesner v. Electric Power Board of Chattanooga, 48 Tenn.App. 178, 344 S.W.2d 766 (1961). Instead, the testimony establishes that Plantations's promise was intended "as a token of appreciation for (Hayes's) many years of service." As such it was in the nature of a gratuity paid to Hayes for as long as the company chose. In Spickelmier Industries, Inc. v. Passander, 172 Ind.App. 49, 359 N.E.2d 563 (1977), an employer's promise to an employee to pay him a year-end bonus was unenforceable because it was made after the employee had performed his contractual responsibilities for that year.

The plaintiff's most relevant citations are still inapposite to the present case. Bredemann v. Vaughan Mfg. Co., 40 Ill.App.2d 232, 188 N.E.2d 746 (1963), presents similar yet distinguishable facts. There, the appellate court reversed a summary judgment granted to the defendant employer, stating that a genuine issue of material fact existed regarding whether the plaintiff's retirement was in consideration of her employer's promise to pay her a lifetime pension. As in the present case, the employer made the promise one week prior to the employee's retirement, and in almost the same words. However, Bredemann is distinguishable because the court characterized that promise as a concrete offer to pay if she would retire immediately. In fact, the defendant wanted her to retire. Id. 188 N.E.2d at 749. On the contrary, Plantations in this case did not actively seek Hayes's retirement. DiMartino, one of Plantations's founders, testified that he did not want Hayes to retire. Unlike Bredemann, here Hayes announced his unsolicited intent to retire.

Hayes also argues that the work he performed during the week between the promise and the date of his retirement constituted sufficient consideration to support the promise. He relies on Ulmann v. Sunset-McKee Co., 221 F.2d 128 (9th Cir. 1955), in which the court ruled that work performed during the one-week period of the employee's notice of impending retirement constituted consideration for the employer's offer of a pension that the employee had solicited some months previously. But there the court stated that its prime reason for upholding the agreement was that sufficient consideration existed in the employee's consent not to compete with his employer. These circumstances do not appear in our case. Hayes left his employment because he no longer desired to work. He was not contemplating other job offers or considering going into competition with Plantations. Although Plantations did not want Hayes to leave, it did not try to deter him, nor did it seek to prevent Hayes from engaging in other activity.

Hayes argues in the alternative that even if Plantations's promise was not the product of an exchange, its duty is grounded properly in the theory of promissory estoppel. This court adopted the theory of promissory estoppel in East Providence Credit Union v. Geremia, 103 R.I. 597, 601, 239 A.2d 725, 727 (1968) (quoting 1 Restatement Contracts s 90 at 110 (1932)) stating:

"A promise which the promisor should reasonably expect to induce action or forbearance of a definite and substantial character on the part of the promisee and which does induce such action or forbearance is binding if injustice can be avoided only by enforcement of its promise."

In East Providence Credit Union this court said that the doctrine of promissory estoppel is invoked "as a substitute for a consideration, rendering a gratuitous promise enforceable as a contract." Id. To restate the matter differently, "the acts of reliance by the promisee to his detriment (provide) a substitute for consideration." Id.

Hayes urges that in the absence of a bargained-for promise the facts require application of the doctrine of promissory estoppel. He stresses that he retired voluntarily while expecting to receive a pension. He would not have otherwise retired. Nor did he seek other employment.

We disagree with this contention largely for the reasons already stated. One of the essential elements of the doctrine of promissory estoppel is that the promise must induce the promisee's action or forbearance. The particular act in this regard is plaintiff's decision whether or not to retire. As we stated earlier, the record indicates that he made the decision on his own initiative. In other words, the conversation between Hayes and Mainelli which occurred a week before Hayes left his employment cannot be said to have induced his decision to leave. He had reached that decision long before.

An example taken from the restatement provides a meaningful contrast:

"2. A promises B to pay him an annuity during B's life. B thereupon resigns profitable employment, as A expected that he might. B receives the annuity for some years, in the meantime becoming disqualified from again obtaining good employment. A's promise is binding." (Emphasis added.) 1 Restatement Contracts s 90 at 111 (1932).

In Feinberg v. Pfeiffer Co., 322 S.W.2d 163 (Mo.App.1959), the plaintiff-employee had worked for her employer for nearly forty years. The defendant corporation's board of directors resolved, in view of her long years of service, to obligate itself to pay "retirement privileges" to her. The resolution did not require the plaintiff to retire. Instead, the decision whether and when to retire remained entirely her own. The board then informed her of its resolution. The plaintiff worked for eighteen months more before retiring. She sued the corporation when it reduced her monthly checks seven years later. The court held that a pension contract existed between the parties. Although continued employment was not a consideration to her receipt of retirement benefits, the court found sufficient reliance on the part of the plaintiff to support her claim. The court based its decision upon the above restatement example, that is, the defendant informed the plaintiff of its plan, and the plaintiff in reliance thereon, retired. Feinberg presents factors that also appear in the case at bar. There, the plaintiff had worked many years and desired to retire; she would not have left had she not been able to rely on a pension; and once retired, she sought no other employment.

However, the important distinction between Feinberg and the case before us is that in Feinberg the employer's decision definitely shaped the thinking of the plaintiff. In this case the promise did not. It is not reasonable to infer from the facts that Hugo R. Mainelli, Jr., expected retirement to result from his conversation with Hayes. Hayes had given notice of his intention seven months previously. Here there was thus no inducement to retire which would satisfy the demands of s 90 of the restatement. Nor can it be said that Hayes's refraining from other employment was "action or forbearance of a definite and substantial character." The underlying assumption of Hayes's initial decision to retire was that upon leaving the defendant's employ, he would no longer work. It is impossible to say that he changed his position any more so because of what Mainelli had told him in light of his own initial decision. These circumstances do not lead to a conclusion that injustice can be avoided only by enforcement of Plantations's promise. Hayes received $20,000 over the course of four years. He inquired each year about whether he could expect a check for the following year. Obviously, there was no absolute certainty on his part that the pension would continue. Furthermore, in the face of his uncertainty, the mere fact that payment for several years did occur is insufficient by itself to meet the requirements of reliance under the doctrine of promissory estoppel.

For the foregoing reasons, the defendant's appeal is sustained and the judgment of the Superior Court is reversed. The papers of the case are remanded to the Superior Court.

McDonald v. Mobil Coal Producing, Inc.

Supreme Court of Wyoming
789 P.2d 866 (1990)

Macy, Justice.

This is an appeal from a summary judgment in favor of Appellees Mobil Coal Producing, Inc., Brad Hanson, Peter Totin, and Bert Gustafson, denying the claim of Appellant Craig McDonald for wrongful discharge from employment.

We reverse and remand.

McDonald states the issues as:

I.   [Whether t]he trial court erred in holding that the Mobil Coal handbook did not constitute an employment contract.

II.   [Whether t]he trial court erred in dismissing Craig McDonald's claim under the covenant of good faith and fair dealing.

McDonald worked at Mobil's Caballo Rojo coal mine in Campbell County, Wyoming, from August 1987 until June 1988 as a technician in the preparation plant. Hanson was the mine superintendent, Totin was the mine supervisor of employee relations, and Gustafson was the preparation plant supervisor. McDonald contends that he resigned his position at the mine following rumors that he had sexually harassed a female co-employee. McDonald also contends the resignation resulted from a meeting with Hanson, Totin, and Gustafson where McDonald was told he had the choice of either resigning or being fired.

When McDonald applied for the position at Caballo Rojo, he signed a statement on his employment application which said in part:

I agree that any offer of employment, and acceptance thereof, does not constitute a binding contract of any length, and that such employment is terminable at the will of either party, subject to applicable state and/or federal laws.

After he started working at the mine, McDonald received an employee handbook. The stated intention of the handbook, as addressed to Mobil employees, was "to help you understand and explain to you Mobil's policies and procedures." Despite that representation, the handbook stated that it was not a company "comprehensive policies and procedures manual, nor an employment contract."

The handbook stated that Mobil was "committed to maintaining an environment of mutual trust, understanding, and cooperation" and that Mobil encouraged communication between employees and supervisors on an informal basis. It informed the reader of the existence of "a Fair Treatment Procedure that afford [ed] an employee the opportunity to be heard, without fear of reprisal." This "Fair Treatment Procedure" was a detailed four-step procedure in which an employee discussed a problem with a supervisor. If the employee was not satisfied with the outcome of this discussion, the employee could take the matter to other supervisory personnel.

The handbook also detailed a disciplinary procedure. It included a noninclusive list of behaviors which Mobil would not condone and a five-step disciplinary process. These steps were: (1) counseling; (2) written reprimand; (3) final written reprimand; (4) three-day suspension; and (5) discharge. The handbook stated that Mobil believed "union representation [was] unnecessary for employees to enjoy job security, career opportunities, consistent treatment, and competitive wages and benefits." The handbook listed seven "fundamental obligations" for Mobil to fulfill. Among these seven were:

2.   To train and guide employees, allow them to develop their job abilities and regularly keep them informed of their progress.

3.   To invite constructive suggestions and criticism and guarantee the right to be heard without fear of reprisal.

4.   To give helpful consideration when an employee makes a mistake or has a personal problem with which we are asked to help.

After resigning, McDonald filed suit, claiming breach of contract, breach of the covenant of good faith and fair dealing, negligence, and defamation. Mobil and Totin moved to dismiss the suit on the bases of W.R.C.P. 12(b)(1) (lack of jurisdiction over the subject matter)2 and W.R.C.P. 12(b)(6) (failure to state a claim upon which relief can be granted). Hanson and Gustafson moved to dismiss on the basis of W.R.C.P. 12(b)(5) (insufficiency of service of process).

Because supplemental documents were filed with the motions, the trial court treated the motions as motions for summary judgment. W.R.C.P. 56. See, e.g., Mostert v. CBL & Associates, 741 P.2d 1090 (Wyo.1987). The court noted that the "tenor" of the handbook could cause it to appear to be a contract. However, the court held that the disclaimer in the handbook defeated any claim that the handbook was part of an employment contract. Thus, despite the "tenor" of the handbook, the court held that McDonald was an at-will employee and that his termination did not violate any concept of good faith and fair dealing. The court also held that the negligence and defamation claims failed to state a cause of action recognized in Wyoming. It granted summary judgment in favor of Appellees.

Summary judgment is proper only when there are no genuine issues of material fact and the prevailing party is entitled to judgment as a matter of law. Baros v. Wells, 780 P.2d 341 (Wyo.1989); Farr v. Link, 746 P.2d 431 (Wyo.1987). We review a summary judgment in the same light as the district court does, using the same materials and following the same standards. Baros, 780 P.2d 341; Roybal v. Bell, 778 P.2d 108 (Wyo.1989). We examine the record from the vantage point most favorable to the party opposing the motion, and we give that party the benefit of all favorable inferences which may fairly be drawn from the record. Baros, 780 P.2d 341; Doud v. First Interstate Bank of Gillette, 769 P.2d 927 (Wyo.1989). A material fact is one which, if proved, would have the effect of establishing or refuting an essential element of the cause of action or defense asserted by the parties. Albrecht v. Zwaanshoek Holding En Financiering, B.V., 762 P.2d 1174 (Wyo.1988); Johnston v. Conoco, Inc., 758 P.2d 566 (Wyo.1988).

Disposition of this case requires us to review the revision of the employee handbook discussed in Mobil Coal Producing, Inc. v. Parks, 704 P.2d 702 (Wyo.1985). We held in Parks that the provisions in the handbook constituted part of the Mobil employee contract and that the existence of the handbook elevated the nature of the Mobil employees' status beyond simple at-will employment. Id. at 706–07. In an at-will employment situation, either party may terminate the relationship for any reason at any time without incurring liability and without violating any implied covenant of good faith and fair dealing. Nelson v. Crimson Enterprises, Inc., 777 P.2d 73 (Wyo.1989); Griess v. Consolidated Freightways Corporation of Delaware, 776 P.2d 752 (Wyo.1989); Parks, 704 P.2d at 704.

Following Parks, Mobil revised its handbook. The most significant revision was the addition of a statement that the handbook was not an employment contract. A contract exists when there is a meeting of the minds. Anderson Excavating and Wrecking Company v. Certified Welding Corporation, 769 P.2d 887 (Wyo.1988). Mobil's express disclaimer demonstrates that it had no intention to form a contract. We cannot say that the handbook was part of the employment contract; however, this determination does not end our analysis. We have recognized limited exceptions to the at-will relationship. Nelson, 777 P.2d at 75. See, e.g., Leithead v. American Colloid Company, 721 P.2d 1059 (Wyo.1986); Alexander v. Phillips Oil Company, 707 P.2d 1385 (Wyo.1985), after remand 741 P.2d 117 (Wyo.1987) (employee handbook without disclaimer is part of the employment contract); Griess, 776 P.2d 752 (employer cannot terminate at-will employee for seeking benefits under worker's compensation statutes); and Parks, 704 P.2d 702. Other provisions of the handbook require us to recognize another manner in which an employer can modify the at-will employment relationship.

As the trial court noted, if it were not for the disclaimer, the "tenor" of the handbook could cause it to be viewed as a contract, and McDonald may have believed that the handbook was a contract. Our reading of the portions of the handbook included in the record reveals language which could be understood to connote promises notwithstanding a lack of a contractual obligation. Even without a contractual obligation, some promises remain enforceable. This Court has adopted Restatement (Second) of Contracts § 90(1) (1981), which states:

> A promise which the promisor should reasonably expect to induce action or forbearance on the part of the promisee or a third person and which does induce such action or forbearance is binding if injustice can be avoided only by enforcement of the promise. The remedy granted for breach may be limited as justice requires.

Hanna State & Savings Bank v. Matson, 53 Wyo. 1, 77 P.2d 621 (1938). See also Tremblay v. Reid, 700 P.2d 391, 395 n. 1 (Wyo.1985). The Restatement (Second) of Contracts, supra, § 2(1) at 8, defines a promise as

> a manifestation of intention to act or refrain from acting in a specified way, so made as to justify a promisee in understanding that a commitment has been made.

Despite the disclaimer of contract, the handbook did indicate its purpose was to explain the company's policies and procedures to Mobil's employees.

Having announced the policy, presumably with a view to obtaining the benefit of improved employee attitudes and behavior and improved quality of the work force, the employer may not treat its promise as illusory.

Toussaint v. Blue Cross & Blue Shield of Michigan, 408 Mich. 579, 292 N.W.2d 880, 895 (1980), quoted in Damrow v. Thumb Cooperative

Terminal, Inc., 126 Mich.App. 354, 337 N.W.2d 338, 342 (1983). Thus, an employee is entitled to enforce a representation in an employee handbook if he can demonstrate that: (1) The employer should have reasonably expected the employee to consider the representation as a commitment from the employer; (2) the employee reasonably relied upon the representation to his detriment; and (3) injustice can be avoided only by enforcement of representation. Cronk v. Intermountain Rural Electric Association, 765 P.2d 619, 624 (Colo.App.), cert. denied (1988). These are issues for the trier of fact to determine. Id. Unless the employee can make this factual showing to overcome the presumption of an employment terminable at the will of either party, the employee's cause of action will fail. Continental Air Lines, Inc. v. Keenan, 731 P.2d 708 (Colo.1987).

Genuine issues of fact exist here. McDonald must prove that his resignation was forced and not volitional. Should McDonald meet this burden, the finder of fact must determine what effect, if any, the representations made by Mobil in its handbook had upon an otherwise at-will employment relationship. McDonald's affidavit in opposition to the motions for dismissal purported that he relied upon the procedures outlined in the handbook. Issues of whether Mobil should have expected McDonald's reliance upon these procedures, whether McDonald's reliance was reasonable, and whether the Mobil termination procedures should be enforced to avoid injustice will need to be addressed if McDonald proves his resignation was forced. The trial court improperly granted summary judgment to Appellees.

Reversed and remanded for further proceedings consistent with this opinion.

GOLDEN, JUSTICE, specially concurring.

I concur only in the result, disagreeing with the application of the principles of promissory estoppel under the facts of consequence in this case.

The trial court found that the disclaimer (stating that the handbook was not a "comprehensive policies and procedural manual, nor an employment contract") was conspicuous because it was located on the handbook's first page. I disagree. The fact that the disclaimer appears on the front page does not by itself make it conspicuous. I would rule, as a matter of law, that a disclaimer's location is not the sole determinant of whether or not it is conspicuous. In this instance, the disclaimer consisted of one sentence—no different in appearance from any of the other sentences contained on the page. It is not even labeled as a disclaimer.

The United States Court for the District of Wyoming, in a case applying Wyoming law, addressed the issue whether a disclaimer in an employee handbook negates the employee's claim that the handbook constituted an employment contract. Jimenez v. Colorado Interstate Gas Company, 690

F.Supp. 977 (D.Wyo.1988) (Johnson, J.). The Court ruled that disclaimers are effective only if they are conspicuous, which is a question of law. Id. at 980. In Jimenez, the employer claimed that it was not bound to follow the handbook because it contained a disclaimer stating that the handbook was not an employment contract. The District Court ruled, however, that the disclaimer was "not set off in any way that would attract attention" and, therefore, was ineffective against the employee. Id. at 980. The Court listed the disclaimer's inadequacies: "Nothing is capitalized that would give notice of a disclaimer. The type size equals that of other provisions on the same page. No border sets the disclaimer apart from any other paragraph on the page." Id. 980. After review of Mobil's employee handbook, I find that its attempted disclaimer suffers from the same deficiencies found in Jimenez.

Employment agreements are typically unilateral offers to persons untutored in contract law. If an employer seeks to offset the contractual tenor of its handbook with a disclaimer, equitable and social policy concerns demand that the disclaimer be presented clearly so that employees are not misled by the handbook. A recent Idaho case involved a disclaimer located on the cover page (the disclaimer was, apparently, the cover page's sole occupant). Arnold v. Diet Center, Inc., 113 Idaho 581, 746 P.2d 1040, 1041 (1987). The personnel manager read the disclaimer to the employee. The employee was then told the disclaimer meant that the handbook was not a contract. Finally, the manager had the employee sign the cover page, below the disclaimer. This court should hold that something similar to what the Idaho employee was afforded is required before a disclaimer is found to be conspicuous.

In addition, I am concerned that the plurality opinion leaves the issue of the disclaimer's effect unresolved. The trial court granted Mobil summary judgment because it found that, as a matter of law, the handbook's disclaimer was conspicuous. The plurality reasons that summary judgment was inappropriate because promissory estoppel raises issues of material fact. On remand, however, the trial court may still rule, as a matter of law, that the disclaimer is sufficiently conspicuous to constitute a defense. For the reasons set forth above, I find this result unacceptable.

Because the disclaimer is ineffective as a matter of law, and its effect now becomes a question of fact, Mobil's attempted disclaimer has rendered the employee handbook ambiguous. The handbook provides that "union representation is unnecessary for * * * job security and * * * consistent treatment, * * *." It also contains a detailed disciplinary procedure. In Jimenez, at 980, the Court observed that "[u]nder Wyoming decisions, handbooks that list misconduct that could result in discharge imply that cause is required." (citing Leithead v. American Colloid Company, 721 P.2d 1059, 1063 (Wyo.1986); and Mobil Coal Producing, Inc. v. Parks, 704 P.2d 702, 705 (Wyo.1985)). When these provisions are juxtaposed against the attempted disclaimer, ambiguities exist as to the parties' intent vis-a-vis the terms of employment.

This court outlined the procedure for resolving ambiguous employee handbooks, stating:

Some handbooks or manuals may be ambiguous or may not have apparent meaning, making the determination of their effect on at will employment a question of fact. * * * If the meaning of a contract is ambiguous or not apparent, it may be necessary to determine the intention of the parties from evidence other than the contract itself, and interpretation becomes a question of law and fact.

Parks, 704 P.2d at 706 (citation omitted).

The handbook's ambiguous provisions create issues of material fact and, therefore, summary judgment is improper.

CARDINE, CHIEF JUSTICE, dissenting.

I dissent.

Mobil did all it could by its disclaimer to assure there was not a contract of employment. Parties are free to contract or not as they choose. Mobil chose not to contract with its employee, and, like it or not, we should accept that decision.

THOMAS, JUSTICE, dissenting.

I agree with the dissenting opinion of Chief Justice Cardine. If I count the votes correctly, it would seem that three justices do not agree on the majority disposition invoking promissory estoppel; four justices agree that there was no employment contract; and three justices agree that the summary judgment should be reversed and the case remanded for trial. There are not many moments of comfort in the life of a judge, but I find one of those in the fact that I do not have to develop the jury instructions in this case.

In prior cases, this court has critiqued employee handbooks in the context of their effect in structuring an employment contract as distinguished from an employment at will. Leithead v. American Colloid Company, 721 P.2d 1059 (Wyo.1986); Alexander v. Phillips Oil Company, 707 P.2d 1385 (Wyo.1985); and Mobil Coal Producing, Inc. v. Parks, 704 P.2d 702 (Wyo.1985). In this instance, Mobil Coal Producing, Inc. obtained a signed statement from McDonald that his employment was terminable at the will of either party. The handbook contained an express disclaimer of its status as an employment contract. As Chief Justice Cardine notes in his dissent, "Mobil did all it could by its disclaimer to assure there was not a contract of employment." Indeed, what more could it have done.

Now, having done its best to have its conduct comport with the prior decisions of this court, Mobil finds that, in any event, anything it may say in the employee handbook can become a binding promise under the doctrine of promissory estoppel. I apologize to my readers for being obtuse, but I cannot distinguish that from the effect of a contract, although the majority concludes that there is no contract. I fear that corporate America, as it lives in the state of Wyoming, will be forced to conclude that the court is toying with it in some cruel and peculiar game of cat and mouse. In my judgment, we offered guidance in the earlier employee at will cases and, now, when confronted with an employer who followed that advice, we should not say that we really did not mean to adhere to our earlier guidance.

I would affirm the summary judgment in this case.

———————